D1523352

UNDER STALIN'S SHADOW

A VOLUME IN THE NIU SERIES IN

Slavic, East European, and Eurasian Studies
Edited by Christine D. Worobec

For a list of books in the series, visit our website at cornellpress.cornell.edu.

UNDER STALIN'S SHADOW

A GLOBAL HISTORY OF GREEK COMMUNISM

NIKOS MARANTZIDIS

NORTHERN ILLINOIS UNIVERSITY PRESS
AN IMPRINT OF CORNELL UNIVERSITY PRESS
Ithaca and London

First published 2023 by Cornell University Press

Library of Congress Cataloging-in-Publication Data

Names: Marantzidēs, Nikos A., author.
Title: Under Stalin's shadow : a global history of Greek
    communism / Nikos Marantzidis.
Description: Ithaca : Northern Illinois University
    Press, an imprint of Cornell University Press,
    2023. | Series: NIU series in Slavic, East European,
    and Eurasian studies | Includes bibliographical
    references and index.
Identifiers: LCCN 2022016861 (print) | LCCN
    2022016862 (ebook) | ISBN 9781501767661
    (hardcover) | ISBN 9781501768347 (paperback) |
    ISBN 9781501767685 (pdf) | ISBN 9781501767678
    (epub)
Subjects: LCSH: Kommounistikon Komma tēs
    Hellados—History—20th century. |
    Communism—Greece—History—20th century.
Classification: LCC HX375.5.A6 M347 2023 (print) |
    LCC HX375.5.A6 (ebook) | DDC 949.507/6—dc23/
    eng/20220819
LC record available at https://lccn.loc.gov/2022016861
LC ebook record available at https://lccn.loc.
    gov/2022016862

To Charis and Alexandros

Contents

ACKNOWLEDGMENTS

This book is the product of efforts over many years, and I wish to acknowledge and express my gratitude to those who have assisted me. Among them, I owe a particular debt to John O. Iatrides, who has been a teacher and a friend, and provided the moral support and encouragement I sometimes needed to keep going. He also offered advice on the manuscript and helped prepare it for its publication. Stathis Kalyvas has been a friend and colleague for more than twenty years and has supported me in many ways. I doubt that without him I would have dared to tackle a subject of this magnitude and complexity.

The adventure of this book began in 2005 in Paris, when I began collecting international documents concerning Greek Communism and the Greek civil war. I was then fortunate to meet Professor Andrzej Paczkowski, who kindly provided me with crucially important Polish documents on the Greek civil war, which led me to the archives of the Institute of National Remembrance. I would not have been able to accomplish this work in Poland without my research assistant, Angelica Wudalas.

Collecting documents from different countries is a complicated and laborious affair. Several fellow scholars and friends helped me to get access to archival material. I am particularly indebted to Kostas Tsivos, Elias Skoulidas, Nikosz Fokasz, Kostis Karpozilos, Nikos Papadatos, Evangelos Kofos, Katerina Tsekou, Apostolos Patelakis, Charis Marantzidou, Marios Markovitis, Stratos Dordanas, and Paris Aslanidis. I also owe special thanks to my research assistants, Victoria Ouroumidou and Irma Papadopoulou, who worked for several years at the RGASPI and RGANI archives, where they collected many documents from the Soviet period.

I owe Karolina Partyga a huge debt of gratitude for her corrections and comments, which made the manuscript eminently more readable than it would have been otherwise. Thanks to our discussions, I gained a much clearer insight into the book's issues. Vladimir Tismăneanu and Stathis Kalyvas read the manuscript and made valuable comments. Kostis Karpozilos and Charis Marantzidou were also kind enough to read the manuscript, or parts of it, and offer critical comments.

Work on this book was supported by a number of institutions. In 2008, thanks to the financial support of Yale University's Program in Hellenic Studies, I was able to consult and translate several documents from the Czech Archives. In addition, the collection and translation of an extensive assortment of documents from different countries became possible during 2010–14, when I assumed the scientific coordination of a five-year research program entitled "Greece from the Second World War to the Cold War: International Relations and Domestic Developments" (Operational Program "Education and Lifelong Learning"). The program was cofinanced by the European Union (European Social Fund) and Greek national funds. With the contribution of almost thirty scholars and research assistants, we located, collected, and translated, when necessary, a large number of archival materials coming from the Balkans, Central and Western Europe, Russia, and the United States. I am also grateful to my colleagues in the Department of Balkan, Slavic, and Oriental Studies and the University of Macedonia for granting me, during these years, two sabbatical leaves, which permitted me to complete this book under very favorable conditions.

An earlier version of chapter 4 was presented at the workshop "Soviet Foreign Policy during the Second World War," organized in collaboration with the University of Udine and Harvard University's Cold War Studies/Davis Center for Russian and Eurasian Studies. I would like to thank Mark Kramer and Tommaso Piffer for the invitation and the participants of the workshop for their comments. Part of chapter 5 is based on an article titled "The Greek Civil War (1944–1949) and the International Communist System," published in the *Journal of Cold War Studies* 15, no. 4 (2013): 25–54. It is reproduced here with the kind permission of the journal's editor.

Last but not least, I would like to acknowledge with gratitude the support and love of Maria Kyriakidou. It is needless to say that she has put up with Greek Communism for far too long.

Abbreviations

AVNOJ	Anti-fascist Council for the National Liberation of Yugoslavia
BCF	Balkan Communist Federation
BKP	Bulgarian Communist Party
CPSU	Communist Party of the Soviet Union
DSE	Democratic Army of Greece
EAM	National Liberation Front
ECCI	Executive Committee of the Communist International
EDA	United Democratic Left
EDES	National Republican Greek League
ELAS	National People's Liberation Army
KKE	Communist Party of Greece
KPJ	Communist Party of Yugoslavia
KUNMZ	Communist University of National Minorities of the West
KUTV	Communist University of the Workers of the East
MOPR	International Red Aid
NOF	People's Liberation Front
OKNE	Federation of the Communist Youth of Greece
PCF	French Communist Party
PCR	Communist Party of Romania
PEEA	Political Committee of National Liberation
SEKE	Socialist Labor Party of Greece
SEKE(K)	Socialist Labor Party of Greece-Communist
SOE	Special Operations Executive

MAP 1. Map of Eastern Europe and the USSR during the Cold War

Introduction
A Global History of Greek Communism

When the Iron Curtain collapsed, the winds
of change swept over not just the former Communist states, but the entire European Communist world. Suffering from a decline that began
well before 1989, Communist parties abandoned Marxism-Leninism
and embraced either social democracy or a new Left radicalism. One
party, however, followed a different path. The Communist Party of
Greece, known by its Greek acronym KKE, was not eager to denounce
its longtime heroes. In February 1991, after passionate and traumatiz-
ing debates, the majority of the KKE members decided the old Communists had been right and the reformers wrong. The party denounced
the "anti-socialist treason" of the reformist Soviet leader Mikhail Gor-
bachev and refused to do away with its Communist name, symbols, and
identity. Although the Union of Soviet Socialist Republics, once the
motherland of Communism, was now moribund, its specter continued
to haunt the KKE. As the peoples of Eastern Europe tore down statues
of Lenin and Stalin, the Greek party revived its Stalinist past.

What prompted such idiosyncratic devotion to the Bolshevik legacy?
We could think of it as a domestic electoral strategy: the KKE bet on
retaining the allegiance of an aging electorate suspicious of reform and
full of nostalgia for a heroic revolutionary era. We could also note that

1

the KKE was not just an ordinary party, but one purporting to provide a secular religion, and thus debasing its own saints could only prove disastrous for the organization.[1] But neither of those explanations addresses the core of this 1990s Stalinist revival. As this book shows, in order to understand the nature of Greek communism we need to look to the party's history. A history, steeped in the world of international communism, that forged the KKE's culture and identity.

Histories of all European Communist parties cannot be easily categorized, placed neatly in the boxes in which we tend to confine stories about the past. In writing histories of Communist parties, we should resist traditional dichotomies between national and international historical perspectives, between the local and the global. From its birth, revolutionary socialism had disavowed narrowly nationalistic narratives and raised fundamental questions of internationalism, intertwining the national and the global spheres of thought and action, involving geographically distant communities in networks and revolutionary projects.[2]

The specific brand of socialism that had emerged in the twentieth century with the birth of the first Communist state—the Soviet Union—built on this tradition, but gave it its own rendition. Since 1919, the Third Communist International—the so-called Comintern—united revolutionaries from across the world. Those revolutionaries organized themselves into national Communist parties, which, in turn, produced sociopolitical communities parallel to national societies—which the French historian Annie Kriegel called *contre-société*. Those communities simultaneously bore values, visions, and social practices foreshadowing a future society and sets of norms, rules, networks of social capital, and selection mechanisms in line with actual needs and the national framework that encompassed them.[3] In other words, those parties embraced a vision of the future that defied existing national frontiers, centering instead on transnational linkages among the workers of the world. As members of national Communist parties, such individuals simultaneously belonged to the Comintern structure defined by an international hierarchy with Moscow at its center. Hence, the Communist parties' past simultaneously belongs to the fields of local, national, transnational, international, and global history.

To better understand this complex intertwining between the national and the international sphere, Stéphane Courtois and Marc Lazar have used the analytical categories of *teleological* and *societal* dimension.[4] According to them, Communist parties consisted of two dimensions. The first, the teleological, was related to the initial revolutionary project and comprised a doctrine (the Marxism-Leninism elaborated by Lenin and codified by Stalin), an organizational model (the revolutionary party conducted by the professionals of the revolution), and an overriding strategy (the unconditional defense of the Soviet Union and the other Communist states). The second, the societal, comprised all of the elements of the Communist party life related to a specific national society to which a Communist party belonged (national traditions, political system, electorate). The teleological dimension had a centripetal role, to impose cohesion and homogenization on the Communist parties all over the world. The societal dimension led to diversification because of the different social, economic, and political conditions prevailing in each country. The Communist parties strove to reconcile the two dimensions; however, this task proved to be a difficult or, more accurately, an impossible mission. In the same direction, but with different terminology, the historian Brigitte Studer, focusing on the Comintern, describes it as a political organization functioning at three levels: the international, which refers to the world revolution and a global network of activity; the transnational, where dense exchanges of persons and information took place; and the national, which refers to the domestic political arenas, the field of concrete political action.[5]

KKE Origins

Unique in the European context, the Communist Party of Greece was hegemonic within the Greek Left for several years. Up to 1977, the country lacked a strong socialist party—the term "Left" in Greece was and partly remains exclusively associated with Communism and radical nonreformist politics. This was due to sociological but also to historical reasons. The latter were strongly connected to the civil war (1944–49), which further aggravated an already sharply polarized political environment, leading to the isolation of the Communist Party from the rest of the political system.

The KKE was born in a turbulent moment when the Communist world had just begun taking shape. While it originated in 1918 as a typical socialist party, the KKE became one of the European Communist parties most loyal to Moscow. By the mid-twentieth century, it had embraced the spirit of Soviet internationalism more ardently than any other party in Western Europe. While other Communist parties embarked on their national roads toward socialism, the KKE maintained unusually strong relations with Moscow and with its Balkan sister parties. No other West European Communist party experienced such intimate contact with the USSR and with the People's Republics for so many years.

Because of this unique distinction, the Communist Party of Greece should not be considered a typical Western European Communist party but, simultaneously, a Western and an Eastern European organization. The KKE is a Western party by virtue of Greece's international orientation, but it is Eastern European by its own history as a party. In fact, from 1947 to 1974, due to the civil war and the Communists' defeat in 1949, the party's headquarters were in three different Eastern European capitals: initially in Belgrade from 1947 to 1948, later on in Bucharest from 1948 to 1968, and finally in Budapest from 1968 to 1974. The KKE's leadership and dozens of thousands of its followers were living for several decades in a vast area extending from Stettin in the Baltics to Tashkent in Uzbekistan, a *refugeeland*, as a veteran Greek Communist has called it, experiencing life and politics under existing Communist authorities. It was in those regions, geographically and politically very close to the Moscow center, that the KKE experienced the turbulent developments unfolding in the Communist Bloc. As a consequence, the dramatic developments that shook the postwar European Communist world—including Khrushchev's rise and fall, the Hungarian Revolution of 1956, the Prague Spring, and the Soviet invasion of Czechoslovakia in 1968—were felt by the Greek Communists not merely as events of historical significance but as traumatic collective experiences whose impact affected their own situation powerfully and directly.

Indeed, for the Greek Communists, their past relationship with world Communism was not merely significant but genuinely controversial. In their memoirs and other published personal accounts of their experiences, many KKE leaders and rank-and-file veterans wrote about various aspects of their party's relations with the Balkan comrades, the Comintern, and the Soviet Union. As a result, such individual accounts of the internal realities of international Communism as perceived by Greeks provide an unvarnished and little-known dimension of the Greek Communist experience in imposed exile. Inevitably, public debates over that painful experience resulted in bitter controversy and endless disagreement. Veterans of the KKE were sharply divided among themselves in their interpretations of, and reactions to, their foreign comrades' role in the life of their party.

Unsurprisingly, the bloody civil war between the Communist-led insurgents and the forces of a right-wing coalition government attracted very intense scrutiny, particularly from popular history writers, some of whom were affiliated with the Communist movement. They raised questions that reflected their deep disappointment over the failure of the civil war to make Greece a People's Republic. Why did the Soviet Red Army not enter Greece in September 1944, as it did across Eastern Europe? Did Stalin "exchange" Greece for Romania in the "spheres of influence agreement" of October 1944? Why didn't the Balkan comrades help the KKE during its first uprising in Athens in December 1944? The tone of such questions suggests that the Greek Communists felt betrayed but could not fathom the idea that the Soviet Union may have actually intentionally abandoned them. For a Communist, such thoughts amounted almost to heresy.

Historiography

Even though the KKE was deeply entangled in the web of worldwide Communism, readers are not likely to learn about those interconnections from scholarly books. In fact, the last book in English on the subject was published in 1989.[6] Politics, and the prevailing official dogma that the KKE was antinational and allied with Greece's enemies among the Slavs, made it difficult for professional historians to evaluate this entangled history as well: in a country with such a fragile political life as twentieth-century Greece, the KKE and its foreign alliances were politically controversial. The post-civil-war political developments, particularly successive right-wing governments and a strong anti-Communist domestic orientation, along with controversial practices and the political repression of Communists and fellow travelers, rendered the KKE's international ties a highly charged subject. In the early Cold War era, when the East-West conflict appeared to be the principal characteristic of international politics and the domino theory of Communist expansionism dominated official thinking in the Western world, it was difficult for researchers to objectively evaluate ties between Communist parties. Later, as the so-called Regime of the Colonels—a military dictatorship—established itself in Greece between 1967 and 1974, any discussion of the political Left had to include a denunciation of the Communist movement as an anti-Greek project.

After the restoration of democracy in 1974, the majority of Greek historians refrained from dealing with the relations between international and Greek Communism, fearing they would be identified with a domestic variant of McCarthyism or the dictatorship's crude anti-Communist propaganda. Altogether, international Communism remained a sensitive and controversial subject, often exploited by governments, political ideologues, and opinion makers, and Greek historians avoided tackling it for fear of being characterized as biased and politically motivated. As a result, for many years Greek Communism's history was limited mainly to its national boundaries.

To the extent that the KKE has featured in historiography, its story has reflected the polarization between two schools of thought on Communism in general. The so-called *cold warriors*, also known as traditionalists, have argued that, like all the other European Communist parties, the Greek party started out as a semi-independent organization whose members initially adhered to their own political views but were rapidly dominated by Communists who were Moscow's ideological slaves. On the other side of the divide are historians who, inspired by the radicalism of the 1960s and the 1970s, have written narratives that ignore global ties and high-level politics. They are not particularly focused on strategies, conspiracies, and intrigues at the top of the International or even at the higher levels of national parties. They are exclusively interested in what the Communists did on the ground.[7] The traditionalists' portrayal of the KKE as a mere Soviet puppet seems almost like a caricature of the actual party. But the revisionists' stories that ignored Moscow, the Comintern, and in general the international networks of national Communists are also misleading.[8] Ultimately, both groups of scholars misunderstand the role that those international connections played in the KKE's history. And this misunderstanding has prevented them from accurately explaining not just the KKE's decisions and the rifts between party members, but also the nature of Greek Communism itself.

In the post–Cold War era, historical writing on Communism underwent a profound transformation. The fall of Communism in Eastern Europe also greatly influenced the historical research on the KKE, particularly as a considerable volume of party archives was made available to historians in the 1990s. But a real breakthrough was possible only with the opening of Eastern European and Russian archives during the same years. New sources helped historians understand the complicated interactions between the national and the international entities in the Communist world.[9] Those documents allowed researchers to examine the KKE's experiences in minute detail and to contextualize them in the wider world of Communist politics. Hence, some scholars began to link the national Communist activity and mobilization with stimuli coming from the international center. They were thus able to better understand the nuanced relationship not just between the center and the periphery but also between different peripheries of the Communist world. This crucial progress in the availability of documentary materials proved vital in correcting the earlier perceptions of 'top-down' pressure faced by those in the periphery. Equally significant, scholars began to show that horizontal links within this alleged periphery were also of great importance. Balkan Communist parties sometimes worked together without necessarily informing Moscow about everything they did. On occasion, they even managed to collectively influence the Soviet leadership. Stories told from the perspective of the southeastern European periphery can thus inform us about the nature of international Communism itself.

An Unclear Frontier

The history of the Greek Communist Party provides a unique opportunity to understand the nature, organizational characteristics, and dynamics of international Communism, particularly in southeastern Europe. In the interwar period, Greeks joined the Balkan Communist Federation (BCF) even before becoming Comintern members. This was neither accidental nor inconsequential. The Comintern's initial idea was to deeply homogenize the parties in the Balkans, because the Balkans were thought to be a region of interdependent states in which revolution in one country would ignite the flame of revolution in the other countries as well. Indeed, initially, the BCF, even more than the Comintern, helped fashion crucial elements of the Greek party's early political identity. This identity, in turn, shaped the KKE's encounters with the USSR, complicating the process of remaking the Greek party into one resembling the Bolshevik political machine.

The Second World War redrew the political map of the region in the direction that the Comintern had wished, as the other Balkan Communist parties established their own states: Yugoslavia, Bulgaria, Romania, and Albania. But despite its efforts, the KKE, unlike the other Balkan parties, never established a Communist state and survived after the civil war in the 1940s thanks to its international network. But this network was crucial to the KKE and to other Balkan Communists from the very birth of the Communist movement in the region. The international

Balkan Communist network, a sort of subnetwork of, first, the Comintern and, later, the Communist Information Bureau (Cominform), played a key role in the KKE's life.

During the 1940s, the KKE's bonds with its Balkan comrades made it possible for the party to dream up ambitious regime-change plans for Greece itself. The dense Balkan Communist network, featuring legendary personalities such as the Bulgarian Georgi Dimitrov and the Yugoslav Josip Broz Tito, exerted great influence on the KKE. For their part, the Balkan comrades allowed the KKE much more independence and room to develop its own repertoire of actions and strategies than did the Soviets. By its very nature, Balkan internationalism was nowhere near as intrusive and inflexible as the bilateral and highly hierarchical relationships the Greeks maintained with the Bolsheviks. This is not to suggest that the Communist network operating in the Balkans acted independently of the Soviets. There is no doubt that, especially after Stalin came to power in the USSR, the Comintern as an organization and, later, its members were placed under close Soviet tutelage. As Studer remarks, one only has to look at the diary of Dimitrov, the longtime head of the international Communist organization, to appreciate Stalin's presence in Dimitrov's decisions.[10] In other words, even though the national Communist parties retained a degree of autonomy from Stalin, the Bolshevik Center in Moscow exerted undisputed symbolic, cultural, and above all political authority over them.[11]

On the other hand, exerting commanding authority is not the same as pulling strings as in a political puppet show. We cannot consider the KKE to be Moscow's pliant tool. Neither the KKE nor the institutions of international Communism in the Balkans were merely agents of Moscow.[12] Their relationships, and thus their histories, were far more complicated and nuanced than the vocabulary of hegemony implies. Specifically, contacts between the KKE and Moscow were not always equally intense and intimate. And although traditionalist historiography paints the KKE as "Moscow's instrument," the two sides were at times not sufficiently interconnected for the Greeks to even know what the Soviets wanted them to do. For years, their loose communication produced much uncertainty, especially for the Greeks, that took a lot of time to resolve. The situation was aggravated by the fact that the Greeks were poorly represented in the Comintern's institutions, and thus lacked access to everyday Communist politics.[13] In several instances, the KKE was informed about new Soviet or Comintern policies at the last minute, causing stress and irritation. To make matters worse, during the critically important years of the Second World War, contacts between the KKE and the Soviets were not even direct, but rather channeled primarily through the Yugoslav or Bulgarian parties.

In several instances, the Soviets themselves appeared ambivalent with regard to Greek issues, and to have no precise ideas about future policies toward that country. This led the Greeks to try their hand at guessing what the Soviets wanted and to attempt to influence their comrades in Moscow. In other cases, however, as in the turbulent circumstances of the 1940s, when the highest Soviet authorities were preoccupied with much more pressing matters, the Greeks felt they had considerable leverage to negotiate policy and achieve a substantial margin of autonomy in their decisions vis-à-vis the Soviet center.

A fresh and more comprehensive perspective on the KKE's international entanglements helps us not only to understand more accurately what really happened, but also to paint a more nuanced picture of the KKE's internal characteristics, crises, and dynamics as well as their deeper causes. It becomes increasingly clear that the impact of Communist internationalism shaped the party's organizational structure, culture, and strategy. KKE members lived through multiple realities engendered by the processes of Bolshevization and Stalinization, both of which transformed the party from a social-democratic group into a Communist organization loyal to Moscow.

Thus, joining the Greek Communist Party, individual citizens were integrated into a particular worldwide community of comrades. They were involved in international networks, legal and illegal, that gave them the opportunity to travel or, even more, to live for months or years in the Soviet Union and the other socialist countries, and to attend international party schools, conferences, and meetings. Through the reading of the party's newspapers and magazines, the followers and the activists became aware of an imagined community of revolutionaries that exceeded the national boundaries. This was not only a form of socialization to Communist values and norms; it was a source of power and pride both for the party and for the members. From this perspective, in the eyes of the insiders, as well as the outsiders, the Communist Party was not a party like all the others. From this perspective, joining a Communist party was far more than an entry to a revolutionary party. It was a full engagement with a worldwide institutional and symbolic network. A global version of the KKE's history thus offers an opportunity to study Greek Communism both in terms of the top-down forces that shaped it and of the grassroots factors that intersected and collided with the leaders' priorities and decisions.

Stalinization

Once the KKE entered the ranks of the Bolshevik camp, the Comintern and the Soviet leadership began to exert influence on the party's organizational structure. Bolshevization introduced the Greek Communists to a unique global community, and Stalinization prompted what Studer describes as "a qualitative change in the relations between the International and the national parties."[14] Stalin's absolute power in the USSR evidently was decisively reflected in the character of the Communist parties across Europe. No less than its sister parties, the KKE, too, underwent a process of Stalinization, a process that the historian Hermann Weber characterizes as consisting of (a) a shift from party governance based on internal democracy to one defined by a strictly centralized command structure presiding over a rigidly disciplined organization; (b) a remodeling of the party's internal structure into a monolithic and hierarchical one, whereby the leadership controlled the party members through a network of professional apparatchiks; (c) an alignment of party policies with the directives issued by the Communist Party of the Soviet Union; and (d) a universal recognition that Stalin unconditionally occupied the leading role in the whole movement.[15] Nevertheless, the European Stalinist party should not be viewed as a simple transmission belt for Soviet policies. The national parties were also producers of substance and the tools for shaping a very particular collective identity, defining the distinctive thinking and actions of their members. Stalinization encompassed many ideological, institutional, ritual, and behavioral patterns that all profoundly shaped a party's dynamics and its very existence and habitus.[16]

Stalinization was also not a natural consequence of Bolshevization, nor was it a sudden volte-face in the course of Communist parties' histories. Rather, the process of Stalinization involved external pressures, internal competition and resistance, personal disputes, and lasting rifts between party members. It was a long and complex affair. In the KKE, as with several other West European Communist parties, resistance to the process of Stalinization led to severe intraparty crises and splits.[17]

The international dimension of Stalinization also left an indelible mark on European Communism. On the one hand, as the KKE grew closer to the hierarchical world of international Communism, it had to report to the Comintern even the most minute details about its day-to-day activities. Even the personal lives of the KKE cadres were now under the scrutiny of the Comintern and its Soviet functionaries. The KKE had to report on its members' private lives, including family origins, skills, and sexual relations. At the same time, the Comintern also began to interfere in the KKE's internal politics. In 1931, directly and without consultation, it appointed new party leaders whom the membership did not even know. The new leaders were trained Bolsheviks who entered the party structure straight from the Moscow political schools. The KKE's most famous leader, Nikos Zachariadis, who was appointed to the position of secretary-general in 1931, had spent much of his life away from Greece and had been a member of the Russian Bolshevik Party even before he joined the KKE.

Communist parties across Europe adopted the transnational Stalinist organizational culture. This imported culture transplanted into the Greek party two fateful phenomena: the *cult of personality* and *centralism*. The former can be understood as a strategy of legitimizing supreme authority through the systemic veneration of leaders who enjoyed an almost divine status.[18] The latter, a disciplinary tool, was instrumental in implementing the cult of personality through highly restricted decision-making procedures. In moments of crisis, the two phenomena produced quick and arbitrary decisions as well as cruel purges and cleansings of the party membership.

Almost every single European Communist party experienced Stalinization, yet each has its own narrative of how this process took place. In Greece, unlike elsewhere, Stalinization was tied to a particular group of Communist missionary apparatchiks. Members of this group, which took over the party in the 1920s and 1930s, were not born in Greece but originated from the Greek diaspora in Turkey and Russia. They had no families or other social bonds in Greece, many were educated in the party schools in Moscow, and they often spoke Russian or Turkish better than they spoke Greek. These "Stalinist Jesuits" were the vanguard of the Stalinization process within the Greek party. The lives of these men and (very few) women were closely tied to the fate of world Communism. And without examining their rise and fall, and their special bonds with the international center, the tragic story of Greek Communism cannot be understood.

The Global Dimension of Greek Communism

This book represents the first systematic attempt to examine in detail Greek Communism from a global history perspective. It traces the KKE's interactions with the Communist parties in neighboring states, and with the Comintern, the Soviet Union, and the Bolsheviks in the years 1918–56. For Greece this period was not merely remarkably turbulent, but also uniquely tragic, encompassing the devastating impact of the Second World War, a triple foreign occupation, and a bloody civil war that continues to haunt the Greek Left. No studies of international Communism are more historically revealing and consequential than that of the KKE and of Greece. This book aims to show how this complicated past helps us understand not just Greek Communism, but also important aspects of Balkan and European Communism during the twentieth century. As a result, through its macromethodological approach and its global history perspective, the book represents more than the history of a national Communist party; it offers a history of international Communism from the perspective of its periphery in southeastern Europe.

The book is divided into two parts. The first part, covering the years 1918–39, focuses on the role played by the Comintern and the Balkan Communist Federation in the KKE's transformation from a minor socialist party to a significant domestic political force, and traces the party's early immersion in the international Communist world. The second part (1939–56) covers the turbulent and transformative time of the Second World War and the early years of the Cold War. It ends with the famous Twentieth Congress of the Soviet Communist Party, where Nikita Khrushchev denounced the crimes of Stalinism.

Chapter 1 ("Becoming Balkan Bolsheviks") focuses on the birth and the early years of Greek Communism, set in a framework of the movement's relations with the Balkan Communist parties and with Moscow. It shows that Bolshevization was not just an imposition of norms, attitudes, and policies "from above," but a more complicated and awkward process involving almost all the Balkan Communists at the same time. The creation of the BCF signaled the first step in the Bolshevization of the Communist parties of the region, which were thought to function not as distinct national parties but first and foremost as an almost unified Balkan revolutionary entity under the Comintern's auspices. Once the KKE joined the Comintern, it was integrated into a "Moscow-centric" network of structures, values, institutions, personalities, and activities. This global network shaped the organizational culture and the political identity of the Greek comrades. In this first decade of the party's existence, many internal tensions emerged as some officials fruitlessly attempted to resist the homogenizing pressure of Bolshevization. Moscow and the Comintern, however, leveraged their abundant human, material, and symbolic resources to bring the KKE under their powerful tutelage.

Chapter 2 ("Balkan Communism and the National Question") highlights the dramatic consequences of the interplay between international Communism and nationalism in the Balkans. A pivotal clash between those two forces appeared with the rise of the "Macedonian question," an international controversy regarding the future of the multiethnic Balkan region, which had devastating consequences for the Greek Communist Party. The earlier disagreements about reform and revolution paled in comparison to the issues brought to the fore by the Balkan Communist Federation's decision to support Macedonian independence in 1923–24. Yet, despite the protracted internal crisis and the party's resistance to the Comintern, the Greek Communists complied with the international Communist center's dictates on the Macedonian question.

Chapter 3 ("Becoming Greek Stalinists") discusses the Stalinization process of the Greek party. It shows Stalinization not as an abrupt ideological shift, but as a gradual process unfolding from 1924 onward. This process began with the reestablishment of the Soviet embassy in Athens, which greatly facilitated the KKE's contacts with Moscow. The process intensified with the arrival of the Comintern's "missionaries" from Moscow, but it was also significantly shaped by Georgi Dimitrov's particular role as leader of the BCF. Because of the multiple stimuli that propelled Stalinization, the process escalated in two different waves, one in the late 1920s and another in the early 1930s. Due to the fact that Moscow's supervision over the Greek party became more stringent, Stalinization went together with a process of de-Balkanization of the Greek party, which resulted in a radical shift on the Macedonian issue policy.

Chapter 4 ("Greek Dilemmas") examines the KKE's encounters with Soviet foreign policy during the Second World War in the context of the wider Balkan strategies for antifascist resistance. The Ribbentrop-Molotov Pact of 1939, and later the British-Soviet agreement on "spheres of influence" in the Balkans in October 1944, created particular difficulties and dilemmas for the Greek party. On the other hand, antifascist resistance transformed the Greek Communists into leading actors in Greek politics, giving rise to the hope that, following liberation, a radical regime change could take place in Greece, as was happening in the rest of the Balkans. Toward the end of the war, Communists in Greece, Yugoslavia, and Albania had a major role in their respective national political scenes. But when the Red Army entered Romania and Bulgaria, the Western powers all acknowledged that the balance of power in southeastern Europe had changed: the USSR now exerted more control over the region than the Western European powers did. While the Greek Communists thought this meant the time was ripe for a revolution, and despite Tito's promise of support for his southern comrades, Stalin chose to remain passive, still tied to his wartime alliance with the British and the Americans, and having different plans for the small but strategic Mediterranean country.

Chapter 5 ("Balkan Decisions") examines how the KKE leadership tried to navigate this uncertain postwar terrain of international politics, and reevaluates the transnational origins of the Greek Civil War. In May 1945, when the KKE's secretary-general, Nikos Zachariadis, returned to Athens from imprisonment at the Dachau concentration camp, a new era began for the Greek party. Having had no involvement in the Communist-led uprising of December 1944, Zachariadis, together with Communist leaders in Belgrade and Sofia, began to draw up revolutionary strategies under Moscow's careful supervision. The civil war that began again in 1946 basically as a KKE initiative was possible only because of this international Communist alignment and the prospect of decisive foreign support. The party leadership moved its headquarters to Belgrade and throughout the civil conflict worked closely with its sister parties in the Balkans and in Eastern Europe.

Finally, chapter 6 ("The Displaced People's Republic") focuses on the early Cold War years from August 1949 to 1956. The KKE's defeat in the civil war transformed the party yet again. Some eighty thousand people left Greece and settled behind the newly emergent Iron Curtain, while the KKE's leaders moved again, this time to Bucharest, Romania. Unlike Spanish Republicans, who found refuge mainly in the West, in the Greek case, it was the Eastern European people's democracies that became a refuge for the defeated, profoundly shaping their political culture and their political and social trajectory and exposing them to different currents occupying the international Communist world. When Stalin died in March 1953, the KKE, already dependent on its international comrades, had to adapt to the changes taking place in the

Soviet Bloc. The new leadership in Moscow had little sympathy for the old Stalinist Greeks. Hence, the haphazard process of de-Stalinization in the international Communist world yet again pushed the KKE into a protracted crisis. Greek Communists, scattered over the entire continent, had to find a way to reconcile their different visions of what Communism meant. While every Communist party engaged in soul-searching after Stalin's departure, no other party's soul was as deeply fragmented as that of the KKE.

PART I

Interwar, 1918–39

CHAPTER 1

Becoming Balkan Bolsheviks

On January 15, 1920, the Third Balkan Social-Democratic Conference took place in Sofia, the capital of the Tsardom of Bulgaria. The conference participants—the Bulgarian Communist Party (BKP), the Communist Party of Yugoslavia (KPJ), and the Socialist Labor Party of Greece (SEKE)—decided to transform the event into the founding meeting of the Balkan Communist Federation (BCF).[1]

This decision signaled a growing radicalism in the Balkan socialist movement. The movement had sprung up in the Balkan Peninsula in the nineteenth century, but since the Balkan Wars (1912-13), the prolonged atmosphere of horror and violence created conditions for the development of radical and antimilitary socialist ideologies. Yet the rise of radical socialism in the Balkans was not merely an expression of a general discontent. Its creation also marked the organizational progress of Bolshevik networks in southeastern Europe, which had been gradually developing in the three years following the October Revolution in Russia.

For the Greek party, the Sosialistiko Ergatiko Komma Ellados, the outcome of the January meeting was both transformative and expected. For several months already, party members had been passionately debating whether to abandon the Second International (1889-1916) and adhere to the Third International (1919–43). The Greeks, like many other socialists in the early twentieth century, had been divided between reform and revolution, a choice that appeared even more potent in the war-ravaged Balkans. The SEKE members thus had been arguing about their international affiliation almost since the party's birth. Finally, in May 1919, the party decided to leave the Second International, which, they proclaimed, had betrayed the socialist ideology during the Great War. Consequently, the SEKE's National Council instructed its Central Committee to prepare the party for joining the Third International.[2]

Party politics of the Greek Left—politics that continue to confuse outsiders with their alphabet soup of acronyms resulting from frequent disagreements and splits—had gotten underway only a few months earlier. At 10:30 a.m. on Sunday, November 4, 1918, in the port city of Piraeus, the SEKE held its founding Congress. In a room belonging to the Union of Steamboat Engineers, thirty-five delegates, representing roughly eight hundred members from all the corners of the country, gathered for seven days. Their objective was to create a political party that could unite the different personalities, groups, trade unions, and newspapers of socialist orientation already active in the industrial areas of Greece.

The press did not pay much attention to the event. Only one newspaper, *Valkanikos tachidromos* (The Balkan post), published a short note about the meeting. The otherwise ubiquitous indifference angered the delegates, who sent a protest letter to the government accusing it of silencing the media.[3] But whether the government was involved or not, there is no doubt that the founding congress of the Greek socialist party did not spur the interest of the general population. Even though socialist ideas had been circulating in Greece since the mid-nineteenth century, the lack of a robust social-democratic party on the political stage meant that left-wing party politics did not excite many.

The Bolshevik Revolution, on the other hand, did stir up some emotions in Greece. The SEKE had been influenced by the events in Russia from the outset.[4] Yannis Kordatos, a prominent socialist intellectual of that time, noted in one of his articles that the Bolshevik Revolution emotionally influenced many members of the party in such a way as to create a "revolutionary romanticism."[5] But despite common cultural traditions between Greece and Russia, particularly the Eastern Orthodox Church, for the Greek socialists the intellectual influences came almost exclusively from the West, unlike those of the wider Balkan Left, which during the nineteenth century was receptive to Russian revolutionary ideas and Russian intellectual life.[6] Several of the leading figures of Greek socialism in the nineteenth century had studied in Western European universities or spoke languages, mainly French and German, that enabled them to read Western socialist pamphlets, books, and newspapers.

Despite its Western social-democratic origins and its principles based on the 1891 Erfurt Program of the German Social-Democratic Party,[7] the new party had a strong revolutionary faction, consisting mostly of a younger generation of students and intellectuals who pushed the party toward Bolshevism.[8] The pressures coming from the revolutionary faction proved effective. On the fifth day of the congress, following a motion by the soon-to-be first secretary of the party, Nikos Dimitratos, the SEKE welcomed the Bolshevik Revolution with enthusiasm.[9]

Despite the early resonance of Bolshevism among the SEKE membership, the party's conversion from a leftist social-democratic party to a revolutionary one was neither simple nor predetermined. For the first five years of its existence, the party had been suffering from severe internal rifts and splits concerning its ideological orientation. Even though, as attested by one of the Central Committee leaders, the majority of the body wished to follow the Bolsheviks, Greek socialism, like socialist movements everywhere in Europe, was traumatized by the demise of the Second International and rather excited by the October Revolution.[10] Hence, until 1924, the new party oscillated between those two prominent currents of old social democracy and the rising Communist movement. The path toward the Bolshevization of the Greek Left was full of clashes, lopsided compromises, and splits.[11]

Nevertheless, Russia was not completely a *terra incognita*—neither for the Greeks nor, especially, for the Greek socialists. It was in the USSR that a group of people who would play a noteworthy role in Greek Communist affairs in the years to come lived: the ethnic Greek Russians. According to different sources, at the time of the October Revolution in the Russian Empire, between 440,000 and 550,000 Greeks lived in two major areas: Mariupol and the Donetsk region, and Kuban and the Caucasus area. In cities such as Odessa, Mariupol, Novorossiysk, Sebastopol, Sukhumi, and Batumi, thriving communities of Greek merchants and farmers had been living since the nineteenth century, or even earlier, as was the case with the so-called Mariupol Greeks, who were descendants of ancient Greek and Byzantine colonists.[12] It was perhaps no accident that in January 1913, a revolutionary socialist from Georgia, later universally famous as Joseph Stalin, disembarked from the Cracow train at Vienna's North Terminal station, bearing a forged passport with the common Greek name Stavros Papadopoulos.[13]

Some of those Greeks were initiated into Communism and joined the Bolsheviks' ranks during the October Revolution and in its aftermath. Actually, in 1921, at least two Greek-language Communist newspapers were in circulation in Russia: *Spartakos* (Spartacus) in Novorossiysk and *Kommunistis* (The Communist) in Batumi.[14] Importantly, those Russian Greeks were not isolated from Greece. Rather, a ceaseless population movement bridged the gap in geography and connected the two worlds.

For instance, Dimitris Sakarelos, the editor of *Spartakos*, represented this cultural bridge that connected Greeks from Russia with Greece. Sakarelos can hardly be called an ordinary person, as his life story reads more like a novel than like a history book. Yet his path demonstrates the complicated and durable interconnections between Greece and the Soviet Union made possible by the rise of Communism and the existing presence of ethnic Greeks in Russia. Born in central Greece in 1900, Sakarelos studied at the Teacher's Academy in the city of Lamia without graduating and took a job as a dockworker in Salonica instead. He deserted from the Greek Army, and in 1920 left the country for Istanbul. In this city he found contacts with Greek revolutionary syndicalists who helped him move to Russia, where he soon joined the Bolshevik Party and became the editor of *Spartakos*. In 1924, on orders from the Comintern, he returned to Greece immediately after the reestablishment of Greek-Russian diplomatic relations. In 1927, Sakarelos was sentenced to twelve years in prison for the murder of a Trotsky follower in Athens. He escaped in 1934 and fled back to the Soviet Union, where between 1934 and 1937 he worked for the Comintern's Greek Section and the Balkan Secretariat of the Executive Committee of the Communist International (ECCI). During the Spanish Civil War (1936–39), he was sent to Spain for five months, where he served in the Servicio de Informacion Militar, the Republican secret police, which maintained close relations with the Soviet People's Commissariat for Internal Affairs during the Spanish Civil War. There is no doubt that Sakarelos's duties in the secret police were to supervise the Greek volunteers in Spain and inform about them to the Comintern. From Spain Sakarelos moved to France, where, in Paris, he coordinated the Communist Greek network until 1939. Toward the beginning of the Second World War, he returned to Moscow again, where he worked for the Comintern's leader, Georgi Dimitrov, as a secretary for Greek affairs. His illustrious career was cut short in 1944 when he died under mysterious conditions in an airplane crash on a mission to Yugoslavia, or, according to other rumors, he fell victim to the Stalinist purges.[15]

But while Sakarelos's career suggests that Greek Communists lived international lives, the *early* Bolshevization process within the SEKE was exclusively a Greek affair.

Paving the Way for Bolshevization

The parties gathered at the January 1920 Sofia conference that established the Balkan Communist Federation were not, at the time, overly preoccupied with organizational details. Those issues had to be resolved soon afterward. The conference resolutions primarily concerned the ideological and political orientations of the new revolutionary organization. The BCF took on the task of coordinating the diverse Balkan Communist parties to promote a vision of a Soviet-style socialist Balkan Federative Republic, a socialist dream dating to at least the early twentieth century and supported by personalities such as Lenin and Trotsky years before the Bolshevik Revolution.

The BCF's first resolution urged the Balkan Communist parties to have close links with each other while preparing to assume power in their respective states, as a Communist takeover would, sooner or later, lead to the creation of a Balkan Soviet Socialist Republic. But the gathered parties identified another urgent duty: defending the Soviet Union. The resolution called on the Balkan Communist parties to support the Bolsheviks and "to paralyze thereby the counterrevolutionary forces moved against it from the Balkans or through the Balkans."[16]

Acting against the anti-Bolsheviks in the Balkans did not remain an empty pledge. The Russian Civil War (1918–20) pitted the Communist Red Army against the White forces supported by Western European countries. Socialist unions, particularly in the Black Sea ports, were encouraged to boycott ships carrying supplies for the White Russians as well as those containing the French-British troops that were coming to aid the counterrevolutionaries. Georgi Dimitrov, later the secretary of the Comintern, for instance, recalled that in May 1920, Bulgarian dockworkers in the port of Burgas heeded the Communist appeals and refused to load supplies destined for the White Army in Russia.[17]

In April 1920, three months after the BCF's creation, the SEKE's Second Congress voted to change the party's name to formalize the new ideological orientation of the organization. From then onward and until 1924, the party was named the Socialist Labor Party of

Greece-Communist. The SEKE(K) decided to adhere to the Third International of Moscow, accepting its principles and resolutions.[18] In line with this shift, the party resolved to send a representative to the Second Congress of the Comintern, which was to be held in Petrograd and Moscow in July.[19]

The SEKE's representative was Dimosthenis Ligdopoulos, a young journalist who served as a Central Committee member. Ligdopoulos was one of those socialist intellectuals radicalized during the Great War. Born in Athens in 1898, he enrolled in the Mathematics School of the University of Athens, but dropped out because of his activism—at eighteen, he joined the "Socialist Youth of Athens." His antiwar activism landed him in a prison cell. He remained in jail until 1918, when he was pardoned and released along with other socialists and antiwar activists.[20] Ligdopoulos was one of the most active leaders of the SEKE's left wing, and one of the first Greeks who had direct contacts with the Comintern. He in fact managed to get in touch with an envoy of the International Propaganda Department, Andriy Ivanov, who had covertly crossed from Odessa to Salonica in order to meet with the leaders of the left-wing faction. With the help of the secretary of the Yugoslav Communist Party, Sima Marković, Ivanov remained for some weeks in Salonica, in effect the capital of Greek socialism (having a massive and influential revolutionary syndicalist movement at that time), where he carried out party activity among activists within the trade unions. He also organized meetings with select revolutionary workers, with whom he discussed the latest developments in Soviet Russia and in the Bolshevik Party.[21]

Ligdopoulos's journey to Russia proved to be a long adventure with an unfortunate ending. First he traveled to the BCF founding conference in Sofia in January 1920, where he received the authorization to participate in the Comintern's Congress.[22] But his trip to Russia lasted two months, during which he lost communication with his comrades in Greece: from Bulgaria he went to Italy and then to Austria, from where he finally found his way to Russia. By the time he arrived in Moscow, the Second Comintern's Congress, which later became famous for the voting through of the "Twenty-One Conditions of Admission to the Communist International," was over.[23] Ligdopoulos, of course, realized the importance of these conditions to the life of the national parties. The parties wishing to belong to the Third International had to thereafter accept that "all decisions by Congresses of the Communist International as well as by its Executive Committee are binding on all parties that belong to the Communist International." The congress also noted that the name of every national party was a political question of high importance. Accordingly, it required every party to bear "the name Communist Party of this or that country (Section of the Communist International)."[24]

Even though he missed this fateful event, with the help of Orion Alexakis, a Greek-Russian member of the Russian Communist Party, Ligdopoulos managed to establish contact with the Bolsheviks and delivered to the Comintern officials a short report, written in French, on the situation within the Greek party. This fact demonstrated one of the usual difficulties the Greek Communists encountered in their efforts to contact the Comintern during the party's early years: they did not know Russian or any other Slavic languages. This linguistic gap formed a real obstacle that placed the Greeks at a significant disadvantage in the new international Communist movement, compared to their Slavic comrades, the Bulgarians and the Yugoslavs.

On September 21, a few days after his arrival in Moscow, Ligdopoulos presented to a specially convened session of the ECCI a report on the situation of the Communist movement and the trade unions in Greece. The Greek representative acknowledged that the SEKE(K) was still following its old reformist social-democratic program, but he informed the ECCI about the party's preparations for a new revolutionary program based on the principles of the Third International. Moreover, he promised that at its next party congress, the SEKE(K) would carry out purges of opportunist reformist elements—that is, socialists who preferred reform rather than revolution. After a short discussion, the Comintern's president, Grigory Zinoviev, announced that the SEKE(K) was to be officially recognized as a full member of the Communist International.[25]

Ligdopoulos did not have the chance to tell the tale of his experiences in the Fatherland of Socialism to his Greek comrades, and to explain the significance of the "Twenty-One Conditions" for the parties that belonged to the Comintern. Returning from the USSR, he tried to shorten his journey by choosing a way through the Black Sea, where he met a tragic death in October 1920. According to the official police version of the story, he was killed on a boat by Turkish smugglers, because they thought he had a large amount of cash on him. But Ligdopoulos was not alone at the time of his death—his comrade Orion Alexakis was on the boat as well, and suffered the same cruel fate. The Comintern had decided to send him as an emissary to the Greek party, a favored

Comintern assignment for all of its foreign-party members. The murder of the two comrades gave rise to questions regarding the possible involvement of the British secret services. There were suspicions that Alexakis was blacklisted by British Intelligence for his role in the Russian Civil War in southern Russia.[26]

Meanwhile, the BCF made its first public appearance at the Baku Congress of the People of the East in September 1920. The Bulgarian leader Ivan Nedelkov (Shablin), the organization's secretary in that year, spoke on behalf of the BCF in front of two thousand representatives from twenty-nine Asian delegations. Shablin was appointed an honorary member of the Presidium of the Congress and took the floor along with other foreign guest members of the ECCI on the very first day of the congress, following the opening addresses by ECCI chairman Grigory Zinoviev and ECCI secretary Karl Radek. He addressed the congress again a few days later in the fourth session, on September 4, and sent a message of solidarity to his comrades, not as a Bulgarian but as a Balkan Communist: "On behalf of the Balkan Communist Federation, to which belong the Bulgarian, Yugoslav, Greek and Romanian Communist Parties, I am authorized to say to you, delegates of the peoples of the East, that we, the Balkan peoples, are also oppressed and enslaved by the world bandits of Britain and France, just like you, that your struggle means our liberation as well."[27] This first public appearance of the BCF clearly signaled the way the Balkan Communists viewed the region's conditions at this time. Presenting Balkan peoples, as a whole, as victims of the Entente Powers' imperialism, the BCF leaders tried to demonstrate the unity of the region and the need to shape a common direction toward the future.

A few months later, in May 1921, the Second Conference of the BCF met again in Sofia. Even though only the Bulgarian and the Yugoslav delegates were able to attend the conference, the representatives present approved the statute of the organization. According to its provisions, the BCF was to be a regional intermediary organ connecting the center of Communist activity with the local entities, a sort of transmission belt between the Comintern and the Balkan parties. The BCF's Executive Committee was to be responsible for guiding the activities of the BCF and of the party members; it was to ensure that all parties developed a unified organizational structure and obeyed democratic centralism's organizational principles.[28]

Actually, the crucial decisions were made not in Sofia, but rather three months earlier, on February 24–28, 1921, in Vienna, the BCF's headquarters. The city was at that time a meeting point for all kinds of Balkan troublemakers, revolutionaries, and conspirators, and the words of the Russian Bolshevik Victor Serge perfectly reflected the city's atmosphere: "In Vienna we breathe the turbulent air of the Balkans."[29] Under the leading presence of the ECCI's representatives, identified at the proceedings as "comrade A and D," the delegates decided the BCF's organizational structure.[30] For unknown reasons, the Greeks were absent. The comrades from Moscow presented to the Bulgarian (Vassil Kolarov and Georgi Dimitrov), the Yugoslav (Djuro Cvijić, Lovro Klemenčić, and Ilija Milkić), and the Romanian (Alexander Dobrogeanu-Gherea, and a certain delegate with the pseudonym Marcu) representatives the Comintern's plan for what the BCF's tasks and role would be. The BCF was to collect information for the Comintern and seek to break the *cordon sanitaire* that the Anglo-French diplomacy had erected to contain Soviet Russia. To fulfill its goals, the BCF needed a permanent organization. Therefore, the delegations in Vienna decided that each party should assign one of its members the monthly task of informing the other BCF parties about its own internal state. Copies of these reports would also be sent to Moscow. And to maintain the comradely spirit, each party should also supply the other Balkan parties with its journals and other political publications.[31]

Even though many of those resolutions remained empty commitments, they had profound consequences for the national parties. In the following years, as the SEKE tried to adopt the BCF's procedures and norms, it became increasingly subordinate to the Comintern. In practice, therefore, the BCF integration was paramount to Bolshevization. Through the fusion of the national and the regional, the Comintern sought to create a particular revolutionary Balkan identity, able to promote both centralization and revolution in the region.

But the plan seemed too ambitious, and not everyone in the SEKE(K) agreed with the direction the party had taken. Some members questioned the Comintern's ability to intervene in the party's decision-making procedure and its internal structure. Opposed to the faithful-to-the-letter implementation of the Third International's decisions, some party officials argued that the SEKE(K) should not follow the Comintern's directives blindly, but rather adapt them to the local conditions.[32] An *à la carte* Bolshevization seemed to them a perfect solution. Unfortunately for these cadres, the Comintern did not share their perspective.

On June 22, 1921, the Third Comintern Congress opened in Moscow. Three men represented the SEKE(K): Nikos Dimitratos, a lawyer and the secretary of the party; Pastias Giatsopoulos, a bank employee; and George Georgiadis, another lawyer. All three were leading figures among the party's intellectuals who spoke fluent French and German (but not Russian), and were typical representatives of the Greek socialist leadership before the Bolshevik era.[33] Dimitratos, born in 1894, hailed from a political family. He was initially the leader of the SEKE's left faction and one of the proponents, together with Ligdopoulos and Giatsopoulos, of joining the Third International. And as unlikely as it probably seemed to them at that moment, all of the Greek delegates to the congress would be expelled from the party in different moments in the 1920s.

In general, the Greek presence at the congress went largely unnoticed. Dimitratos waited twenty days, until the evening of July 12, to take the floor for the first time; he spoke only at the penultimate, twenty-third session. The Greek secretary focused on the Greco-Turkish War in Anatolia and the SEKE(K)'s antiwar mobilization against British imperialism and colonialism. The party had taken a strong position against the Greek Army's participation in the Allied intervention in Ukraine in 1919 and in the Asia Minor campaign that same year, an "antinational" position for which it paid a very heavy price.[34]

The Greek leader made a strong antiwar and anti-British statement: "Greece is now fighting against Turkey. The Greek people have held many rallies to protest the ongoing war in Asia Minor. The proletariat of Greece understands that the war benefits only the capitalists of its own country and the Entente, especially British capitalism. The Greek people are in an even worse situation than the population of the colonies because they pay not only an economic but a political tribute to world capitalism. They pay a tribute in blood, which they are even today still shedding in Asia Minor for British capitalists."[35] He continued his speech by referring to the different actions taken by the party against the war and the human cost paid for it. According to him, just two months earlier, 160 people were arrested for resisting the war, and another forty faced charges of high treason. Apart from Dimitratos, no other Greek delegate took the floor during the congress.

At the Third Comintern Congress, the Greek delegation was the smallest of the Balkan parties' delegations. The Bulgarian, the largest, consisted of twenty delegates, the Yugoslav of fourteen, and the Romanian of ten. As reflected in the size of their representation, the Greeks carried little weight within the Comintern, and had insignificant status within the Communist world. The size and voting power of the national delegations at the Comintern's congresses were based on a variety of factors. The Comintern's secretary, Karl Radek, underlined the fact that the "Credentials Committee" used several criteria to classify member parties, including membership size, the country's political importance in global politics, and, particularly important to the Greeks, the prospects for the development of the Communist movement in that country. The delegations were divided into five groups. Accordingly, the first group, the members of which had forty votes each, consisted of Germany, France, Italy, Russia, and Czechoslovakia. The second group, with thirty votes each, counted Britain, the United States, Poland, Ukraine, Norway, Yugoslavia, and Bulgaria. The third group, with twenty votes each, included Romania, Spain, Finland, Latvia, Switzerland, Hungary, Austria, the Netherlands, and Belgium. Greece, with ten votes, was in the fourth group along with countries such as Lithuania, Estonia, Denmark, Luxembourg, Iran, and Turkey. This group, according to Radek, contained "small countries with an old workers' movement and imperialist countries where a Communist movement already exist[ed]." Finally, the last group, accredited with five votes, consisted of countries like South Africa, Iceland, Mexico, Argentina, Australia, and New Zealand. Hence, most significantly to the Greeks, the SEKE(K) was considered the least crucial Balkan party in the Communist world order.[36]

The importance of this elaborate hierarchy was not limited to the Comintern's congresses; nor did it attest only to the symbolic leverage each party had within the international Communist world. It did not escape the Greeks' attention that the hierarchy in fact signaled how the Bolsheviks saw revolutionary geopolitics, and that such perceptions had multiple organizational and political consequences for the member parties of the Comintern.

The Bulgarian Communist Party was undoubtedly the most prominent party within the Balkan Communist world at the time. From the first day to its end, all the secretaries of the Balkan Communist Federation were Bulgarians: Shablin, Kolarov, Kabakchiev, and, since December 1923, Dimitrov. Led by internationally recognized personalities with close ties to the Russian Bolsheviks, the Bulgarian party also had a prominent role in the Comintern since its very birth. Kolarov, Kabakchiev, and Dimitrov, especially, belonged to the socialist old guard generation within the party. They were leading figures and deputies of the

Bulgarian Workers' Social Democratic Party (Narrow Socialists) that joined the Zimmerwald movement, which first divided the Left into reformers and revolutionaries. Kolarov personally participated in the antimilitary socialist Zimmerwald Conference in September 1915, where he developed close personal relations with the Bolshevik leaders. In the early years of the Comintern, the Bulgarians thus ranked second only to the Hungarians among the international Communist officialdom.[37]

Perhaps even more importantly, the Bulgarians' stature was not just a matter of personal connections, but was related to the geopolitical developments in the Balkans. The Comintern saw Bulgaria as "pregnant with revolution," in the words of Victor Serge.[38] Defeated and territorially reduced after the Great War, Bulgaria was the opposite of its Balkan neighbors, Yugoslavia, Romania, and Greece, which, according to the British historian and diplomat E. H. Carr, were considered by the Soviets to be "agents and protégés of the victorious Powers."[39] The war-related national humiliation and economic deprivation contributed to the spread of revolutionary ideas and trade union agitation that made Bulgaria resemble Russia during its own revolutionary turbulence just a few years earlier. The Communists' self-confidence grew with the outbreak of 135 strikes, involving eighty thousand workers in 1919, and the considerable electoral performance of the Communist Party of Bulgaria in the consecutive national elections of 1919 and 1920.[40] The BKP received 17 percent of the vote in the August 1919 election and increased its performance the following March, gaining 20 percent of the votes, or 51 parliamentary seats (out of a total of 229), which put it in second place, after only Aleksandar Stamboliyski's Bulgarian Agrarian National Union.[41] Hence, many Bolsheviks thought that, at the time, Stamboliyski's government's position was not unlike that of Alexander Kerensky's ill-fated Provisional Government during the summer of 1917 in Russia. And the numbers suggested that the Bulgarian party was even more prepared for a revolutionary takeover: along with the Yugoslav party, the BKP was the strongest Communist party in the Balkans, claiming to have thirty-five thousand members in 1920 and growing to thirty-nine thousand just two years later.[42]

The Yugoslavs were not far behind the Bulgarians in terms of their importance within the Comintern.[43] The Socialist Workers' Party of Yugoslavia (Communists) was transformed into the Communist Party of Yugoslavia (KPJ) at its Second Congress in Vukovar in June 1920 and claimed to have between sixty thousand and sixty-five thousand members.[44] The party's performance in its first national election, on

November 28, 1920, could be considered satisfactory: the KPJ took third place, winning 12.36 percent of the vote and 58 out of 419 seats in the parliament.[45] Compared to their Western comrades, at that time, the Yugoslav and Bulgarian parties were giant electoral machines and organizations ready to seize power. Sima Marković, Filip Filipović, and Ilja Milkić were probably the most prominent communist Yugoslavs at this time. Marković was a mathematics professor at the University of Belgrade until his dismissal in 1920 for his Communist activism. He was elected secretary-general of the party in 1920 and, at the same time, was considered its leading theoretician. His international career took off when he was appointed to the ECCI in 1921. Filipović, also a mathematician, had studied in Russia, in Saint Petersburg. He was elected mayor of Belgrade in 1920 and a member of parliament the same year. Later he became the chairman of the KPJ and, like Marković, a member of the ECCI. Milkić helped create both the Serbian Central Trade Union and the Serbian Social Democratic Party in 1903. In 1918, he was posted at the Soviet embassy in Bern, Switzerland, and in 1920 he also became a member of the ECCI.[46]

In late December 1920, however, following its electoral success, the Yugoslav party was declared illegal and had to relocate its headquarters to Vienna. This development weakened the organization considerably because it lost touch with Yugoslav society and with the trade unions. It entered a long period of internal strife, which the Italian Communist leader Palmiro Togliatti labeled a "permanent crisis."[47]

On the other hand, in Greece the SEKE did not share in the glorious past or the promising present of its fellow Balkan Communist movements. It was the youngest in the region: the Bulgarian party had been formed in 1891, the Romanian in 1893, and the Serbian socialist party in 1903.[48] The SEKE was therefore an infant party with weak roots in Greek society and with no significant intellectual legacy on which to build domestically or capitalize internationally.

Except for the Jewish community of Salonica, which had been developing strong bonds with socialist thinkers and trade union organizers in the late nineteenth and early twentieth centuries, few people in Greece were concerned about socialism. In the early twentieth century, Salonica, a Mediterranean port and a multiethnic city of Jews, Turks, Bulgarians, Armenians, and Greeks, constituted a sociologically complex community within which nationalism competed with socialism and trade unionism. The latter significantly shaped the culture of the city, and forged the collective memory of its inhabitants. For example, many reminisced for years about the thirty-day strike of the tobacco workers in 1911, which united workers from many different national groups in order to secure wage increases and an eight-hour workday.[49] But Salonica, as well as the northern territories of the country, was not a part of Greece's territory until the Balkan wars in 1912 and, subsequently, was not a typical Greek city.[50] Until the 1920s, in the rest of the country, the so-called "Old Greece," socialism appeared a marginal political option. For a number of reasons, including the late industrialization of the country, the trade unions were weak and their membership small.[51] At the turn of the century, nationalism, rather than socialism, was the dominant ideological aspiration in the country.

At its founding conference in November 1918, the SEKE had roughly 1,000 members. Two years later, the progress made was far from impressive: in 1920, the party claimed to have 1,320 members. Its electoral performance was insignificant as well. Despite the discontent caused by the war in Asia Minor and its ensuing disaster for Greece, in the national elections of 1920 and 1923, the party failed to obtain a single deputy.[52] The atmosphere of extreme polarization between the Liberal Party and the Royalists, aggravated by the never-ending disruptions and upheavals of first the Great War and then the Greco-Turkish War, overshadowed the Communists' political platforms and rhetoric. Last but not least, with the notable exception of Avraam Benaroya, Salonica's Bulgarian-Jewish socialist leader who did not belong to the SEKE's revolutionary faction, the party lacked any internationally renowned personalities—the murders of Ligdopoulos and Alexakis in 1920 had left a leadership vacuum that was hard to fill.

To put it simply, Greece and the Greek party were of secondary importance to the Bolsheviks and hence to the Comintern, not only because the SEKE was small and weak, but also because Greece was not considered a crucial country for the international revolutionary movement. As already noted, the Comintern located Greece within the sphere of influence of the British. For their part, even the Bolsheviks saw Greece as "the policeman of the British," a country armed by Britain to enforce the imperialist whims, desires, and interests of "the despot in London."[53]

Accordingly, the Greek party was not entrusted with having representatives in the ECCI until 1928. Therefore, initially the Bulgarians and the BCF informed the ECCI about developments in Greece. At the First Enlarged Plenum of the ECCI in February 1922, for instance, Kolarov delivered a short but optimistic report on Greece, announcing that the Greek party had only 1,500 members but enjoyed great influence among fifty thousand to sixty thousand workers who were organized in trade unions.[54] Despite Kolarov's optimistic assessment of SEKE's influence among Greek workers, the Comintern remained unconvinced: not a single Greek delegate was elected to the Central Council of the Red International of Labor Unions.

The SEKE's second-class status extended to its status within the Balkan Communist Federation as well. Because the BCF was not considered a confederation of national parties but a unified regional organization of the Comintern, the composition of the federation's Executive Committee was not determined according to national quotas. Nevertheless, as secretary of the BCF in 1922, Kolarov insisted that each member country should have a different number of representatives on the committee, and proposed awarding three seats to the Bulgarian party, two each to the Yugoslav and the Romanian parties, and just one to the Greek party. Although they were unhappy with the arrangement, the Greeks ultimately accepted it. And initially Dimitratos represented the SEKE on the BCF's Executive Committee. But it soon became customary to hold committee meetings simply in the absence of the Greek representative.[55]

Such differences among the Balkan parties were reflected in the different amount of subvention from Moscow that each party received. Specifically, 35 percent of the BCF funds went to the Communist Party of Bulgaria, 25 percent to both the Yugoslav and the Romanian parties, and just 15 percent to the SEKE. With regard to the Comintern's direct subvention, the inequalities between the Balkan parties were even more conspicuous. In 1925, for instance, the Bulgarian party received the lion's share, amounting to 160,000 rubles, while the Yugoslavs got 40,000 rubles, the Romanians 30,000 rubles, and the Greeks only 10,000 rubles.[56]

Reactions to Bolshevization

Two days after the Third Congress of the Comintern ended, the BCF met for the third time. The conference took place in Moscow, where, under close Bolshevik supervision, the four Balkan parties reaffirmed the decisions made at the previous conferences. Although the members of the Greek delegation left Moscow immediately after the conference, their short visit to Moscow had a lasting impact on them. The delegates were disappointed by the images of poverty and misery they saw in

Moscow, which made them pessimistic about the future of Soviet Russia. Especially for Secretary Nikos Dimitratos and Georgios Georgiadis, who had previously ardently supported Greek participation in the Third International, their Moscow experience generated doubts that later led them toward adopting social-democratic positions.[57]

They were not alone: the news they brought to Greece, coupled with disturbing domestic developments, made a considerable number of party cadres want to slow down, if not abandon altogether the SEKE's Bolshevization process.[58] Indeed, the party soon began taking decisive steps away from the Third International. Exploiting the absence of the more radical younger party members, whom the war with Turkey had sent to the Anatolia front, a number of old-generation cadres organized a national conference in February 1922. There the delegates adopted two resolutions that departed from the Comintern line.

The first resolution stated that the party needed "a long period of lawful existence" before attempting to take over power. Departing from the revolutionary logic of the Bolsheviks, the February conference decided that the best way to defend working-class interests was through the broadest possible participation in all of the country's parliamentary struggles and institutions. In this way, they resurrected the old rift between reform and revolution that had divided European socialists at the beginning of the century. For years to come, the SEKE would remember this moment in the party's history as a serious effort to return to social-democratic principles. But the decision was not simply about theory. Reform became more appealing after November 1921, when the Greek government took measures against the SEKE and its media organ *Rizospastis* for spreading defeatist slogans while the Greek Army was fighting in Asia Minor.[59]

The second decision proved even more daring. While the conference participants did not openly renounce the Comintern, they concluded that all of the Comintern's earlier resolutions were not binding, but rather constituted "documents of historical significance."[60] In a somewhat confusing manner, the conference stressed its willingness to transform the SEKE into a revolutionary party, but only in the future; for the time being, the conference acknowledged that its priority was to strengthen the party as an organization. Without revoking their affiliation with the Comintern, the delegates nevertheless expressed their opposition to the SEKE's further Bolshevization. In other words, what they wanted was a limited Bolshevization. For them, this *à la carte* Bolshevization strategy was a compromise between reform and revolution that enabled the party to play for time under challenging conditions. But for the SEKE's younger members and, crucially, for Communists in Moscow, the middle road simply did not exist.

The man behind this peculiar social-democratic strategy was Giorgos Georgiadis, one of the three Greek delegates to the Third Congress of the Comintern. Born in 1892, he studied law at the University of Athens and initially pursued a legal career. By 1918, he had become the solicitor general at the Athens Public Court but quit the position in 1919 when he joined the SEKE. While it is difficult to establish whether his trip to Moscow played the decisive role in his shift toward social democracy, Georgiadis was clearly the leader of the "anticentralist" faction in the SEKE. This faction attracted not only the social democrats but also all party activists who felt uncomfortable following the paths of their Russian or Balkan comrades.[61]

Whether the majority of conference participants intended it or not, the SEKE(K)'s February conference gravely undermined the revolutionary character of the party and signaled the rising presence of a strong group of influential pragmatist-socialists within the organization. This reaction to Bolshevization predominantly came from the SEKE's old guard, which identified more closely with the legacy of the Second International. This old guard faced opposition from a younger generation of Communist leaders, radicalized on the fronts of the Great War and the Asia Minor campaign, who insisted that the party had to faithfully follow the Comintern's revolutionary policy. And those young Communists had an important ally: the Comintern promptly acted to realign the Greeks and put them back on the road toward Bolshevism.[62]

The Comintern acted quickly because the Greeks were not alone in harboring hesitations concerning the future direction of their movement. In fact, within the Communist world a number of crises rose to challenge the Comintern's primacy. From the North to the South of the European continent, reactions against the centralized model of "one way toward socialism" proliferated. The 1923 Third Enlarged Plenum of the ECCI, for instance, discussed the Norwegian and the Swedish cases. There, the prominent Soviet leader Nikolai Bukharin reminded his comrades that the new International had to act as a unified organization, in which the national element should be completely subordinated to the international. In other words, the decisions of the national parties should be subordinated to the decisions of the Comintern.[63]

Similar trends against centralism, as the Cominternians called this strategy at the time, also surfaced in the Balkan Communist world.[64]

There, volatile sociopolitical conditions, ethnic conflicts, and national traumas gave even more intense expression to the anticentralist trends. Balkan parties, especially the Yugoslavs, criticized the Bulgarians' leading role in the region, which they saw as a control mechanism applied "from above"—an extension of Moscow's centralizing drive. Indeed, the Soviets felt closer to the Bulgarians, partly because the Bulgarian comrades, examples of discipline, accepted orders without back talk, unlike the Yugoslav comrades, who frequently objected to Moscow's directives. The other Balkan Communists often complained that the Comintern was patronizing them and resented the Bulgarian Communist Party's interventions into what they considered to be the internal affairs of their parties.[65]

But the issues reflected more than a simple clash of personalities and cultures. The thrust of the problem was Moscow's view of Yugoslavia's international position. Lenin himself considered Yugoslavia a result of Serbian expansionism in World War I. The Comintern officials distrusted and detested the pro-tsarist Serbian elites who maintained close relations with their counterparts among the British and the French. Hence, influenced by Lenin's perceptions, the Comintern considered the non-Serbian nations within the Kingdom of Yugoslavia as oppressed nationalities and supported an anti-Versailles separatism, embracing Croatian nationalism as a potential ally for the Communist revolution. On the other hand, Moscow considered a pan-Yugoslav revolution to be unimaginable: for the Bolsheviks, revolution was possible only if the different peoples of Yugoslavia revolted against the "reactionary" Yugoslav state. This vision clashed directly with that of Yugoslav Communists who were committed to an antinationalist unified vision of a Communist future. At both the 1919 First Congress and the 1920 Second Congress, the party declared that it was going to fight for a federal socialist Yugoslavia.[66]

Such diverging views between Moscow and Belgrade aggravated the discord within the BCF. At the Vienna Conference in February 1921, the Yugoslav representative Klemenčić warned about the risk of transforming the BCF into a southern bureau of the Comintern. He insisted that the Balkan Federation had a distinct role to play and should not become merely an instrument of Soviet foreign policy.[67] Despite the different approaches of Yugoslav Communists and the Comintern vis-à-vis the Yugoslavian state, Moscow center did not openly oppose the KPJ's support for Yugoslav unity until 1922.[68] Soon afterward, however, the disagreement between Stalin and the Serb Communist leader

Marcović on the national question had as a consequence the targeting of the latter and his followers by the Comintern's leaders.[69]

Less intense, but equally disruptive, ideological strife had been developing in the Romanian Social Democratic Party since 1920, when joining the Comintern became the central issue on the party's agenda. In the summer of 1920, a delegation went to Moscow to negotiate with the Bolshevik leaders on the party's affiliation with the Third International. Although several party leaders and cadres continued to criticize Moscow's desire to dictate and interfere with the party's internal decisions, at the Congress of Dealul Spirii in May 1921, the Romanian party became a member of the Comintern.[70]

From this point of view, the Comintern's prompt reaction against the resolutions of the February National Conference of the SEKE(K) was not a surprise; nor was the SEKE(K)'s U-turn. In October 1922, at the SEKE(K)'s Extraordinary Conference, following a harsh confrontation between the left and right factions, the delegates clarified that the decisions of the Third International were made compulsory for the party. Moscow's efforts to impede the SEKE(K)'s return to social democracy proved to be successful.[71]

The conference not only made a policy shift, but also elected a new leadership: a new Central Committee and a new secretary, the left-wing trade union leader Nikos Sargologos, who belonged to the ultrarevolutionary faction. His slogans—"Down with intellectuals" and "It's time for the proletarian revolution"—resonated with the working-class base of the party.[72] His rise to power was neither surprising nor merely a result of Moscow's, or Sofia's, meddling. Undoubtedly, beyond a narrow circle of intellectuals and petit bourgeois educated people who led the SEKE(K) at the outset, the party membership consisted of self-educated workers who looked scornfully and suspiciously at the intellectuals. As a result, the Greek party began to resemble the Bolshevik Party not simply through external pressure. The SEKE(K) members were developing a *proletkult*, a Bolshevik-inspired "rejection of the old 'class culture' which was to be swept away," as Isaac Deutscher puts it.[73] At that time, as was noted by a party leader several years later, the party members were deriding the intellectuals as "pen pushers."[74]

But the new developments within the party and the international similarities did not obscure the reality that the SEKE(K) was not thoroughly Bolshevized at this time. The party seemed isolated and without close contact with the international center. As a matter of fact, the Greek delegates hardly attended important Comintern meetings, and not one showed up at the Fourth Congress of the Comintern held in November 1922 in Moscow. Almost two weeks after the opening day of the congress, on November 17, the German Hugo Eberlein announced to the congress that a delegate from the Communist Party of Greece was invited but had not arrived.[75] The attendance of the Greeks at the BCF conferences and the plenums of its Executive Committee was also poor. It seems that a Greek delegation was not present at half of the BCF's meetings.[76]

The low attendance of the Greek party at the Comintern's meetings during the years 1920–23 reveals the presence of three different realities: the low level of Bolshevization of the Greek party, the marginal role of the Greeks in the decision-making process of the BCF and the Comintern, and the inherent difficulties of the Greek party caused by the lack of human capital and material sources. But the Comintern would not let its Balkan members ignore its existence. In October 1922, at a meeting in the city of Ploiesti, the Romanian Communists defined the future of their party as a section of the Communist International whose "goals are identical to those of the International it belongs to," and stressed that the decisions of the Comintern were binding on all members of the Communist Party of Romania.[77]

The Comintern also found it necessary to go to the Greeks, as they were not willing or able to come to the Comintern's meetings. In May 1923, the SEKE(K) held its national conference at the headquarters of the party's organ *Rizospastis*. The conference delivered a final blow to the policy of a "long period of lawful existence," which the party now assessed as dangerous and opportunistic.[78] Crucially, this meeting took place in the presence of a Comintern representative. It was the first time in the SEKE's history that an emissary from the Third International was present at its meeting.[79]

The Greeks now found themselves firmly, and somewhat forcefully, in the international revolutionary Communist camp. But this accommodation did not bring peace within the ranks of the SEKE. On the contrary, new clashes soon broke out as Balkan geopolitics related to Moscow's and the Comintern's revolutionary strategy reminded the Greek Communists that their declarations of loyalty to internationalism hardly provided solutions to their local problems.

CHAPTER 2

Balkan Communism and the National Question

The Balkan states had emerged from the dis-
integration of multiethnic empires. When the peoples began turning
into nations, several so-called national questions appeared. How to give
each nation a national homeland that the other states could agree to?

For twentieth-century Greece, the national question that wreaked
the most havoc in domestic politics was the Macedonian question.
And it was hardly merely a domestic question. As the Bulgarian Communist leader Dimitrov characterized it, from the nineteenth until the
mid-twentieth century, it was "the most complex, most important and
most burning issue for the Balkan nations," involving three traditional
Balkan powers: Bulgaria, Yugoslavia, and Greece.[1] Born in Western Bulgaria in the late nineteenth century, when nationalisms were sweeping
the Balkans, and originating from a refugee family of Ottoman Macedonian descent, Dimitrov knew by personal and familial experience
what was at stake in the region.

A Specter Haunting Balkan Communism

The Macedonian question became an issue of international politics
toward the end of the nineteenth century. After the Balkan Wars in
1912–13, the historic region of Macedonia, which was inhabited by

an ethnically mixed population, ceased to be a part of the Ottoman Empire and was divided between Greece, Serbia (which later became Yugoslavia), and Bulgaria. Under the Treaty of Bucharest, confirmed in August 1913, Greece and Serbia acquired the main part of the Macedonian territories, an outcome of the war that Bulgaria, according to Mirosław Dymarski, saw as its "first national catastrophe."[2] A few years later, as a result of the First World War, in which Sofia joined the losing side of the Central Powers, Bulgaria experienced another bitter defeat. Under the Treaty of Neilly (1919), Bulgaria's aspirations in Macedonia, Thrace, and Dobruja were nullified and its Aegean coastline was ceded to Greece.[3]

Each of the three Balkan states that shared Macedonian territories tried to nationalize its part of the region, laying claims to lands and peoples in the remaining areas. Macedonia thus became a clashing point that combined age-old national antagonisms, great-power politics, ethnic identities, ambitions and suspicions, economic considerations, and conflicting political ideologies and organizations.[4] Over time, the level of complexity only increased. After the First World War and its geopolitical consequences, the stakes multiplied. The Balkans saw the rise of anti-Versailles sentiments, and of revisionist aspirations resulting from traumatic population transfers and the multinational refugee crisis that began during the Balkan Wars and lasted for a decade until the Greek-Turkish population exchange in 1923–24.

The interaction between the national issue and the socialist movement in Ottoman Macedonia led to a deeply complicated situation and a highly controversial dispute. Socialists from the region could not ignore a geopolitical question with such incendiary potential. In the nineteenth and early twentieth century, left-wing intellectuals were aware of the complexities of the Macedonian question, but also wanted to dissociate themselves from rising nationalism. Instead, the early Balkan socialists wanted to reinvigorate an old dream of Balkan unification, an idea that had originated with a Greek political thinker and revolutionary of the late eighteenth century, Rigas Velestinlis (also known as Rigas Feraios). While the great powers had responded to the decline of the Ottoman Empire in Eastern Europe and the resulting instability in that region (the so-called Eastern Question) by promoting the establishment of national states, Velestinlis had advocated an alternative solution: in order to avoid nationalist wars, the Balkan nations should be united in a single multinational and multiethnic state.[5]

Inspired by this proposal, the First Balkan Socialist Conference, held in Belgrade in January 1910, just two years before the outbreak of the Balkan Wars, declared that only a Balkan Federal Republic could provide a cohesive and peaceful solution to the national issue in the Balkans.[6] The outbreak of the Great War, which a majority of Balkan socialists resolutely opposed, did not change their perspective on the desirability of a Balkan federation.[7]

At the Second Balkan Social Democratic Conference in July 1915 in Bucharest, which was attended by such luminaries as Kolarov and Dimitrov (who would play a leading role within the Comintern and within the Balkan Communist Federation), the conference participants reiterated their commitment to the Balkan federation. Their manifesto stressed that "the Balkan social-democracy fights for a Federal Balkan Republic based on national autonomy, which will ensure the independence of the peoples, cause the hate that animates them to disappear, unite them through their federal organization."[8] Putting their idea into action, the participants created the Balkan Workers' Social-Democratic Federation, an organization led by a multiethnic bureau headquartered in Bucharest. Its primary aim was to coordinate socialist antiwar activism in the Balkans. But this "little International" ultimately failed to become more than another ambitious but ineffective venture.[9]

In 1920, after the Great War was over, the newly created Balkan Communist Federation returned to the idea of a regional political union. At this early stage of Balkan Communism, however, national questions receded into the background, as the proletarian revolution was considered a matter of higher priority. In the context of postwar regional irredentism, national questions were perceived as problematic and dangerous, especially by the losers of the Great War. The Bulgarian leader Khristo Kabakchiev expressed this sentiment at the 1920 Second Congress of the Comintern: "Bulgarian Communists cannot fight for national determination, despite the grip of foreign powers on their country and separation of over one million Bulgarians in Macedonia, Dobruja, and Thrace. It was just this Nationalism that led the Bulgarian people through two terrible disasters in 1912 and 1918 into its present condition." According to Kabakchiev, the only way out was a Balkan socialist revolution.[10]

Nevertheless, while many proclaimed their commitment to internationalism and revolution, it was not long before national questions resurfaced within the Communist world. After the failed revolutions in

Bavaria and Hungary in 1919, and anxious to conserve the revolutionary momentum, the Comintern redirected its policy in the Balkans. Now the question of the self-determination of the "oppressed minorities" became a critical issue on the revolutionary agenda.

Already in January 1922, the Bulgarian party displayed the first signs of the policy shift. The Central Committee declared that the party would strongly support the national struggle of the oppressed peoples who inhabited Macedonia, Thrace, Dobruja, and the other Balkan territories. But, attempting to maintain a balance between nationalist and socialist aspirations, the Central Committee stressed that the BKP would also fight against the Balkans' bourgeoisie which, it said, "seeks to use the national movement for its imperialist policy and its reactionary domestic policy."[11]

At the BCF's Fourth Conference in June 1922, the Bulgarian Kabakchiev, supported by the ECCI's Russian representative, Vladimir Milyutin, argued that Communist parties should, in fact, support the liberation struggles of national minorities. The Yugoslav representative, Mosha Pijade, disagreed, claiming that national liberation would simply come along with the socialist revolution and the birth of Balkan Soviet Republics. The Greek representative, Yannis Petsopoulos, sided with Pijade.[12] The Yugoslavs and the Greeks, however, soon found themselves on the defensive. As tensions across Europe subsided after the war, the Comintern began to view national discontent as a potential catalyst for revolution that was beginning to look less likely as peace consolidated.

Accordingly, the Comintern began to press the Balkan comrades to shift their positions on nationalism and, in particular, on the Macedonian question. The Russians made the matter more urgent, as they took the initiative and began negotiations aimed at uniting the different Macedonia-based nationalist organizations into a single force under Moscow's tutelage. As a result, after 1923, the Balkan Committee of the Bolshevik Party launched systematic efforts in support of the Macedonian independence movement.[13]

The Fifth Conference of the BCF, held in Moscow in December 1922, immediately after the Fourth Congress of the Comintern, discussed the future Balkan Federal Soviet Socialist Republic within which Macedonia, Thrace, and Croatia would become autonomous republics. Notably, the conference recognized the existence of a Macedonian liberation movement, and emphasized that the local Communists had a duty to wrest the movement away from the bourgeoisie's control and guide it so that it would benefit the socialist revolution.[14]

Vasil Kolarov, the conference's chairman, pressed for a more targeted discussion on the issue. But the SEKE(K)'s representative, Yannis Petsopoulos, refused to participate and proposed postponing the debate under the pretext of lacking precise instructions from Athens. The Yugoslav and Romanian representatives sided with Petsopoulos.[15] As a consequence, no major steps forward were taken, since apart from the Bulgarians, nobody else in the BCF wanted to open the potential Pandora's box of the Macedonian question. The Yugoslavs, the Romanians, and the Greeks all knew well that any resolution on the subject could severely damage them politically among their respective national constituencies.

Despite the widespread unease with which the Balkan Communists approached the Macedonian question, regional events and Communist politics soon coupled to create the need to address it. In June 1923, in Bulgaria, Stamboliyski's agrarian government was overthrown in a coup d'état and replaced with a new conservative and profascist government led by Alexander Tsankov. The Comintern considered the domestic situation in Bulgaria to be critical, to have a high revolutionary potential, and to be closely tied to the Macedonian question.

A few days after the coup in Bulgaria, at the Third Enlarged Plenum of the ECCI, the Comintern's leader, Karl Radek, explained the reason why the Macedonian issue now loomed so large. First, Radek castigated the BKP for its neutrality during the coup. Drawing a comparison to Kornilov's coup against the Russian Provisional Government in 1917 headed by Kerensky, he maintained that the BKP had facilitated the fascist coup and allowed for a significant shift in the Balkans in favor of the reactionary forces. He also claimed that the coup was hailed by the fascists and would propel them forward across Europe, and, finally, that through the new Tsankov government, Britain had acquired "an outpost for its policy of Eastern containment against Soviet Russia."[16] In short, for Radek, the coup was a momentous event in which the Macedonian question had been a major factor that helped the putschists. Having personally berated Kabakchiev for his underestimation of the issue, Radek argued that Macedonia occupied a critical role in Bulgaria's modern history and had brought about the downfall of Stamboliyski's government because the agrarian leader had signed the Treaty of Niš with Serbia, which helped him suppress Macedonian organizations, permitting the Yugoslav Army to pursue the Macedonian guerrillas into Bulgarian territories, alienating a significant part of the population. Finally, Radek proposed that an appeal on the issue be addressed particularly to the Macedonians. From the Comintern's perspective, the Macedonian question had the potential to set back the Communist cause in the Balkans.[17]

A few weeks later, on July 19, in a lengthy article in *Inprecor*, the semi-official organ of the Comintern, Zinoviev repeated the ECCI's criticism of the "social-democratic attitude" and the "neutrality position" of the Bulgarian comrades. Yet he concluded on an optimistic note, urging his comrades to continue the struggle, because, "after all, the civil war is only just beginning. It can only end with the victory of the Communist Party."[18] But despite Zinoviev's optimism about the revolutionary potential in Bulgaria, in September 1923 the armed Communist uprising ended in a crushing defeat. Hundreds of insurgents were killed and many others were imprisoned or exiled.

While the Bulgarian Communists bore the brunt of the criticism, other Balkan parties were also censured for their supposed indifference to nationalism in the region. At the same Third Enlarged Plenum of the Comintern, Chairman Zinoviev criticized the Yugoslav leaders for underestimating the importance of the issue: "Many of them say, 'Why does the National Question concern us? After all, we are internationalists, and proletarians have no fatherland. . . . The result of this backward viewpoint is that the workers' organizations in entire provinces of Yugoslavia dropped away from us."[19] Subsequently, Manuilsky attacked Marcović for his "passive attitude to one of the most burning questions," as the Bolshevik leader characterized the Macedonian issue.[20]

Pressed by the Bolsheviks, the Balkan comrades held another conference, the sixth, in November 1923, where they finally agreed on how to resolve the Macedonian question. A resolution included a section on "the future of Macedonia and Thrace," which proclaimed,

> A united and autonomous Macedonia is the slogan now of the Macedonians on all corners of their Fatherland which is covered with ruins. . . . The Communist Parties of the Balkans consider it their duty to intervene with the greatest energy in favor of national and cultural rights and of the independence of the oppressed peoples of Macedonia and Thrace. . . . The CP must fight for the political and cultural freedom of national minorities. It must proclaim the right of minorities to self-determination. This

right to self-determination should even give the right to compact national minorities to separate from Greece. . . . [T]he Communist Party will do its best to carry out the resolutions adopted with regard to Macedonia and Thrace.[21]

Understandably, the Balkan Communists were not happy to accept such a strong commitment on a sensitive issue. But the Bulgarians, supported by the Comintern's Balkan experts Dmitry Manuilsky and Christian Rakovsky, exerted strong pressure on their Balkan comrades to yield on this sensitive issue.[22] The Yugoslavs recorded their objections but finally, and reluctantly, accepted the resolution. Despite his initial, albeit unrecorded, reservations, the Greek representative, Nikos Sargologos, also followed the majority position. When he returned to Greece, he apologized to his comrades for his stance and explained that the Bulgarians and the Russians had pressed him firmly.[23] According to Sargologos, the Russians had blackmailed him into voting for the resolution in exchange for the $15,000 subsidy that the Comintern provided to the Greek party.[24]

Sargologos indeed had reasons to apologize for his action, as the Greek party immediately felt the consequences of the BCF resolution. For Greece, an independent Macedonia implied ceding territory paid for with blood in the wars of 1912–13, and an independent Thrace meant the loss of the lands acquired in both 1913 and 1919. The situation became even more complicated with the most recent demographic shifts in the mixed Greek-Macedonian areas: following the crushing defeat in Anatolia in the summer of 1922, 1,200,000 Greek refugees arrived into Greece, half of whom were settled in the Greek-Macedonian territories in the North.[25] As a result, the BCF's resolution signified not only territorial losses, but also another wave of resettlements for a large number of destitute Greek refugees, who were already struggling to survive in and adapt to their new homeland under difficult conditions.

For the Greeks, the acceptance of the BCF resolution on Macedonia constituted political suicide. The country's political establishment denounced the Communists as "antinationals" and "Slavophils," and the party risked losing a crucial electoral base, as the Asia Minor refugees constituted almost one-fourth of the Greek electorate in the 1920s.

The Greek Communists were not the only ones who suffered. The BCF's support for national liberation was also disastrous for the Romanian party, which, although not directly concerned with Macedonian independence, was committed to supporting the self-determination rights of minorities and strengthening their movements until the point of "their complete separation from the existing state organism," according to the BCF's resolution from the Sixth Conference.[26] Like their Greek comrades, the Romanian Communists were placed in an awkward position on their national stage, where they were denounced by their domestic opponents as antinational elements and Soviet puppets.[27]

As a result of these considerations, the BCF's resolution on the Macedonian question was a turning point in the story of the SEKE(K)'s Bolshevization. Earlier disagreements about reform and revolution paled in comparison to the issues brought to the fore by the BCF's decision to support Macedonian independence. Yet despite the protracted internal crisis and the party's resistance against the Comintern, the Greek Communists complied. Although it took more than a year for it to happen, the party's alignment with the Comintern line proved to be a development of major historical significance. And however heavy the price paid for it, the Greek party's compliance with the Comintern's orders was not automatic. On the contrary, it proved to be lengthy, painful, and full of back-and-forth decisions. Being a Bolshevik party in the Balkans in the 1920s was not simple. Difficult choices abounded.

Greek Communism and the Macedonian Issue

In February 1924, the National Council of the SEKE(K) reaffirmed the earlier decision to reject the reformist path of the "long period of lawful existence" that the party had favored in 1922. Now the SEKE(K) committed itself to fighting against all the bourgeois parties and agents of the imperialist powers, which for the Communists primarily meant Britain. Last but not least, the National Council expressed its support for reestablishing diplomatic relations between Greece and the Soviet Union.[28] But far more important than the decisions made were those not made. The council ignored the elephant in the room: the Macedonian question. The published documents did not refer to the BCF's November 1923 resolution on the independence of Macedonia and Thrace. The party's silence on such an important issue was blatant and—for the Comintern—inexplicable, because only a few months earlier, the SEKE(K) had expressed its readiness to support the cause of Macedonian independence. In fact, the party was playing for time, as the majority of its leadership in Greece still had severe objections regarding the resolution on the Macedonian question.

As was to be expected, the Balkan comrades, particularly Georgi Dimitrov, who in December 1923 had assumed the leadership of the BCF, were not at all satisfied with the Greeks' attitude. Accordingly, the BCF intensified its efforts to control the developments in the Greek party and redirect it toward the acceptance of the Comintern's priorities. The international Communists saw the Greeks' hesitation on the Macedonian issue as a symptom of the incomplete Bolshevization of the Greek party.

Appraising the situation as critical, Dimitrov addressed a stern letter to the Central Committee of the SEKE(K) on March 20, 1924.[29] He complained that the party had failed to submit to the BCF any reports on its activities, and informed the Greek comrades about the agenda of the next meeting of the Executive Committee of the BCF, scheduled for April 10. Dimitrov's letter contained a veiled threat: he demanded that the SEKE(K) take all necessary measures to ensure the participation of a Greek delegate in the event.[30] Meanwhile, following Dimitrov's orders, the BCF emissary in the Greek party from 1923 to 1925, Ivan Chonos (pseudonym Mikhail), an ethnic Greek Bulgarian Communist, increased the pressure on the Greeks as well. He informed his comrades that they would soon receive from the BCF's Presidium a manifesto on the Macedonian question, which they should immediately publish in *Rizospastis*, the party's chief publication.

The Greek party resisted. Not only did it not respond to the BCF's appeals to align its policy with the Comintern's directives, but it also did not send any representative to the BCF's Executive Committee meeting on April 10, as a new, angry letter from Dimitrov to the SEKE(K)'s Central Committee revealed.[31] To make matters worse, the SEKE(K) dispatched a letter to the Comintern, expressing concerns over the publication of the BCF's resolutions and manifesto. The Greeks complained that the BCF was pressing them too hard on the issue and warned that publishing the manifesto would unleash a new wave of harsh anti-Communist measures by the Greek government.[32]

Unsurprisingly, the Greeks failed to persuade the Comintern to shift its position. On April 10, 1924, *Inprecor* printed the first section of the BCF's resolution on the Macedonian question; the rest of the text appeared in the May 1 and in May 29 editions.[33] It thus became entirely clear that Moscow fully backed the Bulgarian party on this highly charged issue. Moreover, on April 20, Dimitrov addressed another letter to the Greek comrades, in which he underlined in a severe tone that not only was the SEKE(K)'s position on the Macedonian issue wrong, but it also made him suspicious of the motives behind it. He insisted that the Greek party should want to publish the BCF's resolution on the question "clearly and loudly."[34]

Yet despite Dimitrov's pressures, the SEKE(K) did not break its silence on the Macedonian question. In its publications, the party continued to ignore the BCF's resolutions, probably with the intention of renegotiating the subject in Moscow at the Fifth Congress of the Communist International, scheduled for June–July 1924.

The SEKE(K)'s delegation to the Fifth Congress consisted of Serafim Maximos and Pantelis Pouliopoulos, whose role in party affairs would be catalytic during the next period. The two new leaders had very different personal backgrounds. Pouliopoulos was born in 1900 in Thebes, a small town near Athens, began to study law in Athens in 1919, and joined the SEKE the same year. He was soon conscripted and served in the Greek Army at the Asia Minor front from 1920 to 1922, where he became active in the antiwar movement organized and directed by the SEKE(K). Those activities led to his arrest in August 1922, but he was freed after the collapse of the Anatolian front and returned to Greece. Undeterred, he joined associations of army veterans, seeking to radicalize and initiate them into socialism. Rising through the party ranks, Pouliopoulos made a significant contribution to the Bolshevization of the SEKE and its transformation into a Communist party. While his rise to prominence was domestic, the party's international entanglements helped secure Pouliopoulos's position: the ECCI and the BCF recognized his leading role within the party and contributed considerably to his election as secretary of the newly renamed Communist Party of Greece (KKE) in December 1924.[35]

Maximos's social background and revolutionary trajectory were completely different. Born in 1899 in Gaziköy, an Ottoman town near Istanbul, he was first educated at the Fener Greek-Orthodox College, but in 1916 he was initiated into socialism. In Istanbul he engaged in syndicalist activities, and while visiting relatives in South Russia, he made contacts with Russian revolutionaries.[36] Back in Istanbul, Maximos played a leading role in the formation of the International All-Workers Union (Panergatiki), a multinational organization uniting mostly Greek, Armenian, Jewish, and a few Turkish workers, mainly from the maritime and construction sectors. Several of the Greek members were Communists who later influenced the Greek party.[37] The Panergatiki claimed to have five thousand members, and gradually developed close relations with Moscow-based organizations, joining the Red International of Labor Unions in 1921.[38] In July 1921, Maximos represented the Panergatiki at the Red International's founding congress in Moscow, where he met Nikos Dimitratos and the other members of the Greek delegation at the Comintern's congress.[39] In late 1921, Maximos's activism landed him in trouble with the Turkish authorities, which at that time were particularly hostile toward ethnic Greeks. He was arrested in November and remained in prison for several days.[40] In late 1922 or early 1923, immediately after the Greek Army's retreat in Asia Minor, Maximos, along with thousands of Greek refugees, came to Greece. He immediately got in touch with the SEKE(K), which sent him to work as the party's permanent representative to the tobacco workers' union in the northern city of Kavala. In September 1923, he was elected to the Central Committee, possibly in line with the Comintern's wishes.[41]

Even though only two years had passed since the previous participation of the Greek delegates in the Communist International Congress, the 1924 delegation reflected the changes that had occurred in the Greek party. Dimitratos, Georgiadis, and Petsopoulos, who had represented the SEKE(K) two years earlier, belonged to the generation of the Second International socialists. They also represented a "Western-oriented socialism," based on local elites with ties to Western Europe. On the other hand, the 1924 Greek delegation included much younger activists, brought into the fold of Communist politics by the Bolshevik Revolution and the experiences of World War I and the Greco-Turkish War (1919–22). In addition, the presence of Maximos signaled the rise to prominence within the party of the Greek diaspora from Anatolia and from Russia itself.

Meanwhile, things had considerably changed in Moscow after Lenin's death on January 21, 1924, and Stalin's gradual stabilization in power. The Comintern, at the Fifth Congress in July, condemned as rightist deviation a political strategy of forming coalitions from above with social-democratic parties, a decision that was in reality an apparent attack against prominent Communists Radek and Heinrich Brandler, and their ally Trotsky.[42] In any case, the Comintern's line had no particular impact on the Balkan situation: even if some among the Balkan parties preferred coalitions with social democrats, they could hardly find partners among them, due to the absence or weak position of social-democratic parties on the Balkan political stage.

As might be expected, the national question evoked many negative emotions and gave rise to skepticism and debate. Yet the Bolshevik leader Manuilsky left no doubt regarding his intention to compel the unruly Balkan parties to align themselves with the Comintern's policy. He criticized the Balkan comrades who wanted to postpone solving the Macedonian question by tying it to the potential of a Balkan Soviet Federation. This future-oriented approach, said Manuilsky, "is tantamount to ignoring the acute problems which confront us at present." He was particularly critical of the Yugoslavs and the Greeks, informing the delegates that the Greeks not only failed to publish the manifesto on the independence of Macedonia and Thrace but even sent "a protest against the issue of such a document."[43]

For their part, the Greeks tried to defend themselves, in effect saying yes and no at the same time. Maximos argued that the SEKE(K) was not against the BCF's decision on the Macedonian question. On the contrary, he insisted, the Greek party recognized the significance of the issue and acknowledged that there was no "Greek Macedonia," but rather a "Macedonia occupied by the Greeks."[44] He admitted that the SEKE(K) addressed a letter to the BCF protesting that in issuing the statement on the autonomy of Macedonia, it failed to take into consideration the particular conditions in Greece. He reminded the congress that after the Treaty of Lausanne, all of the Muslim inhabitants of Macedonia were obliged to leave, and the Greek state installed 700,000 refugees in their place: "The Greek Communist Party opposed and will continue to oppose this violence and the Treaty of Lausanne. . . . But the fact remains that there are 700,000 Greek refugees in Macedonia. The workers and peasants of Greece are not prepared to accept the slogan of the autonomy of Macedonia."[45]

As expected, the Greeks failed to persuade their comrades assembled in Moscow. The congress stood behind its earlier slogan, "For a United and Independent Macedonia," which the delegates found "entirely correct and revolutionary," and they thus called on the Balkan parties to back "vigorously the national-revolutionary movements of the oppressed peoples of Macedonia and Thrace for the formation of independent states."[46]

A day after the Comintern's Congress ended, the BCF held its Seventh Conference in Moscow, but little of significance happened at the event. The assembled parties agreed on the policy directives of the Sixth Conference, and, as usual, criticisms were directed to the Greek party for its stance on the Macedonian issue.[47] When Pouliopoulos and Maximos returned to Greece, they pressed their comrades to adopt Moscow's decisions. But soon Maximos was arrested, and the burden to persuade his comrades fell on Pouliopoulos.

Despite Pouliopoulos's efforts, the Comintern's directives on the Macedonian issue continued to meet with resistance from the SEKE(K)'s leadership. For instance, in October 1924, the Greek party's official publication, *Kommounistiki epitheorisi* (Communist review), published the BCF's Seventh Conference resolutions but, again, made no reference to the Macedonian issue. The situation seemed to be leading to a new crisis in the relations between the Greeks and Communism's international center.

During the same month, the BCF's Presidium sent another letter to the Greeks, in which it again complained about the lack of cooperation from the Greek comrades.[48] As a result, relations between the Greek party and the Balkan center again turned increasingly tense. In its letter of November 3, the Presidium of the BCF found with frustration that the Central Committee of the Communist Party of Greece, despite its formal acceptance of the resolutions on the national issue, had not properly considered the appeal for the freedom and liberation of Macedonia and Thrace. The Presidium considered this position unfounded and firmly condemned it.[49] Three days later, Dimitrov wrote to Chonos, the BCF emissary to the Greek party, insisting on the need to implement the resolutions on the national issue.[50] But although the noose was gradually tightening around the Greeks, party secretary Apostolidis and other leading members remained intransigent, and for an entire year, the party continued to ignore the Comintern's pressure.[51]

In the end, however, the Greek dissidents conceded defeat. On November 26, 1924, the Third Extraordinary Congress of the SEKE(K) marked the moment when the Comintern imposed its will on the Greek party in every aspect of its strategy.[52] According to Pantelis Pouliopoulos, at that time a fervent supporter of an independent Macedonia, the SEKE(K) met to launch its own full Bolshevization. Under the watchful eyes of two international comrades representing the Comintern and the BCF—the Russian Boris Danilovich Mihajlov and the Bulgarian Ivan Chonos—Pouliopoulos told the gathered delegates that the party's position on the national question should be perceived as intertwined with the very character of the party as a Communist party.[53]

Pouliopoulos's rising star simultaneously signaled the gradual marginalization of the party's old guard, beginning with the current leader, the typographer Thomas Apostolidis. Born in 1892 in the industrial city of Volos, Apostolidis had been a prominent trade union leader well before the SEKE's creation and had became famous as a strike organizer during the early 1920s. He was a typical case of a socialist radicalized in wartime. Despite his radicalism, Apostolidis was not convinced of the correctness of the Comintern's policy on the national issue and stubbornly defended the party's reservations about it, for which he was severely chastised by the new Bolshevik guard.[54]

For their part, Pouliopoulos and his supporters constantly criticized the outgoing leadership for embracing a latent social-democratic, rather than Bolshevik, policy.[55] During the congress, Pouliopoulos's followers, with the help of the Comintern's representatives, who intervened whenever they considered it necessary, attacked the "rightist deviation" of the earlier leadership and demanded the party's alignment with the Comintern's revolutionary line. In the end, the party complied fully with the Comintern's directives, and the congress made two crucial decisions in that respect. First, the SEKE(K) accepted the resolutions of the Fifth Congress of the Comintern, as well as the decisions made at the BCF's Sixth and Seventh Conferences. The delegates expressed their unconditional support for those documents, calling them absolutely accurate and truly revolutionary. Critically, they thus explicitly embraced "the national revolutionary struggle of the oppressed peoples of Macedonia and Thrace for the creation of independent republics." In addition, the party decided to immediately publish its decision on the Macedonian issue, and one hundred thousand copies were distributed, half of them in northern Greece.[56] As a result, from this moment forward, the Greek Communists were constantly denounced by their domestic opponents as unpatriotic and antinational.

In retrospect, 1924 could be considered one of the most significant and dramatic years in the history of Greek Communism. For many, the official birth of the Communist Party of Greece meant that Greek Communism could properly begin its march toward a revolution guided by the Bolshevized party. But it was not just the Greek Communists who, that same year, fully embraced the Soviet model of a monolithic party model. Balkan Communism as a whole made a decisive shift toward Bolshevization.

A critical factor in the process was that both the Greeks and the Yugoslavs accepted the Comintern's line on the national question. As the Greeks met for their congress, their Yugoslav comrades organized in Belgrade their Third Conference. For the first time in its history, the Yugoslav party rejected the idea of a united and independent Yugoslavia. Instead, the conference accepted the right to self-determination of the Croatian, Slovenian, and Serbian nations, stating that independence was not a necessary step but nevertheless a potentially liberating one. The KPJ also expressed its support for a united and independent Macedonia, which in practice meant ceding the Yugoslav Macedonian territories.[57]

Why would the Greek Communists tie their future to foreign comrades who so blatantly disregarded their interests? As the story recounted here shows, the question has no simple answer. In the literature of the interwar Communist movement, the Bolshevization of the national parties, in effect the gradual Russification of the organizations and their submission to Moscow's directives and decision-making process, was often considered an inevitable path of the development of those parties. But at least in the Greek case, to regard Bolshevization as inevitable underestimates the dilemmas, choices, and strategies of the Greek Communist leaders. The Greeks' submission to the Comintern line regarding the Macedonian question was neither automatic nor predetermined. As shown in these pages, for a period of almost two years, the Greeks refused to follow the BCF's directives. But in the end, their decision to enter the Comintern and all it represented brought them under the control of Communism's center, whose authority and power they might resent but could not resist.

While it might be tempting to stress the instances when the Greeks actively chose their own political direction, an examination of the larger picture points to an important fact: the Greek Communists' experience was not unique. On the contrary, it was the norm: all of the Balkan comrades followed a similar path toward Moscow, even when the Comintern's directives appeared to be too much to swallow. Thus the Balkan parties submitted to the 1923 BCF's resolution on the national question because it was an integral part of a path-dependent process leading to full Bolshevization. From 1920 onward, it became gradually more and more difficult for the Communist officials to dissociate their parties from the Comintern. The Balkan parties' decision to join the Comintern had integrated them into a "Moscow-centric" network of structures, institutions, personalities, and activities that shaped the organizational life, culture, feelings, and personal careers of party officials in the region, including the Greeks. Indeed, the Greek party's international partners mattered greatly in its Bolshevization process. The Comintern became a major tool of international Communist politics and strategic planning and, last but not least, a source of human capital and financial support, so precious for the isolated and hunted Balkan comrades. Since 1924, endowed with a centralized and disciplined apparatus of professional activists directed from Moscow and conforming to Moscow's policy, the Comintern was capable of implementing the centralization process with great success.[58]

One of the Comintern's leading personalities, one who played a significant role in Greek affairs, was Georgi Dimitrov. After December 1923, the Bulgarian sat on the BCF's Presidium, and as its secretary he strengthened Moscow's role in the BCF while also improving its cohesion and organizational effectiveness. A loyal instrument of Bolshevik authority and Stalin's confidant, he was an effective agitator and a great conspirator, who propelled the BCF from insignificance into action.[59]

Dimitrov's vision for the Balkan Communists went beyond coordinating the everyday affairs of the national parties. He made plans for an uprising in the Balkans that all regional Communists would support. To that end, he established the Balkan Revolutionary Center in Vienna in 1924. Its members included not only the BCF member parties, but also the Macedonian revolutionary organization IMRO-United (Internal Macedonian Revolutionary Organization) and a number of separatist organizations from Dobruja, Kosovo, Croatia, and Thrace, as well as pro-Communist agrarians from Romania and Bulgaria. The Balkan Center published a bimonthly review titled La Fédération Balkanique, headed by Dimitar Vlahov, a revolutionary Macedonian politician appointed to the post by Dimitrov.[60] The publication appeared in many languages, including seven Balkan ones. It portrayed itself as not affiliated with any party and committed only to the struggle against European imperialism and national Balkan chauvinism, supporting the self-determination of the Balkan people.[61]

Tightly controlled by ethnic Macedonian separatists and Bulgarian Communists, La Fédération Balkanique reflected elements of the interwar revolutionary culture. For the Balkan Communists in the 1920s, nation-states may have been important arenas of political action, but given the region's highly unstable map, the existing state entities were not foundations for political change. The question occupying them was not just how to achieve Communism, but also whether it could even be pursued within the existing borders. By contrast, as citizens of well-established sovereignties, Western Communists did not have to concern themselves with these sorts of questions. In the Balkans, more than anywhere else, nationalism and internationalism were inseparable from Communist politics. The Bolshevik revolutionary Victor Serge described this complicated Balkan world magnificently: "Around the great conception of the

Balkan Federation there swarmed hordes of secret agents, impresarios of irredentism, peddlers of the influential word, night-walking politicians engaged in six intrigues at a time—and all these smart gentlemen, with their over-gaudy neckties, sought to harness the unbridled energy of the *Comitajis* and sell it to and fro to any buyer."[62]

Inevitably, this revolutionary culture merging with strong doses of romanticism and optimism shaped the development of Greek Communism, especially after Dimitrov assumed the role of the secretary of the BCF and strengthened the regional organization's grip on the Greek comrades with a network of BCF-trusted emissaries.[63] Dimitrov's effort to strengthen the BCF's control over the Greek party was buttressed by another factor: on March 8, 1924, Greece and the Soviet Union formally resumed diplomatic relations, which had been severed since the October Revolution.[64] Greece was the fifth country—following Britain, Italy, Norway, and Austria—to establish relations with the Soviet Union.[65] In June 1924, the first Soviet ambassador to Greece, Aleksei Mikhailovich Ustinov, presented his credentials to the president of the Greek Republic, Pavlos Kountouriotis.

In years past, the SEKE(K) had been consistently calling for this move, arguing that it was in the interest of the Greek commerce and shipping sectors.[66] This development, however, had an altogether different effect on the party itself. With the reestablishment of relations between Greece and Russia, new perspectives and opportunities opened up for the Greek Communists, while Moscow's control over the Greek party became easier to impose and maintain. For the Communists in Greece, the opening of the Soviet embassy in Athens was a critical factor for improving the conditions of their political work. Among other features, the presence of the embassy in the Greek capital could ensure that the Greek comrades would be adequately funded and would be better able to communicate with Moscow.

To be sure, the Comintern's revolutionary activities were theoretically incompatible with traditional diplomatic conduct, and the People's Commissariat for Foreign Affairs (Narkomindel) officially denied the existence of Comintern emissaries within Soviet embassies. The truth was precisely the opposite: Comintern representatives were deeply embedded in the Soviet foreign affairs service. Admittedly, the Narkomindel-Comintern relationship was far from perfect, and their cooperation was hindered by friction and misunderstandings. But at the end of the day, the two institutions found a modus vivendi that ensured that both could achieve their aims.[67]

One of the practical consequences of the peculiar Narkomindel-Comintern collaboration was that the Soviet diplomatic missions facilitated the communication between the Comintern and the national Communist parties; the diplomats helped transfer money, material, supplies, and personnel. Comintern emissaries were on the embassies' payrolls, thus enjoying diplomatic immunity and other protections.[68] In Greece, the Soviet embassy helped the Communists with communication lines, financial transfers, and visits to Moscow, and offered an escape route for the Communist outlaws from the Balkans.

Prior to the reestablishment of Greek-Soviet relations, the SEKE(K)'s clandestine correspondence with the BCF or the Comintern traveled through regular post via Vienna. Disguised as love letters and partly written with invisible ink, the correspondence was sent to a person in Vienna who would transcribe the message and, if necessary, forward it to Moscow.[69] Such communication was not only slow but also risky, as the Greek police closely monitored the activities of the SEKE(K) and its followers. Similarly, the money from Moscow came to Greece through Vienna or Germany, from where individual Greek comrades carried it to Athens personally, and not without risks and obstacles. A particular problem was that the money might disappear in the process, as evidenced by Dimitrov's correspondence with the Greek party regarding "lost money" in April 1924.[70] The same correspondence revealed another aspect of the relationship between the Greek party and the Comintern: the absolute dependence of the Greek party on the Comintern's financial help. Dimitrov often was unhappy with the Greeks, who systematically begged for money and depended for all their needs on the solidarity and generosity of the international comrades. According to the Bulgarian leader, the Greek party made no serious efforts to secure other financial resources.[71] This dependence on external funding constituted a heavy burden on the future activities and development of the party. After 1924, however, the situation improved considerably. The correspondence between the Comintern and the party now traveled in diplomatic bags, while the money passed through the channels of the Soviet embassy, assuring the Greek comrades that their subsidy would arrive safely and regularly.[72]

Another important change pertained to conditions of travel to and from Moscow. The tragic end of Ligdopoulos and Alexakis in 1920 was a traumatic reminder of the difficulties the Communists had to endure while traveling to Soviet Russia and contacting Comintern officials. An equally important improvement was the greater ease with which people

could now travel between Russia and Greece. The first Soviet diplomatic mission, which arrived in the summer of 1924, included a few
Comintern emissaries. They were the so-called Kutvies: Greek nationals, or ethnic Greeks from Russia or Turkey, who had graduated from
the Communist University of the Workers of the East (KUTV). Among
them was Nikos Zachariadis, the future leader of the Communist Party
of Greece.[73]

In short, the SEKE(K)'s submission to the Comintern's directives toward full-accomplishment Bolshevization certainly was not a typical
case of bottom-up conscious ideological choice coming from the party's rank-and-file members. But it was also not merely a case of top-
down intervention resulting from the uneven balance of power between
Moscow and the Greek party.

A close examination of the SEKE(K)'s inner sociological reality reveals in the Bolshevization process competition between the party's
cadres, who were polarized around two competing political cultures
related directly to generational experiences and social class *habitus*: the
sectarian and the innovator culture, to use the terminology of Joan
Barth Urban. The former group rejected alliances between classes, while
the latter accepted intraclass cooperation and looked favorably on political alignments with social democracy, thereby consenting to the rules
and norms of liberal democracy framed by the West.[74] In the case of
the SEKE(K), the sectarian culture gradually gained ground at the expense of the innovator mentality. This process was helped considerably
by the changing demographics of the party during the first few years
of its existence.

Indeed, from its very beginning, the party was dominated by two major groups: an older generation of social-democratic partisans who were
leaning leftward during the Great War, and a new, often younger cohort
comprising what Ben Fowkes describes as "chiliastic ultra-leftists and
anarchists who thought the world socialist revolution was imminent."[75]
The differences were not merely ideological, but related to how party
members experienced their class status. While the former group consisted mostly of intellectuals, middle-class employees, professionals,
and skilled workers, the latter included young students, veteran soldiers, army deserters, and unspecialized workers.

The old guard controlled the party in its early years, but Greece's protracted military engagements, which lasted almost ten years, radicalized
many young people in the trenches, where they heard and embraced

the party's antiwar slogans and the Bolsheviks' revolutionary appeals for peace. After returning from the front, this group of young Communists played a significant role in the party's development. They became the new leadership that pushed the party on a course toward the Comintern, which in turn rewarded and promoted the pro-Bolshevik youngsters.

In view of such changes in the party's leadership and ideological direction, we should view the SEKE(K)'s concession on the Macedonian issue as an outcome of two major factors. First, the Comintern possessed powerful mechanisms of persuasion and insisted on total obedience and loyalty. It demanded absolute compliance with its directives, not a so-called *à la carte* Bolshevization. And it had at its disposal all the resources of the Soviet state—money, human capital, organizational networks, power, and authority—with which to impose its will and strategy. In the majority of cases in the Balkans, the mechanisms of compliance proved to be efficient and adequate for the task.

To understand the nature of loyalty toward the Soviets and the Comintern, however, it is also very important to consider the second factor: the behavior and motives of many of the political newcomers and their demand for radicalism. They shared in the mass psychological disposition of the time, and they embodied the spirit of Bolshevization that swept through the party, mostly among the "proletkult," as a result of the trauma suffered by many young people on the Asia Minor frontline and in the ensuing disastrous retreat to the Aegean coast and the chaotic evacuation to Greece.

Demographic shifts among Left supporters were taking place all over Europe. In some Western European countries, polarization fed into the separation between the Communists and the socialists. In Greece, however, there was no socialist party to which the skilled workers and intellectuals could turn. Instead, factionalism and divisions dominated the life of the single left-wing party. Thus, for the Greeks, becoming Bolsheviks was clearly an agonizing process. Moving from a social-democratic party to a revolutionary Bolshevik-style Communist party caused grave trauma to many members—trauma magnified by the complex and painful road toward the organizational model imposed by Moscow. This strife was so distressing because it raised questions about the nature of their party's relationship to the international center. For the Communists of the interwar era, such questions signified an existential struggle over the very essence and purpose of their party. Communism was an internationalist ideology; its success, after all, depended on the unity of the workers of the world. Now, realizing the dream implied changing how the party worked and whom it answered to. In this fratricidal conflict inflamed by the Bolshevik intervention, fundamental principles and temperaments clashed bitterly. The effects proved lasting. In the first five years of the SEKE's life (1918–23), the outcome of the internal strife between rival factions seemed uncertain. In 1924, however, the party's full capitulation to the Comintern's Macedonian policy signaled a critical moment in the process of the complete Bolshevization of the Greek party.

CHAPTER 3

Becoming Greek Stalinists

The famous "Twenty-One Conditions" approved by the Second Congress of the Comintern held in the summer of 1920 placed special emphasis on the nomenclature used by parties that wished to belong to the Third International. Parties across Europe adopted new names. The party name was not a technical issue or merely a communication device but, as the seventeenth condition stressed, a highly political question of great importance. Activists across the continent recognized the significance of this seemingly marginal point as well. Soon the party name became an identity issue related to the old cleavages within the socialist movement. As per the Comintern's rules, being a Communist meant belonging to a *Communist* party. As a consequence, all across Europe, ex-socialist organizations that wished to be members of the Comintern were transformed into such parties, in the majority of the cases after protracted internal debates and dramatic splits.

In the Balkans, the Bulgarian and the Yugoslav revolutionaries quickly prevailed over those with reformist social-democratic tendencies. In 1919, two months after the Comintern's founding congress, Bulgaria's Narrow Socialists unanimously voted to change the party's name to Bëlgarska Komunističeska Partija (Bulgarian Communist Party, or BKP).[1] In Yugoslavia, the Komunistička Partija Jugoslavije

(Communist Party of Yugoslavia, or KPJ) was founded in June 1920. On July 29, during the Second Comintern Congress, the Yugoslav delegate Ilja Milkić announced proudly to his international comrades that "today Comrade Zinoviev gave me some Serbian newspapers where I read that the Yugoslav Socialist Party has changed its name to the Communist Party."[2] Similarly, but in a more adventurous way, in May 1921, the Romanian Socialist Party initially was transformed into Partidul Comunist Român (Romanian Communist Party), but in October 1922, at the party's Second Congress, it changed the name again, to the Partidul Comunist din România (Communist Party of Romania, or PCR).[3]

The Greek Section of the Communist International

In 1924, in a situation unique in the Balkans, the Greek party continued to bear the old name SEKE, even if the added (K) indicated its ideological orientation. Dimitrov, who had sat on the BCF's Presidium since December 1923, did not hide his exasperation. In April 1924, observing that organizational adjustments toward Bolshevization had not been fully achieved anywhere in the Balkans, he pointed out that in Greece they had not even begun.[4]

The Greeks, as we have seen in the previous chapter, were shifting toward the Comintern's positions, even if they did so haphazardly enough to cause Dimitrov to complain repeatedly. And finally, at the Third Extraordinary Congress held on November 25, 1924, the party transformed itself into Kommounistiko Komma Elladas–Elliniko Tmima tis Kommounistikis Diethnous (the Communist Party of Greece–Greek Section of the Communist International, or KKE). In addition, the party accepted all of the previous resolutions of the Comintern and the BCF, thereby signaling the absolute adjustment of the party elites to the Comintern's dictates.[5]

In fact, accepting the Comintern's hegemony was written into the KKE's new name. Like the Yugoslav and the Romanian party and unlike the Bulgarian one, the KKE was not the "Greek Communist Party" but the "Communist Party of Greece," indicating the Comintern's point of view on the character of the Greek nation-state. The Comintern viewed Greece, Yugoslavia, and Romania not as nation-states but as multinational states characterized by Greek, Serbian, and Romanian domination over other nations, such as the Croats, the Macedonians, the Slovenians, and the Moldavians.

Whether by coincidence or not, the KKE, one of Europe's Communist parties most loyal to Stalin, was officially created in 1924, the year that Stalin, born Ioseb Jughashvili, was freed from Lenin's guardianship because of the death of the Russian leader early that year. From this moment on, the crucial ideological and organizational principle was "The party is always right."[6] This principle dominated the lives of three generations of the KKE's members: the founding generation active roughly until the 1960s, the postwar generation that led the party until the late 1980s, and the postjunta (1974) generation, which assumed leadership following the collapse of the Soviet Union in 1991 and the disappearance of Europe's Communist regimes, and which remains in its role to this day.

The KKE's Third Extraordinary Congress not only changed the party's name but elected a new secretary and a new Central Committee. Evidently, the selection of the party's leadership was an important issue that preoccupied the BCF and the Comintern. As Dimitrov wrote to the KKE's Central Committee in advance of the meeting, the Bolshevization of the party was a primary task to which the congress had to devote its attention, first and foremost electing a leadership capable of action.[7] With such words, the Bulgarian leader made it abundantly clear that Bolshevization was primarily a question of, first, appointing to the leadership the right people and, second, policies: since the Comintern's policies could change, what mattered most was the ability of the national leaders to adjust to these changes. Dimitrov's experiences with the Greek party regarding the Macedonian question had taught him the importance of having leaders who were faithful to Moscow, rather than to their own convictions and principles. Accordingly, on December 1, the Comintern's representative, Mihajlov (Schneider), took the floor to explain to the KKE delegates the importance of voting for the candidates proposed by the Comintern.[8] Meanwhile, the BCF's representative proposed Pantelis Pouliopoulos for the post of the KKE's secretary. And so Pouliopoulos became the first secretary in the history of the Communist Party of Greece.

The KKE's foreign allies chose Pouliopoulos after careful consideration. The Comintern scrutinized him as well as two or three other candidates. But Pouliopoulos was also not the only one whose fortunes began to brighten at that time. Andronikos Chaitas, until then the secretary of the Athens section of the party, was recognized as an exemplary party worker.[9] On the Comintern's recommendation, Chaitas was elected to the Central Committee and nominated representative to the

BCF. This latter post hinted at the future plans the Comintern had for him. But Chaitas, a capable man, was also temperamental. Although he was short-listed for the post of party secretary, his character raised concerns about his fitness for office. The Comintern's emissary, Mihajlov, informed Dimitrov that even though Chaitas appeared to be a good organizer and practical man, he was also a big troublemaker.[10]

Indeed, Chaitas's life revealed his restless and adventurous personality. According to his Soviet security file, he was an ethnic Greek from the Black Sea region of Trabzon, born in 1897. At the end of the Great War, he lived in Ekaterinoslav (Dnipropetrovsk), where he worked as a teacher in the Greek community, but he moved to Greece in 1922. He and his wife and their two daughters settled in northern Greece, near the city of Drama, but he soon left his family to study law in Athens. In 1922–23 he joined the SEKE(K), and not long after that, he rose to the high ranks of the party. According to Soviet sources, having been to Russia, he was able to forge relations with the Comintern and the Soviets, even though he was not fluent in Russian.[11]

The new KKE elites played a prominent role in the party's transformation. Between twenty-three and thirty years old, this new generation of KKE leaders replaced the old guard with the Comintern's endorsement, and came to represent the new face of radical politics in Greece. There is no doubt that since 1923–24 the Greek party took critical steps in its Bolshevization, and that the Moscow-trained cadres—the Kutvies—played a major role in that process. Their personal stories, as Chaitas's and Karakozov's stories suggest, reveal that Bolshevization also meant a trend toward the Russification of the organizational structures and the decision-making process of the national Communist parties.[12]

As already suggested, the Kutvies first appeared in the KKE in 1924, along with the Soviet diplomatic mission in Athens. Their lives had not been ordinary: they had no stable occupation or residence, used many pseudonyms and different passports, and often lacked family ties, or even friends. These "red Jesuits," as the revolutionary Victor Lvovich Kibalchich (later known as Victor Serge) called them, constituted a distinct group within the KKE's life.[13] Such Comintern emissaries had operated across Europe since the organization's birth, and many Communist parties suffered serious disruptions as a result of their meddling.[14] What made the Greek case unique was the fact that these Bolshevik emissaries were of Greek origin.

The idea of sending Soviet citizens of Greek ethnic origin as emissaries to the Greek party did not originate with the Comintern itself.

It was proposed by a Greek Communist from Odessa, E. Gryparis, who in 1921 asked the Bolshevik Party to create a Greek department that would help with propaganda work within the Greek communities of South Russia. These Russia-born Greeks could later be sent as emissaries to the Greek party. The then-leader of the BCF, Kolarov, and the Greek party secretary, Dimitratos, both applauded the plan.[15] For its part, the Greek party not only welcomed the proposal but persistently requested Comintern emissaries. For instance, on Christmas Day in 1924, the Central Committee of the KKE sent a message to the Secretariat of the Comintern, asking for emissaries who could be of great help to the party. The unusual part of the message was that the KKE named three specific emissaries it wanted the Comintern to send: Dimitris Makrogiannis, Stelios Triantafyllidis (or Stilian Panov), and Panagos Tzinieris. The first two were born in Russia, and Tzinieris, while born in Greece, had been living in Russia since 1922.[16]

The Comintern promptly accepted the Greek comrades' suggestion, and in early 1925 sent Makrogiannis to Greece undercover as a diplomat. Makrogiannis, who remained in Greece until 1928, had a minimal effect on the KKE's functioning. In fact, the performance of the emissaries was often disappointing. This was partly because of obstacles they encountered in their activities, including their limited knowledge of the Greek language, the cultural gap between interwar Greece and Bolshevik Russia, which hindered mutual understanding between comrades, and the natives' reservations regarding the emissaries.[17]

On the other hand, while many emissaries failed in their tasks, Konstantin Karakozov's exceptional story showed that the policy could have had a significant impact. Konstantin Stiljanovich Karakozov (also Korkozov or Kostas Eftihiadis) was born in 1902 in Kars, then in the Russian Empire. His father was an Orthodox priest who probably influenced him to attend the Tiflis Spiritual Seminary, a training college for Orthodox priests, where Stalin had studied a few years earlier. Like Stalin, Karakozov did not follow the religious path, and he joined the Bolshevik Party in 1922. Between 1923 and 1925, he studied at the Sverdlov Communist University, an institution designed to train party officials rather than to provide a standard university education.[18] In 1926 the Comintern sent Karakozov to Greece. According to Eleftherios Stavridis, then the KKE secretary, the Russian ambassador to Greece informed Stavridis that Karakozov was part of a mission that came from Russia to organize the Communist Party. Describing Karakozov contemptuously, Stavridis portrayed him as a person without specific skills, ignorant of Greek affairs, and arrogant.[19] Yet from 1926 to 1931, Karakozov played a leading role in party affairs. He became a Politburo member, led the struggle against the Trotskyist faction, and contributed decisively to the KKE's Stalinization.

Karakozov's impressive performance, however, was an exception, not the rule. After some time, both the Greeks and the Comintern conceded that sending Soviet-born Greek emissaries was not as productive as initially expected. While they were respected as Bolshevik emissaries, they usually spoke Greek poorly and did not properly understand the realities of Greek politics. It soon became apparent that the best strategy was the reverse: sending Greek Communists to Russia to attend party schools and universities. With the new strategy, the process of cultural Bolshevization went into full swing.

The Bolsheviks had already recognized that they had to educate international cadres in Russia. In 1921, they adopted a resolution to establish a new training institution, the Communist University of the Workers of the East (KUTV), which, as Stalin himself recounted, subsequently welcomed representatives "of not less than fifty nations and national groups of the East having the aim of creating cadres capable of serving the needs of the Soviet republics of the East, and . . . creating cadres capable of serving the revolutionary requirements of the toiling masses in the colonial and dependent countries of the East."[20] An international department was created in 1922 and a Greek department began operating in 1923.[21] Initially it served students who belonged to the Greek minorities of South Russia or of Turkey. One such student was Nikos Zachariadis, the future leader of the KKE, who belonged to the first generation of Greek Communists educated by the Soviets. The KUTV experience shaped his personality, transforming him into a loyal Bolshevik, but it also gave him the credentials he needed to become a Communist leader. In the Greek Communist culture, to be a Kutvie was considered a great privilege, a sign of in-depth knowledge of Marxism-Leninism. For years, proud of his ideological grooming, Zachariadis used the pseudonym "Kutvie" in his articles for the official party newspaper.

Although the selection of students was the responsibility of the Soviet authorities, the leaders of the Greek minority in Russia had a role in the process, providing recommendations of candidates. For example, before going to Greece and while acting as a secretary of the Greek faction of the Bolshevik Party in the city of Sergiyev Posad, Karakozov recommended six Greek comrades to attend the KUTV.[22]

In August 1921, as the Soviet educational network expanded, the Bolsheviks decided to open the Communist University of National Minorities of the West (KUNMZ). Like the KUTV's, the KUNMZ's purpose was to train cadres for Western countries as well as would-be officials who belonged to national minorities living in European Russia. After 1925 the Balkan comrades thus also attended the KUNMZ. The Greek section was established relatively late, in 1928, in order to train members of the KKE and Russian nationals of Greek origin. This latter group continued to constitute the majority of the Greek students until the 1930s.[23]

In the beginning, the Greek students' delegation did not have a noticeable presence at the institution. As already mentioned in this book, the marginal role of the Greeks in international Communist affairs reduced their role within all of the international Communist institutions, including the party schools in Moscow. The largest section of the student body of Balkan origins was the Bulgarians, another reflection of the significance of the Bulgarian party in the Comintern. In 1929, for example, 132 Bulgarians attended the school, compared to 89 Yugoslavs, 51 Romanians and Moldavians, and only 36 Greeks.[24] In 1934 and 1935, the number of Greek students was 40. A few Greek comrades also attended the International Lenin School, the Comintern's school established in 1926.[25] Beyond the courses they attended at the party schools in Moscow, the Greek students were obliged to perform a variety of tasks for the Russian Greek community.[26]

The Kutvies, and generally all party officials who had attended party schools, regarded themselves as the "transmission belts" of the real revolutionary principles and as committed defenders of Bolshevik discipline. They relentlessly demanded that their party faithfully follow Moscow's decisions. They kept in contact with the international Communist world, maintaining a parallel communication network with the international center. And they corresponded in Russian on developments in the Greek party without feeling obliged to inform their Greek comrades about their activities. In other words, the Kutvies maintained their own secret network within the Greek party.[27]

Having aligned itself with the Comintern and its Balkan outpost, the KKE remained weak within the international Communist world, partly because of its domestic position. Despite hopes and expectations, the reestablishment of Greek-Soviet relations did not strengthen the KKE's standing in Greece. On the contrary, the Macedonian question had a devastating impact on the party, and the damage it caused was profound and, for years, irreparable. In Greece, the KKE members faced arrest, imprisonment, or exile based on charges of national treason and secessionist propaganda.

The year 1925 brought a new wave of repressions. In April, the party's secretary, Pouliopoulos, and several other party officials were jailed or exiled. A few months later, the dictatorship of General Pangalos (June 1925–August 1926), who overthrew the legitimate government of Prime Minister Andreas Michalakopoulos, outlawed the KKE, closed the party newspaper, *Rizospastis*, and exiled hundreds of party members, throwing the party into chaos. The remaining free members of the Central Committee elected as the new secretary Eleftherios Stavridis, a Greek journalist from the Turkish town of Silivri, a district of Istanbul.[28] Despite the KKE's efforts during the summer of 1925, the vast majority of the active rank and file remained under arrest or isolated.[29]

Soon, however, the KKE's fortunes brightened and a new page in the party's history began with the fall of Pangalos's dictatorship in August 1926 and the subsequent free elections. In November 1926, for the first time in its history, the KKE succeeded in securing representation in the Greek parliament, having received 41,982 votes (4.3 percent) and electing ten deputies. The geographic distribution of the KKE's votes reveals that the party performed well in northern Greece; in fact, in some electoral districts the KKE won more than 10 percent of the vote. In Salonica, the country's second-largest city, long considered the Jerusalem of the Balkans due to the strong presence of a Jewish community, the party secured an impressive 39 percent of the vote of the fifty-four thousand Jewish voters, who at that time constituted a quarter of the city's population. On the other hand, the KKE's share of the vote in all of Salonica was 10.8 percent, highlighting a deep social cleavage and the ethnic polarization between the Christian Orthodox majority and the Jewish minority at the time.[30]

In Salonica, the party elected three deputies, two of whom were Jewish. In general, the electoral results demonstrated an important development: the KKE succeeded in representing a large fraction of Greece's national minorities, primarily the Jews and the ethnic Macedonians.[31] In fact, the KKE's position on the Macedonian issue, as well as its friendly position on minorities' rights, helped the party to expand its support among those minorities. Of course, Salonica's Jewish population had already been attracted to socialist ideas and trade unionism several years before the creation of the KKE, but for now the party managed to maintain those sentiments and the image of an organization best suited for promoting socialist policies.

Salonica had shown promise as a potential Communist stronghold a year earlier in October 1925. In the municipal elections held under the anti-Communist authoritarian regime of General Pangalos, the socialist lawyer Minas Patrikios was elected mayor. Inevitably, the KKE's considerable contribution to his election created fears among the city's Greek-Orthodox bourgeois population. The thought that Salonica, which had been incorporated into the Greek state only a few years earlier, would have a socialist mayor elected with the support of the Communists and the Jews terrified the city's establishment. Astonished and panicked, the local press warned that Salonica was becoming a new Odessa, a clear reference to the so-called specter of Judeo-Communism, based on the fact that, like Salonica, Odessa in the Russian Empire had a large Jewish community.[32]

Despite the excitement, the KKE failed to capitalize on its electoral and political successes due to factional divisions within the party, which in 1925 had escalated into a heated struggle. The resulting strife that plagued the party was a Greek version of what happened during this period in the Bolshevik Party in particular and in worldwide Communism in general. The conflict was between the Stalinists (i.e., the Kutvies); the Liquidarists, later called Trotskyists and Spartacists; and the so-called Centrists. Within the KKE, the Stalinists were led by Chaitas and Karakozov, both of whom, as we have seen, had close ties with the Soviet embassy in Athens and with Dimitrov. The leading figure of the Liquidarists was Pouliopoulos, the ex-secretary of the party, while Maximos, Kostas Sklavos, and Tasos Chainoglu led the Centrists. Sklavos and Chainoglu had almost a similar trajectory to that of Maximos. Born in 1901 in Izmir, the second-largest city of the Ottoman Empire, Sklavos became a member of Maximos's Panergatiki labor organization in 1921, and in May 1924 he moved from Istanbul to Greece. There, on Maximos's and the Comintern's recommendations, he immediately took over the party magazine, *Kommounistiki epitheorisi* (Communist review); a few months later, in December 1924, he was elected to the party's Politburo. Chainoglu was born in 1900 in Edirne in the Ottoman Empire's Eastern Thrace and had been a schoolmate of Nikos Zachariadis. During the Asia Minor campaign, he served in the Greek Army, where he met Pouliopoulos, became an ardent antiwar activist, and joined the SEKE. In 1926, he was elected a member of parliament.[33]

Significantly, except for Pouliopoulos, who was born in Greece, all of the other leading figures belonged to the Greek diaspora. Several among them were refugees from Asia Minor, the Black Sea region, and Eastern Thrace. Chaitas came from the Black Sea region of South Russia, Karakozov was a Russian Greek, Maximos and Giatsopoulos were born in Eastern Thrace and educated in Istanbul, Sklavos was born and grew up in Izmir, and Chainoglu was born in Edirne. In the years that followed, the presence of this diaspora within the party leadership would increase. It appeared that the Russification of the party coincided with the increased role of these Greeks who had been born beyond Greek borders. Ironically, the majority of the Stalinist leadership consisted of strongly internationalized individuals, while Pouliopoulos and the Trotskyist circle around him were mostly native Greeks without strong international ties.

Whether native born or of the diaspora, their conflict revolved around a series of issues that had plagued the KKE for years, and that reflected the party's position as a peripheral yet actively involved member of the international Communist world. Greek Communists disagreed over the very character of their party, over the interpretations of and appropriate responses to the sociological and demographical realities they faced, and over the contemporary developments in the Soviet party and particularly the clash between Stalin and Trotsky.

While the Liquidarists and the Centrists had profound disagreements among themselves, they were united in their dislike of the Kutvies. In their view, the Kutvies were unbearably arrogant, lived apart from the rest of the Communists, and considered themselves saviors of the party. The Kutvies' network and their intimate relations with Dimitrov and other Comintern officials did not go unnoticed by the less privileged party members. Their opponents often denounced the close and secret ties Kutvies maintained with the Soviet embassy and the Comintern and blamed these contacts for creating an atmosphere of subservience, intrigue, and corruption.[34]

The most prominent anti-Kutvie figures were the leaders of the Liquidarist faction, Pouliopoulos and Giatsopoulos. In a series of public pronouncements, the two men condemned the Kutvies' behavior and blamed them for the difficulties besetting the KKE. They also criticized the Comintern and the Balkan Communist Federation for creating a network of trusted people who fraternized with the Comintern's and BCF's officials, engendering an atmosphere of defamation against those considered adversaries. Pouliopoulos and Giatsopoulos thought that the Greek party should assume the responsibility of forming its own professional party cadres, and they rejected the Comintern's practice of sending emissaries, which they regarded as Moscow's unsolicited intervention.[35]

Although such accusations were basically justified, it would not be correct to conclude that the dispute pitted the Comintern and its supporters against those who wished for greater autonomy for the party. Such an explanation would be too simplistic, as evidenced by the behavior of one of the chief accusers, Pouliopoulos. Three years earlier, when he had been elected party secretary on the Comintern's recommendation, he had strongly supported both the Bolshevization of the party and the Comintern's position on the Macedonian issue. In 1926, however, Pouliopoulos appeared to have changed his mind on all major issues confronting the party. He was now totally against supporting Macedonian independence, and considered the pressures coming from the Comintern two years earlier to be completely unacceptable. Pouliopoulos's about-face was equally dramatic. Having been the leading proponent of the party's Bolshevization in 1924, two years later he was the leading figure against further steps in that direction.

Until 1927, the Comintern's pronouncements did not fully ignore the Greeks' preferences. Even Dimitrov was personally in favor of a more flexible and tolerant stance toward the more hesitant minority within the KKE. An instance of Dimitrov's nuanced politics was his reaction against the expulsion from the party of the well-known Jewish trade union leader Avraam Benaroya. Benaroya, whom the majority considered a rightist opportunist, was expelled in December 1924. But he was no ordinary man. Born in 1887 in the Bulgarian city of Vidin, he moved to multiethnic Salonica in the early twentieth century, when the city was still part of the Ottoman Empire, and in 1909 he played a prominent role in the creation of the Federation Socialiste, a multiethnic organization dominated by Salonica's Jews. During the Balkan Wars (1912–13) and the Great War, Benaroya was active in the antiwar movement and was one of the few socialists in Greece who had contacts with the Balkan socialist movement. In 1915, after Salonica's incorporation into the Greek state, he was elected to the Greek parliament, and three years later he became a founding member of the SEKE. The Bulgarian-born Jew played such a critical role in the development of trade unionism and socialism in Greece that many considered him to be, as Hüseyin Kazim, the Ottoman governor of Salonica in 1912, put it, "the man who created socialism in Salonica from scratch."[36] As a result, the party's expulsion of

Benaroya did not go unnoticed. Dimitrov, who knew the socialist leader well, was particularly unhappy about the decision and criticized it as arbitrary, urging the Greek comrades to act objectively and discreetly.[37]

Often the disagreements within the party reflected personal ambitions and differences in temperament rather than diverging ideological and political views. It is striking how often Dimitrov wrote his Greek comrades that they had to overcome their personal quarrels and be resilient and patient, placing "the interest of the working class above personal conflicts."[38]

On the other hand, while personalities mattered, the so-called "Kutvies debate" required the KKE to seriously evaluate the extent of its autonomy within the Comintern and the BCF, a question that had haunted the Greek party since its birth in 1918. By 1924, the question had returned with consequences far more profound and devastating than ever before. While the KKE had become entangled in the world of international Communism much earlier, gradually that world itself had been transformed. By 1924, Stalin had reached the highest level of power in the Soviet Union. The KKE thus no longer experienced Bolshevization, but Stalinization, which meant that the KKE, like other Communist parties, came more firmly than ever before under Moscow's control.[39] Over the course of this transformation, the stakes for the Greek party moved from the realm of ideology to the realm of loyalty to a highly personalized authority.

For the KKE, the consequences of Stalinization within the international Communist world were compounded by the socioeconomic status of the rank and file of its membership. While the rival factions did not map perfectly onto the class origins of their supporters, the Stalinist-Kutvies were usually younger blue-collar workers. On the other hand, the Liquidarists' support came from the older middle-class activists: intellectuals, members of parliament, and local councilors, many of whom came from Salonica's Jewish community. From a certain perspective there was no particular difference between the pre-1924 intraparty rivalries and the new divisions. In essence, the new elites who had become enchanted with Moscow's revolutionary aura and authority saw serving the center as a means of furthering their party careers. As time went by, they made themselves more amenable to the Greek rank and file, and their positions in the party and in the institutional network became stronger and more secure.

The star of the intellectuals, on the other hand, was waning. Their position within the SEKE had proved divisive already at the party's birth. Some working-class members resented the fact that the party leadership initially consisted mainly of intellectuals, considering it a social-democratic deviation that made a mockery of the idea that the SEKE was a workers' party. Bolshevization, therefore, provided an opportunity to improve the Communist credentials of the party by demoting the middle-class leaders. Some of the new leaders, including Pouliopoulos, did argue that there was still a need to attract intellectuals, whom he considered to be particularly significant in countries like Greece.[40] During the early 1920s, however, the SEKE faced so many traumatic events—including the highly unpopular and politically costly settlement over the Macedonian question, government attacks against the Far Left, and the ongoing internal purges—that many of the socialist intellectuals who had founded the party or had close ties to it chose to withdraw.[41]

As a result, gradually the KKE became a very different party compared to its predecessor, the SEKE. Whereas the latter had been a fairly transparent party with multiple factions whose cadres came primarily from the middle class, the KKE was an organization created according to the (somewhat pliable) norms of the Comintern. In fact, to some it appeared to be a brand-new party.[42] The key principle of Stalinism—that is, centralism—carried with it a rigid discipline that many intellectuals, for whom freedom of speech was essential, considered unbearable. Domestic conditions, whose harshness was exacerbated by the Comintern-sponsored radicalism, alienated middle-class professionals who could not afford to engage in clandestine activities or live under continuous threats of legal repercussions.

The role of the older intellectuals in guiding the party also diminished as the traditional divide between reform and revolution intensified during the more turbulent times. Those members who favored legal action advocated a reformist agenda and alliances with part of the left-wing bourgeoisie. The others, who prepared for a revolution, did not feel the need for the cautious legalistic plans of the party's founding fathers.

The key question that the party had to address was simple: what kind of policies would the international Communist center tolerate? The younger rank-and-file revolutionaries, who were happy to support Bolshevization from the outset, were soon to find out that, after all their sacrifices to fulfill the mission promoted by the center, Moscow's priorities began to change. As the Soviet Union embraced the policy of socialism in one country, the European Communist parties appeared to acquire a new role. While formally the new policy, in Kotkin's words, "had nothing to do with abandoning world revolution," the approach now favored by Moscow changed, as the Comintern began to promote more cautious plans that were compatible with the Narkomindel policies.[43]

In the Balkans, another Comintern principle caused confusion and havoc, as international Communists began to embrace the "stabilization of capitalism" thesis, elaborated in 1925–26.[44] According to this new thesis, the socialist revolution no longer appeared imminent, and, under certain circumstances, the Communist parties were finally allowed to ally with the nationalists, the agrarians, and the socialists.[45] Consequently, international imperialism, rather than capitalism itself, became the principal enemy. Based on such thinking, the issues of nationalism and colonialism collapsed into one another, confusing many Balkan Communists who lived in ethnically mixed but weak and unstable states that had emerged from recently fallen empires. For workers of the Balkan Peninsula, these novel theoretical tenets did not easily conform to their notions of traditional politics, in which enemies were more easily identifiable.

In Greece, domestic politics required responses that went beyond the simplistic positions of the Communist center's new directions. In 1925–26, the brief dictatorship of General Pangalos prompted the KKE to seek alliances that could help it confront the military government and its harsh anti-Communist measures. In doing so, they were, in fact, following Dimitrov's recommendations. Haunted by memories of the 1923 coup in Bulgaria, when the Bulgarian Communist Party had kept the neutral position that the Comintern leadership of Zinoviev and Radek had so severely criticized, Dimitrov recommended that the Greek party take action against the dictatorship. Even before Pangalos's coup, believing that he had learned the appropriate lesson, Dimitrov argued in favor of an alliance with the "leftist bourgeoisie" to promote the workers' and peasants' demands.[46]

In accordance with Dimitrov's advice, the Greek party began to embrace the slogan of a "Left Democracy" or "Real Democracy," and the Kutvies' group, including Chaitas, Karakozov, and Zachariadis, played a considerable role in pushing the party in that direction. The "Left Democracy" policy was an effort to introduce the Comintern's line of the "workers' and paysans' government" under the conditions prevailing in Greece. From a certain Communist perspective, it was a move toward the right because it promoted interclass alliances from the top, which meant coalition with social democrats and other leftist, non-Communist parties, a sort of prelude to the "People's Republic" concept shaped during the "antifascist front" of later years. According to Joan Barth Urban's classification, the "Left Democracy" was a "moderate sectarian" line combining "strategic and programmatic intransigence with tactical agility."[47] In August 1925, with Dimitrov's full support, the Kutvies leadership promoted the new concept in *Rizospastis* articles.

As might be expected, the new strategy was opposed by radical sectarians who rejected any consideration of an alliance with the class enemy. Pouliopoulos and Maximos reacted promptly against what they called a legalistic and opportunistic position, and their interpretation received the approval of the Comintern. The "Left Democracy" thesis was soon dropped,[48] and the world of international Communism was in flux. As the rules and the centers of power were shifting, the KKE found itself in a confusing and more complicated world in which developments in the Bolshevik Party and internal orientations in the KKE were even harder to reconcile.

Between 1924 and 1927, the Comintern's control over the KKE became increasingly stronger. Despite the government's harsh measures against the party elite and its rank and file, the faithful implementation of the Comintern's line on the Macedonian issue was clear evidence of the KKE's successful Bolshevization. But the party was still far from being the monolithic organization that some in Moscow dreamed of. On the contrary, old cleavages did not completely disappear, while new ones continued to emerge as the party experienced a number of harsh disputes caused by internal and external factors. Undoubtedly, the latter were by far the most significant. But the factional strife within the KKE was not a simple echo of the Russian Communists' squabbles during the post-Lenin period. It also reflected domestic sociological, political, and cultural factors, as well as the specific characteristics of the radical politics of Greece in the 1920s.

The First Wave of Stalinization

Stalin transformed international Communism when the consolidation of his personal power in the USSR sent ripple effects across the wider Communist movement. Already embroiled in the Comintern's elaborate network, Communist parties had to grapple with the consequences of changes in the top leadership of the socialist motherland.

Stalin's rise to uncontested authority included power moves that defied ideological divisions. His first rival was Leon Trotsky, against whom the would-be supreme leader joined forces with Grigory Zinoviev and Lev Kamenev. But frightened by the formidable and ruthless Georgian, the two soon were allied with Trotsky and formed a group called the United Opposition against him. While prominent Bolsheviks swapped sides, Stalin forged a more sustainable alliance with Bukharin, defeated the so-called United Opposition, and in October 1926 placed Bukharin at the head of the Comintern as its secretary-general.

Those turbulent events had great significance beyond Russia, including in Greece, where the KKE's internal dynamics reflected the rise and fall of the United Opposition in the Soviet Union. And the party's international entanglements meant that its leaders had to face Stalin's and Bukharin's new networks and sympathizers in the international Communist movement.[49] In fact, Greece had its own version of the United Opposition, which took the form of a united front between the Liquidarists and the Centrists. The two factions rallied together, united by their anti-Kutvie sentiment. But their alliance soon proved to be no match for the Stalinist organizational machine, which had the full trust and support of the Comintern, and the consequences for the Greek Communists were dramatic.

First, in September 1927, Pouliopoulos and Giatsopoulos, along with a hundred other members of the Liquidarist faction, were purged from the party. This was punishment for an open letter addressed to the general membership in June 1927, in which the leaders of the minority proclaimed their clear opposition to the Stalinist majority.[50] After this first wave of purges, the Centrist faction of the Politburo—Maximos, Sklavos, and Chainoglu—resigned from the body. On November 4, 1927, Maximos and Pouliopoulos presented their new joint platform, which they called the United Opposition, and a few weeks later the pair launched their own publication, the *Spartacus*. The title soon became the group's brand name. But their act of defiance cost them their party membership: in February 1928, the Third Plenum of the Central Committee of the KKE decided to expel the three ex-Politburo members, as well as five other Central Committee cadres who had chosen to follow the former leaders.

Having rid itself of the dissenting voices, the KKE's Stalinist leadership now defined the party's enemies rather broadly. Branded as the new "counterrevolutionary elements" were all of those who disagreed with the purges and the expulsion of the "petit bourgeois intellectuals," or considered the role of the Kutvies damaging or corrupted and the Comintern's interventions detrimental. Also now labeled enemies were those who regarded the KKE's Macedonian policy as bankrupted and asked the party to abandon it, and finally those who disagreed with the strategy of socialism in one country.[51]

Inspired by Moscow's new realities, the purges within the KKE took the form of a hunt against Trotskyism that in February 1928 exploded into a paroxysm of punitive action. During 1927–28, a significant number of party officials, among them eight out of the ten parliamentary deputies of the party, were formally expelled, and hundreds of the rank and file were pushed out of the party. The purges hit the KKE's two most significant urban sections: Piraeus and Salonica. In the Piraeus party organization, the majority of the members took the side of Pouliopoulos, and strongly, but in vain, criticized the majority opinion. Over the next two years, the KKE lost at least one-third of its membership.[52]

Given the members' resistance to such severe measures, the Greek Stalinists did not succeed in imposing their firm control immediately. Between March 1927 and December 1928, two congresses were held in which the battles over the party's future raged. But already in February 1928, the Stalinists took over the leadership when, at the Third Plenum of the Central Committee, the purges were launched and the Kutvies group established its monopoly over power within the organization.

The new leadership was a poor replica of the Soviet Stalin-Bukharin duumvirate. In March 1927, Chaitas and Karakozov took over: Chaitas was elected secretary and Karakozov a Politburo member. The two led the Stalinization process and rose to power aided and supported by the Comintern and Dimitrov.

For his part, Dimitrov and the Comintern's wider network immediately set out to closely supervise the new Greek Communist leadership. Since 1923 the Comintern's monitoring system had developed considerably, as communication between the Balkan center and the Greek party was growing in volume. The shift was caused not only by the volatility of Greek Communist affairs, but also by Greece's changing position within the Comintern's network. Through Greece, and mainly through Salonica and Athens, the Comintern's International Liaison Department in Vienna maintained communication lines with the Comintern's center in Istanbul. According to the Austrian police, in 1926, an alternative Comintern route connecting Moscow and Vienna led through Salonica, Athens, Sebastopol, Odessa, and Baku.[53]

The Comintern network in Greece performed a variety of tasks. It worked on providing escape routes, protection, and material support for Balkan Communist outlaws, including for some Greeks. Soviet steamboats like the *Topolski* also transported Communist cadres to the USSR for health and other apolitical reasons.[54] As the Comintern's network expanded in order to handle those tasks, its members became increasingly more involved in Greek party affairs. In February and March 1927, Dimitrov had a series of exchanges and meetings concerning the KKE with international comrades, including the Czech Bohumir Šmeral, the head of the Balkan Secretariat of the ECCI; the German Hermann Remmele, member of the Presidium of the ECCI; and an ethnic Czech from Sarajevo, Milan Gorkić (born Iosip Čižinský), a Bukharin protégé who later became the secretary of the KPJ.[55]

In turn, Dimitrov regularly updated the ECCI on the KKE's situation. He warned that the party was in critical condition and urged the Comintern to pay serious attention to developments in Greece. But it was not only Dimitrov who urged the center to pay attention to Greece. At the same time, KKE officials themselves also demanded more visits by Comintern delegations, warning that without their presence, the Greeks would be unable to control the situation within their party. It became clear that in this phase of the KKE's evolution, the main source of legitimacy for the Stalinist Kutvie leadership was Moscow.[56]

As a result, the Comintern was kept well informed on all aspects of Communist life in Greece. The purge of the two ex-secretaries, Pouliopoulos and Giatsopoulos, in September 1927 was a turning point in that life, which ensured the further Stalinization of the KKE. Did the Comintern know in advance about the purge of the two leaders? And if it knew, did it approve? At that time, there were rumors, probably spread by the United Opposition, that the Comintern had not been informed about the impending purges and disagreed with the KKE's Central Committee on those drastic administrative measures.[57] The truth, however, was different. The Comintern not only knew about and approved of the purges, but conspired with the new leaders, Chaitas and Karakozov, on the decision. A lengthy article by Šmeral published in *Inprecor* soon after the purges leaves no doubt about the Comintern's involvement in the matter. Such a conclusion is striking not only because the publication rarely covered Greek affairs in such depth, but also because the content of the article made clear that the Comintern worried about the two purged leaders.

In his article, Šmeral set out to destroy Pouliopoulos's reputation as a committed Communist and as an outstanding Communist intellectual. He attacked the "petit-bourgeois anarchist intellectual," as he called him, in every possible way: he criticized Pouliopoulos's personality, his perspectives on the role of the intellectuals and of the Comintern in party affairs, and, finally, his inconsistent views on the Macedonian question. Šmeral did not forget to mention Pouliopoulos's rejection of the theory of "socialism in one country" and his recent conversion to Trotskyism: "He [Pouliopoulos] already announces his solidarity with the standpoints of the Opposition in the CPSU [Communist Party of the Soviet Union], and although he can but cling to them quite artificially he seeks to make use of them for the purpose of strengthening his fractional and disorganizing activity." Finally, Šmeral delivered the verdict: "Pouliopoulos will soon be outside all connection with the international revolutionary labor movement." The article was published in *Rizospastis* a week later.[58]

Not every prominent international Communist had such harsh words for the ousted Greek leaders. In fact, Dimitrov had more sympathy for the purged comrades than many within the Greek party. Even though he perceived the Liquidarist threat as the most critical danger to the party, he understood that a split would also be a catastrophic development for the Greek Communist movement. Accordingly, Dimitrov urged the Stalinist majority within the KKE to do whatever it could to find a modus vivendi with the centrist minority, at least. And indeed, after the Third Congress in April 1927, the two factions coexisted in the Politburo and the Central Committee for some time, giving the impression that a compromise between them was possible. Pouliopoulos's and Maximos's joint presentation of the United Opposition platform on November 4, 1927, was a blow to Dimitrov's hopes for defusing the incendiary disputes of the Greek Communist leaders.[59]

Undaunted, Dimitrov continued to seek a compromise between the two factions. The Bulgarian leader severely reprimanded the KKE's majority for underestimating the dangers of a split and for making wrong and risky moves that would have disastrous consequences for the party. Fearing that the recent turbulent events would spin out of control and propel the party toward an irreversible catastrophe, he decided to send to Athens someone whom he considered the most suitable for such an important and sensitive task: the Bolshevik Boris Mihajlov, who, according to Dimitrov, "knows quite well the people of the party and the relations between them."[60]

Dimitrov's anxiety stemmed from his concern for the broader Communist movement. What was happening in the Greek party also reflected the messy situation of the other Balkan Communist parties. For
instance, the Yugoslav party was in complete disarray, with factional
struggles that had begun in the early 1920s now reaching a new level
of intensity. In May 1926, the ECCI, strongly disappointed by developments within the KPJ, considered it "paralyzed and transformed into a
permanent debating club."[61]

In response, the ECCI took a series of measures and interventions. In
January 1928, Dimitrov proposed that the ECCI take decisive steps to
eliminate the rest of the Liquidarists and social democrats within the
Yugoslav party, stabilize the situation, and elect a "good leadership."[62]
At the Sixth Congress of the Communist International on July 19,
1928, Bukharin, the Comintern's secretary-general, warned the party
that it faced serious damage, due not so much to police intimidation as
to internal factional strife. He concluded that the reorganization that
had taken place, and the new leaders who had taken control following
the reorganization, had miraculously saved the party.[63]

For Dimitrov, while the Yugoslav comrades were in complete disarray,
the Greek party, which faced the same kind of problems, was approaching the cliff even more dangerously. In late January 1928, Dimitrov conceded that the split within the KKE was irreparable. Nevertheless, he
expressed cautious optimism regarding the future of the Greek and the
other Balkan parties.[64] But following the results of the national election
on August 19, 1928, Dimitrov's optimism appeared to have been misguided: the KKE's parliamentary representation had been obliterated.
Having received 23,889 votes (2.35 percent), the party had lost almost
half of its 1926 voters and all of its deputies.[65] Not surprisingly, the
leadership did not show the slightest remorse for the strategy it had
followed and attributed the outcome to the government's repressive
measures against the KKE and to the "degenerative reformism" that
the previous parliamentary group had shown. In its formal statement,
the KKE concluded that "it is imperative to set up a strong clandestine
mechanism and to develop an active organizational work."[66]

But without parliamentary representation to defend the party, the
government's coercive measures against the KKE were only getting
worse. The gravest threat came in 1929 with the enactment of "security
measures for the social status and the protection of civil liberties" (Law
4229/25-7-1929), known as "Idionimo." The law punished with prison
or exile those who advocated the violent overthrow of the regime or

the secession of any part of the country—an apparent reference to the Macedonian issue. It did not expressly ban the KKE, but it clearly targeted its activities and its members. Empowered by the Idionimo law, the authorities broke up strikes and the KKE's public meetings. In the following years, up to two hundred Communist cadres were imprisoned or exiled, and scores of public servants were fired.[67]

Paradoxically, while domestically the KKE's troubles worsened, its position in the international Communist world improved. Probably profiting from the disarray afflicting the Yugoslav and Romanian parties, the Greeks succeeded in strengthening their presence within the Comintern. In July 1928, the KKE's secretary, Andronikos Chaitas, arrived in Moscow heading a three-member delegation to the Sixth Congress of the Comintern, where the Greeks were received more sympathetically than ever before. Giorgos Siantos (pseudonym Saris) was nominated to the Presidium of the congress, a post with much symbolic value, and another Greek delegate was appointed to the Congress's Program Committee.[68] While in 1924 Manuilsky had berated the Greeks for their approach to the national question, now the delegation heard words of support and the party's dog days appeared to be over. The Comintern approved the KKE's mobilization against the "Ultra-Left and Ultra-Right deviation."[69] And the ECCI's Bulgarian leader Kolarov observed that "there was a crisis in Greece, but it has already been disposed of, ending in a complete victory for the Bolshevist majority of the Party and the Communist International."[70] Now it was the Yugoslavs and the Romanians who, according to Kolarov, were in trouble, disorganized, without strong leadership, and detached from the masses. On the other hand, the Balkan Secretariat of the ECCI congratulated the Greek party for implementing the right line and achieving good results overcoming sectarian tendencies observed among its ranks, and it encouraged the party to continue the fight against the Liquidarists and the opportunists.[71]

While the Balkan section of the Comintern had kind words for the KKE, tensions were mounting between the Greeks and the other Balkan organization, the BCF. In a speech to the congress, Chaitas criticized the BCF's work and proposed that the congress create a special commission responsible for discussing the situation in the Balkans and determining the immediate tasks of the Balkan Communist parties.[72] In reality, Chaitas was proposing the dissolution of the BCF, a serious affront to the Bulgarian party and to Dimitrov personally. Nor were the Greeks the only ones dissatisfied with the BCF. The secretary-general of the Romanian party, Vitali Holostenko (Petrulescu), complained that the BCF had not been flexible enough and was thus unable to help the individual Balkan parties correct their mistakes.[73]

Dimitrov sought to respond to his Balkan comrades' complaints. He acknowledged that the Balkan Communists had recently suffered heavy defeats and crises, but argued that, with the aid of the Comintern, the parties had succeeded in recovering from their adversities and "with greater boldness are embarking systematically on the road of their Bolshevization."[74] Dimitrov concluded his speech by reminding his audience of the importance of the old slogan "For a Balkan Federation of Workers' and Peasants' Republics," adding that it was necessary now more than ever to strengthen rather than disband the Balkan Communist Federation. In his view, because the Balkan countries were closely interrelated and their revolutionary potential interdependent, the BCF could help the Balkan Communist parties "fulfill jointly and successfully their revolutionary tasks affecting the Balkans as a whole."[75]

In defending the BCF, Dimitrov expressly disagreed with Chaitas. The clash between the Bulgarian and the Greek had both personal and political causes. A year earlier, Dimitrov had harshly and systematically attacked the KKE's leaders for their treatment of the centrist faction within the party. While the two politicians had little sympathy for one another, their problems were real and went further back in time. Ever since the placing of the Macedonian issue on the BCF's agenda, the federation's relations with its constituent parties were in a state of crisis. The Yugoslavs, and even more the Greeks, considered the organization to be an instrument of the Bulgarian party. These peculiar Balkan intra-Communist rivalries, in which, in the name of internationalism, national interests were at stake, led to the weakening of the regional organization and to the gradual decline of its earlier importance. As a result, by 1926, when the Balkan Secretariat of the ECCI was set up, the BCF essentially merged into the new body and the federation's responsibilities, and influence, evaporated.[76]

Of course, as an organization the BCF did not simply disappear, and in fact it soon became a source of new controversies. Just after the Comintern Congress in July 1928, the BCF met in Moscow for its Eighth Conference and Dimitrov repeated his earlier arguments with greater urgency and desperation. Conceding that there was "a big mess, high uncertainty, and no coordination among the Balkan parties," he did not spare anyone from his criticism. Instead, he implored his audience to accept the BCF as the only means with which to overcome the crisis together.[77]

In its response, the Greek delegation, supported by the Romanians, challenged Dimitrov's defense of the BCF. Chaitas accused the BCF of serving mostly the Bulgarian party to the detriment of the other parties, and this time explicitly proposed the federation's dissolution. His criticism of the Balkan federation revealed the new position of the Greeks in the international Communist world. With the election of Chaitas to the ECCI at the Sixth Congress of the Comintern, for the first time ever, the KKE had a representative in the highest organ of international Communism. No longer protesting external pressures for centralization, the Greek party leaders considered themselves to be closer than ever to the Soviet party and to the Comintern, and believed it was time for the Greek party to be removed from the Bulgarians' tutelage.[78]

In short, the Greeks no longer approved of Dimitrov's and the BCF's supervision. Now that, thanks to Chaitas's ties to Bukharin's international network, they had independently established direct contact with the Soviets, the Greek leaders believed that the balance of power had tilted in their favor. Moreover, their hopes were buttressed by a shift in the fortunes of Dimitrov, who was held responsible for the failed strategy in Bulgaria and for the intensification of the factional strife between the older and the younger generations within the Bulgarian party. As a result, his position within the party weakened and his future as an international Communist leader became somewhat uncertain.[79]

Despite the Greek and Romanian attacks, the BCF survived for three more years and was finally dissolved only in 1931. For the time being, the Soviet leadership decided to intervene to save the BCF and reorganize its structures. Prompted by Moscow, at the BCF's Eighth Conference in 1928, the delegates unanimously decided to reactivate and transform the organization into a supervisory body of the Balkan Communist parties. The BCF was no longer to serve as a mere coordinating center promoting bilateral contacts between its members.[80] Thus in the end, with Moscow's help, Dimitrov emerged victorious. This development hardly made the Greeks more cooperative; in fact it caused them to adopt a new strategy to express their displeasure. For some months after the BCF conference, the KKE turned uncooperative. Specifically, it failed to answer Dimitrov's letters and refused to send a representative to the BCF Executive Committee. On April 29, 1929, an outraged Dimitrov wrote to the Balkan Secretariat of the ECCI, underlining the

fact that he had not received any response from the Greek Central Committee to his letters, or any confirmation that the letters and the material he had sent were received. Shifting to a dramatic tone, he stressed
that the whole behavior of the Greek party was unacceptable, and that
it "raised suspicions of systematic sabotage." He concluded, pessimisti-
cally, that without the active participation of the Greek party, any serious Balkan agitation was impossible.[81]

The meaning of the word "sabotage" in the Soviet vocabulary of the
late 1920s required no explanation. It obviously implied a serious of-
fense and thus conveyed a direct threat for the Greek party leaders. Two
weeks later, as Dimitrov informed the ECCI, Dionisis Piliotis, another
Kutvie and Politburo member of the KKE, arrived in Berlin to participate in the BCF's work.[82] In the end, the Greeks were no match for the
strongmen of the Balkan Communist world.

A year and a half later, in December 1931, the Comintern intervened
openly in the KKE's affairs. While in 1928–29 the Greek Stalinists
had thought themselves invincible enough to take on Dimitrov, their
conflict with the BCF was to play a considerable role in the 1931
intervention. Although the Greeks had learned to engage in the Bolshevik rhetoric of antifactionalism, in reality their leadership that rose to
power in the 1926–28 period no longer enjoyed the absolute confidence
of the Comintern.

Nevertheless, the everyday life of the party seemed normal. On December 10, 1928, the KKE held its Fourth Congress and Chaitas was
reelected secretary. Karakozov, Siantos, and Theos were reelected to the
Politburo alongside three new members. Significantly, almost all of
the Politburo members had attended party schools in Russia. Consequently, this was not a new homegrown generation that had taken over
the reins in the KKE, but a group whose different experiences had also
been shaped in Moscow in the party schools.[83]

Since 1928, the party had reconfirmed its earlier commitment to
remain vigilant against the dangers of "Right deviation," and thereafter
had faithfully followed the policies of the Comintern's Sixth Congress
and the July 1929 Tenth Plenum of the ECCI. At those meetings, Communist strategists had concluded that the period of capitalist stabilization was ending and the masses were radicalizing. They therefore
embraced new theories that were identified under the slogans of *class
against class* and *social fascism*. Those concepts, however, were to create
new difficulties for the European Communist parties.[84]

The concept of social fascism originated with Stalin's 1924 famous statement that social democracy and fascism "are not antipodes; they are twins." It was thus not a new theory, but one harking back to the years of Zinoviev's leadership in the Comintern. The concept resurfaced at the Comintern's Sixth Congress as part of Stalin's strategy against his onetime ally Bukharin, who maintained that Communists should ally with agrarian parties and left-wing social democrats, and who opposed revolutionary "adventurers." Such views made Bukharin the poster child for Right deviation.[85]

Such theories developed to guide the Communist movement had real-life implications. If Communists were to accept that social democracy was "objectively the moderate wing of fascism," as Stalin put it, they had to change their strategies. Communist parties thus intensified their attacks against the social democrats in national parliaments and within the workers' movement, often establishing rival trade unions.[86] In Greece, changes were launched in February 1929 when 289 delegates, claiming to represent 158 unions and twenty-one thousand active members, set up the United General Confederation of Greek Workers. Separate from the socialists, this new labor organization elected an Executive Committee controlled by the KKE. Kostas Theos, the secretary of the new labor confederation, was a Politburo member, a Kutvie who had returned to Greece from Russia in 1926.[87]

Another change pertained to forms of political mobilization. The Comintern's conviction regarding the radicalization of the masses propelled the Greek party toward revolutionary action. The KKE launched preparations to declare a general political strike and passionately hoped for an armed revolt of the peasantry.[88] Such a strategy emerged from two factors: an analysis of the geopolitical developments in the Balkans in the late 1920s, and an increasing commitment to defend the Soviet Union. The two factors merged into a radical conclusion. The KKE came to believe that the British had transformed Greece into a center of military supply for the anti-Soviet Balkan front to prepare a campaign against the USSR. The party thus believed that "the struggle against the prepared imperialist war and for the USSR's defense [was] a struggle for the vital demands of the workers." The interests of the USSR and of the Greek working class were thus viewed as compatible and complementary.[89]

Moscow was not merely an inspiration for this strategy, but its active instigator. The Comintern had sent a delegation to the Third Plenum of the KKE's Central Committee. In late January 1930, the Austrian

Communist deputy Karl Gruber (Karl Steingardt) and the Yugoslav leader Milan Gorkić, with whom the Greeks were already familiar, both arrived in Greece, and the meeting of the committee proceeded unencumbered by major disagreements. A veteran party cadre, Agis Stinas, recalled that the Greeks' trust in the Comintern was at the point where they could not suspect that everything the Comintern's emissaries told them about the activities of the working class all around the world was, in the best case, an exaggeration. As a consequence, the delegates put forward the implementation of the plan: the general strike and the march of the peasants into the towns. Their strategic goal was to take over the government: "We left from the meeting feeling like generals after drawing the plan for the final battle," wrote Stinas.[90]

But although the party appeared united on these issues, dissent brewed below the surface. The Bukharinist Chaitas and a few others were skeptical about the Comintern's revolutionary optimism. Chaitas, however, did not present his reservations openly, but expressed them instead privately to the ECCI representatives during the meeting. Nor was his secretive dissent entirely unique: some in the Comintern also had reservations about the proposed strategy.[91]

Almost two months later, on March 26, the ECCI's Secretariat put Greece on its agenda. At the meeting, Kolarov expressed his ultrarevolutionary position, reflecting his loyalty to Stalin's new line and stating that in Greece the promotion of the slogan for the armed revolt was "too little." According to Kolarov, the KKE had to take concrete steps to transform the slogan into action.[92] Disagreeing with Kolarov, the Yugoslav Milan Gorkić argued that an immediate armed-revolt strategy would be a mistake. Gorkić ridiculed the draft of a KKE declaration for including slogans such as "kill all the policemen" and "revolt today," and concluded that the KKE had to limit its plans to self-defense activities.[93] There is no doubt that Gorkić, who was a friend of Bukharin, was in contact with Chaitas, who belonged to the same Bukharinist cycle, and considered the class-against-class Comintern line suicidal. In the end, Gorkić's admonitions had little impact on the outcome of the meeting. On March 30, the KKE received from the ECCI the final, though somewhat revised, text of its proposed declaration, which the party promptly published.[94]

As a result, frenzied activism took over the KKE. The party tried to mobilize people to attend antiwar days, armed meetings, and demonstrations in support of the USSR, and promoted the idea of a general strike and a massive uprising. Their hopes were not entirely unfounded, as the rank and file were in fact agitated by the prevailing social turmoil. In October 1929 a wave of strikes and violent clashes between protesters and the police broke out in some labor strongholds. In the tobacco-industrial city of Agrinio, the situation appeared serious, as street fighting lasted for days and barricades were erected across the town. To the north, in another tobacco-producing city, Kavala, workers occupied ferryboats to stop the transport of the valuable crop.[95]

While capitalizing on those disturbances, the KKE attempted to faithfully implement the Comintern's instructions. In November 1929, during the Plenary Session of the Executive Committee of the Youth Communist International, Giorgos Douvas, the Greek delegate and secretary of the Federation of the Communist Youth of Greece (OKNE), reported to the Comintern the news of "mutinies in the army, peasant rebellions, conquest of towns by rebellious masses of workers, fights on barricades, great strike movements."[96] But Douvas admitted that due to organizational shortcomings, the party could not exploit the revolutionary mood of the masses. Instead the apparent successes turned into failures and the Comintern's class-against-class warfare proved a disastrous policy. Many party followers were arrested and sent to jail under the Idionimo law and the oppressive measures of the government. Some labor unions controlled by the KKE, including the tobacco workers' federation, a Communist stronghold, were declared illegal. Soon the party lost its capacity to mobilize the public.

In fact, despite the sacrifices and commitment of many members of the movement, the workers' participation in strikes and public demonstrations remained below party expectations. After the May Day strike, the disappointed Politburo estimated that only 3,300 workers, in all, went on strike, and only 1,300 people took part in the demonstrations. "Undoubtedly," it stated, "we have in front of us a significant failure of the May Day Mobilization."[97]

A year later, the KKE's situation became even worse. On August 1, 1931, the party issued a pacifist appeal that revealed the extent to which the KKE's strategy had once again turned into a fiasco. In response to the party's appeal, fewer than 150 participants attended the demonstration in Athens. Some of them were members of rival leftist groups, compelling the organizers to break up the gathering.[98]

In response to such setbacks, the rank and file began to show signs of weariness with an apparently hopeless situation, increasingly expressing their dissent and dissatisfaction with the party's initiatives. Unable to share the revolutionary optimism of the leadership, many supporters voiced their disapproval of the social fascism line, which isolated them from many of the country's progressive and socialist workers and voters. As a result, party membership shrank. According to some estimates, the party had fewer members than the official number of 1,500; some thought there were even fewer than 1,000. Circulation of the party publications decreased from 3,000 in 1928 to roughly 1,600 by 1931. In Athens, the KKE could claim 170 members, and in Piraeus, the most significant industrial city in the country, where the majority of the members left the party to follow Pouliopoulos's Trotskyist organization Spartacus, only 70. The class-against-class strategy threatened to transform the KKE into a small and ineffective group of political activists.[99]

This abysmal state of affairs produced new internal struggles. Chaitas and Karakozov, still loyal to Bukharin's line, along with some representatives of the Central Committee and local sections of the party, began questioning the revolutionary line. They first voiced their dissatisfaction in 1929, but over the following summer, especially after the failure of the August antiwar demonstration, the crisis deepened. In December 1930, the crisis broke out into the open when Chaitas published in OKNE's organ, *Neos Leninistis* (New Leninist), an article titled "Left and Right Opportunism." In it, he criticized the party's ultrarevolutionary tendencies, arguing that the call for a general strike was prematurely launched as an actionable slogan.[100] Although Chaitas was careful not to blame his international comrades but only those in Greece, it was clear that he had now crossed the line of permissible disagreement with higher authorities. The article generated a storm of protests from the majority of the Politburo members, who a few days later responded with a series of harsh statements aimed at Chaitas and denouncing the Liquidarist, rightist danger he posed. The most severe reaction came from the trade unionist party leaders who had earlier argued for the general strike strategy.[101]

Once again, the KKE found itself divided into two factions branded as the Left and the Right: those who favored immediate revolutionary action and those who wanted the party to perform organizational and political preparations before setting off in the same ultimate direction. The latter group included Chaitas's and Karakozov's circle and the majority of the leadership of the youth organization OKNE. On the other hand, the majority of the Politburo belonged to the former faction, which consisted mainly of high-ranking syndicalists such as Siantos, Theos, Paparigas, and Piliotis. Not surprisingly, both groups claimed that they represented the correct line of the Comintern. The rift intensified in September 1930, just as the government's oppressive measures against the KKE escalated. Under the Idionimo law, Chaitas and Karakozov, along with the Central Committee member Ilektra Apostolou, were arrested.[102]

The KKE's adversities were not unique in the Communist world during the late 1920s, a period that came to be known as the Comintern's Third Period, when a wave of conflicts hit the inner circles of Communist parties in Europe and elsewhere. The worst of such crises erupted in the German, US, Czechoslovak, Swedish, and British Communist parties, but turmoil appeared in the French, Italian, and Polish parties as well. As already shown, in the Balkans, too, the Communists were in turmoil. The Bulgarian party had experienced a struggle between the old guard and the new generation in which Kolarov and Dimitrov were pushed out of the leadership by the young cadres. Even though both groups formally accepted the Comintern's doctrine, their mutual suspicion led to a protracted internal conflict. In Moscow, where during the mid-1920s a great number of Bulgarian Communists found refuge, the BKP maintained a fragile balance of power to ensure its survival.[103]

The situation was even worse within the Yugoslav party, where in May 1928 internal strife provoked the ECCI to intervene. The Comintern's organ first published an open letter to the KPJ, characterizing the factional strife as destructive and criminal. More significantly, the ECCI simply removed the secretary-general, Sima Marković, the only Serbian Communist who openly defied Stalin on the Macedonian question, and the entire KPJ Politburo. A provisional secretary, the Croat Djuro Djaković, and a new Politburo were appointed, this time consisting mostly of graduates of Moscow's party schools. In October 1928, the KPJ held its Fourth Congress in the German city of Dresden under close ECCI supervision. The Comintern's emissaries, Manuilsky and Togliatti, forced the delegates to accept the party's new leadership.[104]

Having tried to resist the Comintern's orders, the congress ultimately condemned both factions. In his capitulation, Marković admitted his errors and retracted his opinions, especially on the national issue, which had earlier pitched him against not only the Croat faction but also Stalin himself. The KPJ was thus pacified until April 1929. Djaković's violent death, caused by the organs of the king's Alexander dictatorship, brought about a new round of factional strife. In December 1931, the ECCI intervened again, and in April 1932 it appointed as secretary-general Gorkić, "by disposition a man of the popular front," as the historian Ivo Banac has described him.[105]

The Greeks were not unfamiliar with Gorkić. The Yugoslav leader had been increasingly involved in Greek Communist affairs since 1927 and was well informed about the situation within the party. Several times he had taken part in the KKE's meetings as a representative of the BCF or the Balkan secretariat of the ECCI, and many in the party may have had little sympathy for him. Ironically, Gorkić was to suffer the same fate as his Greek comrade Chaitas: both came to be considered too close to Bukharin's faction and were murdered in the USSR during the Stalinist purges.

The Second Wave of Stalinization

Despite similarities between this new phase of intraparty rivalries and the earlier turmoil of factionalism, there is one crucial difference that distinguishes the two periods: the dispute was now expressed in terms of loyalty to the superior authority. Each faction presented itself as the real interpreter of Stalin's and Moscow's vision and directives. At that time, being a Communist was not about following consistent policies, but about proving loyalty to Stalin, whatever that meant.

The new divisions within the KKE had preoccupied the Comintern at least since September 1930. Dimitrov informed the Balkan Secretariat about the new crisis and urged the ECCI to send an emissary to Greece to address the problem as soon as possible.[106] The situation within the KKE was critical, and the Politburo's left-wing majority had decided to open an internal debate regarding the party's problems. On February 1, 1931, *Rizospastis* published the terms and agenda of the proposed discussion, informing the party members that the ECCI had already approved the procedure.[107] A few weeks later, however, in a dramatic shift, the Politburo announced its decision to stop all discussion within the party and its organs.[108] The embarrassed Politburo explained that it had misinterpreted the Comintern's letter on the subject: the German word *einzustellen* had wrongly been translated as "to take place," instead of the correct "to cease."[109]

With the party exposed to ridicule and the situation appearing to be entirely out of control, the ECCI decided to convene a meeting in Moscow. On September 8, 1931, a joint session of the ECCI Presidium was held, with Greek representatives in attendance. The Greek delegation included KKE secretary Chaitas, OKNE secretary Douvas, and the

Politburo member Siantos.[110] The first two belonged to the right-wing faction and the latter to the left-wing. Chaitas had been in prison, but the Comintern network organized his escape together with those of Karakozov and six other prisoners and brought them by ship to the USSR, not without some adventurous difficulties.[111]

The Moscow meeting of the ECCI resembled a trial rather than a comradely discussion. The attendees included a number of high-ranking Comintern officials and experts on Balkan affairs, such as the legendary Hungarian revolutionary Bela Kun, the Bulgarian leader Vasil Kolarov, and the Ukrainian Central Committee member of the Bolshevik Party Dmitry Manuilsky, among others. Kun and Manuilsky in particular chastised the Greek delegates, regardless of the faction to which they belonged.[112] Although no resolution was passed, the Greek delegation understood well that the meeting presaged a purge of the Greek leadership. In fact, Chaitas and Douvas never returned to Greece: they were removed from KKE affairs and remained in the Soviet Union. Siantos, the more left-wing Communist, returned to Greece. On September 21, he delivered a letter addressed to the Balkan Secretariat and the Political Secretariat of the ECCI, in which he recognized his political mistakes and requested that the ECCI give him a second chance to prove his capacity to correct his faults.[113] Another purged Politburo member, the syndicalist ex-deputy Kostas Theos, sent a self-incriminating letter in which he recognized as completely necessary his removal from the party leadership, and placed himself at the disposal of the new leadership of the party and the ECCI. Meanwhile, in Greece, these developments inspired whispers and the Comintern's anticipated intervention became the talk of the day. The party's Politburo felt obliged to publicly refute the rumors of an imminent solution to the party's domestic problems by the Comintern, stating that they were unfounded and had been circulated to defame the party's leadership and strengthen its enemies.[114]

Unfortunately for the Politburo, the rumors were not unfounded. Beginning on November 1, 1931, and for three consecutive days, the party organ *Neos rizospastis* republished the ECCI's appeal to the KKE members, delivering a crushing blow to both factions. The ECCI branded the clash between the two camps a "criminal and unprincipled factional struggle" fueled by personal motives, and concluded that the KKE needed to purge the leadership of both factions to "finally begin its Bolshevization." The ECCI did not neglect to mention the

Macedonian question, demanding again that the KKE explain broadly and systematically the Comintern's program on the issue.[115]

A new party collective leadership was promptly appointed: Nikos Zachariadis, Giorgos Konstantinidis (Asimidis), and Giannis Mihailidis. All three had graduated from the Moscow schools and had close relations with the Comintern. Zachariadis and Konstantinidis had been living in Moscow for the previous two years and had returned to Greece only shortly before the ECCI's intervention in 1931.[116] The troika was accompanied by a new Politburo.[117] A month after the ECCI's appeal was published, the party affirmed its implementation. In addition, the KKE had to deliver to the ECCI systematic and detailed reports on its progress in enacting the Comintern's orders; otherwise, the ECCI warned in a new letter to the KKE, the center would take the necessary measures to discipline the party.[118]

The significance and the consequences of this intervention remain a subject of interpretation. What was the real nature and impact of the Comintern's interference in the KKE's affairs? Was the ECCI's 1931 intervention a real and decisive turning point, or should it be understood as a phase in the longer and more gradual process of Bolshevization that had begun several years earlier? After all, from the Comintern's point of view, the 1931 intervention was a very ordinary affair: the ECCI intervened frequently and directly to realign the Communist parties with its objectives and to appoint their new leaders.

As already argued in these pages, the KKE carried relatively little weight within the world of the Comintern. Also, in the BCF, nobody had shown much interest in, or great knowledge of, Greek affairs. Over the years, some of the ECCI's cadres had developed personal relationships with the Greek party leaders, but in most cases these relationships were ephemeral: sooner or later, the emissaries had to change their field of interest or their mission. There was nothing special about Greece that made the Comintern intervene in the internal affairs of that particular country. The ECCI wanted to ensure that Greece had a cadre of disciplined Communist leaders who could create and foster a loyal and united party ready to follow the Comintern's directives and the Soviets' recommendations. Basically, factional strife within the KKE worried the Comintern leaders only to the extent that it risked revealing a lack of loyalty among Greek Communists to the Moscow-directed center. The Greeks had therefore already experienced the Comintern's guiding hand several times over the years. Nevertheless, the 1931 intervention was a crucial moment in the party's development. It represented the culmination of the process of Bolshevization that had begun several years earlier, as was apparent in multiple European Communist parties' cases.[119]

For the first time in the KKE's history, the Comintern's intervention in the party's leadership selection process was decisive and overt. Since 1922 the Comintern and the BCF had interfered in the KKE's internal affairs a number of times, but had at least given the impression that the preferences of party members were being formally respected. The 1931 intervention put an end to the remaining elements of autonomy and internal democracy within the KKE. For the following two and a half years, until its Fifth Congress held in March 1934, not only did the party have leadership selected by the ECCI, without consultation with Greek representatives, but the KKE's members did not even know who the new leading figures were. There was also a qualitative change in the relations between the KKE and Moscow, revealed by the volume and the character of the information the party now passed to the Comintern. From 1931 onward, the KKE informed the international center about every little occurrence it experienced. Even the personal lives of the KKE cadres were under the Comintern's and the Soviets' scrutiny, and the party staff were required to declare anything related to their private lives, such as their skills, their sexual relations, and their family origins.[120]

The ECCI selected and advanced a new generation of KKE leaders. Their average age was only twenty-seven years old, which meant they had no personal memories of the socialist movement of the Second International's era. Without ties to the Western European socialist movement, as had been the case with the SEKE's founding generation, these officials were pure products of the Soviet world. They had lived in Russia and had attended the Moscow schools, some spoke Russian fluently, and almost all could understand and read Russian. Therefore, since 1927 but especially after 1931, the KKE's internal culture and the education and acculturation of its cadres underwent a profound Russification. As a result, a process that had been underway for years could now reach its conclusion.

A direct product of this process, Nikos Zachariadis, emerged as the indisputable leader of the Greek party. The third child in a middle-class ethnic Greek family, Zachariadis was born on April 27, 1903, in the Turkish city of Edirne, 230 kilometers from Istanbul. Due to his father's work as an employee at the Regie Company, a French tobacco firm in Turkey, in his childhood and adolescence Zachariadis lived in different places, including in Skopje, Salonica, and Nicomedia. In Nicomedia, a Greek translator who had served in the British Army during the Great War introduced him to socialism. Soon he decided to leave his family and move to Istanbul in search of work, and, once there, he joined the Panergatiki, the trade union organization lead by Serafim Maximos. It was then that Nikos Zachariadis became a Communist. In 1921, he traveled to Russia as a sailor on a tugboat and became a member of the Komsomol, the Communist youth organization. By 1923 he had left Turkey for good and moved to the USSR. That year he enrolled at the newly created Communist University of the Workers of the East.[121]

In 1924 Zachariadis arrived in Athens with the Soviet Legation and assumed a leading position in OKNE, which launched his subsequent remarkable career in the party. Living the life of a professional cadre, he made a reputation as a hardworking and loyal comrade, always difficult and stern. Zachariadis's aggressive and obstreperous personality caused him to get arrested five times between 1926 and 1929. His final arrest was for murder: he was accused of killing an activist from a rival Communist organization. To protect Zachariadis, in 1929 the party decided to send him to Russia, where he remained until 1931.[122]

As his abbreviated biography shows, Zachariadis represented a special type of the interwar-era Communist; he was one of the "Red Jesuits." Rootless since his birth and hungry for adventure, he became a Bolshevik at a very early age. His ascendance to the pinnacle of party power by 1934 inaugurated a new style of leadership within the KKE. And this style fit perfectly into the Stalinist model of the 1930s.[123]

Zachariadis's rise to prominence was thus an unprecedented and unique experience for the KKE. Under his leadership, hundreds of articles in the party press and other party publications praised his personal qualities. In one such article in *Kommounistiki epitheorisi*, entitled simply "Nikos Zachariadis," we read, "The hearts beat faster when his name is pronounced." He is "tireless," "full of life and vitality," "the legend," "the genius," "the Leader of an international scale," "the example of personal life," "the passionate," "the determined," "the brave," "the inspiring example," "the expert of the Greek questions," "the incomparable organizer," and, despite this plethora of commendations, "the humble."[124] No Greek Communist leader before him— and not one after him—received similar praise or commanded such authority.[125]

Many thought that Zachariadis's vanity and arrogance pushed him to expect and require the party's absolute admiration. Even if some of his personal traits suggest that he probably contributed to the creation of his own legend, the cult of personality that surrounded him was not his choice, as many of his enemies believed. There is no doubt that the cult of personality within the KKE was a top-down system of generating admiration for authority and power initiated by Stalin's mechanisms in the 1920s. The personality cult became a common feature of the Communist parties during the Stalinization phase, distinguishing this kind of party culture from Leninism or Bolshevism.[126]

Such ubiquity of adulation of the leader was closely related to changes in how Communist parties functioned. It emerged together with increased bureaucratization and the rolling back of internal party democracy. The new system required a different mechanism of legitimizing control and leadership. Hence, the cult of personality was employed to compensate for the loss of democratic legitimation, enabling Communist parties to maintain a sense of cohesion and unity built around the person of the top leader.

The new era thus affected the social composition of the Communist parties. In Greece, changes in membership structure were already underway before the KKE's complete incorporation into Stalinism. But after 1931 the workers carried much more weight in party affairs, according to the party's data. By 1932, 54 percent of its members were farmers, 42 percent manual workers, 1 percent white-collar employees, and 2 percent people of various professional backgrounds. The membership thus reflected the KKE's priorities during the period. As outlined in the KKE Central Committee's decision in 1934, "The development of the Party can be healthy only if it is primarily on account of the pioneers of factory workers, and on behalf of farmworkers and poor farmers."[127]

As might be expected, the transformed membership was reflected in the party's leadership. During the 1930s, the vast majority of the twenty-eight high-ranking officials were workers and peasants. The intellectuals and middle-class professionals had largely disappeared. After 1931, the party's inner circle included only three teachers, one lawyer, one journalist, and two university students. The few intellectuals who remained performed less important functions; they were usually mere translators of the Comintern's directives and letters. They were welcome, as long as they stayed silent and obedient.[128]

As the Greek party was changing, its presence within the Comintern network became increasingly consolidated. A characteristic feature of this process was the rising number of cadres trained in the Moscow party schools, such as the KUNMZ and the International Lenin School. In 1932, Greeks were the second-largest group among the Balkan student community; numbering 46, they trailed behind only the Bulgarians (96) and exceeded the number of Yugoslavs (39) and Romanians (19). In all, from 1928 to 1936, 120 Greeks attended the Moscow schools, and roughly 70 among them returned to Greece to assume political duties within the KKE.[129]

The KKE's more substantial presence within the Comintern resulted from two regional developments. First, the Greek party was the only Communist party in the Balkans that was permitted to operate legally. Although in 1933 approximatively seven hundred party members were in prison under the Idionimo law, the KKE itself was not outlawed.[130] The other three Balkan Communist parties had essentially moved into exile, maintaining a limited clandestine structure in their home countries. Second, the KKE had considerably improved its position within Greece and had enjoyed some electoral and organizational success, as it was able to connect with Greek society. This conjuncture had probably transformed the KKE into the most influential Communist party in the Balkans in the 1930s. And as the party grew stronger, its membership rebounded. In 1931, optimistic assessments put the number of members at 1,500, but by August 1935 the KKE boasted 5,177 comrades.[131] This growth was all the more significant as the other Balkan parties trailed behind: there were 4,000 Yugoslavs, 3,480 Bulgarians, and 2,500 Romanians, while the Albanian Communist Party, recently formed in Moscow, had just 120 members.[132] Years later, Zachariadis proudly remembered that in 1935, Manuilsky considered the Greek party the leader of the Communist movement in the Balkans.[133]

The increase in membership was directly related to electoral progress. The 1930s were an auspicious time for the KKE. In the September 1932 election, the KKE garnered 58,223 votes (4.97 percent) and secured ten seats in the parliament. A few months later, in the March 5, 1933, election, the party increased its share of the vote to 68,647 votes (6.01 percent), although this gain did not translate into an increase in its presence in the parliament. Two years later, on June 9, 1935, profiting from the Liberals' elections boycott, the KKE received 98,699 votes (9.59 percent). While this impressive increase in votes did not reflect the real electoral strength of the party, it demonstrated that the KKE could attract parts of the republican electorate. Finally, in the election of January 26, 1936, the KKE took 73,411 votes (5.76 percent) and returned to the parliament with fifteen seats.[134]

Undoubtedly, the KKE's influence was growing as a result of the 1929 global economic crisis and Greece's bankruptcy in 1932. The intensified level of poverty hit the urban population especially hard, particularly the working-class neighborhoods of Athens, Piraeus, and Salonica. Deceived by the Liberal Party and its governance, poor people of urban areas gave a ready reception to Communists. Additionally, the Anatolian refugees, who had been cultivating the illusion of returning to their homelands, gradually realized their fate was sealed and became increasingly radicalized by extreme poverty, alienation, and harsh living conditions.[135]

The KKE's fortunes also shifted because the party adopted two crucial and popular positions: it committed itself internationally to a united antifascist front and developed a new approach to the Macedonian issue. The Greeks were driven to follow such new directions because of changes in the Comintern leadership and policy changes that came about when Dimitrov was appointed the head of the Political Secretariat of the ECCI in April 1934.[136]

Soon the Comintern abandoned its commitment to the class-against-class strategy and the social fascism theory. Instead, responding to developments in Europe and elsewhere, international Communists embraced a new concept: the united antifascist front. With the new slogan, the organization renounced its earlier policy of attacking the social democrats as the principal enemy of the Communists and agreed that revolutionary and reformist trade unions had to unite to defend political freedoms and parliamentary democracy against the emerging right-wing authoritarian regimes.

In July 1934, the Political Secretariat of the ECCI instructed the Central Committee of the Greek party to create a "united front," particularly with the reformist trade unions. According to the Political Secretariat's directive, to achieve this aim, the party had to abandon "the ultraradical slogans that do not correspond to the current level of the movement."[137] A few weeks later, in August, *Rizospastis* published an "appeal to all antifascists," in which it promoted the new strategy.[138] On September 9, 1934, the KKE and the United General Confederation of Greek Workers, the KKE-led trade union federation created in 1929, sent an open letter to the Socialist and Agrarian Parties and to the social democratic trade unions.[139] The letter was received positively, and in October 1934, an accord was signed by seven organizations: the KKE, the Agrarian Party, the Socialist Party, the pro-Communist United General Confederation, the General Confederation of Greek Workers, and the Independent Trade Unions.[140] These organizations agreed to defend democratic freedoms against any attempt by royalist and extreme right-wing forces to impose an authoritarian regime.

Although this particular initiative did not last for long, it proved to be a turning point in the KKE's political strategy. For the first time since it embraced the social fascism theory, the KKE was able to break out of its isolation. At its Sixth Congress, the party removed from its program its commitment to a "Soviet government" and substituted the slogan, "For a People's Republic." The new and more moderate concept was considered more suitable for promoting the antifascist front before the January 1936 election.

As the KKE's leadership realized, building political alliances also required the party to shift its policy on the domestically divisive Macedonian issue. Obviously, no political organization could cooperate with a party that openly proclaimed the secession of Greek territory. Accordingly, the March 1935 Plenum of the Central Committee took a few timid steps toward renouncing the independent Macedonia and Thrace thesis. Instead, without making any reference to the prospects for the creation of an independent Macedonia, the party declared its commitment to complete national and political equality for the national minorities who were living in Greece.[141] A few months earlier, in December 1934, during their Fourth Land Conference, the Yugoslav Communists took the same steps, beginning to support the unity of the Yugoslav state.[142] Regarding the national question, in the Balkans the wind was now blowing in a different direction.

Shifting positions on the national question was not a simple task, however. Everyone in the Greek leadership remembered how much the party had suffered trying to resist the Comintern's pressures in the 1920s. And their fears were not unfounded: the assistant chief of the Balkan Secretariat and editor of the Comintern's journal *Kommunisticheskii Internatsional*, the Pole Henryk Walecki, at first reacted angrily, accusing the Greeks of trying to overturn the Comintern's policy. Yet in 1935, despite initial disagreements, the KKE persisted. High-ranking officials discussed the problem within the ECCI, and Dimitrov and Manuilsky came out in support of the Greek position. Zachariadis later described the endeavor as a risky but politically justified initiative.[143]

Finally, in December 1935, the KKE's Sixth Congress introduced the slogan of "complete equality for the minorities," replacing the slogan for a united and independent Macedonia and Thrace. The party justified the substitution by citing domestic and international developments: the change in the ethnographic composition of the Greek part of Macedonia, in close connection with political changes in the Balkans and, more specifically, the duty to cooperate against fascism. In short, through a clever formulation, the KKE formally declared that in view of the new circumstances, the rise of fascism could be defeated only by the people uniting against the common ideological enemy and, incidentally, that recent major demographic changes in northern Greece also rendered obsolete the old slogan for a united and independent Macedonia.[144]

The Greeks now became trendsetters in the Balkan Communist world. Shortly after the KKE's resolution on the Macedonian issue, the Yugoslav Communists abandoned the old policy of dismantling Yugoslavia. Instead, in the summer of 1936, the Communist Party of Yugoslavia adopted a new resolution: "The Party opposes the breaking up of the territory at present occupied by the state of Yugoslavia since it aims at achieving a reorganization of that state by peaceful means, on the basis of national equality of rights. In the present circumstances, any movement aimed at the secession of the oppressed peoples would only assist the fascist imperialists and their warlike aims."[145] For Yugoslavia's Communists, people's rights were no longer subsumed under national liberation. As happened with the KKE, the change on the national issue aided the Yugoslav Communists enormously in increasing their influence on important segments of the population.[146]

How can we explain the timing of this shift in policy on national issues? Why would the Comintern and the Soviet leadership accept this radical change? There is no doubt that the Bolsheviks allowed the Greeks and the Yugoslavs to revise their positions. In doing so, however, Moscow was not losing control over the Communist world. When the Comintern adopted the antifascist front strategy, its attitude toward the national question changed. New geopolitical dynamics compelled the Soviets to revise their attitude toward the post-Versailles international order.

In fact, since the end of the Great War, the Leninist doctrine had been prevailing for years. The exploitation of the minorities' demands for self-determination was a critical component of the revolutionary strategy, already in action during the Bolshevik Revolution. The

Bolsheviks had been going back and forth on the national question, trying to reconcile revolution with existing geopolitical pressures. This intellectual heritage included Lenin's theory that Communists had to exploit the contradictions of international and domestic capitalism. Revolution could flourish when Communists capitalized not only on social class dissatisfaction but on inflamed national sentiments as well.

In fact, in 1919, some in Europe were dissatisfied with the Versailles order. Lenin particularly considered the League of Nations a "stinking corpse" and "an alliance of world bandits against the proletariat."[147] Therefore, the Bolsheviks and the Comintern considered attacking the Versailles order a crucial element of their revolutionary strategy in Europe. In practice, they resolved to support the revisionist claims of the defeated of the Great War (e.g., Bulgaria). But by 1933 it became evident that backing the anti-Versailles revisionist complaints inevitably implied supporting the irredentism of the nationalists and fascists in Germany, Italy, and elsewhere.[148] Already in 1926-27, Maxim Litvinov and Nikolai Bukharin had begun to challenge the Leninist approach. Both thought Germany should be treated not as a victim of Versailles, but as an imperialist and revisionist force paving the way for another world war. Litvinov, whom Stalin had appointed the people's commissar for foreign affairs in 1930, emphasized that *indivisible peace*—his idea for a common front against the war—was in the interest of the USSR.[149] After the Tenth Plenum of the ECCI in 1929, however, the leftward turn (i.e., the Comintern's class-against-class strategy) promoted revolutionary antiestablishment uprisings compatible with the anti-Versailles Soviet sentiments, creating what Jonathan Haslam calls a "curious mismatch" between the Comintern and Litvinov's Narkomindel.[150]

Inevitably, the rise of Nazism in Germany in 1933 radically changed world geopolitics. The Soviets' security concerns for both their western and far eastern borders—heightened by the Japanese threat after the German-Japanese rapprochement—hastened Moscow's rapprochement with the opponents of Nazi Germany. Now Versailles and the class-against-class line were transformed into burning problems for the Comintern, as evidenced by the ECCI Thirteenth Enlarged Plenum in November 1933.[151] At that meeting, Litvinov developed a foreign policy strategy of collective security, intended to separate Communists from the irredentist claims of the Great War losers. Gradually, the USSR became a force that promoted the existing order, seeking desperately to secure international peace.[152] In September 1934, the Soviet Union

joined the League of Nations, less than a year after Germany's departure from the international organization in October 1933.

Litvinov's collective security strategy was the ideological equivalent
of the Comintern's new policy of building a popular front against
fascism.[153] The new policy adopted by the Comintern's Seventh Congress in 1935 was, therefore, at odds with its prior anti-Versailles positions.[154] And the Comintern leaders understood this contradiction. In
his speech at the same congress, the Italian leader Togliatti tried to
explain to the attendees how such a transition was possible: "We do not
have to withdraw a single word of our condemnation of the Versailles
Treaty, but at the present moment . . . it is our duty to face squarely *the
new situation* [italics in the original]. This is still not understood by everyone, especially by certain groups of pacifists, for whom the struggle
against the Versailles Treaty becomes at times a pretext for closing their
eyes to the aggressive policy and war provocation of German National-
Socialism."[155]As fascism gained strength across Europe, and its threat
to the security of the Soviet Union intensified, Communists in Europe
had to revise their theories and tactics.

The Soviet Union's new foreign policy was eagerly awaited and immediately noticed in the Balkans. Until the early 1930s, both the Soviets and the Comintern had been promoting secession as the only
means of securing national liberation for the regions' many minorities.
Especially in Macedonian territories, the Comintern had hoped that
national grievances could trigger an all-Balkan revolution that would
pave the way for socialism in the region and beyond. Litvinov's Narkomindel, however, managed to reorient the Communist movement,
including Stalin himself, toward the acceptance of the international
order, which implied the end of support for national secession.[156] It
was no accident that in 1934, Albania, Bulgaria, and Romania finally
granted recognition to the Soviet Union.

As shown above, after several years of having to support relentless
Balkan internationalism, the KKE received the green light to shift its
policy on the Macedonian issue. Zachariadis thought, wrongly, that it
was only because of his own initiatives and the party's organizational
progress that this great turn became possible. In reality, it was the new
Soviet foreign policy, and the Comintern's united antifascist front
strategy, that permitted the KKE's turn. In general, Stalinist foreign
policy of the antifascist front years had beneficial consequences for the
KKE: it permitted the "de-Balkanization" of the party, a transformation
absolutely necessary in the party's efforts to create broader alliances

and escape its isolation. Still, the stars were aligning to favor the new secretary. At the KKE's Sixth Congress in December 1935, Zacharia-dis was reelected to his position. Some months earlier, in July–August, the Seventh Congress of the Comintern was held in Moscow. Although Zachariadis was not able to attend, he was elected to the ECCI.[157]

In Greece the 1930s were marked by lasting instability, polarization, and social turbulence. A failed republican coup in March 1935 had led to a counteroffensive of royalist forces, who succeeded in impos-ing the restoration of the monarchy and the return of King George II in November of that year. Soon the polarization between the Liberals and the monarchists created a moment of political opportunity for the KKE. As already noted, in the elections of January 26, 1936, the KKE garnered 5.76 percent of the vote and fifteen seats in the parliament. With no party able to form a government, the political stalemate in the country enabled the Communists to promote their policy. On Febru-ary 19, with a secret agreement signed between the Liberal Party and the KKE, the Communists agreed to support the formation of a cabi-net without joining it. In exchange, the government would repeal its anti-Communist measures and grant a general amnesty to all political prisoners and convicts, including Zachariadis.[158]

Although the agreement was supposed to be secret, the strong reac-tion to it from different corners of the establishment made a KKE-supported Liberal cabinet impossible to form. In April, after several weeks of impasse, Ioannis Metaxas, a prominent military personality and the head of a small royalist party, received a vote of confidence from the two major blocs in parliament, the Liberal Party and the roy-alist Popular Party. Only the KKE and a few socialist deputies voted against a Metaxas government or abstained.[159]

The prolonged turbulence and polarization had been accompanied by labor and social unrest. The social turmoil culminated in May 1936 in Salonica, when a wave of strikes actively supported by the KKE led to a bloody revolt: in a week of violence, 12 workers were killed and 282 injured. The events shocked not only the city but all of Greece, and provided the pretext for a dictatorship. On August 4, 1936, Metaxas, with the consent of King George II, dissolved the parliament, imposed martial law, and established a dictatorship. The return of King George in 1935 and the Metaxas regime greatly intensified the polarization and contributed to the creation of new and lasting cleavages in Greek politics and society.[160]

Despite the failure of the KKE to create a successful parliamentary coalition with the Liberal party and, more broadly, with the republican bloc, the events of 1935–36 enabled the Communists to strengthen their contacts with the electoral base of the republican forces. These contacts were to be of critical importance during the Second World War and enemy occupation, when a Communist-led resistance movement emerged.

The Metaxas dictatorship persecuted all political parties, but hunted down the KKE with particular ferocity. According to the Comintern's data, more than three thousand political activists were arrested.[161] The majority of the party's Central Committee and Politburo members were imprisoned or exiled to barren Aegean islands. Roughly 1,500 rank-and-file KKE members—half of the political detainees—were put in jail or exiled as well.[162] Those who escaped lived undercover, fearing arrest. The regime built a vast network of former party members who had become government informers. The security services succeeded in infiltrating the KKE as an organization, spreading confusion and sowing disagreement.

Zachariadis was arrested on September 17, 1936, and the news quickly circulated in the international press.[163] Afraid that the Metaxas regime wanted Zachariadis dead, the Comintern was mobilized and launched an international campaign to save his life. Two organizations responded: the International Red Aid (MOPR) and the Association Juridique Internationale.[164]

On September 23, the ECCI's organizational secretary, Wilhelm Pieck, sent a letter to Yelena Stasova, the head of the MOPR, to inform her about the situation regarding the KKE's secretary-general. Pieck confirmed that the Metaxas regime had arrested Zachariadis and that his life was thus in great danger. He reported that the ECCI had already employed the French, British, Czechoslovak, and US Communist parties to run publicity campaigns for the immediate release of Zachariadis, and asked Stasova to launch a similar campaign immediately. A few weeks later, on October 11, a three-member legal team—the Belgian August Buisseret and two Frenchmen, Joë Nordmann and Renaud de Jouvenel—departed for the Balkans and Hungary. Initially they went to Romania to observe the conditions of detention of two prominent PCR leaders: Ana Pauker and Miron Constantinescu. From Romania, they headed to Greece to see for themselves what happened to Zachariadis and the other Greek political detainees.[165]

They were seriously worried by what they saw in the Balkans. Upon his return, Jouvenel published an article with the significant title "Rumania and Greece Following Hitler's Way," denouncing the harsh anti-Communist measures and inhumane detention conditions.[166] Another lawyer helped mount the pressure on the Greek authorities. In mid-December, Jean Moro-Giafferi Jr., the son of the famous French lawyer Vincent Moro-Giafferi, landed in Athens and gave a press conference on Zachariadis's arrest and incarceration. While in Greece he communicated with Zachariadis's lawyers and tried to help them free the Communist leader.[167]

In the months that followed, the Comintern coordinated from Paris a diverse international campaign. To facilitate these efforts, Moscow sent to Paris Andronikos Chaitas, the KKE's ex-secretary, who assumed responsibility for communications between the MOPR and Athens and tried to mobilize the Greek community in France. During Zachariadis's trial and for several months afterward, articles on the case appeared in newspapers such as the French Communist organ *L'Humanité*, the pro-Communist trade-union-related *Le peuple*, the socialist daily *Le populaire*, the British Communist Party publication *The Daily Worker*, and the British daily *The Manchester Guardian*. Across Europe, the "save Zachariadis" campaign organized public meetings in front of Greek embassies, while prominent intellectuals and politicians sent telegrams to King George and Metaxas.[168]

In October 1936, Zachariadis was sentenced to five and a half years in prison for his political activism, and in late December he received an additional nine years for the murder of the Trotskyist activist Georgopapadatos. Chaitas considered the court's decision fairly lenient and attributed the relative success to the "save Zachariadis" campaign. As he noted, in similar cases and under more favorable circumstances, Greek Communists had been sentenced to fifteen or eighteen years in prison. According to Chaitas, international pressure had forced the Metaxas regime to abandon its initial plan to sentence the KKE secretary to death. Undoubtedly, the international publicity campaign had another consequence that Chaitas did not consider: from then on, Zachariadis became the only internationally recognized Greek leader in the ranks of the Comintern.[169]

As Greek Communists and their international comrades mobilized against the Metaxas regime, Stalin's Soviet Union entered the infamous period of the Great Terror, during which, between 1937 and 1939, at least eight hundred thousand civilians lost their lives. Many of the victims were condemned to death without trial or any other form of due process. Instead of a trial, they received a verdict that could not be disputed in court: they were considered enemies of the people and counterrevolutionary elements.[170]

Stalinist terror reached the Greek Communists as well, and the KKE cadres who had been living in Russia were decimated. They had been students of the Moscow schools and former party leaders who had escaped from Greek prisons to find refuge in the socialist motherland. At the end of 1936, in connection with the liquidation of the KUNMZ, a number of Greeks who were students at the KUNMZ were sent to work in the Greek regions in the South of the Soviet Union—the Sukhumi and Azov–Black Sea regions. Soon they were found to have been involved in an alleged conspiracy against the Soviet state. While their exact numbers are not known, estimates of those arrested and executed, accused of espionage and terrorism, ranged from thirty-eight to fifty. Several years later, Zachariadis stated that of the Greek Communists in Russia, only two had survived the Stalinist purges.[171]

Among the victims of Stalin's regime were the veteran Communists of the 1920s, many of whom appeared in earlier portions of this narrative. The list includes the old KKE leadership: the ex-secretary Andronikos Chaitas, the Politburo members Konstantin Karakozov and Dimitris Piliotis, the OKNE secretaries Giorgos Douvas and Giorgis Kolozov, the *Rizospastis* editor Christodoulos Christodoulidis, the KKE parliamentary deputy Apostolos Klidonaris, and other prominent cadres such as Markos Markovitis. And these well-known Communists were not the only Greeks who suffered under Stalin. So did the ethnic Greeks from the autonomous Greek region in Soviet Ukraine and from southern Russia. The purges took place in four different waves: in October 1937, February 1938, July 1938, and February 1939. In total, tens of thousands of ethnic Greeks were executed, deported to Siberia, imprisoned, interrogated, or simply mistreated between 1936 and 1939. At least twenty thousand died.[172]

Undeterred by suffering and loss of life among its members, the KKE continued to loyally follow the Comintern's directives on domestic and international affairs. Another Greek community abroad proved instrumental in this endeavor: Communists in Paris could act more freely than those who remained in Metaxas's Greece. The Greek Communist presence in France dated to the mid-1930s. Many came from the

dockers' trade union movement, and others from the network of Spanish Civil War Greek volunteers who had found refuge in France.[173] The
Balkan Committee of France, established in Paris, coordinated Communist activities in the country, and its *Bulletin du Comité Balkanique*,
published since July 1936, gave the community a voice.[174]

Paris was a strategic location for another reason. At this time, some
of the Balkans' most prominent Communists, including Tito of Yugoslavia and top officials of the Bulgarian party, had been there. Representatives of the three Balkan parties made systematic contacts with
each other and with some representatives of the French Communist
Party in order to coordinate their actions against the dictatorships in
their respective countries and to facilitate their communication with
Moscow.[175] The Greek network could also cooperate directly with the
Comintern Center established in the city. Thanks to those contacts,
the Greek Communists in France received organizational support and
financial aid. In October 1938, as head of the Comintern, Dimitrov
designated Dimitris Sakarelos, the old director of the Greek-Russian
newspaper edited by the Bolsheviks, *Spartakos*, in Novorossiysk, to represent the KKE in the ECCI. As a result, until Sakarelos left for Moscow
in early 1940, he was sending reports systematically to Moscow, informing the center on his activities in France and the conditions in Greece,
and was communicating the Comintern line to his comrades.[176]

But in Greece in the late 1930s, the KKE's fortunes were anything
but bright. In the last months before the outbreak of the Second World
War, the party tried to embrace the Comintern-sponsored popular
front strategy, but the Metaxas regime's harsh anti-Communist measures made any political agitation extremely difficult. As a result, even
as the KKE's international position finally improved, at home the party
itself subsisted by issuing infrequent and largely unnoticed manifestos.

Between 1918 and 1939, the Greek socialist movement underwent multiple changes, crises, and transformations. The SEKE's early Bolshevization (1918–24) had combined two elements: a gradual radicalization
of its public discourse accompanied by a convergence of its platform
with Bolshevik policies, and an internationalization of its organizational structure. Radicalization was characterized mainly by the rejection of social democracy as a political family, as a strategy of lawful
political activism, and as a parliamentary culture of reformist political
change. Internationalization signified the integration of the SEKE's
policy-making procedures with the decision-making mechanisms of

the Comintern and the Balkan Communist Federation. In reality, this process corresponded more to a *Balkanization* of the Greek party, in the sense that revolution in Greece came to be regarded as an integral part of a Balkan revolutionary process, for which the Greek party's policies had to be closely coordinated with the Balkan international center.

During this phase of the SEKE's evolution, despite the Bolsheviks' growing authority over the Greeks, the Soviets' leadership itself seemed too far away to influence developments in the Balkans in any practical and tangible way. More than a real center of authority and policy-making, it represented a symbolic point of reference. Difficulties in communication between the Greeks and Moscow, and the Bolsheviks' limited interest in Greek affairs because of the SEKE's minor international importance, perpetuated the gap between the Greek Communists and the Soviet leaders.

On the other hand, this situation permitted the Greek party to enjoy a critical measure of autonomy from the Comintern and from its Balkan comrades. Until 1924, the party's decisions had been basically the outcome of internal debates between its two main camps: the semi-social-democratic right wing and the revolutionary pro-Bolshevik left wing. Such autonomy, however, did not mean that the party was healthy and flourishing. On the contrary, the SEKE was plagued by endless factional strife that weakened its effectiveness and had catastrophic organizational results, a situation familiar to all the Balkan parties at this time. This state of affairs explains why the Bolshevization process was not steady and linear but spasmodic and haphazard, as the party swung back and forth between social democracy and Bolshevism, unable to stabilize its orientation. Such turbulence and instability within the Balkan parties was not entirely independent of the parties' predominantly revolutionary strategy. Despite the relative constancy of revolutionary objectives, the Balkan Communists could not overcome the traditional nationalist obsessions that divided states and nations in the region, and they were deeply traumatized by the conflicts those obsessions spawned.

The establishment of Greek-Soviet diplomatic relations in 1924, making Greece the only Balkan country that had recognized the USSR, coincided with the Comintern's and the Bolsheviks' growing interest in the Greek comrades. Undoubtedly, the arrival in Greece of a substantial number of Soviet citizens and Moscow-educated party personnel advanced the SEKE's Bolshevization process. As already suggested, however, even though foreigners carried the prestige of the Bolshevik Party and enjoyed the Comintern's backing, many among them did not appear to understand the Greeks' mentality, political culture, or even language. They thus helped engender new rifts within the Greek party, which became embroiled in the struggle between the Kutvies and the anti-Kutvies.

As the leader of the Balkan Communist center, Georgi Dimitrov contributed considerably to the Bolshevization of the region's parties. From his headquarters in Vienna, Dimitrov tightened his control over the BCF and over the Balkan parties. The imposition on the Greek and Yugoslav parties of the Comintern's line on the Macedonian issue was a clear sign that times had changed, particularly since after 1924, Bolshevization implied submitting to external interference not only in policy-making but also in leadership selection. This led to new waves of disagreements within the Communist organizations in the Balkans. Even though the foreign personnel were finally integrated into the Greek party's ranks, the factional strife that emerged as a result of those competing orientations and loyalties caused, once again, serious and lasting damage to the party.

During the second half of the 1920s, the contradictions within the Balkan parties were, directly or indirectly, related to the struggle for power within the ranks of the Bolsheviks. Stalin's final victory over his enemies led to changes within the Comintern, the Balkan parties, and consequently their relations with Moscow. From the late 1920s onward, Stalinization was, for the KKE, equivalent to Russification. It spelled the de-Balkanization of its organizational structure and the imposition of a powerful and incontestable hierarchy, whereby not just the Soviets but Stalin personally came to define Communism. Russification was both a political and a cultural process, one that followed from a decade-long program of internationalizing the party cadres. Greek Communists traveled to Moscow, where they learned Russian and were educated in Soviet party schools, and from where they returned to Greece to perform important new tasks in the party.

The dissolution of the Balkan Communist Federation in 1931, and the transfer of the coordination of the Balkan parties to the Balkan Secretariat of the ECCI, tightened Moscow's grip on the Balkan parties and limited, if not eliminated, the regional dimension of Balkan Communism. From this moment on, every Communist Balkan party had to maintain vertical bilateral relations with Moscow, while the horizontal bonds between the Balkan parties had to be curtailed. From a certain point of view, this was the direct consequence of the policy of socialism in one country.

Following the Comintern's intervention in 1931, the elevation of Zachariadis to the post of secretary-general expedited the KKE's transformation into a Stalinist organization. In a few years, and always under close Comintern scrutiny, Zachariadis turned the organization into a monolithic entity and soon became known as "the little Stalin." Because of the personal suffering he experienced under the Metaxas regime and the Comintern's mobilization to save his life, Zachariadis became the first KKE leader to achieve genuine prominence on the international stage. But by a strange stroke of fate, the "Great Leader" was absent when Greek Communism experienced its most epic moment: the resistance movement against the Nazi invaders and their four-year occupation.

PART II

World War II and the Early Cold War Years, 1939–56

CHAPTER 4

Greek Dilemmas

Soon after German tanks crossed the Polish border on September 1, 1939, the Comintern announced its new foreign policy priority. All Communists were to struggle against the "imperialist war" that started on September 3, when France and Britain, Poland's allies, declared war on Germany. By that point, the Comintern had become a tool of Soviet foreign policy, which, after August 23, 1939, was abruptly defined by the Nazi-Soviet Nonaggression Pact, also known as the Ribbentrop-Molotov Pact. As Stalin now considered quasi-neutrality the best strategy for the Soviet Union, the Comintern shifted away from promoting the antifascist front. All Communist parties were expected to denounce the war by exposing the "myth" that the war of the European Allies against Germany was antifascist.[1]

On September 8, 1939, Dimitrov, following a consultation with Stalin, the minister of foreign affairs, Vyacheslav Molotov, and Stalin's favorite, Andrei Zhdanov, issued a directive to the Comintern member parties. The Bulgarian noted that "the war is being fought between two groups of capitalist countries for control of the world. The division of the capitalist states into fascist and democratic [camps] has lost its former significance. . . . The strategy of the Communist parties in all warring lands at this stage of the war is to oppose the war, to expose its imperialist character."[2]

Most of the European Communists were shocked by the Comintern's new directive. The Italian Communist Giorgio Amendola remembered the confusion and bewilderment that he and his comrades experienced upon hearing of the Soviet-German Pact.[3] Some were so incredulous that they continued to follow the old strategy. The main publication of the French Communist Party (PCF), L'Humanité, proclaimed on August 26 the "Union of the French Nation against the Hitlerite aggressor," while the PCF issued a communiqué that stated, "In the struggle against the aggressor Fascism, the Communist party claims its place in the first rank."[4] Although Dimitrov instructed the PCF's secretary-general, Maurice Thorez, against providing "unqualified support for the Daladier-Bonnet government,"[5] the French Communists unanimously voted in favor of the Daladier government's war budget on September 2, 1939. The next day, Thorez and the party's underground militants rallied around the national flag.[6]

Nor were the French alone in their defiance of the Comintern. Across the channel, also on September 2, the British Communist Party published a manifesto in the Daily Worker, the front page of which declared, "A war that CAN and MUST be won."[7] The manifesto presented a two-front strategy against both fascism and British prime minister Neville Chamberlain, stressing that military victory over Nazism should be secured along with Chamberlain's political defeat. In Belgium on September 5, the parliamentary group of the Communist Party denounced Hitler and chose to participate actively in the country's defense.[8]

In other countries, confusion and uncertainty reigned supreme. In German-occupied Czechoslovakia, the Soviet-German pact created a truly messy situation within the party. The Communist Party of Czechoslovakia had allied with other antifascist political forces and, following the country's invasion by Germany in March 1939, had implemented the Comintern's earlier strategy, which called for the development of a resistance movement based on a fusion of antifascist unity and national liberation struggle.[9] But on August 23, the party found itself in a state of complete confusion, and chaos reigned for several weeks as the "unholy alliance" between the Nazis and the Soviets shocked many party members. Soon the party secretary, Klement Gottwald, who in 1938 had found refuge in Moscow, denounced the Czechoslovak liberation movement as an organ of British and French imperialism and condemned the London-based government in exile of the social-democratic prime minister, Edvard Beneš, as "an enemy of the Soviets in the service of Western imperialists."[10] In November,

Gottwald rejected Beneš's appeal to create Czechoslovak army units abroad. In July 1940, on the party's instructions, more than five hundred Communists serving in the British Army organized a mutiny in the Cholmondeley Castle military base.[11]

Presented with the Western Communists' defiance, Dimitrov set out to impose discipline and instructed that "Communist parties, especially those of France, England, Belgium, and the United States of America, which have proceeded in opposition to this view, must immediately correct their political lines."[12] His article titled "The War and the Working Class of Capitalist Countries," published in November 1939 in the Comintern's magazine *Communist International*, sent a clear message to all parties about the direction the Communists were expected to adopt. Despite dramatic internal resistance, the pressure worked, and the Western parties ultimately aligned with Soviet foreign policy. Nevertheless, the slow realignment of the European Communist parties indicated that loyalty to the Comintern and Moscow was not an automatic reflex response, but a result of often painful internal and international arguments.[13]

On the other hand, in southeastern Europe, the Communists, either because they were far more accustomed to complying with Comintern policies that were against the national interests of their respective countries or because they did not perceive that the war was imminent yet, were more eager than their Western European comrades to adopt the Comintern's new position. On September 26, 1939, the Yugoslav leader, Josip Broz Tito, who would soon become the symbol of the impressive European guerrilla resistance, argued that the war offered Yugoslav workers and peasants the opportunity to free themselves from capitalism.[14] Although the Nazi-Soviet Nonaggression Pact created confusion among Yugoslavs as well, Tito not only did not lose control over the party but proceeded to purge those members who were thought to deviate from the party's new line.[15] The KPJ's September 1939 manifesto praised the Soviets for "having unmasked the imperialist warmongers' foul trap. German Fascism has been compelled to capitulate before the strength of victorious Socialism, the USSR, and to conclude a nonaggression pact with it."[16] The KPJ not only propagated against the war but also organized strikes and sabotage activities in Yugoslavia's military industry. A strike in the aeronautics industry lasted almost three months, the longest strike in the history of Yugoslavia's trade union movement.[17]

For its part, the Bulgarian party accepted the pact without any discussion. Almost overnight, the country's democratic opposition was considered by the party propaganda to be an agent of Anglo-French imperialism.[18] For the Romanian comrades of the PCR, the situation proved to be extremely delicate, as they were expected to also support the Soviet Union's territorial demands on their own country. In June 1940, the Soviets sent an ultimatum to the Romanian government demanding Bessarabia and Northern Bukovina, a demand that the Communist Party of Romania professed to consider historically justified. Some months earlier, the party secretary, Boris Stefanov, published an article in the *Communist International*, arguing that Romania's interests were aligned with those of the Soviet Union against Britain and France.[19]

Internationalism or Patriotism?

As for Greece, despite some reservations and objections voiced by the KKE membership, the party's leadership accepted the Ribbentrop-Molotov agreement as indispensable to the Soviet Union's security.[20] On November 7, *Rizospastis* criticized the previously popular position that the war against Germany was a just war.[21] In April 1940, a KKE manifesto maintained that such a war had nothing to do with defending the fatherland; it meant only "fighting in the service of one imperialist block or another." The KKE described Metaxas and King George II as enemies of the people "who decided to exterminate the people by pushing Greece into the imperialist war."[22]

The Italian offensive against Greece, launched on October 28, 1940, created new challenges for the Communist Party. The outbreak of the war found the KKE secretary-general, Zachariadis, imprisoned in Corfu. Despite his personal discomfort and suffering, on October 31 he sent a letter to Prime Minister Metaxas, which surprised the dictator and confused Zachariadis's comrades. In fact, its political importance may not have been accurately perceived at the time. Zachariadis declared his unconditional support for the Metaxas government's struggle against Mussolini: "The people of Greece are today conducting a war of national liberation against Mussolini's Fascism. . . .. In this war, directed by the Metaxas government, we shall all give every ounce of our strength without reserve. . . . All into the struggle, everyone at his post." The fervent tone of Zachariadis's letter surprised friends and foes alike. As for Metaxas, the wily dictator did not fail to exploit this opportunity to capitalize on the propaganda value of Zachariadis's expressed sentiments and ordered that the letter be immediately published in the Athenian newspapers.[23]

The Comintern and the Greek party apparatus could hardly conceal their confusion and embarrassment. The issue was not so much Zachariadis's position on the war itself, since Italy was not party to the Nazi-Soviet Pact.[24] What caused serious concern for the Greek Communists and their international comrades was Zachariadis's unconditional and effusive support for the Metaxas regime, which raised for them troubling questions of fundamental importance: Why did Zachariadis make no reference to the hundreds of incarcerated Communists and exiled activists? Or to the authoritarian and profascist nature of the dictator's regime? Given the harsh repression of the interwar period, how could the Greek Communist activists reconcile themselves to their party's unconditional support for the Metaxas war? Should they not, as Greek Communists, oppose both their Italian and domestic fascist oppressors? With such troubling questions in mind, some considered the letter to be a fraudulent product of the regime's propaganda machine, while others raised questions about Zachariadis's loyalties and even mental faculties. Rumors began to appear that the once incorruptible leader had yielded to a compromise with the Metaxas regime.[25]

Zachariadis's first letter—two more were to follow—has remained a controversial issue not only among the Greek Communists but also among historians. But it is unlikely that Zachariadis's initiative was the product of a conscious act of disloyalty or disobedience toward the Soviets. In assessing this letter, it should be kept in mind that Zachariadis had been isolated from the volatile world of Communist politics, buffeted by fast-changing international realities, and that the Comintern's strategy changed frequently, leaving him in his prison cell unacquainted with the most recent changes. It is therefore quite likely that the KKE's leader believed he was following a previously established Communist strategy. In fact, his letter was a virtual repetition of the instructions the party had received from Dimitrov immediately after the ECCI's decisions made in June–July 1939.

In June 1939, Dimitrov had reminded the KKE representative that the Comintern's line consisted of establishing "a national front on a democratic basis for the defense of the country's independence against foreign aggression and the establishment of a Balkan bloc based on peaceful co-operation against the menace of invasion by Germany and Italy."[26] On July 14, in a secret resolution of the ECCI Secretariat, the Greek party had been instructed to recognize the fact that its principal enemy was the fascist Rome-Berlin Axis. The final sentence of this message was remarkably precise: "If an offensive against Greece on the part of the Fascist aggressors (Mussolini, Hitler) takes place during the reign of the dictatorial Metaxas government, then ... there could not be the slightest hesitation that we would spare our weapons against it; if it [the regime] carries out resistance to aggression, then we will fight with all our forces against the Fascist armies, the principal enemy invading Greece. Whether or not it [the Metaxas government] demands any formal declaration against Communism during mobilization, it will not change our stance."[27]

Zachariadis was undoubtedly familiar with this resolution. Almost a month before the Italian invasion of Greece, he had addressed an open letter to Metaxas that revealed his intellectual and emotional struggle to accept the ECCI's position, which was difficult to embrace for a man persecuted by the Metaxas regime. He wrote, "Fascist Italy and the Berlin-Rome axis have effectively decided to abolish Greece's independence and are waiting for the right time to act. . . . [T]he Communist Party, forgetting the past, takes its place in the firing line for national independence and integrity under your command."[28] In his analysis, Zachariadis had clearly tried to combine the Comintern's July 1939 directive with another new Communist foreign policy priority: denouncing Britain's role in Greece. The controversial letter written after the Italian invasion of October 31, known in Greece as the first Zachariadis letter, and the previous one written one month before the Italian invasion, demonstrates Zachariadis's commitment to the Comintern's policies, however uncomfortable and tenuous he found those policies to be.

Despite the similarities in their content, a crucial difference in their impact separated the two letters. While the first went largely unnoticed, the second, which appeared in the national newspapers immediately, had a tremendous impact on Greek public opinion. Zachariadis was not oblivious to that impact. Soon after the publication of his letter of October 31, he realized that it had provoked several objections from the Comintern and from the party ranks. He promptly addressed the criticisms with another letter, dated November 26, 1940, seeking to modify his earlier position. He denounced the war as imperialistic and argued that Greece should not have joined it, suggesting that instead the USSR could mediate a Greek-Italian peace agreement.[29]

Noting the confusion created by the Greek leader's publicized initiatives, the Comintern did not hesitate to criticize him severely. On January 10, 1941, the Presidium of the ECCI took the position that even if the independence of Greece was in danger because of Italy's imperialistic invasion, the war fought by the Metaxas dictatorship did not in fact aim to achieve Greek national liberation, as Zachariadis claimed in his letter. This, argued the ECCI, was leading the Greek people to support Metaxas government in this war instead of opposing his criminal foreign policy. Even if it could not ignore Italy's aggression entirely, the Communist center refused to endorse an antifascist front in the nations attacked by the Axis.[30]

On January 15, 1941, a few days after the Comintern's criticism and following the Greek Army's success in repulsing the Italian invasion back into Albania, Zachariadis wrote a third letter, through which he finally aligned himself with the Comintern's position arguing that the Metaxas war, from its very beginning, was a fascist war of conquest.[31] Yet despite Zachariadis's public repentance, the Comintern remained suspicious of him. In a typically Soviet-style punishment, Zachariadis's wife, Maria Novakova, was sent into exile.[32]

As it happened, Zachariadis was also about to be forcibly relocated. In April 1941, Nazi troops entered Athens and the German occupation authorities transferred the Greek Communist leader from the Corfu prison to the Dachau concentration camp, where he remained until the end of the war. Of the letters he wrote while still in Corfu, only the first was made public during the war against Italy. The second was seized by the Metaxas security services and kept secret until after the war was over, and the third came to light in 1942. By withholding Zachariadis's second and third letters, the Metaxas regime was trying to embarrass the Greek Communists. But as the situation was about to change, the dictatorship unintentionally contributed to the portrayal of Zachariadis as a leader of national importance and facilitated the KKE's efforts to build and coordinate a resistance movement.

When Germany attacked Yugoslavia and Greece in April 1941, the Comintern was compelled to change its position regarding the situation in the Balkans. Unbeknown to the Greeks, some changes in the Comintern's appraisals had already appeared earlier in 1941, or perhaps in May–June 1940.[33] At that time the Comintern still supported the policy inspired by the Ribbentrop-Molotov Pact, but it was becoming increasingly alarmed by the Nazi terror tactics in the occupied territories and the Reich's expansion into southern Europe. On April 9, Dimitrov noted in his diary, "The events in the Balkans do not alter the overall stance we have taken as regards the imperialist war and both of the combatant capitalist alignments. We do not approve of German expansion in the Balkans. But, that does not mean that we are deviating from the Pact with Germany and veering toward England."[34] Publicly, a new approach was taking shape as well. As May Day of 1941 neared, the ECCI prepared new directives for the Communist parties regarding the day's traditional celebrations. On April 17, Dimitrov sent a draft of those directives to Stalin and Zhdanov, noting that "the people who became objects of aggression, like the Yugoslavs and Greeks, are waging a just, defensive war." Stalin agreed.[35]

As already noted, in the early years of the Second World War, the world of international Communism clearly experienced much turbulence and instability. This was principally because, as the historians Dallin and Firsov have shown, the Soviet leadership was determined to avoid any moves that could alarm Hitler or give his regime a reason to respond with hostility against the USSR. While facing an entirely unpredictable partner, Soviet leaders could not ignore their domestic audience or the Communist parties abroad.[36] Striking a balance between those two objectives was not easy, and interpreting the policies of the period remains a challenge for a historian. The story of the Greek party, and specifically the Zachariadis letters, reveals how different parts of this world interacted with one another and how the changes on the war front shaped Communism as an international movement.

When Internationalism Met Patriotism

When Germany invaded Greece in April 1941, the king and a number of political personalities, including remnants of the Metaxas dictatorship, fled the country and a government in exile was formed in Cairo under British tutelage. In Greece, a puppet Athens-based Quisling administration governed under a triple German, Italian, and Bulgarian occupation: Greece's northern neighbor and Germany's ally had been rewarded with Yugoslav Macedonian territories and Greek Eastern Macedonia and Thrace, which Sofia was allowed to annex.

In May 1941, while the swastika was flying over the Acropolis, the KKE was still caught in a balancing act between its desire to organize resistance against the foreign occupation and its commitment to follow the Comintern's second imperialist war policy and the neutrality it implied. At its Third Plenum in May, the Central Committee called for a government that could "assure neutrality, peace, and independence from the great imperialists and their war."[37] For several weeks that followed, the KKE was incapacitated by the embarrassingly unproductive strategy it had adopted.

In the meantime, as Zachariadis was being handed over to the Germans and transported to Dachau, some two hundred Greek Communists escaped from Greek prisons and exile islands, while others were released.[38] Among them was Giorgos Siantos, a tobacco worker and trade unionist who had joined the KKE in 1920, and who had been imprisoned in Corfu since 1939. Siantos had served in the Politburo since 1927, but was dismissed from his post as a "leftist deviationist" after the Comintern's 1931 intervention in the party's affairs. He was then summoned to Moscow, where he conceded his "faults" and a few months later was sent back to Greece. In December 1941, following his prison escape, Siantos was appointed acting secretary-general of the Central Committee.[39]

Soon, however, dramatic developments transformed the war and its geopolitical consequences. On June 22, 1941, Germany invaded the USSR and the shocked Comintern had to abruptly abandon its policy of neutrality. The hastily adopted new strategy called for the creation of "national fronts." In close consultation with Molotov, the Soviet foreign minister, the policy obliged the Communist parties to organize into a unified National Front movement all anti-Nazi forces in each country hostile to the Axis, launch guerrilla warfare operations in the occupied countries, and mobilize as many conationals as possible in support of this armed resistance. In short, the member parties had to immediately abandon their denunciations of the war as imperialist and forge alliances with any political forces committed to the fight against fascism and Nazism, regardless of their previous political stance.[40]

The Comintern acted quickly to enforce its new policy. On June 30, Dimitrov sent Tito urgent instructions to organize guerrilla warfare in the rearguards of the enemy; to burn airports, military mills, and facilities; and to destroy rail tracks and telephone and telegram networks. By mid-July, guerrilla warfare in Yugoslavia was already well developed.[41]

Similarly, in Greece the KKE embraced the new line immediately and enthusiastically. On July 1, at the Sixth Plenum of its Central Committee, the party called on the Greek people, parties, and organizations to unite in a National Liberation Front for (a) the struggle against the German-Italian occupation, (b) the overthrow of the puppet collaborationist government, (c) the defense of the Soviet Union, (d) the support of any coherent antifascist force, and (e) the formation of a provisional government of National Unity.[42] Zachariadis's letter of October 31, 1940, appeared to have been prophetic.

On September 27, 1941, representatives of the KKE, the Socialist Party of Greece, the Union of People's Democracy, and the Agrarian Party of Greece convened in Athens and founded the National Liberation Front (EAM). As stated in its statute, EAM's objectives were to liberate the country and to conduct free elections once the war was over.[43]

EAM's declared goals were unquestioningly moderate and—unsurprisingly—perfectly compatible with the national front strategy of the Comintern. But despite the KKE's persistent efforts to broaden its front and include not only leftist and republican but even royalist elements, EAM remained a left-wing organization dominated by its Communist leadership. The three parties that joined together with the KKE were small and politically marginal leftist groups, while the KKE was unable to incorporate into EAM, or at least attract as allies, the mainstream political personalities and their parties.

Initially, the EAM's activities targeted mainly the cities and chose political forms of mobilization: demonstrations, strikes, and organization of relief assistance for the poor and the most needy. But the Comintern stressed that the most effective form of struggle in the occupied countries was armed activity: sabotage of enemy installations and facilities and guerrilla warfare operations. In October 1941, in its directive to the Communist parties, the ECCI repeated that "in the occupied countries there must be more active development of sabotage, strikes, demonstrations, and, where conditions are ripe for it, partisan movements oriented toward a national war effort."[44]

The Yugoslavs were undeniably the pioneers of such armed struggle. They began to develop serious armed resistance as early as July 1941, and by early 1942, the Yugoslav Partisan movement was considered a model to be emulated. An impressed Dimitrov wrote Molotov that as many as one hundred thousand insurgents fought the Germans in Yugoslavia. In April 1942, a Soviet newspaper article reported that resistance activity in Yugoslavia had caused many casualties among the occupation forces as well as countless other losses, and was more effective than resistance activities in any of the other occupied countries of Western Europe.[45]

In theory, the Greek Communists had also opted for armed resistance early on. On July 1, 1941, the Central Committee stressed the need to organize armed resistance against the conquerors and push for an uprising "for the national and social Liberation of Greece."[46] Six months later, in January 1942, the KKE's Eighth Plenum was even more explicit: "Our national-liberation guerrilla warfare is of paramount importance for the liberation of the country from foreign yoke. The Communists should organize, grow, and expand the guerrilla movement in the countryside."[47] Yet the fiery proclamations produced few tangible results. The party leadership was, in fact, reluctant to embrace a more dynamic form of struggle, the partisan armed resistance.[48] Although a number of factors contributed to their hesitation, the main obstacle was the Communists' insistence on having absolute control over the guerrilla units. On this point, Siantos, the new party leader, was very firm: "The partisan movement is necessary and safe only when it is our own work. Otherwise, it will threaten our heads."[49]

While the KKE's leadership in Athens stalled, the regional party committee in Drama, a town in northeastern Greece now under Bulgarian occupation, had no such reservations. On September 28, 1941, the Communists in the area staged a revolt that lasted only a few days and was a complete failure. The Bulgarian authorities swiftly reestablished control and retaliated ruthlessly, executing hundreds of civilians. Over a period of a few days, more than two thousand people were killed. Shocked by the disastrous failure and the terrible human losses, the KKE in Athens vehemently denounced the uprising as an organized provocation and strictly forbade any such future initiatives.[50]

The Drama debacle drew attention to the international context in which the KKE's policy considerations were taking place. Not coincidentally, during the same period, the Bulgarian Communists were trying to organize an uprising against Sofia's royalist regime and solicited Dimitrov's help. But after consulting Stalin on August 2, Dimitrov responded negatively, considering that initiative to be premature and firmly believing that such an uprising in Bulgaria would only bring harm.[51] When the Bulgarian Communists persisted, Dimitrov took the side of his conationals, and by the end of August, Stalin appeared willing to support the Bulgarians' plan. On September 1, Dimitrov conceded that "in the present situation the issue is not a palace coup, but the uprising of the army and the people."[52]

Bulgarian and Greek Communists in the occupied territories remained in contact until August 1941, when the two sides decided to end the communication for safety reasons. It is certain that the Bulgarian Communists' plan for an uprising against Tsar Boris involved the Greeks from Bulgaria-occupied areas. And even though the lines of communication between them had been cut, the September 28 uprising of the Greeks in Drama was not an isolated event. When Samalidis, the secretary of the Greek party in Drama, proclaimed, "Realize this, we are effecting a revolution," he probably meant a revolution in Bulgaria against the Bulgarian royalist regime.[53] But such a revolution was not underway. Unfortunately for both the Bulgarian and the Greek Communists, the efforts to mobilize the local populations ended in complete failure.

In February 1942, with EAM a growing organization and in line with the Comintern's recommendations regarding organized armed resistance, the KKE decided to create the National People's Liberation Army (ELAS). But progress was slow, and only toward the end of the year did Greek guerrillas make a permanent appearance in isolated mountainous areas. In the first months of 1942, the ELAS fighters numbered just a few hundred, while from March 1942 onward, they were receiving modest support from the British Special Operations Executive (SOE), a clandestine military organization established on orders from Prime Minister Winston Churchill for the purpose of organizing sabotage and armed resistance behind enemy lines in occupied Europe.

The SOE's initially modest and largely ineffective airdrops to small ELAS bands were arranged by a Communist-sympathizer Greek, codenamed "Odysseus," whom the SOE had trained before its evacuation from Greece in advance of the country's occupation by the Axis in spring 1941. Odysseus became an important if erratic link between the SOE and the KKE leadership, primarily through Andreas Tzimas. The SOE provided assistance to various resistance organizations, including the National Republican Greek League (EDES). Violence between EDES and the much stronger and more aggressive ELAS marred the resistance movement and contributed to periodic armed conflict between the Communist-controlled ELAS and its political adversaries. As the resistance movement grew in mountainous areas, SOE liaison officers were assigned to the principal guerrilla armies to organize and coordinate the assistance they received from British commands in the Middle East. In addition to light weapons and supplies, the resistance organizations received from SOE large quantities of gold sovereigns.[54] But beyond providing support, the SOE sought to guide and restrain the resistance organizations, particularly the Communist-controlled ELAS, whose intention to dominate the scene was all too apparent. It was to prove a difficult and frustrating assignment.

In November 1942, in what was to be the only act of cooperation between ELAS and EDES, the two guerrilla armies participated in the destruction of the Gorgopotamos Bridge, an SOE operation of impressive scale requested by the Allied military commands in the Middle East and intended to interrupt the flow of supplies to Marshal Rommel's formidable army in North Africa. The operation could not have been carried out without the active support of more than a hundred armed ELAS men commanded by Aris Velouchiotis, a card-carrying Communist, and about fifty EDES forces led by the EDES leader, Napoleon Zervas, a veteran republican officer who had declared his loyalty to the government in exile and to the king. By the time Italy surrendered in September 1943, ELAS and EDES controlled large areas of the countryside and engaged in skirmishes, while occasionally fighting the German troops. By 1944, with the strength of some twenty thousand guerrillas and having eliminated most of its rivals, ELAS had emerged as the strongest of the resistance armies, and the Communists appeared intent on seizing control of the country.[55]

When in September 1942 the first SOE officers had parachuted into Greece to destroy the Gorgopotamos Bridge, they had no knowledge of EAM and ELAS and of their connection to the KKE. By January 1943, they were so concerned about ELAS's behavior that their second in command, Captain Chris Woodhouse, traveled to Athens in disguise to meet members of EAM's Central Committee, who were in reality leaders of the KKE: Giorgos Siantos, Petros Roussos, and Andreas Tzimas.

The EAM/KKE representatives showed no interest in SOE's proposals for the coordination of resistance activity in the mountains under a unified command, and remained uncommunicative toward their foreign visitor. But Tzimas, who took special care to hide Woodhouse from the occupation authorities who were apparently hunting for him, asked if SOE could arrange for a representative of EAM to meet Greek and British officials in Cairo to discuss issues of mutual interest.[56] Tzimas's suggestion, which SOE recommended to the Greek and British authorities, resulted in a major conference in Cairo in August 1943, with representatives of the Greek government, the Foreign Office, and the Greek political factions. When the Communists demanded participation in a new coalition government and the location of several key ministries in the homeland, while the British refused to consider the king's returning to his throne without a national referendum, the conference broke up and the Communists were sent back empty handed. The failure to reach a workable compromise on the country's burning issues intensified the polarization of the Greek factions and confirmed Britain's commitment to the return of King George as assurance that

Greece would not fall under Communist control. Open violence between the resistance armies was now all but inevitable.[57]

It can safely be assumed that the Greeks' inability to solve their problems peacefully was of considerable interest to foreign observers. In fact, the KKE's initial reluctance in 1941–42 to promote guerrilla warfare did not go unnoticed among Comintern officials. Dimitrov received warnings from ECCI functionaries familiar with developments in Greece, and in particular the KKE's activities, who claimed that the Greek party continued to be more concerned with political and economic issues than with armed resistance.[58] For their part, the Greeks attributed their military inactivity to their isolation from the Communist center and the lack of political and material assistance and support from Moscow. Indeed, already in the final years before the war, communication between the KKE and the Comintern had been weak and indirect, carried out mainly through the Paris center.[59] The situation had its causes. The Metaxas repression and the Stalinist purges had left few Greek Communists unscathed, either in Greece or in the USSR. As the KKE was of relatively little importance to the Comintern, few Greeks could be found in the organization's echelons and bureaucracy. And as the war gained momentum, the KKE became deeply concerned over the lack of direct instructions from Moscow. Rumors began to circulate that the Soviets did not even recognize EAM, which further upset the KKE leaders. They therefore set out to address this problem.[60]

In the early months of the occupation, the KKE had tried to reestablish a network of communication with the Comintern. In 1942 Greek representatives succeeded in contacting the Yugoslav Communists, and the following year the two Balkan groups held three high-level meetings. But the Greeks were unable to contact the Russians. In August 1943, the KKE/EAM delegation in Cairo for the SOE-sponsored conference with Greek and British officials tried to contact the Soviet ambassador but succeeded only in meeting a representative of the official Soviet news agency TASS, an Egyptologist with close connections to the Press Attaché of the Soviet embassy.[61] The meeting did not prove fruitful for the KKE's representatives, whom the TASS man advised to be patient in their aspirations and consider the sacrifices and burdens of the Soviet Union in its heroic struggle against the Nazis. Until the beginning of 1944, and despite their persistent efforts, the Greek Communists had not succeeded in establishing a meaningful connection with either the Comintern or the USSR.[62]

As a result, the Greeks were unaware of major developments, including the Comintern's dissolution in May 1943, which they found out about only when the news was published in the Soviet press and broadcast on the radio.⁶³ In its official statements, the KKE pretended to enthusiastically welcome the decision, claiming that the Comintern's dissolution gave full independence to the Communist parties. Ironically, the party characterized the event as epochal, one "that shook the enemies and enthralled the struggling people."⁶⁴ Actually, the outwardly celebratory remarks hid a profound discomfort. In reality, the Comintern's dissolution inspired more fear and uncertainties than hope in the Greek party, and some cadres did not hide their disappointment.⁶⁵

But it was not only the Greeks who worried about the lack of contact with the center; some close to the center worried too. In March 1943, Dimitrov's assistant, Dimitris Sakarelos (Zografos), reported to the Bulgarian Comintern's leader from Moscow that the KKE was experiencing difficulties and that the center had to restore communication with the Greek party.⁶⁶ In the same month, two other assistants of Dimitrov's, Ivan Plyshevsky and Shtreryu Atanasov (pseudonym Georgiev), also warned him that the Greek party "does not guide the current antifascist movement and the struggle of the Greek people against the German conquerors." They proposed to send one or two Greeks from the ECCI staff in Cairo to establish contact with the KKE. But they acknowledged that under the prevailing wartime conditions, their proposal was not realistic.⁶⁷

Such wartime difficulties were indeed one of the reasons the Comintern was dissolved. But it did not mean that foreign Communists ceased to be concerned with the situation of their comrades, and Dimitrov, for one, was alarmed. On December 26, 1943, while the war between resistance armies in the Greek mountains intensified, the Bulgarian leader sent a telegram to Tito urgently requesting a detailed report on the partisan movement in Greece, the numbers of armed forces in action against the occupiers, the scope of their activities, and the territories they held. Finally, he urged the Yugoslav leader "to establish a liaison with those partisan detachments which are the true friends of the three allied powers and of your own heroic army."⁶⁸

Dimitrov had reached out to Tito because, unlike the Soviets, who displayed limited interest in Greece and repeatedly assured the worried British that they had no information about the situation in that country, the Yugoslavs had an understanding of Greek issues as well as a concrete geopolitical interest in the region. As already mentioned, the

Yugoslav Communists had established a communication network with their Greek comrades in 1942. The two Balkan neighbors had tried not only to maintain that connection but even to create a firmer basis for it. In 1943 their contacts became systematic and permanent.[69] Between June and August 1943, they organized three meetings, where Tito's emissary, Svetozar Vukmanović Tempo, and ELAS representatives discussed the details of their cooperation.[70] As proposed by Tempo and following long discussions, Yugoslav, Albanian, and Greek representatives finally signed an agreement to establish a unified command for the resistance forces. On July 12 they committed to creating the Headquarters of the People's Liberation Army of the Balkans as a military embryo of a future confederation. The initiative addressed not only the need for coordination between the partisans of the three countries, but also the intention to pave the way toward "ensuring people's democratic power" and the formation of a Balkan confederation.[71]

The nature of the future-oriented agreement could not obscure the fact that, at that time, the Greeks were interested in a different kind of alliance as well. The three meetings with Vukmanović Tempo coincided with discussions for the resistance armies to join the Middle East Command, a British military authority directing the war against the Axis from North Africa, which ELAS ultimately agreed to do on July 5, 1943.

Such a two-pronged strategy was, however, not without its problems. The decision to join the proposed Balkan Headquarters raised a lot of disturbing questions and aroused much fear among Greek Communists and non-Communists.[72] In reality, until mid-1943 the KKE appeared to be uncertain about the political implications involved and to have no clear position on the issue of cooperation with British military authorities in the Middle East. The dilemma of working more closely either with the British or with the Yugoslav Communists was hard to resolve.[73]

One of the reasons why the seemingly simple choice was in fact a serious dilemma was that the relations between the Greek and the Yugoslav Communists were far from harmonious. The Greeks felt that the Yugoslavs held an inaccurate view of the Greek resistance movement, showing little respect for it and maintaining a patronizing and condescending attitude toward their southern comrades. But the real bone of contention between the two parties was the Macedonian question. Some of the Yugoslavs, particularly the Macedonians, pressured the KKE to promote policies that would facilitate the establishment of an independent Macedonian state immediately after the war. Others went further, developing plans to include territories of northern Greece in the postwar Yugoslav state. Given how thorny the Macedonian question had been in the recent history of the KKE, the Greeks were understandably troubled by their neighbor's proposals. As a prominent KKE leader, Giannis Ioannidis, recalled, "A bad move risked endangering the entire future of the Greek people's revolutionary struggle."[74]

Aware that relations between his partisans and the Greek guerrillas were far from harmonious, Tito telegraphed Dimitrov to warn that the relationship between the Macedonians and the Greek comrades was "very unhealthy" because each side accused the other of creating obstacles to their cooperation.[75] Finally Tito assured Dimitrov that he undertook to convince the Union of the Macedonian Communists to stop, at least for the time being, any talk of a united independent Macedonia: "We attempted to persuade our Macedonians not to raise the question of the unification of Greek Macedonia with Yugoslav Macedonia now."[76] But he also criticized the Greeks: "I, personally, got the impression that the Greek comrades really do have an incorrect attitude on the question of the Macedonians in Greece. . . . I try to use my influence to put this right without harming the Greek Liberation movement. I hope now that their representative is here we shall be able to avoid such incidents more easily, and bring our influence to bear to help the Greek comrades avoid the mistakes in the party line as much as possible."[77] Although Tito appeared to be balancing the interests of the two sides, he was clearly aware that the Yugoslav Macedonians intended to create a state that would include Greek territories, and he did not oppose their plans.

The complexities of the Greek-Yugoslav relationship obstructed the efforts to form the Balkan Headquarters that the two parties, and the Albanian Communists, had agreed to establish in June 1943. In Greek Macedonia, where ELAS *kapetanios* were very sensitive on the Macedonian issue, ELAS headquarters announced in July that the project for a joint headquarters was to be postponed. Cooperation between ELAS and the Yugoslav and Albanian partisans would not be regulated, but would be occasionally promoted along the border areas, in the spirit of "the development of brotherhood among the peoples of the regions."[78] Probably on Dimitrov's advice, Tito decided to terminate discussions on a Balkan Headquarters, understanding the risks that such a plan entailed.[79]

Despite those obstacles, relations between the two parties grew closer over time. Increased contact began toward the end of 1943, when the KKE sent the high-ranking party official, Andreas Tzimas, to serve as liaison to Tito's headquarters.[80] This decision was motivated by a range of factors, one of which was the Greeks' hope to use the Yugoslavs as intermediaries for approaching the Soviets, particularly the head of the Soviet mission in Yugoslavia, General Nikolai Korneev. The Greeks thought that Korneev could connect them directly with Moscow, a connection they not only desired but increasingly needed.

It goes without saying that while they were trying to determine their party's best interests in their relations with their Communist neighbors, and were glad to receive the SOE's valuable support, the KKE's leaders were not willing to submit ELAS to British control, which would have been inevitable in any joint command for the Greek resistance under the authority of Allied headquarters in the Middle East. Even if the brutal realities of the war against the Axis necessitated a measure of temporary collaboration with the Allies, for seasoned Greek Communists, those realities did not obscure the fact that Britain remained the symbol of capitalist imperialism and their ideological archenemy.

Despite Moscow's limited interest in and knowledge of the Greeks' situation until 1943, Soviet policy toward Greece appeared deliberate. While from the KKE's perspective Stalin seemed to care little about Greece, his apparent indifference to the fate of Communism in Greece was a sign not of his lack of care, but of his larger geopolitical strategy that was slowly taking shape. In Greece and elsewhere, it gradually became obvious that the postwar political map of the Balkans would not be the same as that of 1939. Indeed, the observation of Greek prime minister Emmanouil Tsouderos on February 16, 1942, would prove prophetic: "I heard that Russia has intentions on Bulgaria. Probably [Russia] will raise claims to dominate Bulgaria after the war. Such a claim, if proven true, will create many entanglements in the Balkan region."[81]

The Greeks' premonitions reflected a series of Soviet approaches toward Bulgaria during the early days of the war. After the signing of the Ribbentrop-Molotov Pact, the Soviets proposed to Bulgaria a mutual assistance treaty that the Balkan government rejected. On November 25, 1940, the Soviets made another attempt to persuade the Bulgarians to set aside their objections and accept a treaty of mutual assistance, and Arkadi Sobolev, secretary-general of the Soviet Commissariat for Foreign Affairs, traveled to Sofia to secure the deal. The Soviet Union was to assume the obligation to support "the fair territorial demands of Bulgaria" concerning the region of Edirne in Turkey and the Greek cities of Alexandroupoli (Dedeağaç) and Kavala on the Mediterranean. Yet despite Russia's tempting offer to support Bulgarian territorial revisionism, Tsar Boris refused to sign such a treaty with the Soviets and opted to align his country with the Germans instead.[82]

The Soviet overtures to Bulgaria can be attributed to Stalin's anticipation that a postwar map of southeastern Europe would include spheres of influence established by the Allied powers. As early as February 1942, Moscow may have exhibited such interest in the Balkans when the idea of a spheres-of-influence arrangement in the region was floated by the Soviet diplomat Ivan Maisky.[83] It appears that by the summer of 1943, the spheres-of-influence concept was receiving serious consideration in Moscow.[84]

Yet despite such speculation about the future of the Balkans, Soviets continued to show little interest in Greece, partly due to a genuine lack of information about conditions on the ground. Whatever the reasons, Moscow's apparent indifference toward Greece relieved earlier British anxieties about Stalin's expansionist plans and convinced some Western officials that the Soviet Union did not intend to interfere in Greek affairs in the foreseeable future. In November 1943, one of them, George Allen, the US prewar consul in the Greek city of Patra, who had recently attended a conference with the Soviet officials in Cairo, expressed to his American colleagues his trust in the Soviets, asserting that Stalin was not interested in seeing Soviet governments established in the Balkans.[85]

Unlike Soviet policies that were driven by broader considerations, British concerns with Greece were strongly related to developments in that country's rugged mountains. As we have seen, following a brief period of relatively harmonious coexistence, various resistance groups began to compete over control of territory, and in early 1943, tensions intensified between the Communist-directed EAM-ELAS, commanded by Aris Velouchiotis, and the republican-led EDES under Napoleon Zervas. By the fall of 1943 and following the disastrous political conference in Cairo in August 1943, a localized civil war broke out in the mountains, which was finally stopped by the intervention of SOE officers. As the Germans' departure from Greece appeared imminent, issues that were already troublesome became critical. Thus, among the questions that emerged as particularly pressing were the nature of the postwar regime, the future of the monarchy, and, last but not least, the role of the KKE in the nation's political life.

In their efforts to control the violence between ELAS and EDES, the British at first chose to operate without consulting the Russians. hoping to avert Moscow's meddling in the already messy Greek situation. Moreover, Moscow's position on the escalating violence appeared to be confusing. On December 23, 1943, *Pravda* had published an article strongly criticizing British support of the Greek monarchy and of the country's extreme right-wing parties. In London, Foreign Minister Anthony Eden complained to the Soviet ambassador, Feodor Gusev, about *Pravda*'s article, while in Moscow the British ambassador met Molotov, who downplayed the issue, claiming that the Soviet government lacked any information of its own about the situation in Greece. Nevertheless, the diplomatic intervention worked, and soon criticism of British policy on Greece in the Soviet press stopped, at least temporarily.[86]

But neither the Greek prime minister in Cairo, Tsouderos, nor British officials felt reassured by Molotov's claims of ignorance. Tsouderos's impression was that "in Moscow they are not as ignorant of Greek affairs as they would have us believe."[87] Similarly, Reginald Leeper, the British ambassador to the Greek government in Cairo, believed that Foreign Minister Molotov knew very well what was happening in the Balkans and was waiting for an opportunity to exploit the situation.[88]

The British kept demanding that Moscow exert pressure on the Greek Communists to deescalate the violence against rival organizations. Initially the Soviet government did not comply, prompting a disappointed Foreign Office to send Ambassador Clark Kerr to see Molotov, and if necessary "beg him to reconsider" and issue a statement calling for unity within the resistance movement.[89] This time the Soviets cooperated: on January 2, 1944, Molotov agreed to support Prime Minister Tsouderos's appeal for unity among the resistance organizations. The Soviet government issued a declaration urging all partisan groups in Greece to unite in their fight against the Germans, and Moscow radio broadcast similar appeals for unity.[90]

It may be assumed that Moscow's declarations constituted a clear signal to the Greek Communists to conform to the demands of the government in exile and its British advisers. And by his initiative, Molotov sought to assure the British and the Greek government that the Russians were not behind any aspirations of the KKE to seize power. But as Lincoln MacVeagh, the US ambassador to Greece and Yugoslavia, remarked at that time, the new development also had the effect "of giving the Russian pronouncement when it comes a unique distinction as that of a power peculiarly interested in Greek affairs and specially to be heard and this may have been the Russian aim from the beginning."[91]

Whatever their suspicions and concerns, the British were compelled to bring about an end to widespread violence between Greeks in their strategically important country. Hence, in January 1944, London and Moscow intensified their attempts to resolve the Greek crisis together, and in Cairo, Ambassadors Leeper and Novikov held talks on their possible cooperation regarding Greek issues. Professing to be cautiously optimistic, Leeper afterward noted that the Soviets "will not obstruct us" and stressed the need to press all Greek political parties, but especially the KKE, to stop fighting among themselves. For his part, Novikov underlined the need for the Greeks to establish a genuinely representative government, which, for him, meant one that included the KKE. Despite their positive tone, however, these talks produced little else beyond wishful declarations and gave the impression that the Soviets may have been stalling, waiting for developments on the ground in Greece to provide them with greater leverage.[92]

In fact, in the early spring of 1944, the situation did change. In January, at its Tenth Plenum, the KKE Central Committee decided to create a "Political Committee of National Liberation" (PEEA), and on March 10, 1944, EAM formally announced the establishment of such an authority, whose cabinet included prominent personalities of the Greek Left, in ELAS-controlled territory. By April, the "Mountain Government," essentially a rival to the internationally recognized government in exile, was ready to enter Greek politics.[93]

Undoubtedly the PEEA's appearance marked a point of no return in the polarized political arena, institutionalizing the divide between the left-leaning "Free Greece" and its opponents across the country's political spectrum, officially represented in Cairo by the king's government under Tsouderos. The British were understandably alarmed by such developments, and their fears and apprehension reached new levels when, on March 25, units of the Greek armed forces in Egypt mutinied. They were soldiers who had escaped the country's occupation or were recruited from among the Greek communities of the Middle East. Equipped, trained, and supplied by the British and based in Egypt, they had been formed into regular army units and expected to fight alongside their British allies. But except for two infantry brigades that distinguished themselves in hard-fought battles across North Africa, they had been allowed to languish in inactivity, becoming politicized and feuding, resenting the king, the Tsouderos government, and its remnants of the Metaxas regime. Their mostly royalist officers were soon replaced by republicans who were also politicized, insecure, and undisciplined. Attempts by the Tsouderos government to establish its authority over the military by repeatedly reshuffling commands failed, as did its efforts to stem the increasingly leftist orientation of the lower ranks, caused by the growing number of EAM sympathizers and some Communists arriving from occupied Greece. The situation was no better on the sizeable contingent of navy ships, where republican loyalties, political feuding, and insubordination were common.

In March 1944, the news of PEEA's establishment sparked leftist and antigovernment demonstrations leading to acts of violence and, eventually, to a major mutiny in the army. On some of the navy's ships, sailors were assaulting and imprisoning their officers, with some being thrown overboard. Although the revolt in the army was organized by leftist and Communist sympathizers, there is no evidence that the instigators were acting in response to instructions from the KKE or were in contact with the party. As the Tsouderos cabinet was disintegrating and the government proved incapable of restoring order among its armed forces, British troops took drastic measures, and during April 22–23 succeeded in crushing the uprising with few casualties. The mutineers surrendered, their units were purged of the rebellion's leaders, and a large number were sent to prison camps in desolate areas where they were to remain for many months. As expected, Prime Minister Tsouderos resigned, and after a period of uncertainty and political maneuvering, the British chose as his replacement Georgios Papandreou, a prominent antimonarchist and anti-Communist politician of pro-British sentiments who had recently arrived from occupied Greece with SOE assistance.[94]

During the Greek crisis, British fears and actions were fueled by Moscow's reactions to the developments in the Middle East. On April 7, the Soviet press had published a TASS dispatch on the troubles within the Greek armed forces, which criticized the Greek government for arresting patriots and for cooperating with fascists. The British also suspected possible Soviet involvement in the mutiny, with Ambassador Novikov in Cairo becoming the principal target of suspicion.[95] The Soviet diplomat did not hesitate to express to his Western colleagues his profound disapproval of British actions in this affair, and to add that he and his government agreed with the interpretation of events contained in TASS's dispatch. He hoped that the Greek government would not ignore, as did other governments in exile, the will of the Greek people, and he reiterated his point by asking "why they were arresting so many Greeks there, civilian as well as military, and why only members of the Left." In a conversation with Ambassador MacVeagh, the Soviet diplomat argued yet again that the Greeks were merely seeking a change in their own government, and that under such circumstances to menace them with tanks and deprive them of food was unjust.[96]

Both Leeper and former prime minister Tsouderos were convinced that the Soviet embassy in Cairo had been behind the mutineers, while the staunchly anti-Communist Papandreou agreed with the more experienced politicians.[97] Presented with this problematic situation, British officials appealed to a higher authority for understanding and support. Following requests from Leeper and the Foreign Office, Prime Minister Churchill wrote to Molotov demanding that Moscow stop its propaganda on Greek issues.[98] As he had done before, Molotov answered that the Soviet government had extremely limited information on Greek affairs and that the British government, which had a military mission in Greece, was in a more favorable position. Regarding the TASS telegrams, Molotov promised to instruct the TASS press agency to verify its information more strictly. Churchill could do little more than accept Molotov's response and thank him for his promise.[99]

While the Soviet response was diplomatic as always, Britain's ally was not about to become a reliable partner. Even though the British asked Molotov to recognize and support Papandreou as the prime minister, Ambassador Novikov showed disrespect toward the new political leader, postponing an official visit and labeling him a British puppet who was not qualified for the position. Novikov's attitude was fully in line with Manuilsky, who characterized Papandreou as "pro-fascist," an "anti-left element," and a "new Metaxas." The Soviets' strange rejection of Papandreou, a well-known republican with socialist tendencies, dismayed British diplomats and prompted Leeper to speculate that perhaps Russia aspired to supplant Britain as the dominating foreign power in Greek affairs.[100] In fact, by the summer of 1944, most top British officials had come to believe that the Soviets were now seeking to control the Balkan region, including Greece, through Communist-controlled resistance movements. They feared that their own wartime policy of supporting the Communist-dominated resistance movements had backfired and was undermining their interests in the Mediterranean. According to a top-secret paper dated June 7, 1944, and presented to the War Cabinet, "The Russians are, generally speaking, out for a predominant position in Southeastern Europe and are using Communist-led movements in

Yugoslavia, Albania and Greece as a means to an end. If anyone is to blame for the present situation in which the Communist-led movements are the most powerful elements in Yugoslavia and Greece, it is we ourselves. The Russians have merely sat back and watched us doing their work for them."[101] To British, US, and Greek officials, Communism in the Balkans appeared to be a regional phenomenon that was not confined to a single country. In fact, foreign governments considered the PEEA a replica of the Anti-fascist Council for the National Liberation of Yugoslavia (AVNOJ), the wartime umbrella organization for the Yugoslav resistance that by 1944 Tito had transformed into a de facto government. The diplomats believed not only that Tito prompted the Greeks to follow in his footsteps, but that Tito's influence in Greece enjoyed the approval of the Soviets.[102]

Initially the Yugoslavs, and particularly Tito, had, in fact, become a source of fear for the British and of concern for the Soviets and the Comintern. The latter increasingly worried that Tito's ambitions would negatively affect Moscow's relations with the Western Allies, and therefore Soviet plans for the future. In 1941–42, the still-existing Comintern had lectured Tito to hide the Communist character of his guerrilla movement ("Do not call your proletarian brigades proletarian; instead call them shock brigades," Dimitrov urged Tito in August 1942), make peace with the Serb nationalist resistance of Draža Mihailović, and improve his relations with Yugoslavia's exiled government in London, so as not to create problems between Russia and Britain.[103] Tito, on the other hand, protested the Soviet portrayals of Yugoslav resistance. In September 1942, he complained to his friend Dimitrov, "Why does Radio Moscow in its Serbo-Croat program not speak of the Chetnik atrocities? Why does it not give publicity to our struggle? That is what many people are asking, and justifiably they demand at least moral support. Many are dissatisfied with the programs of Radio Moscow in Serbo-Croat."[104]

Nevertheless, for the Balkan Communists, Tito's resistance movement constituted a compass to be followed. Dimitrov himself expressed his admiration for Tito's victorious partisans, and championed Tito's cause in Moscow, lobbying Molotov and Stalin in favor of the Yugoslavs. In addition to Dimitrov, everyone in the region understood that the Yugoslavs were the leading force paving the way for a victorious socialist revolution in the Balkans, and that the KPJ was the pioneer party in the peninsula. Tito was undeniably the rising star in the Balkans. In April 1944, despite initial reservations, Stalin and Molotov assured Tito that they considered Yugoslavia a key ally of the Soviet Union, and that they wanted it to be their principal partner in south-eastern Europe.[105]

The Greeks would not have been offended to be seen as the Yugoslavs' replica and saw obvious similarities between the two countries. Both Yugoslavia and Greece suffered triple German, Italian, and Bulgarian occupations, both had seen their country plundered and destroyed, and both had governments in exile under British tutelage. Finally, both had built a powerful, if divided, resistance. And it was the Communists, who had been persecuted and marginalized before the war in both Greece and Yugoslavia, who led that resistance. In the spring of 1944, Communists in both countries began to think that the old dream of the Balkan Socialist Federation was not a distant utopia anymore.

Before that dream could be realized, however, the liberation struggle had to be won. At that stage of the war, the international Communist world seemed supportive of both Greek and Yugoslav ambitions. The Greeks looked at how Dimitrov approached the Yugoslavs and thought their path could be similar. Several months before the PEEA's creation, Tito informed Dimitrov of his intention not to recognize the king and to maintain AVNOJ as the only government in the country. In February 1944, Dimitrov agreed with Tito to defend AVNOJ as the legitimate government against the policy of the British government: "The Cairo government must be eliminated. . . . The government in Yugoslavia, that is, the AVNOJ government, must be acknowledged by England and the other allies as the sole government of Yugoslavia, while the king must submit to the laws of AVNOJ. If King Peter accepts all these conditions, then AVNOJ has no objections to cooperating with him, given that the question of the monarchy in Yugoslavia is [to be] decided by the people following the liberation of Yugoslavia." In sending this message to Churchill, Tito had followed almost without alteration the wording of the text he had received from Dimitrov.[106]

But while the KKE believed that the Yugoslav path was available to them as well, it also realized that the reason why Tito could maintain a hard line against the British was the superior military situation of the Partisans. Yet at that stage, the Balkan Communists' main obstacle was not only the British imperialism that threatened to follow the Nazi occupation of their countries. While appearing to approve of the resistance movements, the Soviets were not particularly keen to support the ambitions of the Yugoslav and Greek Communist Parties. Although in early 1944 Stalin had shown a restrained internationalist attitude toward the Yugoslav and Greek Communists, he personally restricted their revolutionary plans.

Despite the fact that it considered the PEEA a political factor that deserved to be taken into account, Moscow offered the Greeks' "Mountain Government" no recognition and clearly kept its distance from it. The Greek Communists were further disappointed when, on March 25, Greece's Independence Day, the Soviet government sent a congratulatory message to the Greek government in exile, but not to the PEEA. For the Greek Communists. the day of national celebration got only worse when a telegram from Moscow informed the KKE that the Soviet Union had recognized the newly formed government in Cairo as the legitimate government of Greece.[107]

In March and April 1944, preoccupied with their own intense struggle against the retreating Nazi armies, and focusing on securing Soviet interests in Romania and Bulgaria, officials in Moscow chose to avoid involving themselves directly in the Greek-Yugoslav situation, which would have angered the British. At that time, however, contacts between the PEEA and AVNOJ had intensified and Tito had sent to the PEEA a warmly worded telegram of congratulations and declared his full support and willingness to cooperate with it. "The aims of our struggle are the same," he proclaimed. Andreas Tzimas immediately left for Tito's headquarters to become the liaison between AVNOJ and the PEEA.[108] And even though relations between the Greek and Yugoslav Communist Parties were far from harmonious, Tzimas kept the Yugoslavs systematically updated about developments in Greece and often requested from Tito material and political assistance. The Yugoslav and Greek Communists were developing a common regional strategy, based on the strength of their armed resistance and Britain's inability to control it.

Despite their common ideology and the similarity of their objectives, Yugoslav, Greek, Albanian, and Bulgarian Communists continued to disagree on the ever-recurring Macedonian question. And despite Tito and Dimitrov agreeing that it was "unacceptable for Communists to quarrel for future borders and territorial issues of their countries," as Dimitrov stressed in his letter to Molotov, increasing uncertainty affected the future of the Balkans. Dimitrov's anxieties in April 1944 clearly reflected this uncertainty: "What will concretely happen with Macedonia after the war, is impossible to be said now and personally I don't assume the responsibility to do it. Everything will depend on a number of currently unknown factors."[109]

And, of course, those factors remained unknown because despite the Balkan Communists' strength in resisting foreign occupations, their future still depended on the geopolitical ambitions of the great powers that were emerging victorious in the global war against Nazism.

Imperial Agreements

Although the war was to last another year, British officials, among others, were increasingly focusing their attention on introducing changes in the world order that might prevent major wars, perhaps forever. Avoiding war, however, was possible only if dangerous antagonisms between states could be defused or quelled. The creation of the PEEA and Moscow's ambivalence regarding the political situation in Greece intensified British fears of the Soviets' ambitions to establish their hegemony in the postwar Balkans, challenging Britain's vital interests in the Mediterranean and beyond. Accordingly proceeding carefully, British officials decided to reach an understanding with Russia and conceded that the Greek government in exile had to soften its position on the most thorny issues affecting the Balkan region.

On May 2, Ambassador Clark Kerr in Moscow discussed with Foreign Minister Anthony Eden the idea of openly bringing up with the Soviets the future of Romania and Greece.[110] Three days later, Eden met with the Soviet ambassador in London, Fedor Gusev, and proposed an Anglo-Soviet agreement on the Balkans, while in Moscow, Molotov continued to express his puzzlement about Greek situation.[111] The US ambassador to the USSR, Averell Harriman, informed President Roosevelt that it was Stalin's understanding that the proposed agreement gave the Soviets a free hand in Romania, but, in exchange, they would keep their hands off of Greece.[112] On May 18, Gusev relayed to the British his government's consent to the proposal, on the condition that the United States approved. Admitting that he had not consulted the Americans, Eden expressed the hope that Washington would not object.[113]

On May 30, in Washington, Lord Halifax, London's ambassador, explained the British initiative to the US secretary of state, Cordell Hull, and inquired about possible US reactions to it. The British diplomat stressed that tensions had developed between Moscow and London over the Balkans, especially over Romania.[114] Sensing the United States' reservations about such deals, the following day Churchill telegraphed Roosevelt a lengthy explanation of British motives in proposing the arrangement and appealed to the president for his understanding and support.[115] On June 8, in a follow-up letter to Roosevelt, Churchill added Bulgaria to the agreement and stressed that his was not a strategy of creating permanent zones of influence but only a temporary solution to avoid friction in the Balkans. Two weeks later, in a new effort to persuade the skeptical Roosevelt, Churchill argued that the only way he could prevent EAM's "reign of terror in Greece" was by convincing the Russians to stop propping up that organization. He had therefore proposed to the Russians "a temporary working arrangement for the better conduct of the war."[116] News of the Anglo-Soviet negotiations regarding the Balkans arrived rapidly in Cairo. Already on June 1, Leeper informed MacVeagh that London and Moscow had agreed that "in Romania the Russians shall be allowed the initiative and in Greece, the British, to avoid divergencies of action and policy."[117]

While the British government was pursuing with Moscow a policy of mutual accommodation and reciprocity in the Balkans, it was also pressuring the Greeks to stop their infighting and reconcile their differences through a new coalition government under Papandreou, which the KKE would agree to join. Organized and monitored by Leeper, a conference was convened in Lebanon from May 17 through 20, 1944, to which representatives of all political parties, including the KKE, were invited. Planned in anticipation of the liberation of Greece, its principal goal was the formation of a Government of National Unity, with the participation of all political forces and with the power to address the critical issues left unresolved by the failed conference in Cairo in August 1943. Although the urgent need for such a conference was obvious to all, its timing was exceptionally difficult for the KKE representatives, who were very much on the defensive because of recently committed acts of violence attributed to ELAS. The most reprehensible was the murder of a leading resistance figure and committed republican, Colonel Dimitrios Psarros. He was killed when his independent resistance group was attacked by Communist guerrillas on April 17, a death for which the KKE could offer no explanation beyond its determination to monopolize armed resistance. With Papandreou taking the lead, most of the other participants piled on to the KKE representatives, depriving them of any bargaining leverage they could have derived from ELAS's superior strength and achievements.[118]

Even though the KKE's three representatives risked their comrades' wrath by their initial positive response to the proposed Lebanon plan, the Communists ultimately refused to join Papandreou's Government of National Unity. Confident in its guerrilla army and keen to follow in Tito's footsteps, the KKE was not ready to accept the role of a minor partner in the proposed coalition government. The party recalled its representatives, asking for explanations for their initially flexible position.

Immediately after the Lebanon conference, the KKE began considering a violent confrontation with the British in Greece, a bold move for which it needed more military equipment and the Soviets' backing. On June 12, the KKE's Secretary Siantos sent a telegram to Tzimas, the party's liaison to the KPJ: "You know that we have no contact with the Soviet Union. Immediately forward through Tito the party's appeal [to the Soviets]. Remember that the lack of equipment and ammunition affects all our policy." A few days later, another telegram stressed the situation's urgency: "Inform Field Marshal Tito and the Soviet government and ask for political support and material aid. Recall the need to equip us with weapons and ammunition."[119] Finally, Tzimas met the head of the Soviet military mission to the Yugoslav partisans, Lieutenant General Nikolai Korneev, and requested a Russian mediator to solve the Macedonian problem between EAM and Tito, a Soviet mission to Greece, and military assistance for ELAS. He also handed Korneev a report on the situation in Greece as well as a letter addressed to Stalin. The letter stated that there were about forty thousand Greek partisans and requested military supplies as well as Moscow's diplomatic support against British interference in Greek affairs. Tzimas also informed the Russians about the difficulties in Greek-Yugoslav relations and the need for Soviet mediation to solve such bilateral problems. The letter was not without a positive tone: Tzimas concluded that "our army is completely under the influence of the party."[120]

Moscow did not need the Greek Communists to understand the Greek comrades' problems. Soviet officials were now well aware of EAM-ELAS's leading role in the Greek Resistance. On June 3, 1944, a Soviet report stated that EAM controlled large swaths of territory and three-quarters of the resistance armed forces.[121] The data they received, however, did not convince the Soviets to openly and directly support an immediate Communist takeover in Greece because they were not eager to clash with their Western Allies over issues of secondary importance to Moscow. Instead, beginning in early May 1944, the USSR responded positively to the British initiatives and the two Allied powers gradually began to move toward an arrangement of "sharing responsibilities" in the Balkans.

The news of an Anglo-Soviet understanding on the Balkans did not, however, reach the KKE leaders, who knew nothing of the proposed deal. In theory, such a deal meant that the Communists had to join Papandreou's government, and that they would receive such guidance from Moscow. But until mid-June, there appeared to be no concrete moves either from the Soviets or from the EAM/KKE side. And while the British hoped Novikov would persuade the Greek Communists to conform to the proposed agreement, MacVeagh was less optimistic: "The Russians are not any longer criticizing the British, but they are not helping them in any positive way either."[122] On July 11, Churchill politely reminded Stalin that the British believed they had reached a working arrangement about the future of Romania and Greece. Stalin gave a frosty reply: "One thing is clear to me: it is that the American Government have some doubts regarding this question, and that it would be better to revert to this matter when we receive the American reply to our enquiry."[123]

Stalin's less-than-cordial response was not unjustified. On July 15, after deliberations between the State Department and President Roosevelt, Washington informed Moscow that it accepted the proposed plan as a three-month temporary arrangement for the duration of the war. While explicitly giving their consent only for the remainder of the war, the Americans continued to worry that the Anglo-Soviet agreement could permanently divide the Balkans into spheres of influence. It is also possible that Stalin was still unsure about the EAM/KKE's real strength in confronting the British in Greece and played for time to reexamine the situation.[124]

The Greeks also experienced the ambiguities in the Soviets' behavior. In June 1944, EAM's representatives once again visited the Soviet embassy in Cairo for consultations. And once again, they were not able to see Novikov. A few days later, the embassy's first counselor, Daniel Solod, told the KKE's representative, Petros Roussos, that the Soviet government did not reply on the issue of EAM's participation in Papandreou's government, and the ambassador's personal opinion was to support the arrangement made at the Lebanon conference: EAM should join Papandreou's government.[125]

The KKE did not consider Novikov's "personal opinion" a decisive factor and chose to maintain a hard line. According to MacVeagh, EAM's proposed conditions for joining the Papandreou government, dispatched on July 3, were obviously impossible to accept. EAM demanded that its guerrilla army be kept intact until Greece's liberation and that the Left receive seven out of the fifteen cabinet positions. Papandreou rejected the demands, and a final break between the two sides appeared imminent. In Moscow, the British ambassador, Clark Kerr, told Molotov that the Greek Communists' proposal was unacceptable, as it would turn the Greek government into nothing more than a branch of EAM. The Soviet embassy in Cairo thus made another effort to persuade EAM's representative that the Communists' demands were unrealistic. But this was to no avail.[126]

The Soviets finally pulled out their big guns. On July 27, a twelve-member mission under Lieutenant Colonel Grigori Popov landed in central Greece in order to meet the Communist leadership and the PEEA representatives. The mission did not remain secret.[127] Initially, the British and Papandreou were upset by this Soviet move, fearing that the Soviets would offer support to the EAM-ELAS forces. On Churchill's instructions, the Foreign Office protested the unexpected arrival of Soviet officers.[128] If, as suspected, the purpose of the Popov mission included reconnaissance to evaluate ELAS's fighting capabilities, its reported findings would have come as anything but good news to the KKE leadership. According to an SOE report, one of the Soviet visitors remarked to a British officer, "What they cannot understand in Moscow is why you have put up with this rabble so long."[129] But apparently the mission's main task was to advise EAM and the KKE leaders to join the Government of National Unity. This time the KKE budged, and the party agreed to participate in the government on one condition: Papandreou, whom the Communists continued to characterize as reactionary and divisive, had to resign.[130]

The brute reality was that some in Papandreou's cabinet shared the KKE's disapproval of the prime minister and sought to hide their feelings about him behind Communist objections. But demands for his resignation were dismissed by Ambassador Leeper, and on August 9, 1944, the representatives of other parties who had previously favored Papandreou's resignation changed their minds, leaving the Communists isolated on that crucial issue, and the stalemate continued. The day after, on August 10, the KKE's Politburo sent a desperate telegram to Dimitrov, Molotov, and Stalin demanding ammunition. But there was no turning back the clock for the Greek Communists. On August 14, KKE's Politburo informed Molotov, Dimitrov, and the deputy chief of the Foreign Affairs Department of the Bolshevik Party, Leonid Baranov, about the latest political developments and asked for advice. Refusing to be drawn into the dispute, Molotov urged that the Greeks "resolve the questions they raised themselves."[131] Finally, on August 17, the KKE capitulated and announced its intention to join Papandreou's cabinet. In an internal document, the party leadership conceded that the entry into the government encompassed risks and created questions, saying, "We ought to explain that we decided this under pressure."[132]

On September 2, the EAM coalition formally agreed to enter Papandreou's government without any conditions and received six cabinet posts: ministers of finance (Alexandros Svolos), communications (Nikolaos Askoutsis), national economy (Elias Tsirimokos), labor (Militiadis Porfyrogenis), and agriculture (Giannis Zevgos), and deputy minister of finance (Angelos Angelopoulos). Even if this was not what the KKE had hoped for, it was not a negligible position, and one that, before the war, it could have only dreamed of.

Once the Communists joined the Government of National Unity, and as the day of liberation approached, everything began to change—but not the determination of British officials to prevent a sudden move by ELAS to seize control of the Athens area as the last Germans were leaving and before the government and its British escort force could arrive. On September 26, the ELAS commander, General Stefanos Sarafis; the EDES leader, Napoleon Zervas; Prime Minister Papandreou; the British minister resident in the Mediterranean, Harold Macmillan; and the supreme Allied commander in the Mediterranean, General Henry Wilson, met in the Italian town of Caserta and concluded a comprehensive agreement on the security arrangements under which Greece was to be liberated. According to the Caserta agreement, ELAS and EDES were placed under the authority of the new Greek government, which in turn authorized a British lieutenant general, Ronald Scobie, to assume supreme command of all Greek armed forces.[133] Papandreou had informed Sarafis before the meeting that Scobie had been appointed Allied commander for Greece, and with his signature, Sarafis committed the KKE to the agreement.

The KKE's decision to accept a British officer as commander of its military forces shocked ELAS's kapetanios and caused great consternation within the KKE, while Aris Velouchiotis, ELAS's top kapetanios, urged that ELAS should take action immediately and seize Athens. But the KKE leaders were uncertain as to how to react to the challenge posed by their more aggressive members. On the one hand, after the Caserta agreement, an armed clash with the British appeared to them to be illegitimate and risky. The Soviets could be presumed to be opposed to it and most Greeks would almost certainly disapprove of such an aggressive strategy just as the country was celebrating the end of a terrible enemy occupation. On the other hand, the Communist leaders were unwilling to surrender control over the party's armed forces or to submit to British military authority. Hoping to find a compromise, they continued to negotiate while also trying to preserve the option of resorting to armed force. This "dual strategy," as the historian David Close characterizes it, allowed the Communists to buy time against their domestic adversaries and their British support while remaining loyal to Moscow.[134]

The KKE leaders had reasons to hope that their strategy would work. In what may in retrospect be seen as a case of wishful thinking, they anticipated that the Soviet Army, which in September 1944 was in control of Bulgaria, would continue its southward advance and enter Greece.[135] In fact, in late September several hundred Soviet officers and support teams toured the Greek towns of Xanthi, Komotini, and Drama, apparently in advance of the arrival of their units, and rumors circulated that Soviet troops were soon to liberate Salonica from the retreating Germans.[136] And ever since the new Bulgarian regime established itself in early September, the KKE representatives in northern Greece had made contact with officials of the Bulgarian Communist Party and, through them, pleaded with Red Army officers for a military advance into Greece. Moreover, and probably without obtaining prior authorization from their leaders, a group of ELAS kapetanios addressed a letter to the top Soviet commander in Bulgaria, begging the Red Army to come into Greece.[137]

As already indicated, the new Bulgarian government maintained close relations with the KKE and with the ELAS forces in northeastern Greece. Between September 12 and 16, Bulgarian ministers Dobri Terpeshev and Dimitur Neikov visited the still Bulgarian-occupied Greek Thrace to discuss the region's future with the KKE representatives.[138] The secretary of the KKE Eastern Macedonian Bureau, Giorgos Erithriadis, obtained Bulgarian assistance for ELAS's struggle against British-backed nationalist resistance organizations and later traveled to Bulgaria to persuade the Soviet general Fyodor Tolbukhin to send the Red Army to Greece. As might be expected, the Bulgarians had become increasingly involved when Greek nationalists and the government in exile made demands to the Western Allies for border changes at Bulgaria's expense. Uncertainty and anxieties led to increasing tension between Greece and Bulgaria.

In coordination with the temporary government, the Bulgarian Communist Party sent two hundred men to fight with ELAS against Greek nationalist groups. And on September 28, the Bulgarian party sent a telegram to Moscow, stressing the need for arms and ammunition for the Greek comrades.[139] For its part, the Greek government was becoming increasingly alarmed by the situation in Thrace, where the Bulgarian occupation of Greek territories continued even after Bulgaria's capitulation. On September 20, Papandreou told Leeper he feared that the Bulgarians were trying to hand Thrace over to EAM and to the Bulgarian partisans.[140] The following day, King George sent Churchill an even more dramatic letter, complaining that the British were abandoning the Balkans.[141] Aware of the instability in the region, British officials feared that either Soviet troops would move into Greece or Moscow might support Bulgarian claims to Greek Thrace.[142] Accordingly, British Army officers and military missions were sent to the Greek-Bulgarian border area, while in Moscow, Ambassador Kerr informed Soviet authorities that the British government was about to send troops to Greece. The Soviets replied that they had no such plans of their own.[143]

A month later, the Soviet government addressed the unstable situation clearly and decisively. On October 6, Stalin instructed Dimitrov that "Bulgaria ought to withdraw its troops from Thrace and Macedonia,"[144] making it apparent that the Russians had no intention of advancing into Greece. The Soviet officers and support personnel who had briefly appeared in the borderland cities of Komotini, Xanthi, and Drama now left. Not surprisingly, for years the KKE would lament this loss of a rare opportunity. In 1946, in a private meeting with Stalin, Zachariadis asked the Soviet leader why the Soviet army had not entered Greece. Stalin reportedly replied that the Soviets did not have a fleet, with which, presumably, it could control the sea coast of Greek Thrace and Macedonia. In fact, however, on October 9, 1944, in Moscow, Stalin told Churchill that he agreed that England could have the decisive voice in Greece, and on that basis, the two leaders settled the Balkans' future with the so-called Percentages Agreement: while the Soviets' share of influence in the other Balkan states would range between 50 percent (Yugoslavia) and 90 percent (Romania), in Greece it would be a marginal 10 percent.[145]

Although Stalin was to remain steadfast in his position on Greece, other top Communist officials raised questions about the arrangement. On October 17, a few days after the Stalin-Churchill Moscow talks, Dimitrov and Leonid Baranov sent Molotov a detailed report on the

Greek resistance movement. While they recognized that due to Greece's international position the Soviets could not provide direct assistance to EAM-ELAS, they suggested that the USSR should at least offer moral support, for instance in the Soviet press. While agreeing that the Soviets should support the Greek comrades in some way, Molotov warned against antagonizing the British. Stalin, on the other hand, protested that he wanted to remain faithful to his agreement with Churchill.[146]

The terms of the Moscow Percentages Agreement were never communicated to the Greeks, and in fact were kept secret, in part because the agreement had never been fully accepted by the United States. Stalin also saw no need to explain to the KKE leaders the Anglo-Soviet deal on Greece and the rest of the Balkan Peninsula. The Greeks continued to hope for Soviet help and would have been devastated with what, to them, appeared to be a betrayal and a Communist defeat. For Stalin, on the other hand, the agreement constituted a practical arrangement and a peculiar strategic victory that allowed the Soviets to remain detached and flexible on future developments in the Balkans. For instance, the USSR could not be held responsible for the forthcoming Communist victory in Yugoslavia, which had been attributed to the noncooperating Tito, whom Moscow could not control. Needless to say, Stalin would have welcomed a Communist takeover in Greece if it would succeed without Soviet involvement. But in the face of strong British opposition and while the war against Nazi Germany had yet to be won, he wished to avoid the dire consequences of taking any initiatives that might make Communist Greece a reality but in the process antagonize the Western Allies and particularly Roosevelt.[147]

Shattered Dreams

Although the Greek Communists were not pleased with their Soviet patrons, in the fall of 1944 they still continued to hope that they could seize control of their country, particularly since they could see that Communism in the Balkans was clearly on the rise. To be sure, in late 1944, their comrades in Yugoslavia, Bulgaria, Romania, and Albania were not yet properly in power. Yet there were definite indications that with the strong presence of the Soviet military, the region was moving closer to the day when they would be in power. Success seemed likely because the Red Army was not staging a colonial invasion of the Balkans but was pursuing interests and strategies that were closely interconnected with those pursued by popular and victorious Communist parties. At the same time, the situation was far from simple, as each Communist party had its own plan, interests, and concerns, and pursued them independently of Moscow's wishes or directives. And the game each party was playing was taking place simultaneously, but to varying degrees, on the local, national, and international levels. And, of course, ideology and comradeship remained significant factors in the quest for Communism in the region.

Greece was in a unique position among the Balkan nations. On October 12, 1944, Athens was liberated from the Nazis, and when the Government of National Unity arrived in the capital six days later—under pressure, King George had agreed to remain abroad pending a plebiscite on his return—most of the country was under EAM's control. In fact, the KKE exercised control over 80 percent of the country establishing in those areas its own institutions and rules. This anomalous situation indicated that the specter of Communism continued to hang low over Greece, and Papandreou's government and its escorting British patrons faced many difficult problems ahead. Over the years of occupation, the Communist-led resistance had established an extensive organizational and administrative network that regulated public life, distributed resources, and controlled the courts and policed the rural areas. It was a process of both state building and new civil society building that the Greek Communists called *laokratia*, a Greek adaptation of the term "people's republic." From a certain perspective, the situation had enormous similarities to conditions in postwar Eastern Europe, where antifascist ideology combined with mass mobilization and the control of public life by the Communist Party and its organs constituted the transition to socialism.[148]

In the countryside, during the last months of the enemy occupation and gradually following liberation, in the majority of the cities and towns, the only organizations permitted to exist were those related to the KKE and EAM. Their young Communist and fierce antifascist activists brought to the country's periphery new modes of conduct and behavior. Colonel Chris Woodhouse, the British commander of the Allied Military Mission to the Greek guerrillas, who knew Greece and its traditions well, became convinced that the Communists were succeeding in transforming the countryside. According to him, "EAM was set to destroy the tradition of patronage and to substitute a modern habit in social relations. It was often a brutal process, impatiently imposed by urban revolutionaries on a rural proletariat."[149] The key element in this regime-change process was the organizational growth of the party: by 1944 the KKE boasted 73,845 members in the country's forty biggest

cities, at least twenty times more than before the war. But this phe-
nomenal growth in the numerical strength of EAM/KKE mechanisms
should not lead us to exaggerate the Communists' ability to impose
their will on the local populations without obstruction. Traditional values and practices, as well as local particularities, were often so deeply
ingrained in people's attitudes toward EAM that the radicalism of the
Communist resistance movement was extensively diluted and adapted
to the regional culture and convictions of the local societies.[150] As liberation approached, however, the radicalism of EAM became clear, and
as the number of KKE members and followers continued to grow, their
dogmatic political and institutional orientation acquired a common
point of reference: the compulsory monopolistic reform of local society
by the combined efforts of EAM and the KKE.

Exercising control over 80 percent of the country, the KKE was preparing for a dynamic confrontation with the Papandreou government.
To this end, the Communists continued to request military supplies
from their Balkan neighbors as well as from their Soviet authorities. On
November 15, a KKE mission visited Sofia and Belgrade. In Belgrade,
Tito promised to help, but did not miss the opportunity to complain
about the KKE's unchanging position on Macedonia. In Sofia, the reception was not as warm.[151]

In Athens, tensions were mounting as the two antagonistic forces,
the Papandreou government and the KKE's *laokratia*, could no longer peacefully coexist. The violent clash came in early December when
ELAS refused to obey orders issued by General Scobie in the name of
the government, under which the resistance armies were to disarm and
disband, to be replaced by a new national army. The leftist cabinet ministers resigned in protest, and on December 3, a massive Communist-
organized demonstration in the center of Athens was fired on by the
police, with a considerable number of casualties. It was stopped by British troops, who marched between the demonstrators and the police, but
it was followed by sporadic attacks on police stations by ELAS squads.
Between December 3, 1944, and January 5-6, 1945, a bloody conflict,
often referred to as Ta Dekemvriana (The December Events), engulfed
the Athens-Piraeus area,. In the ensuing widespread fighting, ELAS
forces dominated the suburbs, restricting the government-controlled
area to a small zone in downtown Athens. But during the first ten days
of December, ELAS failed to defeat the government forces, which, in
addition to several battalions of British troops, consisted of small units
of infantry, officer cadres, and police.

After that critical period, the battle's momentum changed as British troops in considerable numbers arrived from Italy with tanks and aircraft. Despite widespread international criticism of the Churchill government and a media campaign demanding the end of hostilities and the withdrawal of British troops from Greece, the British reinforcements remained, and the Battle of Athens was won by the rump government and its British supporters. ELAS was forced to withdraw from the capital, taking along as hostages hundreds of prominent and elderly Athenians, many of whom perished from their tragic ordeal. On January 10, 1945, a truce agreement ended the fighting, and a month later, on February 12, the Varkiza Agreement defined the conditions for a peaceful transition to a new political regime, starting with a plebiscite on the king's return and new parliamentary elections. The Communist leadership agreed that ELAS would be disbanded, and that there should be provisions for granting amnesty for political offenses, for punishing irresponsible criminal acts committed in the context of resistance activity, and for bringing wartime collaborators to justice. But while restoring stability, legality, and justice in principle was relatively easy, implementing them was to prove difficult, if not impossible.

Why did the KKE move to an armed confrontation with its domestic opponents? Undoubtedly, the KKE's leaders underestimated the British determination to secure their interests in Greece by military force, if necessary. Some years later, in 1952, Giannis Ioannidis, the KKE's second in command, admitted to his comrades in the Central Committee that he had not expected that in December 1944 Britain would intervene militarily. "Britain would not dare," he had thought at the time.[152] On the other hand, the Greek Communists overestimated the willingness and ability of their foreign comrades to provide the assistance that was needed. Neither Bulgaria nor Yugoslavia sent aid to ELAS. And as the Battle of Athens unfolded, Moscow, to the relief and satisfaction of the British, remained silent and refused to offer any support to the KKE and its army.[153]

It appears that the Soviets never considered supporting their comrades in any way. Within days after the fighting in Athens had begun, the KKE's liaison in Sofia, Petros Roussos, appealed to his international comrades for support. On December 8, Dimitrov, still in Moscow and working closely with Stalin, noted in his diary that he had dealt with Roussos's appeal. He informed his comrades in Sofia "that in the current situation our Greek friends will not be able to count on active intervention and assistance from here [Moscow]." And he also advised the Bulgarian Communist Party not to become directly engaged in the civil war in Greece.[154]

Churchill later confirmed that during the six weeks of fighting in Athens, Stalin had respected the Anglo-Soviet agreement fully. Even moral support from the Soviets was not forthcoming. *Pravda* had no correspondents in Greece and published only short pieces based on dispatches from London and New York. The reports were colorless briefs under simple headings such as "The Situation in Greece," whose contents could not be interpreted as expressing a Soviet position favorable to the Greek insurgents. Such reporting left little doubt that Soviet officials were pessimistic about the prospects of a Communist victory in the Greek civil strife and were determined to remain uninvolved.[155]

While the undisputed leaders of the Communist world seemed to care little about the situation in Greece, the Balkan comrades increasingly showed growing interest in their neighbor's troubles. In fact, officials in Sofia and Belgrade saw the fighting in Athens as a favorable opportunity for the Balkan Communist movement. In their view, a Communist victory in Greece might mean the further strengthening and stabilization of the new regimes, as old regional conflicts could be settled more easily with a friendly government in Athens. As the Second World War neared its end, the geopolitical map of the region could be transformed. For some interested observers, the prospect of a Macedonian state that "would include Salonica and Kavala and form part of a federated Yugoslavia" emerged as a worrying scenario.[156] Naturality, the possibility of such a transformation revived dreams of a common Communist future in the Balkans, which were in sharp contrast with old conflicting nationalist aspirations and fears, and painful memories of bloody Balkan conflicts.

The Yugoslavs were torn between their preferences, their earlier commitments, and the need to secure their own regime. The Communist press sympathized with the Greek comrades, who were now fighting a civil war against their domestic opponents and their British patrons. In December 1944, *Politika*, Yugoslavia's oldest newspaper, printed a number of articles criticizing the Greek government and its British backers while praising the EAM-ELAS insurgents. For his part, Tito refrained from providing military assistance at this moment of the unfolding crisis in Greece. Later, the Yugoslavs justified their policy by claiming that they did not want to give a pretext to the British, who were supposedly ready to invade in order to destabilize their newly born socialist regime.[157]

The Bulgarians were more active. Many articles and comments appeared in their press, which had been universally favorable to the KKE's struggle.[158] In addition, Sofia resumed its role as the intermediary between Moscow and the Balkan Communists, and daily telegrams were exchanged between Dimitrov in Moscow, the Bulgarians, and the Greek Communist leaders. These messages reveal how differently the Balkan Communists felt about the December fighting in Athens. On December 5, the Bulgarian secretary-general, Traicho Kostov, expressed his sympathy for the Greek comrades, asking Dimitrov how the Bulgarian party could help the KKE in its struggle.[159] On December 13, Kostov sent two telegrams to Dimitrov, informing him that the struggle in Athens was going well for the Communists, who did not show any intention to surrender. Two days later, Kostov informed the KKE that Dimitrov was advising that the fight must continue. Yet on December 19, Kostov advised the Greeks that, according to Dimitrov, foreign support was unlikely given the current situation.[160]

Although officials in Sofia did not give up easily on their hope to help their Greek comrades, they realized that they could do little without the cooperation of other Communist parties. The day before the January 10 armistice in Athens, Kostov sent another telegram to Dimitrov, informing him about the difficulties faced by the Communists in Greece and the danger of a new wave of violence close to the northern border. Kostov emphasized that the Greek comrades were in urgent need of ammunition, food, and fuel, and, despite his party's impotence, his country's sensitive international situation, and Russian cautiousness, he expressed his will not to leave the Greeks without aid.[161]

Moscow did not take long to provide its final verdict on January 10: having been defeated, the Greek Communists were told to sign the armistice. As Stalin put it, "I advised not starting this fighting in Greece. The ELAS people should not have resigned from the Papandreou government. They've taken more than they can handle. They were evidently counting on the Red Army's coming down to the Aegean. We cannot do that. We cannot send our troops to Greece either. The Greeks have acted foolishly."[162] On January 15, the KKE informed Dimitrov and Tito that it had signed an armistice.[163]

While the KKE leaders did not consider themselves to be fools, they had to admit that the Dekemvriana struggle had caused them much pain. The Varkiza Agreement essentially meant that the party had lost its army and therefore the chance to seize power. Understandably, as

the ELAS fighters surrendered their weapons, many experienced a political, ideological, and emotional tragedy. But as Greek Communists
mourned their military defeat and the crushing of their dreams, Stalin
remained indifferent. In February 1945, at the Yalta Conference, after casually asking Churchill about developments in Greece, the Soviet
leader stated that he had full confidence in British policy in that country and did not wish to interfere; he merely wanted to know what was
happening there. A relieved Churchill thanked Stalin and invited him
to send witnesses to the Greek elections scheduled for 1946.[164]

Some within the KKE could not accept the catastrophe that had
befallen them. The top kapetanios of ELAS, the notorious Aris Velouchiotis, who during the Battle of Athens had destroyed Zervas's EDES
forces in Epirus, publicly denounced the Varkiza Agreement, an act of
insubordination for which he was expelled from the party. Despite
Velouchiotis's harsh punishment, the KKE leaders continued to believe
that the dreams of a Communist Greece were not dead. The expelled
leader had argued that instead of waiting for Stalin to help it defeat
its domestic opponents, the KKE should strengthen its military ties
with Greece's Balkan neighbors. Exploring the possibilities of that
suggestion, the KKE sent a number of its military officials to Yugoslavia to receive training, a clandestine operation that involved other
Communist neighbors as well. In April 1945, following an agreement
between the KKE and Communist Albania's new leader, Enver Hoxha,
around four hundred KKE cadres found refuge in Rubik in central
northern Albania. They remained there until they were transferred to
Bulkes in Vojvodina, northwest of Belgrade, the Yugoslav capital. By
the early summer of 1945, more than three thousand KKE military
and political cadres had gathered in Bulkes, and their numbers kept
growing.[165]

Just as the KKE recruits were leaving Greece for the security and
training offered by the neighboring regimes, the party's leader was making his way back to his homeland with the help of the nemesis of Greek
Communism: on May 29, 1945, Zachariadis landed in Athens aboard a
British military aircraft.[166] His return opened a new phase in the KKE's
quest for closer ties with Moscow and Balkan Communism.[167]

The defeat of the Axis powers and the end of the Second World War
brought not only peace in Europe but also freedom to millions who,
like Zachariadis, had been held in horrible concentration camps or under harsh enemy occupation. The ensuing changes in global geopolitics

included shifts in Soviet policy toward Greece as, roughly a year after the Moscow Percentages Agreement of October 1944, the USSR started pursuing a more aggressive policy toward the anti-Communist Greek regime and its British backers.[168] Excited over the prospects for a more favorable environment for its own aspirations, the KKE expected that, once again, the Balkan comrades would support the cause of revolution in the region.

Chapter 5

Balkan Decisions

The rank and file of the KKE celebrated the return of Nikos Zachariadis, their legendary leader, and saw in him the hope and the promise that the prospects for Communism in their country could turn bright once again. Optimism was needed badly. Following the defeat of the Dekemvriana and the Varkiza agreement, the Communists' morale had sunk and they badly needed reasons to regain their optimism. But if for his party members Zachariadis embodied the hope for a Communist revival, for their opponents and their pro-West government he was a big question mark and, potentially, a serious threat. In June, following a conversation with the KKE leader, Ambassador MacVeagh found him to embody "sweet reasonableness."[1] Could Zachariadis bring about a shift in the party's orientation, or was he just a skilled diplomat trying to keep all of his options open?[2]

If Zachariadis's attitude seemed ambiguous to the Americans, it was the opposite to his followers. In his address to his party, ignoring the defeat suffered recently by the KKE and its organs, Zachariadis made it clear that he was not going to settle for anything but victory. In late May 1945, in an article published in *Rizospastis*, he proclaimed that the KKE faced a dilemma: it could either accept a return of a Metaxas-style dictatorship or follow the example of other Balkan comrades and establish in Greece a people's republic.[3] Of course, when framed in such a loaded way, the situation hardly appeared to be a dilemma, and without questioning the wisdom of Zachariadis's words, the KKE leadership interpreted them as the clarion call to once again set out to follow a strategy for regime change.

Great Disorder under Heaven

To be sure, the KKE leaders still hoped to take over power not just because Zachariadis had returned full of optimism and ready to reenergize the party's revolutionary aspirations. They had good reasons to believe that the situation in Greece continued to be ripe for drastic change and that much of the public had no sympathy for the post-Varkiza regime, or for the king whose return to Greece after a plebiscite was considered to be all but certain. The bloodshed and destruction of the Dekemvriana, including the tragic fate of hundreds of prominent Athenians who died as hostages of the retreating ELAS, intensified the fear of the KKE and Communism among Greeks who might otherwise have welcomed radical reforms and progress toward a more democratic, egalitarian, and progressive society. The country remained marred by political instability, a war-devastated economy, a bloated and incompetent bureaucracy, virtually no social services, and right-wing extremism terrorizing the towns and rural population.

Political tension intensified in the period between the Varkiza agreement of February 1945 and the parliamentary elections scheduled for March 31, 1946. Perhaps the most divisive issue was the future of the monarchy. With King George II being blamed by much of the population for the Metaxas dictatorship, many Greeks considered his reign synonymous with interwar authoritarianism and fascism and opposed his return; some wished to abolish the monarchy altogether. But the polarization and violence of the resistance movement had complicated matters, compelling many republicans to view Communism and its Greek representatives as an even more dangerous threat than an ultraconservative royalist regime. As a result, some republican leaders of the interwar period decided to support the monarchy and confront the KKE first, in an alliance of necessity with their old royalist enemies. And so it was that on September 1, 1946, when a referendum regarding the future of the monarchy was held, 68 percent of the voters supported the king's restoration. The referendum's results reasonably accurately reflected the popular mood, even if terror and electoral fraud contributed to the scale of the pro-monarchy victory.[4]

While eliciting strong passions, the future of the monarchy was not the only pressing political issue. Widespread poverty, severe economic problems, and lawlessness and anarchy in the countryside combined to create an impression of a serious national crisis. One government after another failed the challenge of bringing the situation under control, exacerbating the problems and undermining any prospects for political stability in the near future. Inevitably, polarization between the Communists and the anti-Communists deepened and became more violent. On January 13, 1946, in Volos, an industrial city and one of the KKE's strongholds since the interwar period, four KKE supporters were killed in clashes with the police that followed a public appearance by Zachariadis. While the crisis in Volos appeared to be out of control, on January 20, Vasilis Manganas, a chieftain of a Far Right paramilitary gang in southern Peloponnese, invaded the city of Kalamata, attacked a police station, and released prisoners who had been arrested for assailing local leftist activists. Manganas and his men looted and destroyed the facilities and printing presses of the KKE and EAM, and kidnapped about a hundred civilians, whom they kept as hostages outside the city. In the bloodshed that accompanied the event, fourteen people lost their lives.[5]

Domestic violence, combined with new international developments, made a new round of civil warfare a realistic possibility. Until 1945, the Soviets' attitude had created the impression, at least for one US diplomatic observer in Athens, that in Greece the Soviets were not inclined "to do more than fan the flames with a sympathetic press and radio and keep the local communists in a constant state of hopeful expectation of more definite assistance to come."[6] Conditions, however, appeared to have changed, and Zachariadis now hoped to ensure that this time a Communist uprising would not fail. His first move was to secure political and material support from the KKE's sister parties in the Balkans, and his overtures met with a warm reception. Dimitrov, still Stalin's confidant and adviser, personally undertook to help the Greek party: he urged a number of Soviet officials to provide the KKE with materials, including printing machines and paper, needed to mobilize the Greek population into action.[7]

More important, in early 1946, the KKE sent a high-level mission to Moscow to present its case at the highest levels. The head of the mission was a forty-one-year-old trade unionist leader and former tobacco worker, Mitsos Partsalidis, who had joined the KKE in 1923 and who had already visited Moscow in 1936 as a Greek delegate to the International Communist Youth Congress. He had risen to fame as the first elected Communist mayor in Kavala, an industrial city in the north of Greece. Partsalidis and his entourage went to Moscow to consult top Soviet officials and request their material and political assistance. On January 18, 1946, the Greek delegation met with Leonid Baranov, the deputy head of the International Department of the Central Committee of the Communist Party of the Soviet Union, and with two other officials.[8] In addition to securing promises of assistance, the Greeks' main objective was to obtain Soviet advice on the crucial dilemma they faced: should they participate in the forthcoming national election or boycott it and take up arms instead?

Although the Soviets recommended that the KKE participate in the election, their advice left another option open. According to Partsalidis, the message he received was, "Take part in the elections now. Later, review the situation. In accordance with the way it develops the center of gravity may move as necessary, either to legal methods or to armed struggle."[9] Partsalidis's critically important account is confirmed by Dimitrov's memoir: on February 9, the Bulgarian noted in his diary, "Received an answer from 'Alekseev' [Molotov] to a question posed by the Greek comrades—shall they prepare for an armed uprising against the reactionary monarchist regime, or shall they organize their self-defense, combined with the political mobilization of the popular masses? The second is recommended."[10]

International problems, however, began to intensify and Moscow began to revise its positions on a number of fronts. In particular, Soviet relations with Britain and the United States were no longer what they had been a year earlier, when the war was still the Allies' unifying factor and highest priority. Unexpectedly, on February 1, 1946, the Soviet delegate to the UN General Assembly accused Britain of inciting political violence in Greece and demanded that British troops be withdrawn from the country. On February 9, in a major speech on domestic and international issues, Stalin declared that socialism and capitalism were incompatible, that peaceful coexistence with the West was not feasible; and that the interests of the Soviet Union required rapid industrialization and the expansion of its power. Stalin's speech was received by many in both the East and the West as the prelude to more muscle flexing, and by Communists around the world as a signal to launch radical initiatives.[11]

Particularly alarmed were officials of the Truman administration, who were puzzled by Stalin's bellicose tone. Recent Soviet offensive behavior over divided Germany, expansionist moves in Iran, and territorial pressures on Turkey appeared to call for a policy of more vigorous and robust opposition to Moscow. The new strategy, labeled "containment," was in principle based on a lengthy analysis of Soviet conduct sent to the US State Department from Moscow on February 22, 1946, by George Kennan, a senior diplomat and respected expert on Russia. In his "long telegram," Kennan blamed the growing East-West tensions entirely on the Soviets and attributed their hostility toward the West, and especially the United States, to the Russians' traditional feelings of insecurity and inferiority, now compounded by discredited and misguided ideological theories of Marxism-Leninism. Although he thought that meaningful compromise was not at present possible, Kennan was not pessimistic about the future: he argued that if the West could remain patient and vigilant in blocking further Soviet expansionism, solutions to international problems could eventually be found without recourse to military conflict. And if "contained" by the West, the Soviet system would stagnate and collapse under the weight of its backwardness, brutal authoritarianism, and total disregard for human dignity and values.

Kennan's containment thesis included ambiguities and contradictions that in later years he acknowledged and disavowed. Among its simplistic premises was the belief that Communists around the world were united in their loyalty to their Bolshevik motherland and served as pliant tools of Moscow, whose goal was world conquest. But whatever its shortcomings, the simplicity of its logic and its interpretation by Washington's more action-oriented officials made Kennan's containment strategy widely accepted and the centerpiece of US foreign policy throughout the Cold War.

A more restrained and less intellectually grand version of containment was presented on March 5, 1946, by Churchill, on a visit to the United States as a private citizen. At a ceremony in Fulton, Missouri, with President Harry S. Truman in attendance, Churchill delivered his famous "Iron Curtain" speech, in which he described in stark terms how the Soviet Union's brutal domination of Eastern Europe had split the continent, and by extension much of the world, into two hostile armed camps. Decrying such a dangerous division, Churchill thought that negotiated settlements of conflicts with Stalin were still possible and should be pursued. But the speech was not received particularly well, and his faith in diplomacy appeared to be an illusion. Among the world's many trouble spots, the Greek Civil War was emerging as the first proxy war of a global East-West conflict that would last for decades.

Undoubtedly, international developments played a part in perpetuating political turmoil in Greece. Influenced by the growing signs of antagonism and hostility among the erstwhile Allies, and the atmosphere of instability and terror in the Greek periphery, the Second Plenum of the KKE's Central Committee decided on February 12, 1946, to boycott the upcoming national election scheduled for March 31. Although the majority of the committee members apparently preferred to launch an insurgency immediately, Zachariadis wanted to develop a strategy of slow and careful escalation so as not to give the British the pretext to intervene militarily. This was a new version of a "dual strategy" that combined legal political activities with a slow and gradual buildup toward a popular uprising.[12] In guiding the party forward, Zachariadis tried to avoid crossing any of the red lines drawn by the Soviets regarding an eventual resort to military action. Although he had not been in Greece during the Dekemvriana battle, when according to Stalin the Greeks had acted foolishly, he understood better than many of his comrades the consequences of lacking discipline and inadequate preparation for dangerous initiatives. The controversial letter Zachariadis had written when Italy invaded Greece had given him a personal experience of rejection, which he had brought on himself by defying the Soviets. He knew that an insurgency without the green light from Moscow was unlikely to succeed. And, of course, this last conclusion had been a bitter lesson he shared with his comrades after December 1944.

Zachariadis came up with a plan to escape the dilemma of election or revolution. The KKE would boycott the election, but it would also escalate the violence, which could turn into a revolt only gradually, allowing the KKE to keep all the options open. The party could play for time, avoiding a direct British intervention and gathering supplies and aid from its Balkan comrades in case a civil war became a reality. At least that is what Zachariadis told the Soviet ambassador in Athens, Admiral Konstantin Rodionov, during their meeting in May 1946. The previous month, the Soviet diplomat had already reported to his superiors in Moscow that despite the boycott of the elections, the Left "will not proceed to an open insurrection."[13] This despite the fact that Zachariadis had expressed to the ambassador his optimism about the possibility of guerrilla warfare in Greece, even in the presence of the British troops, because the latter, according to Zachariadis, were not capable of conducting operations in mountainous areas inaccessible to the action of the tank forces.[14]

Zachariadis's strategy appeared to be working, as the Communist world slowly realized that the Greeks were not going to give up their struggle for power. The KKE leader took a long trip to the Balkans and to Eastern Europe, lobbying the more established Communist parties for support. On March 27, 1946, he went to Prague, where he informed the Czechoslovak leader Klement Gottwald that the situation in Greece was inevitably leading toward a civil war and that the KKE was counting on the sister parties of Eastern Europe for material aid. Without much enthusiasm, Gottwald assured Zachariadis that he could count on aid from Czechoslovakia. On April 1, Zachariadis left Prague for Belgrade, where he met Tito, Aleksandar Ranković, and Milovan Djilas. Tito received him warmly and encouraged the Greeks to go ahead. He added, however, that the KKE's leader needed to see Stalin to proceed with any military action.[15]

From Belgrade, the KKE leader flew to Moscow and then to the Crimea, where he met Stalin, Andrei Zhdanov, the head of the International Department of the Central Committee of the Soviet Party, and the Soviet foreign minister, Vyacheslav Molotov. Although the Soviets criticized the Greeks for boycotting the March elections, they agreed with their visitor that an armed struggle in Greece was imminent, and Stalin instructed Zachariadis to arrange the details with Tito. Once again, Stalin drew Zachariadis's attention to the need to avoid a British military intervention and to move toward armed struggle gradually, leaving open the possibility for compromise in the future. In short, Stalin gave his Greek comrades a first faintly green light for armed insurrection.[16]

With Stalin's cautious approval in hand, Zachariadis traveled back to Belgrade, and from there proceeded to Sofia to see Dimitrov. In this meeting, the KKE leader specified what the party needed to succeed: training centers for its guerrilla fighters in Yugoslavia, Albania, and Bulgaria, as well as weapons, military supplies, printing presses, paper, and a wireless communications system. On April 26, the day after his meeting with Dimitrov, Zachariadis asked Moscow's top-level officials, Mikhail Suslov, Georgy Malenkov, and Andrei Zhdanov, to approve this request for fraternal assistance. The Soviets approved the proposal, and in October 1946 the KKE proceeded to combine existing guerrilla bands and form the Democratic Army of Greece (DSE).[17]

In much of the Greek countryside, the civil war was already underway. A few hours before Election Day on March 31, a band of Communist guerrillas attacked a police station in the northern town of Litochoro, located at the foot of Mount Olympus. The major difference between this and earlier Communist armed struggles like those of the Dekemvriana, was that now the international Communist world was involved. How did this change in circumstances occur?

As already discussed, the USSR had been particularly cautious in becoming entangled in the conflict. But by mid-1946, the Soviets had begun to show more flexibility in their attitude toward the future of Communism in Greece. They had gone from inertia to careful, but clear, support for the KKE's ambitions. In particular, they paid increasing attention to the needs of the Greek insurgents. This gradual shift indicated that Zachariadis's strategy of playing for time and escalating the tension gradually and carefully had been justified. While boycotting the March 1946 election may have seemed a risky move since the Soviets did not approve of it, time was on the Greeks' side. The KKE's leader was convinced that relations between the former wartime allies would deteriorate, and over the course of the year, Zachariadis was proven right. As time passed, Moscow's faint green light became brighter, and the planning for the Greek insurrection had become a preoccupation of Communists in Europe.

In early October 1946, Baranov traveled to Belgrade twice to meet the KKE Politburo leaders Giannis Ioannidis and Petros Roussos and discuss with them the party's aid requests. The Greeks informed the Soviet official that four thousand insurgents were already in the mountains, and that with appropriate assistance, their number could grow to twenty thousand in a few months. Ioannidis and Roussos asked for medicine, clothes, and weapons, and for a cash subvention of at least $150,000 per month. The KKE request also included training for fifteen to twenty Greek guerrilla officers in Soviet military schools.[18]

Baranov discussed the Greeks' requests with the Yugoslav leadership: the marshal Josip Broz Tito and his minister of interior affairs, Aleksandar Ranković. The Yugoslavs declared that they were ready to help the Greeks with weapons, munitions, and military training. They could also provide a radio station and a refuge facility in Belgrade for the KKE's Central Committee. The only request they refused to meet was that for cash, because, they claimed, they did not have enough for their own needs.

Baranov returned to Moscow and immediately proceeded to arrange for the details of what had been agreed to. In response, the Soviet bureaucracy went into action. On October 7, 1946, Suslov wrote Zhdanov and told him to dispatch to the Greek insurgents funds, food, and medical supplies.[19] A few days later, all of the top Soviet figures—Stalin, Lavrentiy Beria, Anastas Mikoyan, Malenkov, and Zhdanov—were briefed on the scale of the fraternal assistance.[20] The formidable machinery of international Communism had gone into action because, finally, Soviet policy had become consistent. Until the end of 1946 it had remained unchanged: the armed struggle in Greece should not escalate too quickly, in order to keep the opportunity open for political activity, which could protect the party cadres from arrests, systematic persecution, and extermination. This was exactly what Dimitrov had advised Ioannidis, the Greek representative, in November 1946 in Sofia.[21] But while the priority was caution, this policy framework no longer specified that Greece should remain under British, or generally Western, influence. In other words, while the "how" of building socialism had not been determined, the "if" was also no longer removed from consideration. When the leaders of the Communist world began supporting the KKE's cause, the other Communist parties were no longer constrained in their desire to assist the Greeks in achieving their aspirations. Some European Communist parties immediately provided financial support: for instance, the Czech party gave 1 million crowns ($20,000), and the French contributed almost $100,000.[22]

Balkan Internationalism

As a result of these developments, the people's republics in the Balkans became actively and directly involved in their neighbor's future. Unquestionably, the greatest champions of this cause were the Yugoslavs, as Tito early on had made explicit his intention to support the Greek Communists in their struggle. And the KKE tried to take full advantage of this connection. Already on August 25, 1946, the KKE's leading cadres, Ioannidis and Roussos, came to Belgrade to set up improved communications with the Yugoslav Communist Party and secure aid for the insurgency. As we know, however, the Greek-Yugoslav relationship was not free of some thorny issues, the most important of them being the old Macedonian question. Now that preparations for the insurgency had turned serious, the Greeks and Yugoslavs had to find a way to put their differences aside. Ioannidis and Roussos spoke to the Yugoslav hosts not only about the need for assistance, but also about the KKE's attitude toward the Macedonian organization NOF (Narodni Osvoboditelen Front, or People's Liberation Front). Created in 1945, NOF's goal was to secure the self-determination of Slav-Macedonians, which in reality meant the secession from Greece of Aegean Macedonia (the Greek-Macedonian territories). As had been the case before the war, the issue of Macedonian independence remained a matter of grave concern to the Greek party and a threat to the Greek state.[23]

Nevertheless, the KKE could not afford to alienate its Balkan allies. Therefore, on October 14, 1946, at a meeting presided over by Ranković, Ioannidis, representing the KKE, and Ivan Karayanov, representing NOF, signed a special accord on the KKE-NOF relationship. The agreement represented a compromise: NOF would cease to demand the creation of independent Slavic Macedonian units within the Greek guerrilla forces, while the KKE would accept that Slav-Macedonians could maintain their own centralized political leadership, a de facto recognition of the Macedonians' autonomy. At the time, the arrangement benefited the KKE because the party could now recruit Slavic Macedonian autonomists into its DSE and, of course, count on the support of Yugoslavia, which exercised great influence over this Slav-speaking population.[24]

But although, for the time being, the compromise heralded a success for both sides, the Macedonian question continued to bedevil leftists in the Balkans. Throughout the entire civil war, the KKE would be compelled to walk a tightrope between its two conflicting support bases. On the one hand, it would have to speak of national unity and seek to galvanize its domestic audience in traditionally Greek nationalistic terms, while on the other, it would have to cater to the political elites of the country's Slav-Macedonian population, which constituted the largest single ethnic group within the Democratic Army of Greece. It was a delicate and challenging exercise in balancing antagonistic nationalisms that often ended in feelings of bitterness and resentment. And such experiences of discrimination and hostility within the DSE would later also adversely influence Yugoslav-Greek relations, as NOF leaders would bring their complaints to Belgrade, which in turn would pressure the KKE to be more accommodating to NOF.

Despite persistent mutual antagonism, in late 1946 it was the Yugoslavs' support for the insurgency that helped the KKE march confidently into the armed conflict. Tito's unconcealed sympathy and support carried a lot of weight in the international Communist world, more than any other country in Eastern Europe. Soviet officials praised Yugoslavia as a bastion of peace and democracy, while its wartime resistance won Moscow's acclaim as a model of partisan organization and effectiveness. But it was their thorough Bolshevization that truly elevated the Yugoslav Communists above other Eastern Europeans. Although in the interwar period the KPJ had resisted the Bolsheviks, toward the end of the war it moved closer to the Soviet Union, and by 1946, the Soviets were heralding the "Yugoslav path" as a model of transition to socialism.[25]

Cordial relations between the Soviets and the Yugoslav Communists reached their apogee in the early summer of 1947. When, as a follow-up to the Truman Doctrine, the United States announced on July 5 the European Recovery Program (the Marshall Plan) for the economic reconstruction and recovery of Europe, the Yugoslavs rejected the Americans' offer immediately and with vigor, as a capitalist scheme administered by Washington, while other Communist comrades remained briefly ambivalent, waiting for Moscow's response.

As the Soviets' most trusted partners, the Yugoslavs assumed a special place in the Balkan region. Among their other pursuits, they began to coordinate Communist activities related to Greece and to provide the KKE with guidance. Yugoslavia became the site of a Greek affairs management center, where Ioannidis, the KKE's representative in Belgrade, cooperated with Soviet representatives Baranov and Vasily Mosetov. Most of the weapons, munitions, and other provisions destined for the insurgents in Greece started to flow from Yugoslavia in 1947. Initially the weapons were of German origin, so as to conceal the Yugoslav regime's involvement in the affair. Belgrade also channeled to the insurgents the aid arriving from Albania, Romania, and Bulgaria.[26]

As the KKE had requested, Yugoslavia also set up a large guerrilla training and rehabilitation camp in the village of Bulkes, in Vojvodina, whose ethnic German population had been expelled. More than five thousand people passed through Bulkes, which gained international notoriety as the site of a camp administered under harsh discipline by KKE cadres. Such camps also existed in Bulgaria, in the towns of Ivaylovgrad and Svilengrad, as well as in Berkovitsa. Although the Greek government persistently protested against the existence of such training camps in Balkan countries, they continued to operate until the very end of the civil war.[27] Yugoslavia also helped the KKE with propaganda efforts. The party's "Free Greece Radio Station" broadcast from

Yugoslav territory, and the KPJ financed the foreign travel and accommodations of prominent Greek Communists, facilitated their contacts with important figures, and provided all kinds of other services that promoted the insurgency's cause.[28]

While the Yugoslavs were the Greek Communists' closest allies, other Balkan parties could not remain indifferent, especially at a time when both their more esteemed neighbor and the Soviets were actively involved. Bulgarian aid to the KKE began in the fall of 1945. Immediately after the Dekemvriana, Bulgarian Communists had urged Dimitrov to use his influence to help their Greek comrades. As already mentioned, Dimitrov, who had always displayed a special interest in the whole Balkan region, lobbied Molotov to send material assistance to the Greeks. In November 1945, Molotov finally authorized Dimitrov to send $100,000 to the KKE.[29] In mid-1946, the Bulgarians became more active in dispatching material and other assistance. In the fall of 1947, they provided the DSE with fifteen trucks to facilitate the transport of military equipment and other materials to the insurgents. The trucks crossed into Greece through nine different entry points on the Greek-Bulgarian border, and their loads consisted of army supplies, provisions, paper, sanitary goods, and other materials. The Bulgarians' energy and dedication prompted the KKE's envoy in Sofia, Kostas Siaperas, to report enthusiastically, "Especially now, the friends supply us with everything. They give us probably more than we receive from anywhere else."[30]

Elsewhere in the Balkans, the Communists also organized assistance to the insurgents. The Greeks developed contacts with the Romanians in 1946. According to the Romanian official Vasile Posteucă, Markos Vafeiadis, the veteran kapetanios of the wartime ELAS and now commander of the DSE, as General Markos, had come to Bucharest to discuss material aid for his troops. A few months later, in 1947, the Romanian supply operation began, supervised by a high-ranking officer of the Romanian Army, Mircea Haupt, and the leading Romanian Stalinist, Minister of Finance Vasile Luca, while two Soviet military officials assisted in the efforts. Soviet agents transported the arms through Bulgaria and Yugoslavia and ensured that the operation remained secret.[31]

With the Balkan Communists mobilized for this cause, the Albanians could not refrain from demonstrating solidarity with their struggling Greek comrades. Although for a while the two parties had serious disagreements over portions of northern Epirus (southern Albania), in April of 1945, Enver Hoxha, the Albanian leader, had welcomed approximately four hundred persecuted KKE cadres who a few months later left for Bulkes. In May 1946, munitions transport points began operating along the Albanian-Greek border and contacts between Greek and Albanian officials gradually intensified. Initially the DSE had asked for large-caliber mortars and further assistance in food and clothing, but in 1947, General Markos also asked the Albanian comrades to recruit three to four thousand members of the Cham community to join the Greek guerrillas. The Chams, an ethnic Muslim-Albanian minority in northwestern Greece, had fallen victims to an operation organized by Greek nationalists in 1944. The entire community had been persecuted and expelled to Albania, and Markos's request was a very sensitive issue. But although Hoxha was happy to have these Greek citizens join the DSE, few Chams volunteered to do so. At first the Albanian authorities considered ordering the community to fight, but soon they abandoned the idea. Hoxha promised Tito that Albania would send some mortars, but as far as mobilizing troops from the Cham population was concerned, Hoxha was pessimistic.[32]

The ubiquitous, though unequal, involvement of the Balkan Communists in the Greek Civil War was formalized in August 1947, in Bled, in the Yugoslav Republic of Slovenia. The army chiefs of staff of Yugoslavia, Bulgaria, and Albania officially agreed to supply the DSE with whatever assistance it required for its armed struggle, to organize within their own territories military training camps and hospitals for the insurgents, and to call on the governments of Hungary and Romania to actively participate in this collaborative effort. The Albanians also agreed to place at the KKE's disposal a naval base and to further develop it for the Greeks' use. But the chiefs were not just pledging support unconditionally and with no strings attached. They also agreed to appoint representatives to the DSE headquarters to serve as an advisory committee. In particular, no change or removal of DSE commanders could occur without the agreement of the tripartite Balkan advisory committee. Despite that restriction, the terms of the Bled agreement were quite generous toward the Greek insurgents, prompting some observers to suspect that in return for assistance in the civil war, the KKE had to consent to a future independent Macedonia. But no archival evidence confirming this suspicion exists.[33]

Unavoidably, the Bled meeting generated a variety of rumors, because, like most of the assistance provided to the Greeks, the tripartite agreement was surrounded by secrecy. Characteristically, Stalin, who ratified the agreement without enthusiasm, made sure to point out that there was no need to publicize it, because the same aims could be achieved without clamor. Almost certainly the Soviet leader feared that these plans would provoke a negative reaction from the West and especially from the United States.[34]

For the Greek Communists, the USSR remained a critical partner that held the whole Balkan assistance together. In May 1947, Zachariadis traveled again to Moscow, where, on May 13, he prepared a memorandum explaining the situation in Greece. It was first sent to Suslov, who forwarded it to Zhdanov, and it finally reached Stalin through Molotov. Zachariadis asked to see Stalin, and on May 20, he secured a private meeting with the Soviet leader.[35] Their discussion was officially described as cordial and productive. Two days later, on May 22, Zachariadis met Zhdanov, who claimed that Stalin had charged him with the task of finding out what the Greek comrades were requesting. In his response, Zachariadis painted a very optimistic picture and declared that one-third of the Greek territory was under Communist control. But he also claimed that Yugoslav support was not enough to secure victory and that the DSE needed more weapons and supplies with which to raise an army of fifty thousand troops. Before ending the meeting, Zachariadis also struck an emotional chord of comradeship: "I think you could help us financially. You should buy weapons. We know the difficulties the Soviet Union faces. We have no right to ask for anything from the Soviet Union. She would give us what she can. We do not want anything bad to happen to her because of us. For the Soviet Union, we are ready to sacrifice everything." Having pleaded his case, Zachariadis left Moscow satisfied, and a few days later the leadership in Greece was informed by telegram that "Zachariadis met the Old Man [Stalin], and our problems were thoroughly discussed. We should be completely satisfied with the results."[36]

The Greek comrades had good reason to be happy. On September 23, 1947, responding to Stalin's query about the Greeks' need for support, Molotov informed him that Zachariadis's requests had been fully met—including the $100,000 cash sent to Zachariadis through Suslov's international network—except for two points: instead of the sixty mountain cannons requested, the Russians sent the corresponding quantity in German 37 mm antitank cannons and ammunition for them. Molotov informed Stalin that such cannons had been sent previously to the Greek comrades, and that the Greeks were satisfied. Moreover, the request for the supply of footwear and clothing could not be fulfilled, due to the lack of the foreign type of military uniforms and footwear in the Soviet Army and industry.[37]

Significantly, at a time when tensions between West and East were beginning to escalate, Stalin found time to discuss details of the military aid being sent to the Greek comrades. Indeed, it is surprising that military assistance to the DSE was in some instances micromanaged at the highest levels of the Soviet government. But such preoccupation with details ensured Moscow's ability to monitor and control the assistance effort and the parties involved in it.

The Greek Civil War attracted the attention of many among its contemporaries, much of it critical of the insurgents and their supporters. It is therefore hardly surprising that so many of the KKE's international comrades wanted to keep their involvement in the conflict secret. During 1946–47, they faced international sanction for arming a guerrilla army in southeastern Europe. For its part, the Greek government lodged repeated charges and formal complaints at the United Nations against the Balkan regimes, and Greek officials bombarded foreign diplomatic missions and international organizations with letters about Communist meddling in the country's internal conflict. Eventually their pleas were heard when the Special Committee on the Balkans, established by the UN General Assembly in October 1947, confirmed that the Balkan neighbors were involved in the Greek Civil War.

To be sure, Greece's neighboring Communist regimes chose to risk international criticism partly in pursuit of their geopolitical interests. But the Communist insurgency in Greece cannot be reduced to a purely geopolitical and regional affair. For many in the West and elsewhere, the conflict took on much greater significance as the first ideological battle line in Europe in the aftermath of the Second World War. Many European Communists saw the violent crisis in Greece as an opportunity for the revival of popular Revolution with a capital R, which had been almost forgotten since the Spanish Civil War. As a result, European Communists followed the conflict closely and with concern about its outcome. The French Communist Party even lent the KKE its platform for a major announcement: in June 1947, at the French party's Eleventh Congress, the KKE proclaimed that it would form a government in the areas of Greece under its control.[38]

Such a dramatic declaration was a message to the international community that the insurgency of the Greek Communists was morally and politically backed by Moscow. A few months later, on Christmas Eve in 1947, the KKE's radio station in Belgrade announced the creation of the "Provisional Democratic Government of Greece," a bold step that was certain to provoke a quick and strong response from the Greek government in Athens. On December 27, in accordance with law 509/1947, the KKE was declared outlawed and the party's newspaper, *Rizospastis*, was shut down. To avoid confiscation, the party transferred its archives to Moscow, where they remained before being transferred to Bucharest in 1950. From then on, and for several years, the KKE and its archives had no home of their own and relied on their foreign comrades to host them.[39]

But the aim of the bold declaration was to set up a proper home for all Greek Communists. Creating a government was meant to help transform the guerrillas into a conventional army capable of positional warfare and of holding territory. The plan for the DSE anticipated that between fifty and sixty thousand combatants would be armed and trained to seize and control wide swaths of northern Greece, with Salonica at their core. Significantly, this project did not originate with the Greek insurgents. This ambitious strategic plan, which came to be known as Operation Lakes, was drawn up by Yugoslav officers and was approved on September 12, 1947, by the KKE at the Third Plenum of its Central Committee. Translated from Serbian to Russian, the decision was sent to the Soviet Communist Party and approved by its Central Committee. Operation Lakes constituted the crystallization of military and political contacts that Zachariadis had had with Tito, and was the result of Moscow's commitment to providing the necessary support to the insurgency.[40]

The Yugoslav-Greek plans proved unrealistically optimistic, particularly as the DSE would not manage to recruit and train the targeted number of combatants: at the peak of their combat strength, in the early months of 1948, the guerrillas numbered roughly twenty-six thousand to twenty-eight thousand troops. As government troops gradually expanded their control over small towns and rural areas, the DSE was no longer able to easily replenish its ranks with new recruits, even though they increasingly included women and adolescents forcefully inducted. By March 1949, there were about twenty-two thousand DSE fighters; in July 1949, toward the end of the conflict, they had been reduced to only seventeen thousand.[41]

Between Tito and Stalin

In September 1947, right after the DSE had introduced its dream of a great conventional army, another event in the international Communist world began to shape the fate of the civil war. On September 22, the Communist parties met in the Polish mountain resort of Szklarska Poręba and established the Cominform—the Communist Information Bureau—which essentially worked as a coordination center for the fraternal parties of Europe. The civil war and Greece's future were hardly the primary interests of the assembled parties. The Soviets, and initially also the Yugoslav Communist leadership, wanted unity, which they considered lacking following the Comintern's dissolution in 1943. And the new Communist International had been in the making since early 1946, or even earlier. The Soviets in particular were concerned about the new era evolving in international relations. Stalin had concluded that only iron discipline over ideological and party issues would enable him to manage the new state of affairs in postwar Eastern Europe and hinder any "contamination" originating in the West with such temptations as the US-sponsored Marshall Plan. Through the Cominform, Moscow hoped to further Stalinize or Sovietize Eastern Europe and the main Western Communist parties.[42]

This new Communist International was in many ways significantly different from its predecessor. The Cominform suffered from organizational inefficacies, while the expired Comintern had been a truly impressive organization.[43] But other differences were even more important. The Comintern had aspired to foment a worldwide revolution and had invited all the Communist parties of the world to join and participate in its activities, while the Cominform was designed as a geopolitical tool to be employed in European politics. Only one person held a top-level position in both organizations: Andrei Zhdanov, the Cominform's key personality and the leader in all negotiations, according to the Italian representative Eugenio Reale. The European party leaders present in Szklarska Poręba quickly realized that Zhdanov was Stalin's omnipotent representative and behaved accordingly.[44] They sat and listened as Zhdanov delivered his now-famous report "On the International Situation," which presented global affairs as divided into two hostile camps.[45] In addition to Zhdanov's report, the European Communist leaders received specific tactical instructions from Moscow. It was generally understood that in such a hostile environment, Communist survival required absolute obedience to the center, even in the seemingly most mundane affairs.

The Soviets' domination of the conference in Szklarska Poręba was softened somewhat by the fact that another party enjoyed much attention at the event. The Yugoslavs, represented by Milovan Djilas and

Edvard Kardelj, were treated as shining stars. Despite myths, advanced later by Tito's regime, that since its beginning Communist Yugoslavia had chosen to follow a different path than that of the Soviet Bloc, in September 1947 Yugoslavia was indisputably regarded by the Communist world as second only to the USSR. It was symbolically significant that the Cominform headquarters were established in Belgrade, where the Yugoslavs worked closely with Zhdanov. In fact, some matters addressed in the founding congress had already been discussed between Zhdanov, Malenkov, Djilas, and Kardelj well before the proceedings were launched.[46]

On the other hand, while aware that the USSR was their undisputed leader, European Communists nevertheless dared to express their own views. Among them, the Poles, represented by the first secretary of the Polish Communist Party, Władysław Gomułka, and the Czechoslovak Communists, led by their secretary-general, Rudolf Slánský, proposed the formation of left-wing coalition governments, a strategy termed "pluralist." Their suggestion did not carry the day, as the congress explicitly favored promoting single-party regimes that would follow the Soviet model. In that discussion, the main proponents of the winning strategy were the Yugoslavs, supported by the Soviets.[47]

Choosing the way forward politically resulted in criticisms of the strategies already adopted by Communist parties to date. The harshest critique was directed at the French, Italian, and Czechoslovak parties. All three faced censure over their predisposition toward broadly left-wing wider coalitions, and the conference expressed its disapproval of their fascination with parliamentarism. Finally, and perhaps most importantly, the three parties had sinned by believing in a national path to socialism—that is, the conviction that there could exist diverse models of socialism besides that of the USSR.[48]

Significantly, those who were actually fighting against the ideological enemy they all shared were not invited to this crucially important meeting. Despite Tito's efforts to persuade officials in Moscow to increase the guest list and invite the KKE to Szklarska Poręba, the Greeks were not allowed to participate. The Soviets responded to Tito, and at the same time informed Gomułka, who had assumed the organizational burden of the conference, that inviting the Greeks to the conference was not a good idea because such an initiative could be exploited by enemies in the West to denounce the Greek insurgents as agents and proxies of foreign Communist parties and forces.[49] As a consequence of the Soviets' cautious attitude toward the civil war in Greece, deafening silence on the Greek issue, as the historian Lilly Marcou has called it, also characterized the first official Cominform publication, *For a Lasting Peace, for a People's Democracy.* The journal did not mention the Communist struggle in that country, which must have come as a great disappointment to the Greek comrades.[50] In reality, the conference mainly involved the European Communist parties already in power, or those in Western Europe that participated in national coalition governments, like the French and Italian parties, and as a result their decisions could, directly or indirectly, affect the Soviet Union.[51]

It appears that in addition to the Greek Communists, the limited list of invitees to the conference in Szklarska Poręba disappointed the Spanish comrades as well. The latter had hoped that the insurgency in Greece might benefit the Communist guerrilla movement against Spain's fascist dictator Franco, and had developed contacts with Tito's Yugoslav regime, asking for financial and material support. Unfortunately for them, Stalin advised their leaders to reduce their guerrilla activity and develop instead other forms of political opposition.[52]

Although the KKE was not represented at the Cominform's inaugural gathering, the delegates assembled in Szklarska Poręba were hardly indifferent to the Greeks' struggle. The minutes of the meetings leave no doubt regarding the sympathy that other Communists felt for their Greek comrades. Certainly, the Yugoslavs' powerful position at the conference helped the Greeks. Kardelj spoke about the duty to assist the Greek comrades, and the attendees praised Yugoslavia's policies in the Balkans and in particular its aid to the Greek insurgency. But the most significant point Kardelj made in his speech was his comparison between the "wrong way" followed by his Italian and French comrades, and the "right way" of the Greek Communists: "The 'Greek situation' is at the present time an incomparably better situation than what prevails in France or Italy," Kardelj stated, directly attacking his Western comrades.[53]

The Bulgarian delegate Valko Chervenkov heralded the tripartite Bled agreement as an important moment for Bulgarian-Yugoslav relations, stressing that "decisions were taken at Bled on coordinated action and common defense of peace in the Balkans."[54] In his turn, after recalling that Romania had also taken concrete measures to help the Greek people, its leader Gheorghe Gheorghiu-Dej proposed an even more radical idea: that "giving aid to the Greek Communist Party should be made obligatory upon all other Communist Parties, without writing that in a resolution."[55] Finally, Poland's Gomułka suggested that Greece should become the banner of the struggle of all Communist parties and democratic forces.[56] Thus, the reactions of the Cominform members showcased that most of them felt that the Greek Civil War was, in fact, a conflict between the two enemy camps that Zhdanov had outlined at the congress in his report. The Yugoslavs, closely allied with Moscow on this issue, were particularly strongly convinced that the civil war in Greece was the first armed conflict of the two hostile camps on European soil.

Not everyone in the audience, however, was as optimistic as the Yugoslavs. Some in the Balkans worried that a defeat of the KKE could trigger a series of setbacks for Communism in the region. In February 1948, not long after the first Cominform congress and as the Greek government forces were on the offensive against the insurgents now fighting a conventional (static) war, Balkan Communist leaders met with top Soviet officials at the Kremlin. Stalin, Molotov, Zhdanov, Malenkov, and Valerian Zorin met the Bulgarians Dimitrov, Vasil Kolarov, and Traicho Kostov, and the Yugoslavs Kardelj, Djilas, and Vladimir Bakarić. Addressing Stalin, a skeptical Kostov voiced his personal concerns: "If the partisan movement in Greece fails, it would create a very difficult situation for the rest of the Balkan countries," because, he wondered, "will the Americans allow the victory of the partisans?" Stalin's response sounded confident even if subtly qualified: "No one will ask them. . . . If there are enough forces to win and if there are people capable of utilizing people's forces then the struggle should be continued." To bolster Kostov's confidence, the Soviet leader pointed out that this was precisely what had happened in China's case. Although he himself had advised Mao to compromise with the nationalist Chang Kai-Shek, Mao had defied Stalin's advice and instead built up his forces, and pushed ahead to victory. A seemingly contrite Stalin conceded, "The Chinese proved to be right, and we were wrong."[57] What the Balkan Communist leaders were probably thinking, but did not dare point out to Stalin, was that, unlike Mao, Zachariadis did not have the capacity to expand his army indefinitely: the DSE's numerical strength was shrinking.

In fact, Stalin was not as confident of Communist victory in Greece as his confession about being wrong about the civil war in China suggested. But he tried to reassure his comrades by arguing that a defeat of the DSE would not reverse any of the achievements already made in the Balkans: "One shouldn't think that if nothing comes up in Greece, everything else is lost." On the other hand, he advised caution: "The neighboring countries have to be the last to recognize the [Communist] government of General Markos. First, let the others recognize it."[58] As a consequence, despite dramatic appeals from the KKE, the Balkan regimes did not recognize the "Provisional Democratic Government" and remained cautious in their dealings with Greece.[59]

Stalin's stance on the Greek Civil War was typical of the spirit of "guarded internationalism" he displayed in those years. And it was that same spirit that shaped the position of other Communist parties toward the KKE at that time. The Eastern European Communists were being encouraged to navigate the treacherous terrain with two priorities in mind: first, help Markos's army to succeed, and second, ensure that the gains that Communism had made in the course of the Second World War were not lost.[60]

As already indicated, during 1947, the Soviets did their part in supporting the Greek insurgents, raising the subject with Communist regimes outside the Balkans. On June 14, 1947, Molotov met the Polish ambassador to Moscow, Marian Naszkowski, and among other issues they discussed the situation in Greece. A few weeks later, following discussions between the Polish president, Bolesław Bierut, and Marshal Tito, a significant shipment of aid to the Greek insurgents was shipped from Poland. Begun in September 1947 and code-named "Transport," this operation lasted until mid-1948. It was kept secret, and only a small circle of individuals were aware of its existence. General Wacław Komar, who played a major role in Operation Transport, traveled to Dubrovnik in September, where he met with Tito and the head of the Yugoslav security apparatus, Ranković, to organize this important supply project.[61] Komar was a capable and experienced officer who could be trusted with the highly sensitive task at hand. A Polish Jew and a Communist from an early age, he had been trained in intelligence in Moscow between 1927 and 1931, where he met Zachariadis. After spending six years in Germany, Poland, and Czechoslovakia working in the Comintern intelligence network, he was sent to Spain in 1937. There, he took command of the 129th Czech-Balkan Brigade and met people who later occupied responsible government posts in Yugoslavia. In 1939, he joined the Polish Army in France, where the following year he was arrested by the Germans and spent the rest of the war in a concentration camp. He survived to return to Poland and to become the head of the Polish Army's intelligence service.[62]

For his new assignment, Komar designed a fittingly complex and covert operation. The aid for the Greek insurgents was transported from

Poland to Yugoslavia by train. At least ten airplanes, as well as radio equipment, explosives, guns, medical supplies, and other materials, also traveled by train. As previously mentioned, the weapons were only of German and Italian origin, in an attempt to conceal the fact that Communists were arming the Greek insurgents. Officially, the equipment was being supplied to the Yugoslav Army and then was clandestinely transferred to the DSE in Greece.

With the support they were receiving from Eastern Europe, the Greek comrades, and Zachariadis in particular, could have considered themselves lucky. But the KKE leader's auspicious streak of good fortune ended abruptly when, in the summer of 1948, the international Communist world was shaken by its gravest crisis since its foundation. The crisis, which was to have severe repercussions for the Greek Communists' cause, was the totally unexpected Tito-Stalin split and Yugoslavia's expulsion from the Cominform. The potential significance of this historic development for the East-West conflict was especially momentous since the West did not hesitate to indicate its sympathy for Belgrade's David in his dangerous feud with Moscow's Goliath.

Relations between the two Communist leaders had been deteriorating as their geopolitical strategies began to diverge. Specifically, Stalin was furious when, in early 1948, Dimitrov, in a press conference from Bucharest, announced that plans existed for a future Balkan-Danubian Federation, which apart from the region's people's republics might include Czechoslovakia and Greece. The enraged Soviet leader argued that Dimitrov's plan would harm the Communist cause and destabilize the new regimes in Eastern Europe. It is entirely possible that Stalin's rage also had to do with his concern that such a proposed union would make Tito the undisputed ruler of a large region of the Communist world, over which Stalin was presumed to be the leader. Stalin was also increasingly wary of Tito's apparent intention to annex Albania, a plan that, Stalin believed, would legitimate a US military intervention in the Balkans. Whatever the specific reasons for Stalin's displeasure, soon Stalin and Tito were in open disagreement on the future of the Balkans. In June 1948, Yugoslavia was expelled from the Cominform.[63]

For the KKE, the Stalin-Tito split spelled a real catastrophe, particularly since the party had to pick sides. On the one hand, the Greek Communists saw Stalin as the incontestable leader of the Communist world; Zachariadis and the party's Stalinist cadres could hardly imagine not remaining faithful to the Great Stalin. On the other hand, Tito had been their staunchest foreign supporter, and most of the assistance for their insurgency was coming from or through Yugoslavia. Efforts to navigate between their two patrons were very difficult to contemplate and virtually certain to fail, with disastrous consequences. The KKE could not stop the inevitable. Although the flow of aid from the Yugoslav comrades remained significant throughout 1948, relations between the two parties soon deteriorated.[64] In October 1948, Ranković wrote Roussos, the foreign minister of the KKE-sponsored Provisional Democratic Government, lamenting that "our relations have recently worsened." In November the crisis in the relationship between the two parties was confirmed when Ranković and Roussos met and each of the two former comrades blamed the other for the difficulties.[65] As relations between the two parties deteriorated, and anxious to demonstrate his loyalty to Stalin, Zachariadis published in the Cominform's journal an article, reproduced in *Pravda* in August 1949, denouncing Tito's stab in the back of Greek people's republic.[66] By then, the Yugoslavs had closed their border with Greece, preventing the insurgents from crossing it in either direction.

The cooling in Greek-Yugoslav contacts as a result of the Stalin-Tito split had wider implications and helped revive an issue that had strained bilateral relations for years: the Macedonian question. In January 1949, the KKE Central Committee's Fifth Plenum declared that with the victory of the Democratic Army of Greece, the Macedonian people would realize full national rehabilitation.[67] Ironically, this time it was the Greeks who were promoting independence for Macedonians. Unsurprisingly, this move gave fresh ammunition to the Greek government to brand the KKE as antinational. But in the new geopolitical setting, the Central Committee's resolution acquired another meaning: the KKE intended to maintain its influence among the Slavic community at the expense of Tito's influence. And in doing so, the KKE hoped to stir up domestic tensions within Yugoslavia, a multiethnic state that had to appeal for loyalty and support to all the nationalities inhabiting it. Tito correctly interpreted the Fifth Plenum's decision as an element of Stalin's plan to destabilize Yugoslavia and remove Tito from power.[68] The relations between the Greek and Yugoslav parties thus turned hostile, and the assistance to the insurgents that had been coming from Yugoslavia ceased.

Gradually, the other people's republics took over the task of assisting the Communist cause in Greece. As already suggested, the aid operation was an exceptionally complex, almost titanic task, with unprecedented financial, logistical, political, and even intelligence challenges. Yet the effort brought results. In fact, as a coordinator of the support system based in Tirana recalled, the flow of the aid in 1949 was greater than ever before.[69]

This accomplishment was made possible by a well-coordinated effort of the Communist world. A series of meetings that included Polish, Czechoslovak, Hungarian, Romanian, and Greek officials were organized. They discussed once again the details of what kind and what quantities of aid the Greeks needed, as well as the most efficient means of transportation. Four such meetings took place, starting on September 8, 1948, in Warsaw, Poland.[70] There, the attendees—high-ranking party officials and military officers—established a special committee based in Poland's capital that would coordinate the deliveries of arms and munitions to the DSE. Following the initial Warsaw meeting, the officials also met in Prague on January 20–21 and Budapest on February 15–16. Their final meeting, on March 10, 1949, took place in Bucharest.[71]

Surviving documents from the final meeting demonstrate the significance and scale of the operation. The list of participants shows how many officials were needed to accomplish the task. Poland sent General Komar and another military officer, Major Borhovich, while Czechoslovakia's delegation was more diverse, consisting of Bedřich Geminder, chief of the International Section of the Secretariat of the Czechoslovak Communist Party, Colonel Stanislav Palla, and Jiří Gregor, chief of EU-PEX, a state-affiliated foreign trade enterprise experienced in covert and overt transport of goods.[72] The Hungarian representatives were Aleksandr Sebes and Zoltán Fodor, while Romania's official was the Politburo member and leading party member Alexandru Moghioroş. Finally, from Greece came the leading party leaders Ioannidis and Roussos and a DSE colonel, Ilias Karas. Those important personalities discussed the cost of buying arms and other equipment for the DSE. At that time, the cost of the aid requested by the Greeks was estimated at $11 million in US dollars. The delegates raised a total of $2.5 million pledged by Poland ($2 million) and Hungary ($500,000) and decided to devote half of this money ($1,224,000) to the purchase of explosives and mines, which were considered urgently needed, and use the rest of the funds to pay for trucks, telecommunication equipment, and other supplies.[73]

Although the final aid package fell short of the Greeks' expectations, the pledged amount was not negligible. The people's republics' spirit of internationalism may have been "guarded," but their assistance was crucial for the insurgency and testified to their commitment to the revolutionary cause. After all, by helping the Greeks they were taking away from their own weak economies' significant resources, needed for the reconstruction effort in the aftermath of a devastatingly destructive war. In addition to a large variety of weapons, supplies of every kind, and funds they dispatched, they also trained Greek officers and troops in camps scattered across the people's republics, treated the wounded DSE fighters at Eastern European hospitals, and took care of refugees, both children and adults, whom they transported from Greece into their own states.

The Communists' support efforts were all the more burdensome because, unlike the United States, which assisted the Greek government openly and with much fanfare, the Eastern European regimes had to keep their aid a closely guarded secret. The Czechoslovak intelligence service discovered that the US government had sent agents to follow the transport of arms passing through Hungary and Czechoslovakia and to report the senders, recipients, and contents of the shipments. As a result, the providers of aid to the Greek insurgents took additional conspiratorial measures and designed a clandestine route that carried supplies through Poland and Albania. The need for secrecy complicated the work of furnishing the Greeks with assistance and generated complaints about the system's inefficiency. In one case, in December 1948, Romania sent 3,000 tons of fuel for the DSE, which was first shipped to Poland, from where it traveled to Albania. Four months later, in April 1949, only 1,800 tons had reached the DSE, which promptly complained to Soviet officials.[74]

Poland was not only the coordinating supply center, but also actively helped the Greeks in other ways as well. In the summer of 1948, the Polish secret service began an operation code-named "S," coordinated by the Second Bureau of the General Command of the Polish Army. The purpose of Operation S was to provide enough supplies for a guerrilla army of fifty thousand troops. Between October 1948 and September 1949, twelve ships left Poland carrying fourteen thousand tons of war supplies and fuel, as well as thirty thousand tons of food and other items. Another twelve shipments were airlifted from Polish airports, carrying explosives and medical supplies. For this, Poland paid four billion złoty (roughly $15-$16 million in US dollars,) which constituted between 8 and 9 percent of its annual military spending.[75]

The Polish government's support activities went beyond Operation S. In June-July 1949, Poland established a secret military hospital, code-named "No. 250," in the northwestern Polish town of Dziwnów, on the Baltic Sea island of Wolin. Hospital No. 250 had a capacity of five hundred beds and treated the most severely wounded DSE partisans, brought to Poland from three major Albanian hospitals in Korçë, Elbasan, and Suk. As the operation had to remain secret, the wounded either had to first travel to the port city of Durrës and there board the Polish merchant ship *Kościuszko*, or go to Tirana and fly over two thousand kilometers north to Poland. Between July 1949 and November 1950, around two thousand wounded DSE insurgents made this journey and received treatment.[76]

The Czechoslovak Communists were not far behind in their efforts to assist the Greek insurgents, and they named their program "Operation Ř," code-named for the Czech word "Řecko," which meant "Greece." Geminder, one of the participants in the Bucharest meeting, was in charge of the operation and regularly reported to Klement Gottwald, the chairman of the Communist Party and president of Czechoslovakia, and Rudolf Slánský, the secretary-general of the party. The Czech Politburo estimated the cost of aid to the Greeks at 750 million Czechoslovak crowns, or $15 million.[77]

Despite the significant sums involved, the money contributed by the Czechs and Poles could not replace the services that Yugoslavia, as Greece's neighbor, used to provide to the DSE. From the fall of 1948 onward, Albania thus took over many of the tasks that previously were performed by the Yugoslavs. As a result, contacts between the Greek and Albanian parties intensified, with the KKE working closely with Albanian comrades to facilitate the transport of aid to Greek territory or solve administrative and financial issues.[78] The port city of Durrës became the main hub for DSE-bound aid, from where the supplies traveled to the main fronts of the civil war.[79] But Albania was not Yugoslavia. The country was small and poor in resources, and worried about an invasion from Greece. The Albanian leader Enver Hoxha had personally expressed his fears to Stalin at their March 1949 meeting in Moscow. Although Stalin reassured his Albanian comrade that the independence of Albania was guaranteed by a declaration of three powers—the United States, Britain, and the USSR—Hoxha remained skeptical.[80]

Although such clandestine activities in support of the insurgency remained invisible to the wider European public, the war itself did not. On the contrary, the KKE employed a great variety of public events, publications, and meetings to appeal to European public opinion to promote the Greek Communist cause. Special citizens' committees set up after 1947 played a considerable, and peculiar, role in this effort. Committees to aid the "struggling Greek democratic people" were founded in Eastern as well as Western Europe. According to Roussos, the foreign minister in the KKE's Provisional Democratic Government, in 1948 seventeen countries had such a committee: all of the people's republics, as well as France, Italy, the United States, Austria, Switzerland, Belgium, Holland, Denmark, and Canada. Although pressure by Communists in Western Europe on the Greek government, as well as their own governments, to recognize the Communist cause in Greece as legitimate had little or no impact, support to the KKE coming from Eastern European comrades was invaluable. Despite some reluctance to advertise the Greek Communists' needs and requests, in general the comrades in Eastern Europe helped as much as they could.[81]

Indeed, the committees in Eastern Europe featured important personalities of their regimes: for example, in Bulgaria, Dimitrov's wife, Rosa, was a committee member. For the most part, the committees rallied the public in order to collect supplies for the DSE, and citizens were asked to contribute in cash or in kind. But the Eastern European committees also facilitated intense, albeit disguised, state activity. Even the national Committees of the Red Cross were mobilized in this propaganda war. The Soviet Red Cross, for instance, sent a letter to the International Red Cross complaining about the situation in Greece, and pressured its headquarters in Geneva to take initiatives to stop the violence and the cruelty "against the innocent Greek patriots."[82]

To the Bitter End

Foreign assistance to the Greek insurgents, estimated at $100–$150 million, was not enough to enable the DSE to prevail over the armed forces of the US-backed Greek government. Between June 1947 and the end of the civil war in 1949, US military aid amounted to $476 million. Together with economic assistance, US assistance totaled a staggering $1.2 billion. In other words, US aid to the Greek state was ten times greater than what the DSE received from the Communist world. But money was not the only factor that made it impossible for the DSE to challenge its adversary successfully. While the number of the insurgents' troops never came close to 50,000 (the target of the planners of Operation Lakes), by 1949 the Greek government had a total of 244,000 men under arms.[83] And those troops were better trained, armed, fed, and clothed, and had more experienced officers and vastly greater resources at their disposal. Most importantly, the government forces had clear superiority in positional warfare, for which the DSE lacked essential assets, including mountain artillery and especially air support. In retrospect, the story of the DSE armed struggle appears to be a chronicle of a defeat foretold.

Professional observers of the civil war had anticipated its outcome. In early 1949, the Soviets concluded not only that the insurgents had failed to fulfill the expectations of their leadership, but that their defeat could also destabilize the entire region in ways that would benefit the United States. Despite Zachariadis's assurances to Dimitrov at their June 11, 1948, meeting that the conditions were favorable for continuing the struggle, between the summer of 1948 and February 1949 the DSE sustained severe losses.[84] Growing impatient with the Greek comrades, Stalin initiated talks with the United States and Britain, searching for an end to the bloody conflict in Greece. The chances for peace appeared to be real, even if its terms were bound to be catastrophic for the KKE, whose military power had been obliterated. By that time, and on the heels of the festering Stalin-Tito split, the Soviets did not want to further aggravate Europe's Cold War tensions.[85]

In early April 1949, Moscow summoned Zachariadis to give him the bad news: the insurgency had to end. Aid to the DSE was immediately stopped, and crossings of the Greek borders with Albania and Bulgaria shut down. On April 9, 1949, Zachariadis returned to the DSE headquarters in the war zone, and promptly informed his comrades about the new development.[86] A day later, at the United Nations, the Provisional Democratic Government announced that it was ready to make the maximum possible concessions.[87] It was not the first time that the KKE had made such a peace proposal: since 1946, the Greek Communists had made at least twenty-one offers of peace. While many of the peace offers may have been intended as propaganda rather than genuine proposals, the evidence for assessing their motives and intent objectively and reliably does not exist.[88]

The KKE's international partners tried to lend this offer legitimacy, an effort in which Soviet diplomats took on a more decisive role. On April 29, a few days before the Berlin blockade was lifted, Andrei Gromyko, deputy minister of foreign affairs and chairman of the Soviet delegation to the UN General Assembly, received clear directives from Moscow for his upcoming meeting with Dean Rusk, the US assistant secretary of state for United Nations affairs, and Hector McNeil, chairman of the British delegation to the UN General Assembly. Gromyko was instructed to state that since the English and US governments would propose a peace process with the participation of the USSR, the latter would not refuse to participate in this project.[89] But the Soviet diplomat's proposals for a ceasefire were not received positively in Washington, or in Athens. In fact, the US State Department suspected that the impatient Soviets were trying to save the insurgents in Greece from extinction. The Western capitals also supposed that the Soviet initiative was intended to protect Albania's sovereignty, which Moscow considered threatened by Yugoslavia, Greece, and its foreign patrons. They therefore branded Gromyko's proposals a "Soviet trap" and chose to allow the fighting to continue, leading to the defeat and the total destruction of the DSE.[90]

Faced with the rejection of the Soviet attempts to end the fighting through diplomatic means, the KKE and its allies opted for attack as the best form of defense. In May 1949, following the failure of the Soviet peace initiative, the northern borders of Greece were opened again, aid to the DSE resumed, and the KKE leadership prepared for a big counteroffensive. But the KKE did not have the military strength to reverse its desperate situation. On August 1, 1949, the Hungarian leader, Mátyás Rákosi, advised his Greek comrades that "the time had come to draw in their horns."[91] And although Zachariadis stubbornly insisted that the fighting continue, by the end of August 1949 the last artillery shells had fallen on the insurgents' final stronghold on Mount Grammos. On August 29–30, a few thousand insurgents retreated into Albania. By the time the guns were silenced, around forty thousand combatants on both sides had lost their lives in battle (twenty to twenty-five thousand insurgents and fifteen thousand government officers and troops). In addition, four thousand civilians were killed, caught up in the fighting.[92]

Although the civil war was effectively over, the KKE's leadership was in no hurry to admit the defeat of its military strategies and the collapse of its political ambitions. In September 1949, Zachariadis sent a letter to Stalin in which he announced the retreat of the DSE but, at the same time, expressed his intention to maintain and enforce partisan struggle throughout the country. He insisted that the KKE forces in Albania had to be supported and reinforced politically, organizationally, and militarily.[93] In short, Zachariadis sought to make the Grammos defeat appear to be merely a temporary withdrawal in his policy of "perpetual readiness" or, as it was usually called at the time, the policy of holding the "guns at the ready."[94] But his Albanian comrades, whose country bordered the Grammos mountains where most of the heavy fighting had taken place, did not approve of this policy. Relations between the KKE and the Albanian Communist Party had soured during the war. The animosity between the two parties had deeper roots: Hoxha had never ceased to be wary of Greek nationalist demands on the territory of southern Albania, and had never forgiven the temporary alignment in this nationalist policy of the KKE, made back in 1945.[95] The two parties had also disagreed on a number of issues related to the managing of the aid flow as well as the military tactics pursued by the DSE along the Greek-Albanian border.[96] The latter issue had a particularly negative impact on their comradely relations. The border's porosity had became an argument for Athens when it sought to blame Hoxha's regime for border incidents and to persuade US officials and the United Nations that the Greek Army should be permitted to invade Albania.[97]

As might be expected, tensions between the two parties reached a record high when Zachariadis informed Stalin and the Albanians that he intended to set up a coordination center in Albanian territory to support the remaining guerrilla forces in Greece.[98] In view of threats already made by Athens, Albanian officials were especially sensitive on this issue, and soon the two sides were pointing fingers at each other regarding who was to blame for the Communists' defeat in Greece. The Soviets, unhappy with this blame game, summoned to Moscow the leaders of the two parties to get their problem solved.[99] On January 14–16, 1950, Zachariadis, Partsalidis, Hoxha, and Mehmet Shehu met in Moscow in the presence of the Soviet officials Molotov, Malenkov, Suslov, and Valery Grigorian.[100] Hoxha, now employing a less aggressive tone, repeated his grievances against the KKE leaders concerning their policies and tactics in the civil war. For his part, defeated and humiliated in the war and therefore in a difficult position, Zachariadis understood that the only support he might receive was from Stalin's sympathetic understanding and goodwill. Accordingly, the Greek was apologetic and, on Moscow's orders, agreed to move the DSE forces out of Albania. To his comrades he had to confess that he had been more optimistic than objective conditions allowed.[101]

With no safe base for the Greek insurgents, the fight was unquestionably over. Stalin had foreseen the tragic end of the Greek Communist insurgency at least as early as July 1949, when he remarked that "the guerillas are isolated from the population. . . . You cannot wage a guerilla war in isolation from the population."[102] But the Greek Communist leadership had been convinced that support from international allies, rather than mainly domestic factors, could determine the outcome of the conflict. Although Stalin had been right about the reason for their failure, the Greeks were also not wrong in thinking that international involvement could determine the course of their country's history.

The Greek Civil War was the first and only hot war of the Cold War on the European continent. For much of the rest of the world, this conflict was a harbinger of a new kind of localized war, in which external factors actually played a decisive role—a phenomenon that would become known as a proxy war. The intervention of Western powers in the Greek conflict and the extensive assistance received by the Greek government, initially from Great Britain and subsequently from the United States under the Truman Doctrine and the Marshall Plan, is widely known because of its official intergovernmental nature, the wide publicity it generated, and its magnitude. Its relative transparency and the plethora of archival evidence it generated also made that foreign intervention relatively easy to study. On the other hand, in large measure because of the secrecy that surrounded it and the resulting paucity of documentary evidence, the involvement of the Eastern European Bloc in the Greek crisis has, until recently, remained a relatively unexplored subject. In retrospect, as this chapter has demonstrated, the fellow Communists were deeply involved in the Greek Civil War. Backed by Stalin's "faint green light,"[103] first the Yugoslav and then gradually the Bulgarian, Romanian, and Albanian comrades organized a huge military aid operation in support of the insurgency. Such extensive international involvement has been rare in twentieth-century civil conflicts and, until that point, virtually nonexistent. Even compared to the support given to the Spanish democratic government during the Spanish Civil War (1936-39), the assistance offered to the KKE required far more complicated and riskier strategizing. And this foreign assistance, as well as its shortcomings and inadequacy, truly determined the course and outcome of the conflict.

During the Second World War, every belligerent country had to wage its own battle with whatever support, if any, it received from its allies. Ironically, except for minimal military support from military agents of the British government (SOE), the Communist-led resistance (EAM-ELAS) did not receive any kind of "green light" or help from either the Soviets or its Balkan comrades, who were all in war themselves. Between 1946 and 1949, however, the Greek insurgents depended entirely on their own initiatives and support from their foreign comrades. In reality, the start of the civil war was possible only because of the external political and material support provided to the insurgents. The conflict would also not have lasted as long as it did without the somewhat erratic but crucial Soviet approval, without the steady flow of ammunition, provisions, and other vital supplies, without the training and sheltering of Communist combatants in neighboring territories, and without the hospitalization of the wounded and help for the refugees.

As shown in this book, during the years 1946–49, the KKE worked closely with the Soviets and with the people's republics. The party had permanent representatives across Eastern Europe whose aim was to coordinate with its sister parties and to maximize the aid it received. Therefore, the war cannot be reduced to a domestic affair, and its course cannot be attributed to Zachariadis and his circle of fanatic supporters among senior party officials and DSE commanders. This bloody conflict can be understood only as a result of a complex matrix of policies, conjunctures, ideologies, ambitions, and misunderstandings. And all of those factors interacted on both the domestic and the international levels. Within this dynamic matrix, Zachariadis's obsessive devotion to the idea of a Communist Greece intersected with Tito's plans for Yugoslavia's hegemonic role in the region, the internationalism of the Balkan Communists, and the emerging Cold War that pulled the wartime Allies apart.

The civil war followed the course it did because of what was, for the KKE, a remarkably auspicious coalescence of international factors. In the new and unstable international context of the early Cold War, however, Zachariadis and his comrades misperceived whatever they saw as a positive sign, and underestimated or chose to ignore those factors that indicated that they would encounter obstacles and difficulties in carrying out their ambitious plans. In particular, they considered the existence of the Balkan people's republics a decisively positive condition for the success of their revolution, while they underestimated the resolution of their domestic opponents to fight back and the determination and capacity of the United States to support the Greek government in defeating the Communist insurgency.[104]

Considering how tightly the Greek Communists had been integrated into the international Communist world, it would be naive to argue that they could launch their insurgency without securing the consent of their Soviet and Balkan comrades. But it would be equally unrealistic to assume that such a fortuitous confluence of positive factors in the Communist world would last forever. International support for the DSE was tenuous and conditional, and it depended on the vicissitudes and fluctuations in international geopolitics, especially in a region as "smoldering" as southeastern Europe and the eastern Mediterranean. In reality, international support for the insurgents was tied to the prospects of DSE success and the resulting profits—material, political, and ideological—that Communists worldwide could expect to obtain. The Greek Communists, therefore, had to prove they could win the civil war with their guns and bodies. In such a proxy war, there are many countries happy to offer encouragement and even some support and to share the spoils of victory, but none want to associate closely with a loser.

CHAPTER 6

The Displaced People's Republic

Since the nineteenth century and the Paris Commune in 1871, socialism all around the world was full of traumatic experiences. More often than not, twentieth-century Communist movements in Europe had experienced their own traumas resulting from defeats in uprisings and civil strife. Often the shattered dreams of the Communists were followed by forced migration. In the early twentieth century, cases abounded where revolutionaries had been transformed into refugees. Between 1918 and 1920, thousands of Finnish, Hungarian, German, and Bulgarian Communist leaders and their rank-and-file followers left their countries and fled to Russia or other safe places following defeats in civil wars and armed confrontations with state authorities at home. During the interwar years, an international community of Communist émigrés flourished in the USSR.

Similarly, the Spanish Civil War ended with a major refugee crisis. Following Franco's seizure of power in 1939, over 400,000 republicans left Spain, many going to France and Latin America. A smaller number, 4,221, went to the USSR, among them the legendary secretary-general of the Spanish Communist Party, Dolores Ibarruri, "La Pasionaria" (the Passionflower), accompanied by a relatively small contingent of high-ranking Communists.[1] During Stalin's years, living in Moscow as a political refugee leader or cadre of a Western Communist party was to be in a peculiar position fraught with insecurity and danger. Such émi-grés found themselves under harsh supervision by Soviet authorities and experienced the cruel turmoil of the Stalinist purges. Many among them suffered hardships and casualties that had a profound impact on their lives and their mental state.

In some respects, as we will see in this chapter, the Greek émigrés shared the same experiences as other Communists who fled their homelands. But the Greek situation had its own particularity. While the other émigré leaders in Russia were isolated from their followers, who remained either at home or in Western countries (in France, for instance, after the Spanish Civil War), the Greek Communist leaders were followed into exile by a significant number of their compatriots. Moreover, the KKE had far more members in the *refugeeland* than in Greece, and the party was leading abroad a community of eighty thou-sand to one hundred thousand people, living scattered across a vast region, which was determined by Cold War developments.

Exodus

By late August 1949, the defeated Communist guerrillas, some accom-panied by their families, were in retreat and on the move. Of the eighty thousand who left Greece for the Communist side of the Iron Curtain, not all were fighters. Some twenty-five thousand had fought with the Democratic Army of Greece, while the rest were civilians who, willingly or not, joined the journey north: relatives of the combatants, inhabit-ants of the northern borderlands who had lost their homes, even several hundred captive officers and soldiers of the national army, and, last but not least, some twenty-eight thousand children, whom the KKE had already begun to evacuate to Eastern Europe in 1948. In February of that year, around five thousand children had left Greece heading to the people's republics, but the relocation of all these people from Greece lasted several years, with the last refugees arriving at their final destina-tions only in 1950.

Who could organize such a large-scale operation? It was the Comin-form countries that undertook the enormous challenge of coordinat-ing and providing for the safe transport of the numerous refugees from Greece. The USSR and almost all of the people's republics worked together to host the displaced. The exception was Albania, which ac-commodated in its territory only a few dozen wounded Greek guer-rillas and three hundred soldiers of the Greek national army who had been taken prisoner.[2] The USSR, Poland, and Czechoslovakia hosted 12,000–13,000 people each, Romania 9,000, Bulgaria 6,000, Hungary 7,500, and East Germany 1,250. Although not cooperating with the Cominform, Yugoslavia hosted almost 20,000 people, mostly ethnic Macedonian refugees.[3]

The farthest journey from their homeland took the displaced all the way to Tashkent in the Uzbek Soviet Socialist Republic. In late September 1949, following a decision of the Communist Party of the Soviet Union (CPSU), 12,020 troops—male and female DSE fighters who had participated in the final battles of the civil war, as well as children and civilians—were secretly transferred from the Albanian city of Durrës to Tashkent, in a long and tiring journey that lasted twelve days.[4] They first boarded the Soviet ships *Taiganos*, *Pulkovo*, *Chiatouri*, *Sukhona*, and *Vladivostok* and made their way to the Georgian port city of Poti, and then proceeded by train to Tashkent. Upon their arrival, the Soviet authorities placed them in thirteen different neighborhoods in Tashkent's suburbs.[5] Between July 1949 and January 1950, another 13,868 people departed Albania by ship and headed to Poland.[6] Onboard the Polish ships *Kościuszko*, *Wisła*, *Lechistan*, and *Białystok*, and the Romanian ship *Transylvania*, they traversed the Mediterranean, passed the Gibraltar, circled around Western Europe, and reached Gdańsk, Kołobrzeg and Świnoujście, the Polish ports on the Baltic Sea. The Poles settled the refugees primarily in the previously heavily German-populated regions of Lower Silesia and Western Pomerania.[7]

Approximately 8,500 refugees arrived in Bulgaria and Romania by crossing the Mediterranean and the Black Sea. They disembarked in Varna (Bulgaria) and Constanza (Romania), and from there were settled at various locations in the two countries. By June 1948, Bulgaria was hosting 1,793 adults and 1,752 children, the majority of them distributed in the northwestern cities of Berkovitsa and Belogradchik.[8] Czechoslovakia received several waves of refugees, a total of 12,095 individuals arriving there by train through Romania and Poland. First came 5,185 children, some of whom were in Czechoslovakia already in April 1948;[9] the first group of adults arrived on August 30, 1949.[10] The majority of the Greek refugees were settled in Moravia and in the rural regions of Northern Bohemia and Moravia (Krnov, Žamberk, and Jeseník).[11] In Hungary, which received 7,500 refugees, train stations were busy receiving small groups of refugees—mostly children—throughout April 1948. By month's end, Hungary had received 2,187 Greek children and 38 adult refugees.[12] Finally, 1,153 children and 93 adults, the latter being members of the KKE, were installed in East Germany after August 1949.[13] The first mission, comprising 342 children, adolescents, and young adults, arrived in the Soviet Occupation Zone of Germany on August 6, 1949, and most of them were sent to Radebeul, a town near Dresden, which became the headquarters of the Greek Communists in East Germany.[14]

As this chronicle of the refugees' journeys shows, the evacuation of thousands of refugees from Greece required detailed preparations and careful attention, particularly as the massive project needed to be conducted in secrecy. Moreover, given the vast distances involved and the diverse destinations, transporting and settling the refugees was a costly operation with diplomatic and security problems. Although the KKE kept top-level Soviet officials well informed concerning the movement of the refugees, information on the refugees alone could not prepare the host countries for the daunting task of resettlement.[15]

Even for the richest among the people's republics, transporting and taking care of thousands of sick and traumatized foreigners was a heavy economic and administrative burden. For instance, in 1950 the Soviet Ministry of Finance told Molotov that the transport and rehabilitation costs for the period between September 1949 and April 1950 amounted to 106 million rubles ($26 million in 1950 dollars, or $280 million in 2020 dollars).[16] And yet, Molotov proposed extending financial support for the Greeks until July 1950, because many could not survive without public aid.[17] In the end, the Soviet authorities fully funded the refugees' program until December 1950.[18] If the Soviet Union could barely afford to cover the cost of solidarity, the financial and administrative burden was much heavier for the smaller and economically weak countries of the Eastern Bloc. For instance, for Bulgaria, only for the years 1947–49, the total cost of providing for the livelihood of the Greek refugees amounted to 1,318,340,000 leva ($4.5 million), provoking a reaction in the local population, who disapproved of the granting of financial support and other privileges to the Greek Communist refugees.[19] In Hungary, the cost for approximatively seven thousand Greek refugees was 2.8 million forint per month, or $238,000.[20] Even for a wealthier country such as Czechoslovakia, the cost was not negligible: from April 1, 1949, to October 31, 1950, it was equivalent to 339,220,000 Czechoslovak crowns ($6.8 million).[21]

For the host countries, money was only a minor problem compared to the sensitive international issue created by the refugee children. As in the case of the *niños*, the three thousand Spanish children who were evacuated to Russia by the Second Republic, which the Franco regime condemned as "a communist machination concerning the children stolen from Spain,"[22] the removal of the children from Greece sparked an emotionally charged propaganda war between the Athens government and the KKE. The Greek authorities denounced the Communists as kidnappers and sought recourse through the United Nations. For its part, the KKE defended its actions as humanitarian, claiming to be saving the children from the dangers and hardships of battleground regions.[23] As a result of those highly emotional controversies, the people's republics had reservations about taking in the Greek children, and the top leadership of each state repeatedly examined the potential diplomatic fallout.[24]

Despite the controversy and the considerable adverse publicity caused by the resettling of the Greek refugees and their families, the program continued. In coordination with the Committee for Child Support, an organization created by the KKE in 1948, the people's republics devoted substantial resources to the welfare of the Greek children, who thus received systematic and high-quality care. Immediately upon their arrival, the medical authorities examined them so that those in poor health could be placed in sanatoriums and hospitals, while others could find a stable environment in residential centers.[25] Although such care may have been no substitute for the children's own families, reunification was a particularly difficult task. The parents were scattered all across the region, and the Eastern European authorities struggled to process and match the unfamiliar-sounding names. Although most families were reunited after 1951, in some cases this proved to be impossible.[26]

The host republics also applied themselves to the difficult task of integrating the newcomers into their new surroundings as soon as possible. But the Greeks were burdened by obstacles that were mostly beyond their control and impeded their ability to adjust to the new environment. Above all, their lives were complicated by their inability to speak the local languages, which they found hard to learn, especially since few had had any formal education. In addition, the cold and rainy climate of some of the Eastern European countries made some of them feel unwell and resentful. Those who were sent to East Germany, and had bitter memories from three and a half years of German occupation, felt embarrassed seeing that those they considered ex-Nazis were now their hosts. A similar situation was observed in Bulgaria, where old mutual national hatreds and suspicions impeded the integration of the newcomers into Bulgarian society.[27]

But it was in Tashkent that the refugees experienced the harshest conditions. Besides the fact that Uzbekistan was far away from Greece, and that the local population had a very different culture and lifestyle than that of the Greeks, the refugees in Tashkent were placed under close supervision. In one of the classic ironies of history, the DSE's Communist fighters were settled in barracks destined initially for Japanese POWs during World War II. Their life was organized according to military-style discipline, and, for security reasons, they were not even allowed to correspond with their relatives in Greece.[28] The feeling of isolation and resentment caused fighters to suffer from depression and homesickness. One of them, Dinos Rozakis, a DSE fighter, wondered, "Why did they bring us here?"[29] Although Rozakis probably never received a satisfactory response, the answer was simple. The first reason that the Soviets had settled the Greek refugees in Tashkent was obvious: to keep them as far away as possible from Greece. But there was another reason as well. Hoping to industrialize the remote Uzbekistan, the Soviets were keen to bring in men and women who, without a penny to their names, would have little choice but to replenish the local labor supply. The refugees could be a perfect workforce, as they had nothing else and nowhere else to go.

In the first years of their stay in their new homelands, everything seemed difficult to the newcomers. They were homesick, and, keeping alive their dream of returning to Greece one day and nurturing this hope in their hearts, they struggled to preserve their Greek identity. Significantly, the KKE played a major role in helping them maintain their cultural links to Greece. Like the Spanish, whom the exiles imagined as a community bound by their memories of the Spanish Civil War,[30] the Greek Communist leaders tried to hold together their fellow refugees by cultivating the idea that the exile was only a temporary situation, and a continuation of their struggle of the previous years. The basic idea was that the struggle would continue until the refugees returned to their socialist homeland. With substantial aid from the host countries, the KKE set up schools to teach the illiterates among the refugees and their children to read and write in the Greek language. All over Eastern Europe, the party created community centers and cultural and sports clubs, and ensured that party-approved Greek textbooks, literature, newspapers, and magazines were published. Maintaining their "Greekness" and returning someday to Greece became the life dream of the first generation of refugees.[31]

Although most refugees yearned to return to Greece, they were not a unified and coherent national group. While they predominantly came from rural and mountainous areas and had a lower socioeconomic background, an ethnic cleavage separated them: some identified as Greeks and some as Macedonians. The latter, who constituted at least 30 percent of the refugee population, cultivated a separate national identity and sought to preserve it through independent schools and cultural clubs. And even though for purposes of administration they depended on the KKE, they also had their own political organization, the National Liberation Slav-Macedonian Organization, or Iliden, founded in 1952 in the isolated village of Krościenko in Poland.[32]

Although the shared experience of harsh exile from their common homeland drew the less politicized Greeks and Macedonians closer together, relations between ethnic Greeks and Macedonians did not always reflect ties of "comradeship" and "brotherhood," as the party proclaimed. On the contrary, the party itself contributed to the alienation of the Macedonians from the ethnic Greek refugees. In the early 1950s, the KKE suspected Macedonians of "Titoism" and "chauvinism" and surveilled them intensely, and many of them fell victim to the anti-Titoist purges that spread across Communist Europe.[33]

The politically active KKE members were hardly a uniform bloc either. For the 16,448 KKE members among them, the trauma of the civil war and its aftermath became the dominant factor shaping their lives, giving rise to constant arguments and quarrels within the refugee community. They were haunted by the key questions of their misfortune: what had gone wrong with the guerrilla movement, and who was to blame for its defeat. Not surprisingly, they were sharply divided in their interpretations of the past and in their willingness to assign blame, and their quarrels, at times violent, created concerns for the security forces of the people's republics.[34]

Whether they were active members of the KKE or not, none of the refugees could ignore the party, which continued to play a critically important role in their daily lives. And like the Spanish Communist exiles earlier, they looked to the party for guidance in all aspects of their lives.[35] Until the late 1950s, the KKE served as the main arbiter of any disputes among the refugees and was the only authority to which they could address their grievances. As they lived in isolated communities with little contact with the local population, they had hardly anyone else but the KKE to trust with their concerns and demands. How did the KKE manage to keep so many refugees under its influence and control until the 1960s? To handle its daunting task, the party put considerable effort into maintaining strong links with the refugees. Among its most effective tools of communication and propaganda were the publishing house New Greece and the radio station Free Greece. Both were headquartered in Bucharest following the Tito-Stalin split, when Belgrade was no longer an option. The Free Greece radio station started its broadcasts in March 1949 with a staff of 10–15 and an annual budget of $36,000. The publishing house was created in December 1949, initially employing 20 and with an initial annual budget of 30 million lei ($200,000). Soon, New Greece expanded, with its staff rising to 145 employees, and its budget to $360,000. It proved to be very productive. In 1951, for instance, New Greece published 223 leaflets and books in a broad range of genres (literature, party propaganda, popular science, etc.), addressed to the refugee communities and, also, to the Greek minority in Albania.[36]

The Bucharest Party and the Making of the Republic

While life for the displaced from Greece was clearly not easy, the same cannot be said of the KKE leaders. With the financial burden fully assumed by the Romanian party, the KKE leadership was installed close to the Cominform headquarters in Bucharest, where they acted as if they were the elite of another Communist state. Zachariadis, for instance, was housed on Avenue Gradina Bordei, in the city's "Red neighborhood," close to the Romanian *nomenklatura*.[37]

In their relative comfort, the KKE leaders engaged in extended discussions about the insurgency's collapse and deliberated on their options and next steps. They perceived their defeat in Greece as temporary, but were not so unrealistic as to consider their situation unchanged. Instead they developed yet another and even more peculiar "dual strategy," aiming for both revolution and peace at the same time. Given its shaky foundation, the new strategy appeared contradictory and unrealistic. It professed to pursue a bizarre mixture of objectives: an aggressive *revolution from abroad*, with unspecified international implications and risks, combined with lawful participation in electoral and parliamentary politics at home. However bizarre it may seem in retrospect, this "war and peace" strategy was not concocted by the intransigent Greeks themselves but was derived from Andrei Zhdanov's Cominformian theory of the two international camps, which was being prominently discussed at that time.

As might be expected, the Soviets had been monitoring the KKE's deliberations and activities since the end of the civil war and the DSE's defeat in August 1949. Supervising the Greek party, a representative from the International Relations Department of the CPSU sat in on what proved to be one of the most fateful KKE Central Committee meetings. Ostensibly in pursuit of its dual strategy, on October 9, 1949, in Burrel, Albania, the KKE declared its determination to maintain within Greece a limited number of armed groups and to support an undercover network that would keep the pressure on the government in Athens.[38] Undoubtedly, this tactic could only intensify the suffering of the party's faithful supporters who remained inside Greece and who, obeying the party's decision to keep the banner of insurgency flying, were to be subjected to the government's measures of mass repression and imprisonment. In August 1950, one year after the end of the civil war, almost twenty-seven thousand Communists and fellow travelers were either in prison or in exile.[39]

To keep armed groups and clandestine operations in Greece, the KKE needed money, weapons, dedicated militants, safe houses, and training locations, for which, once again, it called on the international Communist network to provide them with immediate assistance. In November 1949, Giannis Ioannidis and Petros Roussos sent a letter to the Czechoslovak leaders Klement Gottwald and Rudolf Slánský requesting military supplies—specifically, flame throwers, 1,500 pairs of boots, one hundred radios, and so forth—and military training for three hundred individuals. A few weeks later, Slánský informed the Soviets about the Greeks' demands and confirmed that the Czechoslovaks had partially satisfied some of them and denied others. Soon the Czechoslovaks set up a "saboteurs' school" for Greek Communists, and training began on February 14, 1950.[40]

Similar secret military schools began operating with Soviet approval in other Eastern Bloc countries. In the summer of 1950, the Polish People's Republic authorities established "a school for leaders of partisan groups" in Komorów near Warsaw. Earlier, a school for officers appeared in Dziwnów, close to the military hospital where wounded Greek insurgents had been recovering. Training began in April 1950 with 169 cadets and was concluded in April 1951. In Romania, in the small town of Dorohoi, 480 kilometers northeast of Bucharest, a military school for the Greeks was opened under the control of the Higher Political Directorate of the Romanian Army. The deputy minister of the armed forces, Major General Nicolae Ceauşescu, the later president of Romania, personally supervised this facility, where approximately eighty young Greeks received instruction in military tactics, sabotage, and espionage.[41]

Other groups studied at the Frunze Military Academy in Moscow and at the Military School of Fergana, a city 420 kilometers east of Tashkent. Their training was a mixture of conventional and informal military training, with a considerable dose of political Marxist-Leninist education. As the Greek students hardly spoke Russian, they faced considerable difficulties in completing their studies As a result, many were rather dissatisfied with their experiences at the Frunze Academy, complaining that they were alienated and distant from the Soviet culture and the Soviet way of life.[42]

Military training, which proceeded somewhat haphazardly, was only one part of the KKE's strategy. The other was designed to pursue the political and eventually parliamentary road to victory within Greece. Accordingly, in August 1951, the KKE clandestine apparatus in Athens helped establish the United Democratic Left (EDA) as the party's political arm in the homeland. The EDA had originated as a loose coalition of small center-Left and antimonarchist groups; in 1951, at its first Panhellenic conference, it decided to transform itself into a unified coalition party created to represent the Left as a whole in the September election. To the surprise of its domestic and foreign adversaries, the EDA coalition started off with an impressive performance, winning 180,640 votes (10.57 percent) and electing ten deputies to the parliament.[43]

Considering the prevailing repression against the Left, the general atmosphere of fear, and the fact that several thousands of exiled or imprisoned KKE voters and cadres could not participate in the election, this electoral result was unquestionably a major success. Although the Communists had appeared on the ballot for the first time in fifteen years following a disastrous defeat in the civil war, the KKE had obviously not lost its popular appeal. In fact, seven years later, in the 1958 elections, the EDA, receiving 24.42 percent of the vote, delivered its best-ever electoral performance. That was the highest percentage that a left-wing party in Greece had secured up to that date, and it placed the EDA as the largest opposition party in the Greek parliament. Both the Greek establishment and the US State Department feared that a new Communist wave was rising.

Such fears, however, were not justified by the complex reasons for the EDA's unanticipated popularity, or by the party's orientation and political character. On the one hand, it was true that Communist voters regarded the EDA as the legal alternative to the KKE, and many of the EDA's grassroots cadres were in fact KKE affiliates. On the other hand, the EDA was neither the KKE in disguise nor an autonomous Communist party. Actually, the EDA was hardly revolutionary, and, unlike the real KKE, it was not a group of intransigent and militant ideologues. As the EDA's logo indicated, the party's avowed principles were peace, democracy, and amnesty; in other words, its political program was the defense of civil rights and of liberal political institutions.

Such a program made the EDA very popular with a broad spectrum of left-leaning voters in Greece. But its platform was very different from the one that the KKE continued to embrace. In its pronouncements, the Communist Party's leadership in Bucharest glorified the 1946–49 revolt and stressed its ties to the Soviet Bloc. For its part, the EDA was basically silent about the civil war, focusing mainly on the conflict's negative consequences for human rights and the rule of law, defending liberal democratic institutions, and seeking to build alliances with political personalities outside the Communist world. As a result, Greek Communists faced a choice between two fundamentally different and incompatible political programs and identities, a dilemma that was hardly unique. Every Western Communist party at that time featured parallel and centrifugal forces, and each party had to grapple with revolutionary and reformist tendencies, as well as with Stalinist and anti-Stalinist dispositions. But in the Greek case, with the EDA in Athens and the KKE in Bucharest, the split was shaped by geography too.

While the EDA celebrated its early popularity and political success, the KKE in Bucharest went into a protracted crisis that reflected internal tensions and personal feuds that had surfaced during the civil war. The most vicious and damaging clash was between Markos Vafeiadis, top commander of the DSE, and Zachariadis, who in August 1948 dismissed Markos and other seasoned veterans of the wartime ELAS, replacing them with party officials loyal to the KKE chief but inexperienced in fighting a civil war. In part, the quarrel was over Zachariadis's insistence that in accordance with Operation Lakes, the DSE switch to conventional (static) warfare, whereas Markos believed that the DSE was best suited for guerrilla warfare. Markos lost the argument and Zachariadis led the DSE to its defeat. Shortly after the insurgency's collapse, the acrimony not only grew in intensity but became highly personal. Markos sent letters to the Soviets, accusing Zachariadis of having had suspicious relations with his Nazi captors in Dachau, and

Zachariadis counterattacked, denouncing Markos as a Titoist agent and requesting Moscow's official backing.[44]

The Soviets did back Zachariadis, but without much enthusiasm. Alarmed by Moscow's lukewarm response, the KKE leader promptly expressed his dissatisfaction with the Soviets' ambivalence. He informed the chairman of the International Department of the Central Committee of the CPSU, Vagan Grigorian, that he was ready to travel to Moscow to clarify any doubts the Soviet leaders might have concerning his leadership.[45] In the end, Zachariadis managed to persuade Molotov and Stalin that it was Markos who had played a negative role in Communist politics and the conduct of the insurgency. The blame game between Markos and Zachariadis, and the power struggle among the émigrés in Moscow, did not surprise the Soviets. Communist parties in exile had often experienced fratricidal infighting, whose outcome was predictably determined by where the Soviets would lean on the scales. Only a few years earlier, for instance, within the defeated Spanish Communist Party, a bitter struggle for the post of secretary-general had erupted between La Pasionaria and Jesús Hérnandez. Supported by the Soviets, La Pasionaria prevailed, and Hérnandez was soon expelled from the party.[46]

The challenge from Markos was only one of Zachariadis's problems. Two other prominent Communists—the former mayor of Kavala and KKE Politburo member Dimitris Partsalidis, and the editor of *Rizospastis*, Kostas Karagiorgis (real name Gyftodimos)—had also strongly criticized Zachariadis's decisions and tactics. Although the two seasoned Communists hardly saw eye to eye on many issues, they agreed that Zachariadis had made fatal mistakes and also considered him disloyal to the Soviets, reopening old wounds. Once again, the KKE and the Soviets began reexamining and reevaluating past disagreements, including the KKE's decision to boycott the 1946 election against Moscow's advice.[47]

With the backing of the KKE Politburo, Zachariadis moved decisively against his critics and major dissidents, whom the party swiftly purged as troublemakers. On October 10, 1950, the party met for its Third Conference in the mountain resort of Sinaia, in Central Romania, where the assembled 184 delegates came exclusively from the refugee communities.[48] In addition to confirming the party's dual strategy, the conference took further measures against the dissidents. It expelled Markos as a "Trotskyist Liquidarist and factionist element," as well as Partsalidis and Chrysa Chatzivasiliou (the only woman in the top echelons of the KKE) as antiparty factionist elements, and Karagiorgis as an enemy agent.[49] Even Georgios Siantos, the ex-secretary of the Central Committee during the occupation years, who had died in 1947, was posthumously denounced as an agent of the enemy class.

All of those condemned by the conference would soon be rendered incapable of representing any threat to Zachariadis. While Chatzivasiliou died of leukemia in November 1950, others were neutralized by the wider Communist network. Karagiorgis was arrested by the Romanian police and died in prison two years later. Although Zachariadis pressured Romanian leader Gheorghe Gheorghiu-Dej to also arrest Markos, the old guerrilla commander managed to flee to Moscow, where he might have been safe but could not challenge Zachariadis's hegemony.[50] The only dissident who survived and remained in Romania, even though Zachariadis humiliated him frequently, was Partsalidis. But he, too, was moved away from the center of power. Partsalidis was transferred four hundred kilometers away from Bucharest to the Transylvanian town of Cugir, where he lived for a year, marginalized and isolated from the Greek community in Romania.[51] Several months later, in October 1951, the Second Plenum of the Central Committee confirmed its previous decision to dismiss Partsalidis and asked the Soviets for help with his "reeducation."[52] Even though Partsalidis begged Zachariadis to allow him to return to Bucharest and to be accepted back into the party, he was formally ousted from the KKE in October 1952.[53]

With the expulsion of his critics, Zachariadis may have averted an immediate challenge to his leadership, but his position was far from secure. As the Greek Communists were discrediting and neutralizing their rivals and dissidents, the Soviets and Stalin personally were kept informed fully and in detail about the recurrent crises within the KKE.[54] As may have been expected, before long, top Soviet officials began to have serious doubts about Zachariadis's ability to manage his party's affairs successfully.

After Stalin's Death

On March 5, 1953, Stalin died, and soon his unexpected departure reverberated across the Communist world and the international stage. Across the Soviet Bloc, long dominated by the cult of the dictator's personality, haphazard efforts at reform began amid much uncertainly, fears, and confusion. While it was unclear where those reforms would lead, one thing was clear: conditions had to change within both the Soviet Union and its orbit states, and the pressure to move away from the capricious rule of a single leader was irresistible. Aware of his own vulnerability, Zachariadis—the Greek "Little Stalin"—tried to adjust to the winds of change, by, ironically, denouncing the cult of personality within the KKE. But his position had become highly precarious, and mere pronouncements of intended changes within a party he had ruled with an iron fist were hardly sufficient to mollify his antagonists and victims. In the USSR, post-Stalinism meant not only structural and institutional reform, but the emergence of a new leadership that would carry it through. As was to be expected, the ensuing power struggle affected not only the Soviet party but also the other Communist parties of Europe, making it clear that no one leader could ever again command the undisputed authority enjoyed by Stalin. In the Soviet party's internal power struggle, Zachariadis chose to back Lavrentii Beria instead of Nikita Khrushchev. This proved to be an unfortunate choice, causing the Greek to clash with the International Department of the CPSU's Central Committee, and specifically with Boris Ponomarev and his patron Mikhail Suslov, the department's two top officials.[55] Though Molotov continued to support Zachariadis, before long everyone within the Greek party understood that Zachariadis's omnipotence was at an end.

Soon, signs that Zachariadis's days as the party leader were over appeared. In a desperate attempt to retain his place as the top policy maker, he reported on the situation in Greece and insisted on a course of action based on the prospect of an imminent socialist transformation, a program entirely incompatible with the EDA platform. In December 1953, the Fourth Plenum of the KKE Central Committee deliberated on Zachariadis's draft program. But the Soviets intervened and vetoed it, claiming that the proposed plan was inappropriate for the prevailing political situation, would harm the EDA's political opportunities, and needed a radical reconstruction. In November 1954, when the KKE withdrew its support for the draft program, Zachariadis's humiliation became all too evident.[56]

With Zachariadis discredited, the entire Greek party was soon engulfed in turmoil and divisions that were spinning out of control. Chaos reigned supreme even in the KKE's most disciplined outpost of the displaced people's republic, the 8,173-member community in Tashkent.[57] The Uzbekistan-based organization was divided into two factions: the "Zachariadists" and the "anti-Zachariadists," who accused each other of anti-Soviet positions and of corruption. While the infighting itself was dramatic, the members of the anti-Zachariadis faction, backed by the Soviets, felt confident enough to publicly criticize the KKE, a development that alarmed the party's Politburo.[58]

In early 1955, the KKE established a special committee of high-level functionaries who flew to Tashkent to calm tempers and avert a potential rebellion through official internal channels. In May and August, Zachariadis met with Suslov and other officials of the CPSU International Department in Moscow. The Soviets refused to take sides in the Greeks' disputes and advised Zachariadis to cooperate with the Uzbekistan authorities to appease the rebels and to seek compromises, rather than further aggravate the strife by trying to impose his views on the party.[59] In August 1955, Zachariadis went to Tashkent, where he discussed the situation with several KKE officials and convened a meeting for hundreds of local cadres. Completely ignoring the Soviets' advice, and accustomed to conducting himself in an authoritarian manner, he opted to deal with the dissenters with an iron hand. He ousted the dissidents' leaders from the meeting and imposed a new local committee loyal to him.[60] Not surprisingly, Zachariadis's high-handed behavior led to another round of infighting and put a strain on the relations between the KKE and the Communist Party of Uzbekistan.[61] Soon, Suslov summoned Zachariadis to Moscow, and immediately following his departure, on September 9–10, 1955, riots broke out in Tashkent between the Zachariadists and the anti-Zachariadists. In the street fighting between the two opposing groups, approximately 120 people were injured, and the local police arrested 25 persons.[62]

With tensions already running high before Zachariadis's visit to Tashkent, his latest imperious behavior was the straw that broke the proverbial camel's back, and for the Soviet authorities, responsibility for the riots lay largely with the KKE leader.[63] Amin Niyazov, the secretary of the Communist Party of Uzbekistan, believed that everything Zachariadis had done during his visit had been harmful.[64] One week after the violent events, the Central Committee of the Soviet Bolshevik Party determined that Zachariadis was indeed partly responsible for the whole debacle, because some of his decisions and initiatives had incited violent reactions.[65] This time, it was the Soviet authorities who nominated a special committee to examine the situation in the KKE. In November, the committee concluded that the accusations made by Zachariadis against many of the party dissenters were entirely unfounded. On December 10, the Central Committee of the CPSU advised the Greek leader again to show restraint and to readmit to the

KKE all those recently expelled as antiparty and factionist elements. In addition, embracing a radically different strategy than the KKE leadership, the Soviets proposed organizing a meeting in Tashkent to discuss the Greek party's problems, reconcile the various factions, and elect new local KKE leaders.[66]

Zachariadis rejected all of this advice, and at the Fifth Plenum of the KKE's Central Committee, held in Bucharest on December 26–28, 1955, he remained intransigent toward the Tashkent dissidents. The plenum branded Zachariadis's opponents a corrupt and antiparty clique consisting of individuals who had betrayed the people, the party, and the Soviet Union.[67] Only one Politburo member, Kostas Koligiannis, voted against this resolution. His overall conduct at the plenum was surprisingly aggressive toward the KKE's leader, and he shocked the other delegates with his audacity. In the end, Koligiannis walked out of the room, shouting, "Zachariadis, forget what you knew!"[68] Undoubtedly, it was a brazen challenge to Zachariadis's authority. Although not obvious to all at that heated moment, Koligiannis had pronounced the end of Zachariadis's regime and the coming of a new era for the Greek Communist party. As most of the assembled understood, the CPSU was behind Koligiannis's bold outburst. And just over a month later, in February 1956, Koligiannis would become the KKE's new leader.

The Twentieth Congress of the CPSU, at which the new Soviet leadership presented its agenda of de-Stalinization, became the site where the actual drama of the Greek Communist leadership unfolded. On February 21, 1956, a week after the congress opened, in a small room in the Grand Kremlin Palace, Zachariadis was informed that, on Soviet initiative, an international committee composed of representatives of six sister parties had been formed to solve the "anomalous situation" within the KKE.[69] On February 25, the same day that Nikita Khrushchev gave his "Secret Speech" on the cult of personality and its consequences, Zachariadis and the international committee met to discuss the most burning issues of the previous fifteen years of Greek Communist politics and tactics. The group excoriated the Greek leader for every misstep attributed to him, past and present: for his letter to Metaxas in 1940, for the boycott of the 1946 national election, for the launching of and defeat in the civil war, and finally for the turmoil and tensions within the party in recent years. In his defense, Zachariadis rejected the committee's criticisms of his past decisions, and argued that such an international committee was a highly inappropriate forum for judging his performance.[70] In desperation, he asked to see Khrushchev to personally explain to him the situation within the Greek party, but his efforts were futile and his request for a meeting with the top Soviet leader was denied. Finally defeated, he resigned from his post as the KKE's secretary-general, along with three other Politburo members who were then in Moscow, and promised not to obstruct the work of the international committee.[71]

As Zachariadis rightly sensed, the committee was merely the instrument of the Soviets' highest authority for carrying out its intervention to remove him. But in order to justify establishing the committee, the top Soviet officials first needed a pretext, which they found in what they labeled an "anomalous situation" that purportedly existed within the KKE. And they demonstrated that an anomalous situation did in fact exist, by referring to letters from the Greek Communists themselves. In early 1956, the CPSU and the Cominform received a barrage of letters from several hundred KKE members in Tashkent, which praised the care they were receiving from the Communist states and accused the "Zachariadis regime" of ruining the refugees' lives. Most of the letters concluded by urging the Soviets to intervene in the internal affairs of the KKE in order to help solve its problems.[72]

To be sure, many Greeks in Tashkent were unhappy about living in an inhospitable foreign land and resented their party's oppressive supervision. Yet in its broader context, the situation reveals a more complicated picture of just how "anomalous" the KKE experience truly was. Such letters of denunciation had been a common practice in the USSR since the 1920s. Ostensibly coming "from below" but usually incited "from above," these written charges and condemnations provided incriminating evidence against the accused during the purges.[73] The letters of the Greek Communists bore a striking similarity to the typical letters of denunciation prevalent in earlier years of Soviet Russia. Apparently incited by the International Department of the CPSU for the particular purpose at hand, their authors did not present general complaints concerning specific matters, but rather argued that Zachariadis had to be removed.

The KKE secretary-general was experienced enough in Bolshevik tactics to realize that his end was approaching, primarily based on his interactions with the Soviets. For example, he was not invited to speak as a foreign representative at the Twentieth Congress of the CPSU, as he had been two years earlier, at the Nineteenth Congress. In fact, *Pravda* did not even list the KKE among the guest parties attending the Twentieth Congress, placing it in the category of the *drugiye* (others). For those not unversed in the Soviet idiom and habits, the message was crystal clear.

The international committee convened to investigate the KKE leadership problems faced pressure from Moscow as well. Its chairman, the Romanian secretary-general, Gheorghiu-Dej, was a friend of Zachariadis who might have been expected to advocate leniency toward his Greek comrade. But Gheorghiu-Dej assumed his task seriously, suspecting that the Soviets nominated him to the position because of his friendship with Zachariadis, in order to test his loyalty to the USSR's post-Stalin leadership. And of course, the Romanian leader did not want to jeopardize his office, particularly as he was already under attack from his own party, where his ambitious rivals accused him of promoting the cult of personality. After his return from Moscow, Gheorghiu-Dej was careful to inform the Romanian Politburo of the latest developments and his new duties.[74] He was thus determined to have proven himself capable of adapting to the new requirements of de-Stalinization.

While Gheorghiu-Dej was trying to pass his test of political loyalty, the real chief of the committee was a Finnish Communist, Otto Kuusinen, who had fled to the USSR after the Finnish Civil War and had become a Soviet citizen. Kuusinen was an eminent Comintern official with international prestige, and once he was in power, Khrushchev had promoted him in the CPSU hierarchy as well.[75] Kuusinen made sure that the investigative committee worked closely with the CPSU's International Department, thus ensuring Zachariadis's removal.

On March 11–12, 1956, the Sixth Extended Plenum of the KKE met near Bucharest, without Zachariadis in attendance and with Gheorghiu-Dej taking the floor first. His speech, delivered in Romanian and only partially translated into Greek, explained to the KKE delegates why the international committee had been convened and reiterated the main accusations against Zachariadis.[76] As during the Comintern intervention in 1931, when Stalinization was easily imposed on the Greek Communist Party by Moscow, this time, too, the international center did not encounter the slightest resistance, as even Zachariadis's closest colleagues had abandoned him. The plenum unanimously decided to depose Zachariadis and to readmit all those expelled from the party during the previous few years.

The initiative of Soviet authorities in precipitating the fall of Zachariadis signaled that a new era had begun in the Greek party, which was immediately noticed in the West as a sign of a shift in Soviet foreign policy.[77] Just as Stalinization had been imported from Moscow, de-Stalinization was launched on Moscow's instigation as well. And as had happened in some people's republics, where Moscow's calls for de-Stalinization met with hostility from some parties' leaders, the new KKE leadership perceived the proposed de-Stalinization changes in the USSR with a measure of suspicion and fear. But, as in the past, they had neither the will nor the capacity to resist Moscow.[78]

A few months after the fateful plenum, the Soviets offered the defeated and ousted Zachariadis several options to consider for his own future. He could take up a place at a party school, where he could complete his studies, or work at a policy institute, where he could help evaluate Greek political issues. The Soviets' offers were undoubtedly quite lenient and attractive compared to the fate that had awaited other fallen party leaders in the past, including Chaitas, Zachariadis's predecessor, who was executed during the Stalinist purges. But in another sign that, even if times had changed, Zachariadis had not, he refused to accept the offers he was given; instead he requested a job in a factory, or preferably a quarry. He was, however, far from being finished with politics. For reasons that remain unexplained, during October and December 1956 he went on the offensive one more time, sending letters to the CPSU Central Committee denouncing the role that the international committee had played in his removal from his party post.[79]

Zachariadis's challenge to higher Soviet authority came at a time when the world of international Communism had experienced strong disturbances and changes, particularly following the Hungarian Revolution and the Soviet invasion of that troubled country. The Soviets were determined not to allow Zachariadis's unruly spirit to be a bad example for international Communism. They therefore decided to put an end to their problem with the Greek Communist Party by dealing with Zachariadis once and for all. In February 1957, at the Seventh Plenum of the KKE's Central Committee, Otto Kuusinen, in "a boss-like style," as the veteran Communist leader Giorgos Gousias described him contemptuously,[80] mercilessly attacked Zachariadis and his closest associates. This time Zachariadis was present at the meeting, and he defended himself stubbornly. Perhaps the most striking of his arguments, recalled by Nikos Yangoglou, an alternate member of the Central Committee, was that the KKE had no right to expel him because he was a member of the Bolshevik Party, which had sent him to Greece to lead the KKE, a statement that shocked the audience.[81] Despite, or perhaps because of, his fiery and erratic self-defense, the plenum voted to expel Zachariadis from the KKE as an antiparty, factionist, anti-internationalist, and anti-Soviet element. Anyone who refused to renounce Zachariadis was to face similar punishment and isolation.[82]

Although the party leadership dutifully complied with Soviet commands, many grassroots members refused to do so. Across the *refugee-land*, differences appeared, and in some cases, as in Czechoslovakia in 1957, many members of the local KKE continued to express their support for Zachariadis.[83] But wherever there was disagreement, repression followed. Once again, hundreds of letters of denunciation were addressed to the authorities and to the security services of all the Eastern European countries, accusing Zachariadists of antisocialist and anti-Soviet behavior.[84] As before, nowhere was this process of denunciation more dramatic than in Tashkent, where 2,400 KKE members were ousted from the party, and forty to forty-five of the local leaders were exiled to Siberia. Altogether, seven thousand dogmatists and sectarians, as the party called Zachariadis's supporters, real or suspected, were expelled from the party branches all over Eastern Europe.[85]

Finally, in June 1962, the Soviet authorities exiled Zachariadis to Surgut, a city in Western Siberia. Despite his persistent efforts to break away from his isolation, and repeated appeals to Soviet and Greek authorities to be allowed to return to Greece, Zachariadis never left Siberia. After going on a hunger strike and writing warnings to Soviet and KKE officials that he would take his own life, on August 1, 1973, he committed suicide. The Soviet authorities buried him under a false identity as Nikolai Nikolaivitch Nikolaev, a Soviet citizen who had never even been a Communist Party member. For obvious reasons, until September 1990, his suicide was kept top secret by the CPSU and the KKE's Politburo.[86]

Zachariadis was a special kind of leader. Born and raised in two different empires outside the Greek borders, his knowledge of Greece and the Greeks was superficial, distorted, and dated. He was a product of a unique lifelong commitment to Bolshevism, which nurtured his faith in strict discipline and self-confidence and directed his activism toward loyal service to the Communist center. He was bright, energetic, stubborn, arrogant, inflexible, and believed to have been (not without some justification) one of Stalin's favorite foreign comrades. He regarded himself as a loyal and valuable instrument of Bolshevism-Stalinism, and the Greek Communist movement's undisputed leader. He was over-awed by Soviet ingenuity, power, decisiveness, organizational discipline, and endless dynamism. On the other hand, he lacked understanding of and appreciation for the strengths and capabilities of the West, and particularly the postwar United States, to mobilize its vastly superior resources and industry and project its influence and raw power to remote and historically weak and marginal states like Greece, in order to block the further expansion of Soviet-controlled Communism, then perceived as the West's mortal enemy. Once deprived of Stalin's backing, Zachariadis felt betrayed by his Greek comrades and abandoned by Stalin's successors, who had their own agendas and favorites. Ironically, the "Little Stalin's" end was brought about by the very tools he had so much faith in: blind obedience and loyalty, rather than genuine consideration of policy; and cynical exploitation of people's grievances, rather than their real democratic input. Those tools were, of course, those of his Bolshevik hero. Fundamentally, it was Zachariadis's and the KKE's Communist internationalism that shaped both his meteoric rise and his tragic fall.

Epilogue

The KKE could probably claim the world's record in dramatic party leadership turnover. From its creation in 1918 until 1956, the ten persons who had occupied the post of secretary-general were all forcibly deposed and expelled from the party. And the last two, Chaitas and Zachariadis, also both suffered tragic deaths.

The highly irregular and violent fate of the KKE's top leaders reflected the party's turbulent political life. Long before its military bid for power, the KKE had been transformed from a party rooted in social-democratic traditions into a disciplined Stalinist entity that became completely subservient to Moscow and its obedient organs. This is not to say that the KKE was merely a pawn in the power games of Communist agencies. In reality, the international institutions, such as the Balkan Communist Federation, the Moscow center, the Comintern, the Cominform, and the sister parties in the Balkans, were not merely external factors determining the KKE's policies. Rather, those institutions, as well as the geopolitical interests of the Soviets and of the sister parties, all shaped the KKE's leadership, its character, its way of life, and its decision-making mechanisms over the years. Unavoidably, this process was full of internal conflicts: the Greek Communists were pulled apart by centrifugal domestic and international forces emerging from political developments in Greece, the Balkans, the Soviet Union, and the shifting dynamics of the international order.

As a component of this complex and unstable international Communist world, the KKE faced a daunting and dangerous task. It had to simultaneously respect Moscow as the fountainhead and arbiter of international Communism, promote the international cause, and defend the Soviet Union's strategic interests as defined by Moscow's top leaders, while at the same time developing a cohesive and respectable party capable of gaining power or at least competing effectively in the domestic electoral arena. Given the realities of prewar and postwar Greece, those ambitions proved excessively demanding, if not contradictory and unrealistic.

Between its birth in 1918 and the 1931 Comintern's intervention into its internal affairs, the Greek party underwent a series of internal crises related to its public profile, its policies, and its model of management. While seemingly no more than petty quarrels, in reality all of those conflicts concerned the very nature of the party's Bolshevization. In short, the crucial debates within the KKE pivoted around the question of loyalty to Moscow's version of socialism, to the Balkan Communist Federation and the Comintern, and to the Bolsheviks' institutional demands that the center should determine every aspect of the party's life, organization, and policies. The internal quarrels about the "parliamentary road," the attitude toward social democracy, or the Comintern's intrusive role in the party's affairs were different components of the Bolshevization process. By far the most divisive issue within the party and its relations with its sister parties, however, proved to be the Macedonian question. The consequences of the Comintern's position on Macedonian independence were inevitably catastrophic for the Greek party's position in domestic politics, and for its own internal coherence. Increasingly controlled by and dependent on the Comintern's network and support, the KKE stood by this disastrous policy for a decade.

On the other hand, although Moscow's apparent control of the KKE signaled the party's submission to Soviet influence and commands, the persistent internal strife between a "Right" and a "Left" faction revealed that the Stalinization process among Greek Communists remained incomplete at least until 1931. This anomalous situation was to be corrected by the Comintern's intervention, which tightened Moscow's control over the Greek party and its leadership. Thus, the KKE became a monolithic Stalinist organization. From that moment on, the KKE was transformed from a national section of a revolutionary world party to an organization devoted to serving the interests of *socialism in one country* above everything else. That country was, of course, the Soviet Union and not Greece.

As has been shown in these pages and elsewhere, the Second World War dramatically changed the role of the Communist parties in the Balkans, including Greece. Especially in Yugoslavia, Greece, and Albania, the Communists became ambitious and significant protagonists of their respective postwar national political scenes. While the Yugoslav and Albanian leaders, Tito and Hoxha, succeed in their dreams of establishing and heading Communist regimes in their countries, the Greeks failed to do so. This was not for lack of trying. Rather, Soviet policy in the Balkans, shaped by the consequences of Stalin's "spheres of influence" power politics agreement with Churchill, impeded the KKE's bid for power, and compelled the party to seek temporary compromise with its rivals. But many in the party were unwilling to accept the postwar international order contemplated by the Western Allies. Rejecting a British-supported centrist-conservative regime, the KKE leaders stumbled into an armed uprising in Athens in December 1944, which was suppressed largely by British troops.

Their defeat in the armed confrontation with their adversaries did not quell the ambitions of the Greek Communists. As the Allies' victory over Nazi Germany and imperial Japan began morphing into an East-West cold war, the Soviet Union shifted its view on the future of the Balkans, which, with the exception of Greece, were now ruled by Moscow-dominated regimes. Growing US-Soviet hostility, combined with the KKE's and Tito's aggressive ambitions for the political future of their region, prompted Moscow to become more responsive to the Balkan comrades' demands for increasingly assertive policies in their region. In 1946, however, it was not Stalin who imposed his will on the Greek party. On the contrary, despite initial Soviet reservations about an armed conflict in Greece, it was the Greek-Yugoslav common strategy, backed by the Bulgarian leader Dimitrov, that persuaded a reluctant Stalin to endorse a Communist revolution in Greece. But the Tito-Stalin split in 1948 and Yugoslavia's expulsion from the Cominform, the defeat of the KKE's guerrilla army in the 1946–49 civil war, and the subsequent flight of the KKE leadership and thousands of its supporters to Eastern European people's democracies all deepened the Greek party's disarray and dependence on Moscow.

The civil war and its catastrophic outcome for the KKE also radically changed how Greek Communists could engage in their country's domestic politics. Two parallel political centers emerged: the old KKE leadership, now in self-imposed exile in Bucharest, and a remarkably resilient left-wing political party in Athens, functioning under the umbrella of the EDA. Their separate and different, yet vaguely complementary, interests, structures, and ideological positions generated significant friction for all Greeks devoted to the cause of Communism. The old KKE leaders no longer commanded absolute authority over the movement, as such authority was now fragmented not merely politically but also geographically. Nevertheless, as long as the world of international Communism itself had a clear center of authority, the KKE leadership could stave off a full-fledged crisis and navigate the incompatible desires of their bifurcated membership. The de-Stalinization process, and the uncertainties it generated, exacerbated the internal rift in the ranks of Greek Communism. For the time being, the differences were assuaged when Zachariadis, who as Stalin's favorite had imposed his will on party politics, was removed from power in 1956.

Despite the loss of thousands of its members, the KKE itself survived the persistent turbulence, but it never achieved the internal unity it had hoped for when Zachariadis was deposed, and its feuding and divisions festered for several more years. Moreover, new rifts within the global Communist world, Khrushchev's fall from power in October 1964, and, closer to the Greeks, Nicolae Ceaușescu's ascension to power in Romania in March 1965 created instability and protracted crisis.

After Ceaușescu rose to power and built his international popularity promoting a vision of national Communism and defiance of Moscow, the Romanian Communist Party actively intervened in support of the "pro-Romanian" faction in the KKE.[1] This support enabled some of the high-ranking members to include in the KKE's agenda old themes with a new vocabulary: according to Ioannis Balampanidis, this was "Communism adapted to national circumstances, wider political and social alliances, democracy, and transition from the revolutionary matrix to the prospect of governance."[2] Undoubtedly, developments in the USSR and the global Communist community played a catalytic role in the rise of this new trend, which later acquired the name of Eurocommunism. Particularly in Europe, new ideas and policies were developing within the Italian, French, and Spanish Communist Parties, influenced by their distance from increasingly discredited Soviet models of Communism. New schemes for national paths to Communism emerged, giving rise to new variants within the Communist family, to which the Soviets never gave their blessing.[3]

In the Greek case, the roots of the internal schism also included an intense conflict among party elites, augmented by peculiar geographic factors. A chasm arose between the KKE leadership located outside Greece and the Interior Bureau, the group of Communist cadres placed within the EDA, to oversee the implementation of the KKE policy in Greece. Presumably, the KKE leadership abroad feared that the EDA's political success would make them irrelevant. This rivalry was aggravated further by the increasingly deeper involvement of the Romanians in the KKE's internal affairs. Yet despite the Romanian effort to control the Greek party, the KKE "Muscovite wing" won the internal struggle at the Twelfth Plenum held in February 1968, for obvious reasons this time not in Bucharest but in Budapest. As a result, the KKE split into two political groups: the pro-Soviet "orthodox," and the pro-Romanian "revisionists."[4]

Having to choose between submission and expulsion, the minority, backed materially and politically by the Romanians, announced the formation of the KKE Esoterikou (Communist Party of Greece-Interior). This label carried a crucial symbolic significance, as it implied that the pro-Soviet KKE, often mockingly referred to as the "KKE Exoterikou" (KKE Exterior), a nickname that the pro-Moscow KKE always rejected angrily, was not an independent party but a Soviet puppet.[5] In August 1968, only a few months after the Twelfth Plenum in Budapest, the Soviet invasion of Czechoslovakia and the crackdown of the Prague Spring shocked many European Communists, but at the same time presented them with a political opportunity.[6] In the Greek case, Soviet aggression fomented processes already underway since February of that year.

The 1968 events bring to mind two crucial features of Greek Communism. First, and not accidentally, since its founding, the major crises of Greek Communism, occurring in the 1920s, 1956, 1968, and 1989–91, were echoes of major crises of Soviet and worldwide Communism. Second, since the very early days of its existence, an enduring, central, and most distinctive feature of the Greek Communist movement was its dual character: a sectarian party, loyal to the international Communist center, coexisted and competed with "Liquidarist" tendencies (in other words, keen to forge alliances with social democrats) that invariably coincided with the desire for a measure of independence from the center. Contrary to what happened in other Communist parties, however, in the Greek case the strategy of ideological and organizational rigidity and loyalty to Moscow had consistently outperformed the strategy of ideological and organizational modernization—until 2012, when the Coalition of the Radical Left, better known as SYRIZA, rose from a marginal position in Greek politics and became not only dominant within the Greek Left but a party that a few years later won the elections and formed a government. As a consequence, the failure of reformist trends acted as a selection mechanism that alienated reform-minded modernizing individuals, who might otherwise have turned the KKE in more social-democratic directions.[7]

Following the fall of the military dictatorship in 1974, the restoration of parliamentary democracy, and the legalization of Communist parties, the Moscow-oriented KKE and the Eurocommunist KKE Esoterikou competed in the political arena. As expected, the KKE Esoterikou cultivated relations with Communist parties in Western Europe and adopted a reformist strategy modeled after the Italian Communist Party. In 1975, the KKE Esoterikou and the Spanish Communist Party issued a joint declaration approving the main Eurocommunist precepts. The Greek party gradually moved away from strict Marxism-Leninism, and on a symbolic level, it adopted a label that associated the traditional hammer-and-sickle symbol with the Greek flag. Its program advocated parliamentary democracy, a mixed economy, and a pluralistic model of socialism "with a human face." It also supported the accession of Greece to the European Economic Community.[8] The new organization quickly attracted a considerable number of intellectuals, artists, and young scientists and students, as well as an important number of the EDA's leadership and cadres who had remained in Greece during the 1950s and 1960s, creating expectations that Greek Eurocommunism could outperform Marxist-Leninist orthodoxy.

On the one hand, the KKE followed a rigidly Marxist-Leninist stance, staunchly supporting the Soviet Union, including its intervention in Afghanistan in 1979 and the Jaruzelski coup in Poland in 1981. It also fought against each manifestation of the country's pro-West orientation.[9] It was something of a commonplace that the KKE, together with the Portuguese party, had been the most loyal ally of Moscow among the Western European Communists.[10] On the other hand, although Greek Eurocommunists presented themselves as modern and pro-European, independent from Moscow's dictates and enjoying the support of an important part of the country's intelligentsia and younger generation, the KKE Esoterikou never developed into a real threat to the KKE, the country's orthodox Communist party. The KKE continued to receive the political and financial support of the Soviet Union and of the

Eastern European people's republics, which helped it considerably in its development of a strong and disciplined organization and an impressive propaganda and public mobilization machine, and rallied behind it the working class, a good portion of the peasant world, and a number of young people and students originating from working-class strata.[11] Despite its close connections with the Soviet Union, or because of them, the Greek leftist electorate, for reasons related to the country's history and political culture, seemed to be more keen to support an original version of Communism than what it considered to be heresy.

With the approaching end of the Cold War, the Greek Communists experienced their final major crisis in November 1989, when the Berlin Wall fell. After the demise of the Soviet Union in 1991, global Communism everywhere received a fatal blow. The Moscow center had collapsed, and "without a global party with its center in Moscow the communists would be like the Roman Catholic Church without a pope," as the American sociologist Seymour Martin Lipset remarked in 1964.[12]

In Europe, the collapse of the Soviet Bloc triggered a major crisis. Some parties, like the PCI in Italy, decided to abandon their Communist identity altogether. Others, like the PCF in France, tried to keep some distance from the past without totally throwing away the whole system. As for the KKE, it remained loyal to its Marxist-Leninist identity and turbulent Communist past without showing any regrets. In February 1991, at the party's Thirteenth Congress, the hard-liners won a close but decisive victory: of the 111 members elected to the new Central Committee, 60 belonged to the hard-line faction.[13] Thus, the KKE remained the last Stalinist party in Europe.

Notes

Introduction

1. Sassoon, *One Hundred Years*, xiv; Marc Lazar, "Fin de Siècle Communism in Western Europe," *Dissent*, Winter 2000, 62-65; Marantzidis, "Exit, Voice and Loyalty," 169-84; Kalyvas and Marantzidis, "Greek Communism," 689-90.
2. Mazower, *Governing the World*, 55-58; Conrad, *What Is Global History?*, 9.
3. Kriegel, *Les communistes Français*; Roux, "Annie Kriegel," 541-43.
4. Courtois and Lazar, *Histoire*, 12.
5. Studer, *Transnational World*, 4.
6. Stavrakis, *Moscow and Greek Communism*.
7. Thorpe, "Comintern 'Control,'" 637-38.
8. Thorpe, "Comintern 'Control,'" 639.
9. See, for example, Konstantakopoulos, Patelis, and Materi, *1931–1944 fakelos ELLAS*; Kondis and Sfetas, *Emfylios polemos*; Farakos, *B' Pagosmios Polemos*; Marantzidis and Tsivos, *O Ellinikos Emfylios*; Kondis, *Sosialistika krati*; Papadatos, *Akros aporrito*.
10. Studer, *Transnational World*, 28.
11. McDermott, "History of the Comintern," 32.
12. McDermott, "History of the Comintern," 32.
13. Farakos, *B' Pagosmios Polemos*, 88-89.
14. Studer, "Stalinization," 50.
15. Weber, "Stalinization of the KPD," 22-23, 30.
16. Studer, "Totalitarisme et Stalinisme," 48, 53.
17. Studer, *Transnational World*, 30.
18. Rees, "Leader Cults," 3.

1. Becoming Balkan Bolsheviks

1. On the Balkan Communist Federation, see Fišera, "La dimension régionale," 88; Fišera, *Les peuples Slaves*, 199; Grišina, "I proti fasi tis drastiriotitas," 174; Njagulov, "Early Socialism," 267, 272.
2. "Decision concerning the International," May 30, 1919, in KKE, *Episima keimena* 1:31.
3. KKE, *To proto synedrio*, 43, 72-73; Kordatos, *Istoria*, 309-21; Katsoulis, *Istoria*, 1:110.
4. Katsoulis, *Istoria*, 1:109-27; Potamianos, "Internationalism," 516.
5. Kordatos, *Arthrografies stin Kommounistiki epitheorisi*, 34.
6. Dimou, *Entangled Paths towards Modernity*, 20.

7. Katsoulis, *Istoria*, 1:130.

8. Marantzidis, "Greek Intellectuals," 84-85.

9. KKE, *To proto synedrio*, 113.

10. Benaroya, *I proti stadiodromia*, 100, 112, 124, 126.

11. Noutsos, *I sosialistiki skepsi*, 2:25-27.

12. Karpozilos, "Greeks in Russia," 19; also see Zapantis, *Greek-Soviet Relations*, 13; Agtzidis, *Paraefxeinios diaspora*, 243-45.

13. Morton, *Thunder at Twilight*, 6.

14. Karpozilos, "Greeks in Russia," 24-25; Agtzidis, *Paraefxeinios diaspora*, 260-79; Ulunian, "Communist Party of Greece," 188.

15. On Sakarelos, see "Spravka: Zografos Dimitrios Georgiou," August 29, 1940, RGASPI, fond 495, opis 207, delo 91, l. 2; Tréand to Dimitrov, January 22, 1941, RGASPI, fond 495, opis 184, delo 5, l. 21, in Bayerlein et al., *Moscou-Paris-Berlin*, 369; Karpozilos, "Greeks in Russia," 24-25; Papathanassiou, "To Kommounistiko Komma," 82; Karpozilos, "Ellinikou Laikou Metopou," 46-47; Palaiologopoulos, *Ellines antifasistes ethelontes*, 47, 69, 136; Pantelakis, *Los buenos antifascistas*, 183-84, 291.

16. "The Balkan Communist Federation: The Resolutions of the First and Second Conferences," *Kommounistiki epitheorisi*, June 1921, 384-86; Rothschild, *Communist Party of Bulgaria*, 224; Papapanagiotou, *To Makedoniko Zitima*, 30; Grišina, "I proti fasi tis drastiriotitas," 177; Ter Minassian, "Le Komintern et les Balkans," 62; Zečević, "Russian Revolution," 325-26.

17. Rothschild, *Communist Party of Bulgaria*, 224.

18. "Resolution on the Third International," April 11, 1920, in KKE, *Episima keimena*, 1:61-62, 68.

19. Riddell, *Workers of the World*.

20. Nikos Dimitratos, "Dimosthenis Ligdopoulos," *Kommounistiki epitheorisi*, February 1921, 75-79.

21. Ulunian, "Communist Party of Greece," 189.

22. Farakos, *B' Pagosmios Polemos*, 23-24.

23. Tsintzilonis, *OKNE 1922-1943*, 26.

24. Riddell, *Workers of the World*, 2:985-86.

25. Ulunian, "Communist Party of Greece," 190; Tsintzilonis, *OKNE 1922-1943*, 26.

26. Dagas, "Kommounistiko Komma Ellados," 194-95; Tsintzilonis, *OKNE 1922-1943*, 28-29.

27. White, "Communism and the East," 499; Pearce, *Congress of the Peoples*, 17, 23, 75.

28. Rothschild, *Communist Party of Bulgaria*, 230; Fišera, "La dimension régionale," 88-89; Fišera, *Les peuples Slaves*, 213-14; Grišina, "I proti fasi tis drastiriotitas," 177-78.

29. Serge, *Memoirs of a Revolutionary*, 208.

30. Rothschild, *Communist Party of Bulgaria*, 227.

31. Rothschild, *Communist Party of Bulgaria*, 228-30.

32. Katsoulis, *Istoria*, 1:282.

33. KKE, *Dokimio istorias tou KKE*, 126.

34. Elefantis, *I epagelia*, 26.

35. Riddell, *To the Masses*, 839–41.

36. Riddell, *To the Masses*, 177–78.

37. Rothschild, *Communist Party of Bulgaria*, 233; Bell, *Bulgarian Communist Party*, 31; Carr, *History of Soviet Russia*, v. 3, part 1, 203; Banac, *Diary of Georgi Dimitrov*, xvi–xxii; Lazitch and Drachkovitch, *Biographical Dictionary*, 224–25, 372, 424.

38. Serge, *Memoirs of a Revolutionary*, 208.

39. Carr, *History of Soviet Russia*, v. 3, part 1, 31.

40. Stankova, *Georgi Dimitrov*, 43.

41. Rothschild, *Communist Party of Bulgaria*, 97, 102; Bell, *Bulgarian Communist Party*, 27; Crampton, *Bulgaria*, 224.

42. Rothschild, *Communist Party of Bulgaria*, 106; Bell, *Bulgarian Communist Party*, 31.

43. Kahan, "Communist International," 154–55.

44. Avakumović, *History of the Communist Party*, 185; Cicak, "Communist Party of Yugoslavia," 17–21; Banac, "Communist Party of Yugoslavia," 188–230; Djilas, *Contested Country*, 63. Lešnik, "Development of the Communist Movement," 60.

45. Lešnik, "Development of the Communist Movement," 45.

46. Lazitch and Drachkovitch, *Biographical Dictionary*, 116, 302–3, 316.

47. Avakumović, *History of the Communist Party*, 62; Cicak, "Communist Party of Yugoslavia," 152; Swain, "Tito," 206.

48. Dimou, *Entangled Paths towards Modernity*, 302.

49. Dimou, *Entangled Paths towards Modernity*, 302; Yalimov, "Bulgarian Community," 93–94.

50. Harris, *Origins of Communism*, 16–18, 30; Mavrogordatos, *Stillborn Republic*, 253–62; Mazower, *Salonica, City of Ghosts*, 269–71, 351–52.

51. Benaroya, *I proti stadiodromia*, 217–19.

52. Dagas, "Kommounistiko Komma Ellados," 159; KKE, *Dokimio istorias tou KKE*, 87; Mavrogordatos, *Stillborn Republic*, 31.

53. Egatrin, "The Greek Defeat and Its Results," *Inprecor*, October 17, 1921, 14; Riddell, *Workers of the World*, 2:1034.

54. Tiber, *Communist Movement*, 93.

55. Grišina, "I proti fasi tis drastiriotitas," 177–78.

56. Grišina, "I proti fasi tis drastiriotitas," 181; Diac, "Între intransigenţă şi complicităţi asumate," 122.

57. Katsoulis, *Istoria*, 1:229–30.

58. Kofos, *Nationalism and Communism*, 70–71; Benaroya, *I proti stadiodromia*, 153; Elefantis, *I epagelia*, 42–43; Noutsos, *I sosialistiki skepsi*, 2:31.

59. Kousoulas, *Revolution and Defeat*, 8.

60. "Resolution of the SEKE's First National Conference," February 19, 1922, in KKE, *Episima keimena*, 1:213, 219–20.

61. Kordatos, *Arthrografies stin Kommounistiki epitheorisi*, 127–29, 133–51; Georgiadou-Katsoulaki, *I proti syndiaskepsi*.

62. Elefantis, *I epagelia*, 29.

63. Tiber, *Communist Movement*, 529, 536-37.

64. The term "Bolshevization" emerged later, during the Fifth Congress of the Comintern in 1924 and the Fifth Enlarged Plenum of the ECCI in March–April 1925. Degras, *Communist International*, 2:188-200; McDermott and Agnew, *Comintern*, 45.

65. Rothschild, *Communist Party of Bulgaria*, 229; Fišera, "La dimension régionale," 89; Fišera, *Les peuples Slaves*, 214; Grišina, "I proti fasi tis drastiriotitas," 180.

66. Djilas, *Contested Country*, 55-57, 62; Connor, *National Question*, 132; Bataković, "Communist Party of Yugoslavia," 63-65.

67. Rothschild, *Communist Party of Bulgaria*, 227-29.

68. Connor, *National Question*, 133; Haug, *Creating a Socialist Yugoslavia*, 20.

69. Connor, *National Question*, 136-41.

70. Stănescu, *Moscova*, 18-19; Tismăneanu, *Stalinism for All Seasons*, 44-47.

71. "Extraordinary conference of the SEKE(K)," October 20-31, 1922, in KKE, *Episima keimena*, 1:268.

72. Katsoulis, *Istoria*, 1:277; Tsintzilonis, *OKNE 1922-1943*, 51.

73. Deutscher, *Prophet Unarmed*, 139.

74. "Meeting of the CC of KKE," November 21, 1952, in Papadatos, *Akros Aporrito*, 487.

75. Riddell, ed., *Toward the United Front*, 440.

76. Grišina, "I proti fasi tis drastiriotitas," 178.

77. Stănescu, *Moscova*, 20; Tismăneanu, *Stalinism for All Seasons*, 50-51.

78. "The National Council of the SEKE," May 21-23, 1923, in KKE, *Episima keimena*, 1:297.

79. Elefantis, *I epagelia*, 30.

2. Balkan Communism and the National Question

1. Dimitrov, *Selected Works*, 1:213.

2. Dymarski, "Macedonian Question," 17.

3. Naxidou, "Bulgarian Historiography," 97-98.

4. Kofos, *Nationalism and Communism*, 2-6; Rossos, "Macedonianism and Macedonian Nationalism," 219-27.

5. Adanïr, "National Question," 27-28; Nicolas Pitsos, "'Peuples des Balkans, fédérez-vous!'"; Njagulov, "Early Socialism," 274.

6. Bell, *Bulgarian Communist Party*, 15-16; Papapanagiotou, *To Makedoniko Zitima*, 21; Perivolaropoulou, "La Fédération Balkanique," 32-33; Njagulov, "Early Socialism," 267-69.

7. Georgi Dimitrov, "La Guerre et le mouvement ouvrier dans les Balkans," *L'Internationale Communiste*, May–July 1924, 235.

8. "Manifesto of the Socialist Parties of the Balkans," *Bulletin of the Social-Democratic Workers Federation of the Balkans*, July 1, 1915.

9. Dimitrov, *Selected Works*, 1:62-65; Papapanagiotou, *To Makedoniko Zitima*, 21; Perivolaropoulou, "La Fédération Balkanique," 32-33; Njagulov, "Early Socialism," 267-69.

10. Riddell, *Workers of the World*, 2:1104–5.

11. Vasil Kolarov, "Après le coup d'etat," *L'Internationale Communiste*, October–December 1923, 71.

12. Kofos, *Nationalism and Communism*, 70–71; Dagas and Leontiadis, *Komintern kai Makedoniko Zitima*, 31.

13. Dagas and Leontiadis, *Komintern kai Makedoniko Zitima*, 36; Dagas, "Kommounistiko Komma Ellados," 161; Rossos, "Macedonianism and Macedonian Nationalism," 236–37.

14. Dagas and Leontiadis, *Komintern kai Makedoniko Zitima*, 31; Fowkes, "To Make the Nation," 212.

15. Petsopoulos, *Ta pragmatika aitia*, 47; Barker, *Macedonia*, 50.

16. Tiber, *Communist Movement*, 637–39.

17. Tiber, *Communist Movement*, 648.

18. Grigori Zinoviev, "The Lessons of the Bulgarian Counterrevolution," *Inprecor*, July 19, 1923, 523–25.

19. Tiber, *Communist Movement*, 410–11.

20. Connor, *National Question*, 137–38.

21. "Resolutions of the Conference of the Balkan Communist Federation," *Inprecor*, April 10, 1924, 224–26; and May 1, 1924, 259–62.

22. Kofos, *Nationalism and Communism*, 72–73; Papapanagiotou, *To Makedoniko Zitima*, 47.

23. Stavridis, *Ta paraskinia tou KKE*, 174–78.

24. Rothschild, *Communist Party of Bulgaria*, 235–36. The money itself is the hero of another story. Sargologos, after his return to Greece, told his comrades that he no longer had the money because he was the victim of a robbery by Italian fascists during his journey. Some months later, he left the party, and along with his wife he moved to the United States, where he pursued a career as a Protestant pastor. His ex-comrades were certain that he was able to obtain the visa after providing the authorities with information on the party. See Stavridis, *Ta paraskinia tou KKE*, 178–79.

25. Pentzopoulos, *Balkan Exchange of Minorities*, 96–100.

26. "Resolutions of the Conference," *Inprecor*, May 1, 1924, 262.

27. Tismăneanu, *Stalinism for All Seasons*, 53.

28. "SEKE(K)'s National Council," February 3–8, 1924, in KKE, *Episima keimena*, 1:395–413.

29. "Dimitrov to Chonos," April 5, 1924, in Leontiadis and Bujaska, *To KKE*, 54–55.

30. "Dimitrov to the CC of the SEKE(K)," March 20, 1924, in Leontiadis and Bujaska, *To KKE*, 50–51.

31. "Dimitrov to the CC of the SEKE(K)," April 5, 1924, in Leontiadis and Bujaska, *To KKE*, 52–53.

32. Dagas and Leontiadis, *Komintern kai Makedoniko Zitima*, 57–58.

33. "Resolutions of the Conference," *Inprecor*, April 10, 1924, 224–25; May 1, 1924, 259–62; May 29, 1924, 312–14.

34. "Dimitrov to the CC of the SEKE(K)," April 20, 1924, in Leontiadis and Bujaska, *To KKE*, 58–59.

35. Elefantis, *I epagelia*, 30; Livieratos, *Pantelis Pouliopoulos*, 16–25.

36. Lane, *Biographical Dictionary*, 2:630–31.

37. Noutsos, "Role of the Greek Community," 85–86; Apostolou, *Nikos Zachariadis*, 29.

38. Harris, *Origins of Communism*, 97–98.

39. Stavridis, *Ta paraskinia tou KKE*, 119.

40. Harris, *Origins of Communism*, 105

41. Stavridis, *Ta paraskinia tou KKE*, 118–21; Elefantis, *I epagelia*, 385.

42. McDermott and Agnew, *Comintern*, 47.

43. "Dmitri Manuilsky's Speech on the National and Colonial Session," June 30, 1924, in Fifth Congress of the Communist International, *Abridged Report*, 190–91.

44. Dagas and Leontiadis, *Komintern kai Makedoniko Zitima*, 130–34.

45. "Serafim Maximos, Intervention on the National and Colonial Session," July 1, 1924, in Fifth Congress of the Communist International, *Abridged Report*, 205–6.

46. "Theses and Resolutions Adopted by the V Congress of the Communist International: Resolution on the National Question in Central Europe and the Balkans; I. Macedonia and Thracian Questions," *Inprecor*, September 5, 1924, 683.

47. Georgi Dimitrov, "The VII Conference of the Balkan Communist Federation," *Inprecor*, August 7, 1924, 597–98; "Balkan Communist Federation: The Resolutions of the 7th Communist Conference," *Kommounistiki epitheorisi*, October 1924, 336–40.

48. "Letter of the Presidium of the BCF to the CC of the SEKE," October 10, 1924, in Leontiadis and Bujaska, *To KKE*, 96.

49. "Meeting of the Presidium of the BCF," November 3, 1924, in Leontiadis and Bujaska, *To KKE*, 97–98.

50. "Dimitrov to Chonos," November 6, 1924, in Leontiadis and Bujaska, *To KKE*, 99.

51. Papapanagiotou, *To Makedoniko Zitima*, 67–68; Dagas and Leontiadis, *Komintern kai Makedoniko Zitima*, 66–68.

52. KKE, *To trito ektakto synedrio*.

53. KKE, *To trito ektakto synedrio*, 113–15, 127.

54. *Kokkini simaia*, November 7, 1944.

55. KKE, *To trito ektakto synedrio*, 81–82, 86–88, 108, 128.

56. KKE, *To trito ektakto synedrio*, 132–37; "Pouliopoulos to the Presidium of the BCF and the ECCI," Athens, February 20, 1925, RGASPI, fond 495, opis 173, delo 100, l. 3.

57. Aleksa Djilas, *Contested Country*, 72–73, 173; Haug, *Creating a Socialist Yugoslavia*, 29.

58. Broué, *Histoire de l'internationale Communiste*, 384–85.

59. "Review of the Activities of the Presidium of the Balkan Communist Federation," April 20, 1924, in Leontiadis and Bujaska, *To KKE*, 60–70; Dagas and Leontiadis, *Komintern kai Makedoniko Zitima*, 42; Stankova, *Georgi Dimitrov*, 66; Fišera, *Les peuples Slaves*, 213.

60. Fišera, *Les peuples Slaves*, 213.

61. *La Fédération Balkanique*, July 15, 1924. On *La Fédération Balkanique*, see also Fišera, "Communisme et intégration supranationale," 497; Basciani, "Screditare un sistema," 79.

62. Serge, *Memoirs of a Revolutionary*, 211. The Comitadjis were Bulgarian and Macedonian nationalist insurgents in the Macedonian territories of the Ottoman Empire in the late nineteenth and early twentieth century. Their name comes from the Committee of the IMRO.

63. Ulunian, "Communist Party of Greece," 191.

64. Kondis, "Re-establishment," 151.

65. Eudin and Fisher, *Soviet Russia*, 189–92; Zapantis, *Greek-Soviet Relations*, 140–41.

66. "Memorandum," January 18, 1924, in KKE, *Episima keimena*, 1:391–93.

67. Carr, *History of Soviet Russia*, 17.

68. Kocho-Williams, *Russian and Soviet Diplomacy*, 66–68, 93–94.

69. Stavridis, *Ta paraskinia tou KKE*, 228–30.

70. "Dimitrov to the CC of the SEKE," April 5, 1924, 52–53; "Dimitrov to Chonos," April 9, 1924, in Leontiadis and Bujaska, *To KKE*, 56–57.

71. "Dimitrov to the CC of the SEKE," April 5, 1924, 53.

72. Stavridis, *Ta paraskinia tou KKE*, 306–7.

73. Stavridis, *Ta paraskinia tou KKE*, 232–33; Zapantis, *Greek-Soviet Relations*, 168.

74. Urban, *Moscow*, 19.

75. Fowkes, "To Make the Nation," 207.

3. Becoming Greek Stalinists

1. Bell, *Bulgarian Communist Party*, 25.

2. Avakumović, *History of the Communist Party*, 43; Riddell, *Workers of the World*, 1:421.

3. Stănescu, *Moscova*, 18–19; Tismăneanu, *Stalinism for All Seasons*, 47–51.

4. "Review of the Activities of the Presidium of the Balkan Communist Federation," April 30, 1924, in Leontiadis and Bujaska, *To KKE*, 60–70.

5. KKE, *To trito ektakto synedrio*, 138.

6. Fitzpatrick, *Everyday Stalinism*, 15.

7. "Dimitrov to the CC of the SEKE(K)," November 25, 1924, in Leontiadis and Bujaska, *To KKE*, 112–13.

8. KKE, *To trito ektakto synedrio*, 188–89.

9. KKE, *To trito ektakto synedrio*, 188.

10. "Mihajlov to Dimitrov," Athens, November 1924, RGASPI, fond 509, opis 1, delo 50, ll. 243–47.

11. "Spravka: Andronikos Chaitas," August 17, 1939, RGASPI, fond 495, opis 207, delo 67, ll. 5, 7.

12. McDermott and Agnew, *Comintern*, 42.

13. Serge, *Memoirs of a Revolutionary*, 207.

14. Fayet, "Paul Levi," 107; Studer, *Transnational World*, 23.

15. Grišina, "I Proti fasi tis drastiriotitas," 181.

16. Karpozilos, "Ektos orion," chapter "Refugee Communism."

17. Stavridis, *Ta paraskinia tou KKE*, 303–6.

18. "Personal Files of Members of the Communist Party of Greece: Konstantin Karakozov," August 14, 1963, RGASPI, fond 495, opis 207, delo 339, l. 2.

19. Stavridis, *Ta paraskinia tou KKE*, 315.

20. Stalin, *Works*, 7:135–54.

21. Ulunian, "Communist Party of Greece," 190.

22. "Personal Files of Members of the Communist Party of Greece: Yani Tsatsakos," January 7, 1925, RGASPI, fond 495, opis 207, delo 176, l. 2.

23. Ulunian, "Communist Party of Greece," 190; Ter Minassian, "Le Komintern," 64–65.

24. Ter Minassian, "Le Komintern," 64–65.

25. Nefeloudis, *Martyries*, 194.

26. "Belov to Makenkov," August 26, 1937, RGASPI, fond 495, opis 207, delo 630, l. 72; "Shatsky to Burminstrenko," October 25, 1937, RGASPI, fond 495, opis 207, delo 630, l. 93.

27. "Dimitrov to Karakozov and Ivanova," September 2, 1926, in Leontiadis and Bujaska, *To KKE*, 154–56.

28. Kousoulas, *Revolution and Defeat*, 18; Elefantis, *I epagelia*, 60.

29. Katsoulis, *Istoria*, 2:155–57.

30. Georgantidis and Nikolakopoulos, "I exelixi tis eklogikis dinamis," 452–53; Mavrogordatos, *Stillborn Republic*, 35.

31. Elefantis, *I epagelia*, 304; Georgantidis and Nikolakopoulos, "I exelixi tis eklogikis dinamis," 455; Mavrogordatos, *Stillborn Republic*, 251, 262–63.

32. "The Electoral Results," *Makedonika nea*, October 27, 1925.

33. Elefantis, *I epagelia*, 69–73.

34. Elefantis, *I epagelia*, 71; Livieratos, *Pantelis Pouliopoulos*, 30–34.

35. Pouliopoulos, *Dialechta erga*, 81, 85, 88.

36. Ilicak, "Jewish Socialism," 124. Also see Dumont, "Jewish, Socialist and Ottoman Organization," 53–54.

37. "Dimitrov to Ivan Chonos," March 20, 1924, in Leontiadis and Bujaska, *To KKE*, 48.

38. "Dimitrov to Chonos," March 20, 1924, in Leontiadis and Bujaska, *To KKE*, 48–49.

39. Thorpe, "Stalinism and British Politics," 626.

40. Pouliopoulos, *Dialechta erga*, 86.

41. Elefantis, *I epagelia*, 368; Marantzidis, "Greek Intellectuals," 84.

42. Elefantis, *I epagelia*, 113–21; Farakos, *B' Pagosmios Polemos*, 25–27.

43. Kotkin, *Stalin*, 532, 555; Carr, *History of Soviet Russia*, 19.

44. "Theses and Resolutions Adopted at the VI Plenum of the Enlarged ECCI, February 17–March 15," *Inprecor*, May 13, 1926, 613.

45. Fišera, "La dimension régionale," 91; Fišera, *Les peuples Slaves*, 208.

46. "Dimitrov Speech in the Enlarged Plenum of the ECBCF," April 24, 1925, in Leontiadis and Bujaska, *To KKE*, 133–35.

47. Urban, *Moscow*, 19.

48. "Resolution of the Central Committee of KKE and OKNE," October 27, 1926, in KKE, *Episima keimena*, 2:159–62; KKE, *Dokimio istorias tou KKE*, 178–79; Ulunian, "Communist Party of Greece," 195–96.

49. Cohen, *Bukharin*, 216–17.

50. "Resolution of the Politburo," September 25, 1927, in KKE, *Episima keimena*, 2:437–38; Kousoulas, *Revolution and Defeat*, 26; Elefantis, *I epagelia*, 75–76.

51. "The Plenum of the Central Committee of the KKE," February 15–18, 1928, in KKE, *Episima keimena*, 2:508–9.

52. Elefantis, *I epagelia*, 76; Stinas, *Anamniseis*, 1:127–28; Dagas, "Kommounistiko Komma Ellados," 159.

53. Dagas, "Kommounistiko Komma Ellados," 194.

54. "Konstantinidis to KKE," June 1, 1928, RGASPI, fond 495, opis 207, delo 589, ll. 27–28.

55. "Dimitrov to Mitskevitch," March 12, 1927, in Leontiadis and Bujaska, *To KKE*, 171. On Gorkić, see Gužvica, "Retrospective Lessons," 35.

56. "Dimitrov to Mitskevitch," February 26, 1927, in Leontiadis and Bujaska, *To KKE*, 169–70.

57. "Dimitrov to the Balkan Secretariat of the ECCI," October 26, 1927, in Leontiadis and Bujaska, *To KKE*, 193.

58. Bohumir Šmeral, "The Struggle in the Communist Party of Greece against the Liquidatory Tendencies of the Right Wing," *Inprecor*, October 9, 1927, 1189–90; *Rizospastis*, October 16, 1927.

59. "Dimitrov to the Politburo of the KKE," October 28, 1927, in Leontiadis and Bujaska, *To KKE*, 194.

60. "Dimitrov to the Balkan Secretariat of the ECCI," December 1, 1927, in Leontiadis and Bujaska, *To KKE*, 199.

61. Carr, *History of Soviet Russia*, 228–32; Avakumović, *History of the Communist Party*, 79, 84; Swain, "Tito and the Twilight," 206–7; Gužvica, "Learning Leninism," 21–22.

62. "Dimitrov to the Balkan Secretariat of the ECCI," January 30, 1928, in Leontiadis and Bujaska, *To KKE*, 201.

63. Nikolai Bukharin, "The International Situation and the Tasks of the Comintern," *Inprecor*, July 30, 1928, 739.

64. "Dimitrov to the Balkan Secretariat of the ECCI," January 30, 1928, in Leontiadis and Bujaska, *To KKE*, 201.

65. Georgantidis and Nikolakopoulos, "I exelixi tis eklogikis dinamis," 453.

66. "Resolution on the Political Activities of the Party, 4th Congress of the KKE(ETKD)," December 10–15, 1928, in KKE, *Episima keimena*, 2:569.

67. Katsoulis, *Istoria*, 3:111; Alivizatos, *I politiki thesmi se krisi*, 359, 390–91, 397–98.

68. "Sixth World Congress of the Communist International, Opening Session 17 July 1928," *Inprecor*, July 25, 1928, 706. Kahan, "Contribution," 185; "Sixth World Congress of the Communist International, Fourth Session, July 19, 1928," *Inprecor*, August 1, 1928, 750.

69. "Schüller's Report on the Activity of the Young Communist International: Third Session, 6th World Congress of the Comintern, July 19, 1928," *Inprecor*, August 1, 1928, 747.

70. "Kolarov's Intervention, Seventh Session, 6th World Congress of the Comintern, July 24, 1928," *Inprecor*, August 3, 1928, 785.

71. "Resolution of the Balkan Secretariat of the ECCI on the KKE Activities," September 13, 1928, in Leontiadis and Bujaska, *To KKE*, 214.

72. "Syfneios [Chaitas] Intervention, Eighth Session, 6th World Congress of the Comintern, July 25, 1928," *Inprecor*, August 8, 1928, 817.

73. "Petrulescu's [Holostenko] Intervention, Tenth Session, 6th World Congress of the Comintern, July 26, 1928," *Inprecor*, August 11, 1928, 854.

74. Dimitrov, *Selected Works*, 1:314.

75. Dimitrov, *Selected Works*, 1:317.

76. Fišera, *Les peuples Slaves*, 212; Ter Minassian, "Le Komintern," 62–63; Dagas, "Kommounistiko Komma Ellados," 161.

77. Stankova, *Georgi Dimitrov*, 88.

78. "Georgi Dimitrov's Report in the 2nd Enlarged Plenum of the CC of the Bulgarian Communist Party," August 19, 1929, in Leontiadis and Bujaska, *To KKE*, 225–26.

79. Stankova, *Georgi Dimitrov*, 83, 88–91.

80. "Georgi Dimitrov's Report," 225–26.

81. "Dimitrov to Mihajlov," April 20, 1929, in Leontiadis and Bujaska, *To KKE*, 222.

82. "Dimitrov to Mihajlov," May 5, 1929, in Leontiadis and Bujaska, *To KKE*, 223.

83. The new politburo members were Piliotis, Paparigas, and Karagiannis. "The 4th Congress of the KKE(ETKD)," December 10–15, 1928, in KKE, *Episima keimena*, 2:559.

84. Broué, *Histoire de l'international Communiste*, 483–84; Wolikow, "Aux origines," 306–8.

85. Stalin, *Works*, 6:294; Cohen, *Bukharin*, 292–93, 329–30; Broué, *Histoire de l'international Communiste*, 381, 493.

86. Stalin, *Works*, 6:294; Cohen, *Bukharin*, 329–30.

87. Kousoulas, *Revolution and Defeat*, 30; Liakos, *Ergasia kai politiki*, 145.

88. "Open Letter of the Politburo," November 26, 1929, in KKE, *Episima keimena*, 3:120; "Third Plenum of the CC," January 28–31, 1930, in KKE, *Episima keimena*, 3:148.

89. "The 2nd Plenum of the CC," June 10–15, 1929, in KKE, *Episima keimena*, 3:36–38.

90. Stinas, *Anamniseis*, 1:146–47.

91. Stinas, *Anamniseis*, 1:146–47.

92. "Vasil Kolarov's Intervention, ECCI Meeting," March 26, 1930, RGASPI, fond 495, opis 3, delo 210, ll. 26–27.

93. "Milan Gorkić's (Iosip Čižinský) Intervention, ECCI Meeting, March 26, 1930," RGASPI, fond 495, opis 3, delo 210, ll. 28–30; Gužvica, "Learning Leninism," 24–25.

94. *Rizospastis*, March 30, 1930.

95. Elefantis, *I epagelia*, 95–96; Tsintzilonis, *OKNE 1922–1943*, 162.

96. "Khitarov's Concluding Speech, Plenary Session of the EC of the YCI, November–December 1929," *Inprecor*, March 21, 1930, 293.

97. "Resolution of the Politburo," May 24, 1930, in KKE, *Episima keimena*, 3:188–89.

98. *Rizospastis*, August 1, 1931; *Rizospastis*, August 17, 1931.

99. Stinas, *Anamniseis*, 1:148–49; Kousoulas, *Revolution and Defeat*, 32; Nefeloudis, *Stis piges tis kakodaimonias*, 58.

100. Kousoulas, *Revolution and Defeat*, 34.

101. "Resolution of the Politburo," December 13, 1930, in KKE, *Episima keimena*, 3:218–19; "Manifesto of the Politburo," January 9, 1931, in KKE, *Episima keimena*, 3:222; "Manifesto of the Politburo," January 28, 1931, in KKE, *Episima keimena*, 3:223–25.

102. Ulunian, "Communist Party of Greece," 198; Nefeloudis, *Stis piges tis kakodaimonias*, 58–61; Katsoulis, *Istoria*, 3:115–36; Elefantis, *I epagelia*, 98–103; Stinas, *Anamniseis*, 1:149–57; Koutsoukalis, *I defteri dekaetia*, 24–35.

103. McDermott and Agnew, *Comintern*, 83; Stankova, *Georgi Dimitrov*, 96–97.

104. Avakumović, *History of the Communist Party*, 90; Bataković, "Communist Party of Yugoslavia," 63; Cicak, "Communist Party of Yugoslavia," 230, 232–33; Gužvica, "Learning Leninism," 23.

105. US Senate Committee on the Judiciary, *Yugoslav Communism*, 41–43; Cicak, "Communist Party of Yugoslavia," 178–85; Swain, "Tito and the Twilight," 206–7; Banac, *With Stalin against Tito*, 64.

106. "Dimitrov to the CC of the BKP," September 25, 1930; "Dimitrov to the Balkan Secretariat of the ECCI," September 29, 1930, in Leontiadis and Bujaska, *To KKE*, 236–37.

107. *Rizospastis*, February 1, 1931.

108. *Rizospastis*, February 24, 1931.

109. *Rizospastis*, March 4, 1931.

110. Ulunian, "Communist Party of Greece," 198.

111. "Personal File of Greek Communists: Ochallis (Markovitis) Konstantin Vasilyevich," February 17, 1953, RGASPI, fond 495, opis 207, delo 630, ll. 4–5. On this story, also see Gritzonas, *Kokkinoi drapetes*, 21–22.

112. Ulunian, "Communist Party of Greece," 198.

113. "Siantos, Personal File," April 18, 1944, RGASPI, fond 82, opis 2, delo 1186, ll. 17–18; "Siantos Informative Report," April 18, 1944, RGASPI, fond 495, opis 207, delo 149, ll. 16–17.

114. *Neos rizospastis*, September 10, 193; Kousoulas, *Revolution and Defeat*, 37.

115. *Neos rizospastis*, November 1–3, 1931.

116. "Zachariadis Dossier," November 17, 1940, in Papadatos, *Akros aporrito*, 540–41; "Konstantinidis Georgy, Personal Dossier," RGASPI, fond 495, opis 207, delo 589, l. 19; Antaios, *N. Zachariadis*, 512.

117. "Giannis Ioannidis, Informative Report," June 2, 1955, RGASPI, fond 495, opis 207, delo 8, ll. 6–7.

118. "ECCI to the KKE," December 4, 1931, RGASPI, fond 495, opis 69, delo 128, ll. 310-13.

119. Studer, "Stalinization," 50.

120. Farakos, B' Pagosmios Polemos, 27-28.

121. "Zachariadis Dossier," 540-41; Lazitch and Drachkovitch, Biographical Dictionary, xxviii; Ulunian, "Communist Party of Greece," 190; Antaios, N. Zachariadis, 150-54; Apostolou, Nikos Zachariadis, 29-30.

122. Daniilidis, O Polydoros thimatai, 60; Apostolou, Nikos Zachariadis, 46-49.

123. Studer, Transnational World, 31.

124. "From the Editor: Nikos Zachariadis," Kommounistiki epitheorisi, November 6, 1942.

125. Nefeloudis, Documento, 52-57.

126. Rees, "Leader Cults," 3; Laporte and Morgan, "Kings among Their Subjects?," 125.

127. "The Fifth Plenum of the CC," December 1932, in KKE, Episima keimena, 3:473; "The Sixth Plenum of the CC," January 1934, in KKE, Episima keimena, 4:33.

128. Elefantis, I epagelia, 386; Marantzidis, "Greek Intellectuals," 83-84.

129. Ter Minassian, "Le Komintern," 64; Nefeloudis, Martyries, 194.

130. "Traicho Kostov's Report in the Balkan Secretariat of the ECCI," March 28, 1934, in Leontiadis and Bujaska, To KKE, 244.

131. "KKE, Membership Inventory in August 1935," October 23, 1935, RGASPI, fond 495, opis 11, delo 83.

132. Papathanasiou, "To Kommounistiko Komma," 80-81. According to Vladimir Tismăneanu, the Romanian Party had 1,200 members at that time. Tismăneanu, Stalinism for All Seasons, 58.

133. "Zachariadis's Notes," July 29, 1973, in Antaios, N. Zachariadis, 518-19.

134. Georgantidis and Nikolakopoulos, "I exelixi tis eklogikis dinamis," 453-54; Mavrogordatos, Stillborn Republic, 41-52.

135. Elefantis, I epagelia, 316-18; Mavrogordatos, Stillborn Republic, 221-25.

136. Stankova, Georgi Dimitrov, 116; Vatrin, "Evolution of the Comintern," 192.

137. "Directives of the Political Secretariat of the ECCI to the KKE," July 1934, RGASPI, fond 495, opis 3, delo 419, ll. 5-7.

138. Rizospastis, August 17, 1934.

139. Rizospastis, September 9, 1934.

140. Rizospastis, October 6, 1934.

141. "Decision of the CC," March 23, 1935, in KKE, Episima keimena, 4:166.

142. Gužvica, "Learning Leninism," 27.

143. Antaios, N. Zachariadis, 519; Nefeloudis, Martyries, 203-5.

144. "The 6th Congress of the KKE(ETKD)," December 1935, in KKE, Episima keimena, 4:296-97.

145. Slijepčević, Macedonian Question, 205.

146. Avakumović, History of the Communist Party, 117.

147. Mazower, Governing the World, 168.

148. Jacobson, Soviet Union Entered World Politics, 203, 280; Jacobson, "Soviet Union and Versailles," 460.

149. Dunn, "Maksim Litvinov," 227; Jacobson, "Soviet Union and Versailles," 465.

150. Haslam, *Soviet Union*, 53.

151. Carr, *Twilight of the Comintern*, 113–14.

152. Haslam, *Soviet Union*, 15.

153. Haslam, *Soviet Union*, 4, 51.

154. "G. Dimitrov's Report on the Fascist offensive and the Tasks of the Communist International," August 2, 1935, in *VII Congress*, 124–93.

155. "Ercoli's [Togliati] Report on the Preparations for Imperialist War and the Tasks of the Communist International," August 13, 1935, in *VII Congress*, 393.

156. Aganson, "Versailles Order," 198.

157. Kahan, "Communist International," 178; KKE, *Dokimio istorias tou KKE*, 280.

158. Kousoulas, *Revolution and Defeat*, 109–11; Mavrogordatos, *Stillborn Republic*, 48–54; KKE, *Dokimio istorias tou KKE*, 293–94; Koliopoulos and Veremis, *Greece*, 103.

159. Mavrogordatos, *Stillborn Republic*, 48–54.

160. Anastasiadis et al., *To ergatiko syndikalistiko kinima*, 109–20.

161. "EC of MOPR to the European Representative Bureau," November 23, 1936, in Papadatos, *Akros aporrito*, 544.

162. Linardatos, "Antistassi sti diktatoria," 96.

163. "Arrestation d'un dirigeant du Parti Communiste de Grèce," *L'Humanité*, September 20, 1936; "Nikos Zachariadis's Autobiography," August 15, 1946, in Petropoulos, *Nikos Zachariadis*, 25.

164. The MOPR was established by the Comintern in 1922 to "render material and moral aid to all captives of capitalism in prison." The organization provided legal aid and financial assistance for the families of those convicted, and helped create press campaigns. See Elbaz and Israël, "L'invention du droit," 32. The Association Juridique Internationale was a satellite organization of the MOPR. It was officially created in December 1929 "to struggle against bourgeois justice." See Israël, "Cause Lawyering," 148–49.

165. "Wilhelm Pieck to Yelena Stasova," September 23, 1936, in Papadatos, *Akros aporrito*, 542–43. Also see Levy, *Ana Pauker*, 50–54.

166. Israël, "Cause Lawyering," 151–52.

167. "Being in Athens the Son of Moro Tzaferi Talks about the Trials That Made His Father a Great Lawyer," *Akropolis*, December 16, 1936.

168. "Pour sauver Zachariadis," *Le populaire*, December 15, 1936; "Il faut sauver Zachariadis," *L'Humanité*, December 21, 1936; "Melchiorre Vanni to Togliatti and Stasova," December 23, 1936, in Papadatos, *Akros aporrito*, 548–50.

169. "La condamnation de Nikos Zachariadis n'est qu'un épisode de la terreur fasciste," *L'Humanité*, January 1, 1937; "Chaitas to Valecki," February 14, 1937, in Papadatos, *Akros aporrito*, 552–54.

170. Getty and Naumov, *Road to Terror*, 1; Ellman, "Soviet Repression Statistics," 1162–63.

171. Nefeloudis, *Documento*, 27–30, 230–31; Markovitis, *Ochi, den eimai exthros*, 221–23, 234–35, 240–60.

172. "Central Committee of the CPSU, August 26, 1937," RGASPI, fond 495, opis 207, delo 630, ll. 72–76; "ORPO to the Krasnodar Committee of the CPSU(b)," RGASPI, fond 495, opis 207, delo 630, ll. 96–105; Agtzidis, "Persecution of the Pontic Greeks," 374; Agtzidis, *Paraefxeinios diaspora*, 471; Nefeloudis, *Documento*, 27–30; Markovitis, *Ochi, den eimai exthros*, 271.

173. Almost four hundred Greeks and Cypriots volunteers traveled from several different places to Spain to fight on the republican side. See Pantelakis, *Los buenos antifascistas*, 243.

174. Karpozilos, "Ellinikou Laikou Metopou," 38–39. Another Greek Communist network was created in Marseille and received support from the Comité Balkanique de France in Paris.

175. Gužvica, "Learning Leninism," 99–102.

176. Kouzinopoulos, *Georgi Dimitrov*, 64–65; Fleischer, *Stema kai svastika*, 1:133–41; Farakos, *B'Pagosmios Polemos*, 51–53, 92–96; Papathanasiou, "To Kommounistiko Komma," 82; Karpozilos, "Ellinikou Laikou Metopou," 46–47.

4. Greek Dilemmas

1. Courtois, *Le PCF dans la guerre*, 53.

2. Banac, *Diary of Georgi Dimitrov*, 115–17.

3. Amendola, *Storia del Partito Comunista Italiano*, 450; Urban, *Moscow*, 151.

4. *L'Humanité*, August 26, 1939.

5. Banac, *Diary of Georgi Dimitrov*, 114.

6. Courtois, *Le PCF dans la guerre*, 44.

7. Beckett, *Enemy Within*, 90.

8. Gotovitch, "Histoire," 26; Lebedeva and Narinski, *I Kommounistiki Diethnis*, 9.

9. "ECCI May Day Manifesto of 1939," in Degras, *Communist International*, 3:438; Luza, "Communist Party of Czechoslovakia," 565.

10. Luza, "Communist Party of Czechoslovakia," 567.

11. Kudrna, "Podivní Vstenectví."

12. Banac, *Diary of Georgi Dimitrov*, 117.

13. Amendola, *Storia del Partito Comunista Italiano*, 450–53; Courtois, *Le PCF dans la guerre*, 59, 88–89; Beckett, *Enemy Within*, 93–97; Donald Sassoon, "Rise and Fall," 141; Lebedeva and Narinski, *I Kommounistiki Diethnis*, 17.

14. Swain, *Tito*, 26.

15. Haug, *Creating a Socialist Yugoslavia*, 53–55.

16. "KPJ Manifesto on the Outbreak of the Imperialist War," September 1939, in Clissold, *Yugoslavia*, 115.

17. Lazitch, *Tito et la Révolution Yugoslave*, 43.

18. Oren, *Bulgarian Communism*, 146; Bell, *Bulgarian Communist Party*, 55.

19. Tismăneanu, *Stalinism for All Seasons*, 80; Ionescu, *Communismul în România*, 87.

20. Ioannidis, *Anamniseis*, 63–64; Fleischer, *Stemma kai svastika*, 1:137.

21. Fleischer, *Stemma kai svastika*, 1:135.

22. "Manifesto of the CC," April 20, 1940, in KKE, *Episima keimena*, 4:487.

23. "Open Letter of the Secretary General of the KKE, Nikos Zachariadis," October 31, 1940, in KKE, *Episima keimena*, 5:9–10.

24. Firsov, Klehr, and Haynes, *Secret Cables*, 177–78.

25. Papapanagiotou, *To Kommounistiko Komma Elladas*, 10.

26. Ulunian, "Communist Party of Greece," 200.

27. Ulunian, "Communist Party of Greece," 201.

28. Papathanasiou, "To Kommounistiko Komma," 87.

29. "The Three Letters of Nikos Zachariadis," *Rizospastis*, October 29, 2011.

30. "Presidium of the ECCI to the KKE," January 10, 1941, in Farakos, *Aris Velouchiotis*, 191–96.

31. On Zachariadis's letters, see Smith, "Zachariadis's First Open Letter"; Fleischer, *Stemma kai svastika*, 1:137–39; Farakos, *B' Pagosmios Polemos*, 64–65; Papathanassiou, "To Kommounistiko Komma," 86–89.

32. Dagas, "Kommounistiko Komma Ellados," 193.

33. Firsov, Klehr, and Haynes, *Secret Cables*, 179; Lebedeva and Narinski, *I Kommounistiki Diethnis*, 32–33.

34. Banac, *Diary of Georgi Dimitrov*, 154–55.

35. Firsov, Klehr, and Haynes, *Secret Cables*, 183; Banac, *Diary of Georgi Dimitrov*, 155; Dallin and Firsov, *Dimitrov and Stalin*, 186.

36. Dallin and Firsov, *Dimitrov and Stalin*, 184.

37. "Manifest of the CC of the KKE," May 3, 1941, in KKE, *Episima keimena*, 5:29–34.

38. Mazower, *Inside Hitler's Greece*, 103.

39. Kousoulas, *Revolution and Defeat*, 148; KKE, *Dokimio istorias tou KKE*, 380, 387.

40. Lebedeva and Narinski, *I Kommounistiki Diethnis*, 87.

41. "Dimitrov to Tito," June 30, 1941, RGASPI, fond 495, opis 184, delo 11; Lebedeva and Narinski, *I Kommounistiki Diethnis*, 90.

42. "6th Plenum of the CC of the KKE," July 1, 1941, in KKE, *Episima keimena*, 5:35–40.

43. "The Founding of the National Liberation Front (EAM)," September 27, 1941, in KKE, *Episima keimena*, 5:54–56.

44. Banac, *Diary of Georgi Dimitrov*, 203.

45. Urban, *Moscow*, 157; Lebedeva and Narinski, *I Kommounistiki Diethnis*, 117.

46. "6th Plenum," 5:40.

47. "Resolution of the 8th Plenum of the CC," January 22, 1942, in KKE, *Episima keimena*, 5:67–68.

48. Farakos, *O ELAS kai I exousia*, 1:56–57.

49. "Giorgos Siantos to Ioannidis," January 5, 1942, in Farakos, *Aris Velouchiotis*, 213.

50. Chatzianastasiou, *Antartes kai kapetanii*, 28.

51. Dimitrov, *Stalin's Cold War*, 50; Lebedeva and Narinski, *I Kommounistiki Diethnis*, 90.

52. Lebedeva and Narinski, *I Kommounistiki Diethnis*, 96.

53. "The Heroical Uprising of Drama, December 1941," *Rizospastis*, December 13, 2015.

54. Iatrides, "I politikopiisi," 268.

55. Farakos, *O ELAS kai I exousia*, 1:47–48, 2:54–56; Farakos, *B' Pagosmios Polemos*, 102.

56. Woodhouse, *Something Ventured*, 57–58.

57. Iatrides, *Revolt in Athens*, 36–41; Papastratis, *British Policy*, 104–12.

58. "Plyshevsky and Georgiev to G. Dimitrov," March 26, 1943 (RGASPI, fond 495, opis 74, delo 174), in Konstantakopoulos, Patelis, and Materi, *Fakelos ELLAS*, 84–86.

59. Farakos, *B' Pagosmios Polemos*, 88.

60. Ulunian, "Communist Party of Greece," 202.

61. "Ambassador Leeper to FO," April 11, 1944, AOA, FO 371/43685/4.

62. Roussos, *I megali pentaetia*, 1:453–54; Iatrides, "Revolution or Self-Defense?," 10; Nation, "Balkan Union?," 131, 141; Farakos, *B' Pagosmios Polemos*, 117–18; Farakos, *O ELAS kai I exousia*, 1:347–48; Papathanassiou, "To Kommounistiko Komma," 125–27.

63. Farakos, *B' Pagosmios Polemos*, 81.

64. "On the Dissolution of the Communist International," May 1943, in KKE, *Episima keimena*, 5:328, 333.

65. Farakos, *B' Pagosmios Polemos*, 81–82; Chatzis, *I nikifora epanastasi*, 2:37; Ioannidis, *Anamniseis*, 472; Mazower, *Inside Hitler's Greece*, 268.

66. "Zografos to Dimitrov," March 14, 1943, in Konstantakopoulos, Patelis, and Materi, *Fakelos ELLAS*, 82–83.

67. "Plyshevsky and Georgiev to Dimitrov," March 26, 1943, in Konstantakopoulos, Patelis and Materi, *Fakelos ELLAS*, 86.

68. Banac, *Diary of Georgi Dimitrov*, 291–92.

69. "Ambassador Leeper to FO," December 27, 1943, AOA, FO 371/37210/R1379b.

70. Lukač, "I sinergasia," 480; Kofos, "I Valkaniki diastasi," 427–29.

71. Nation, "Balkan Union?," 125; Gibianskii, "Federative Projects," 45.

72. Kofos, "I Valkaniki diastasi," 428.

73. Clissold, *Yugoslavia*, 47.

74. "Tzimas Report on the Situation in Greece," June 29, 1944, RGASPI, fond 495, opis 74, delo 176, ll. 53–59. Also see Sfetas, "Autonomist Movements"; Gibianskii, "Federative Projects," 50; Ioannidis, *Anamniseis*, 135; Haug, *Creating a Socialist Yugoslavia*, 106–8.

75. Neshovich, "Correspondence," 275.

76. Kofos, "I Valkaniki diastasi," 470–71.

77. Neshovich, "Correspondence," 275.

78. Farakos, *O ELAS kai I exousia*, 1:127, 131; Farakos, *Aris Velouchiotis*, 268–70; Rossos, "Incompatible Allies," 48–49; Kofos, "I Valkaniki diastasi," 430–38.

79. "Fitin to Dimitrov," August 16, 1944, in Konstantakopoulos, Patelis, and Materi, *Fakelos ELLAS*, 145; Lukač, "I sinergasia," 484; Neshovich, "Correspondence," 272–73; Mastny, *Russia's Road*, 89.

80. Farakos, *B' Pagosmios Polemos*, 106.

81. "Prime Minister Tsouderos to the Ankara Greek Ambassador Rafail," February 16, 1942, in Tsouderos, *Istoriko archeio*, A:554.

82. "Kolarov and Dimitrov to the Central Committee of the BKP," RGASPI, fond 495, opis 184, delo 11, ll. 125–26. Also see Oren, *Bulgarian Communism*, 156–58; Bell, *Bulgarian Communist Party*, 55.

83. "Prime Minister Tsouderos to the Moscow Greek Ambassador Pipinelis," February 12, 1942, in Tsouderos, *Istoriko archeio*, A:545–46.

84. Roberts, *Stalin's Wars*, 220.

85. Iatrides, *Ambassador MacVeagh Reports*, 389.

86. "British Embassy in Moscow to FO," December 30, 1943, AOA, FO 371/43674/R21. Also see Esche, "I politiki tis ESSD," 555–56.

87. "Leeper to FO," December 27, 1943, AOA, FO 371/37210/1379b; "Leeper to FO," January 5, 1944, AOA, FO 371/43674/R258.

88. Iatrides, *Ambassador MacVeagh Reports*, 422.

89. "FO to British Embassy Moscow," December 22, 1943, AOA, FO 371/37210/R13498; "Greek Ambassador Politis to Molotov," December 23, 1943, in Papadatos, *Akros aporrito*, 138–42; "FO to British Embassy Moscow," December 28, 1943, AOA, FO 371/37210/R13724.

90. "Dekanozov to Balfour," January 3, 1944, in Papadatos, *Akros aporrito*, 144.

91. "Ambassador Agnidis to Prime Minister Tsouderos," March 18, 1944, in Tsouderos, *Istoriko archeio*, C2:1095; "The Ambassador in the Soviet Union (Harriman) to the Secretary of State," FRUS, 1944, 84; "The Ambassador to the Greek Government in Exile (MacVeagh) to the Secretary of State," January 5, 1944, FRUS, 1944, 85–86.

92. "Ambassador Leeper to FO," January 6, 1944, AOA, FO 371/43674/R402.

93. "The 10th Plenum of the Central Committee of the KKE," January 20, 1944, in KKE, *Episima keimena*, 5:209. Also see Mazower, *Inside Hitler's Greece*, 291–92.

94. Iatrides, *Revolt in Athens*, 49–56; Papastratis, *British Policy*, 165–72.

95. "FO to Ambassador Leeper," April 21, 1944, AOA, FO 371/43686/R26; "FO to Ambassador Clark Kerr," April 22, 1944, AOA, FO 371/43702/R6356.

96. "Ambassador Politis to Prime Minister Tsouderos," April 8, 1944, in Tsouderos, *Istoriko archeio*, C2:1167; "Ambassador Leeper to FO," April 11, 1944, AOA, FO 371/43701/R5848; "The Ambassador to the Greek Government in Exile (MacVeagh) to the Secretary of State," April 11, 1944, FRUS, 1944, 95.

97. Iatrides, *Ambassador MacVeagh Reports*, 503; "Leeper to London," April 5, 1944, AOA, FO 371/43685/2.

98. "FO to Ambassador Leeper," April 18, 1944, AOA, FO 371/43685/11.

99. "Molotov to Churchill," April 22, 1944, PRO-FO 371/43686/R6642; "Churchill to Molotov," April 23, 1944, AOA, FO 371/43686/38.

100. "Leeper to FO," May 1, 1944, AOA, FO 371/43686/R7003; "Leeper to FO," May 8, 1944, AOA, FO 371/43686/R7332; "Leeper to FO," June 19, 1944, AOA, FO 371/43688/R9652; "Leeper to FO," July 9, 1944, AOA, FO 371/43689/R 10739; "Manuilsky's Report on the Formation of the New Greek Government of Papandreou, June 9, 1944," June 21, 1944, RGASPI, fond 82, opis 2, delo 1186, ll. 19–30. Also see Xydis, *Greece and the Great Powers*, 34.

101. Barker, "Some Factors," 48.

102. Woodhouse, *Struggle for Greece*, 77; "Ambassador MacVeagh to Roosevelt," March 17, 1944, in Iatrides, *Ambassador MacVeagh Reports*, 473; Stavrakis, *Moscow and Greek Communism*, 17.

103. "The Comintern to Tito," March 5, 1942, and "Tito Replies to the Comintern," March 9, 1942, in Clissold, *Yugoslavia*, 145–46; Banac, *Diary of Georgy Dimitrov*, 234; Swain, *Tito*, 50; Piffer, "Stalin," 422–26.

104. "Tito to the Comintern," September 9, 1942, in Clissold, *Yugoslavia*, 150.

105. Banac, *Diary of Georgi Dimitrov*, 337; Gibianskii, "Federative Projects," 52; Piffer, "Stalin," 425, 434.

106. Banac, *Diary of Georgi Dimitrov*, 298–99; Piffer, "Stalin," 430, 433.

107. "Manuilsky's Report on Greece: General Information on the Resistance Movement," June 3, 1944, RGASPI, fond 82, opis 2, delo 1186, l. 10. Also see Stavrakis, *Moscow and Greek Communism*, 17; Ioannidis, *Anamniseis*, 244–45; Farakos, *B' Pagosmios Polemos*, 123.

108. Papapanagiotou, *To Kommounistiko Komma Elladas*, 83.

109. "Dimitrov to Molotov," April 15, 1944, RGASPI, fond 495, opis 74, delo 599, ll. 50–52.

110. Reynolds and Pechatnov, *Kremlin Letters*, 413–14, 437–38.

111. "Eden to Ambassador Clark Kerr," May 5, 1944, AOA, FO 371/43686/R7214; "Ambassador Clark Kerr to FO," May 6, 1944, AOA, FO 371/43868/R7274.

112. "Tele [no number] Harriman to President," Caserta, May 29, 1944, FDRPL, Roosevelt Papers, 051 Balkans: "Spheres of Influence, 5/19–6/30/44."

113. Reynolds and Pechatnov, *Kremlin Letters*, 413–14.

114. Hull, *Memoirs*, 2:1451.

115. "Churchill to Roosevelt," May 31, 1944, FRUS, 1944, 115.

116. "Churchill to Roosevelt," June 22, 1944, FRUS, 1944, 127.

117. Iatrides, *Ambassador MacVeagh Reports*, 533.

118. Papastratis, *British Policy*, 177–78; Mazower, *Inside Hitler's Greece*, 318.

119. "Siantos to Tzimas," June 12, 1944, RGASPI, fond 495, opis 74, delo 176, ll. 207–20; "Siantos to Tzimas," June 25, 1944, RGASPI, fond 495, opis 74, delo 176, ll. 207–20.

120. "Report on the National Liberation Movement in Greece," June 29, 1944, RGASPI, fond 495, opis 74, delo 176, l. 175; "Tzimas's Report on the Situation in Greece," June 29, 1944, RGASPI, fond 495, opis 74, delo 176, ll. 54, 58.

121. "Plyshevsky to Baskakov," June 3, 1944, RGASPI, fond 82, opis 2, delo 1186, l. 3.

122. Iatrides, *Ambassador MacVeagh Reports*, 552.

123. Reynolds and Pechatnov, *Kremlin Letters*, 438–39, 441.

124. Woodward, *British Foreign Policy*, 3:123; Kuniholm, *Origins of the Cold War*, 105.

125. Roussos, *I megali pentaetia*, 2:179–89; Iatrides, *Revolt in Athens*, 65–74, 294–303; Stavrakis, *Moscow and Greek Communism*, 28–29; Baerentzen, "I afixi," 567.

126. "The Chargé Near the Greek Government in Exile (Shantz) to the Secretary of State," July 8, 1944, FRUS, 1944, 129; "Ambassador Kerr to Molotov,"

July 27, 1944, in Papadatos, *Akros aporrito*, 154–55. Also see Baerentzen, "I afixi," 562–67.

127. "Red Army Mission in Greece," *Times* (UK), August 1, 1944; Macrakis, "Russian Mission," 391.

128. "Leeper to FO," July 29, 1944, AOA, FO 371/43690/R11832; "Extract from War Cabinet Conclusions," July 30, 1944, AOA, FO 371/43772/R11847; "Eden to Ambassador Clark Kerr," August 3, 1944, PRO-FO 371/43772/R12090; Goulter-Zervoudakis, "Politization of Intelligence," 183–84.

129. Iatrides, "Revolution or Self-Defense?," 12.

130. "Resolution of the CC of the KKE," August 3, 1944, in KKE, *Episima keimena*, 5:218–21.

131. "The Politburo of the KKE to Stalin, Molotov, Dimitrov, Baranov," August 10, 1944, RGASPI, fond 82, opis 2, delo 1187, l. 1; "The Politburo of the KKE to Molotov, Dimitrov, Baranov," August 14, 1944, RGASPI, fond 82, opis 2, delo 1187, l. 3; Banac, *Diary of Georgi Dimitrov*, 327.

132. "Notice of the Politburo of the KKE," August 17, 1944, in KKE, *Episima keimena*, 5:224–25.

133. Iatrides, *Revolt in Athens*, 115.

134. Close, *Greek Civil War*, XX; Baerentzen, "I afixi," 91–92; Kalyvas and Marantzidis, *Emfylia pathi*, 309–12.

135. Kondis and Sfetas, *Emfylios polemos*, 16; Farakos, *B' Pagosmios Polemos*, 129–39.

136. Kondis and Sfetas, *Emfylios polemos*, 123–41.

137. Kondis and Sfetas, *Emfylios polemos*, 232–33.

138. Baev, "Ta Valkania," 171.

139. Baev, "Ta Valkania," 173.

140. "Leeper to FO," September 20, 1944, AOA, FO 371/43692/R14971; "Ambassador Leeper to FO," October 8, 1944, AOA, FO 371/43693/R15413.

141. "George II to Churchill," September 21, 1944, AOA, FO 371/43693/R15413.

142. Dimitrov, *Stalin's Cold War*, 75, 137.

143. "FO to Clark Kerr," September 21, 1944, AOA, FO 371/43716/R15153. Also see Volkov, "Soviet Leadership," 59; Reynolds and Pechatnov, *Kremlin Letters*, 472.

144. Banac, *Diary of Georgi Dimitrov*, 338–39.

145. Roussos, *I megali pentaetia*, 2:418; Roberts, "Moscow's Cold War," 60.

146. "Dimitrov and Baranov to Molotov," October 21, 1944, RGASPI, fond 82, opis 2, delo 1186, l. 32. Also see Lebedeva and Narinski, *I Kommounistiki Diethnis*, 167.

147. Iatrides, "Revolution or Self-Defense?," 15.

148. Haug, *Creating a Socialist Yugoslavia*, 116–19. Also see Applebaum, *Iron Curtain*.

149. Woodhouse, *Struggle for Greece*, 62.

150. Mazower, *Inside Hitler's Greece*, 269–84. On the KKE's membership, see "Bartziotas's Report to the 11th Plenum of the KKE," April 5–10, 1945, in KKE, *Episima keimena*, 5:435.

151. "Record of Tito's Conversation with the Representative of the KKE," November 15, 1944, in Kondis and Sfetas, *Emfylios polemos*, 155–58.

152. "Meeting of the CC of the KKE," November 21, 1952, RGASPI, fond 495, opis 207, delo 8, ll. 66–104.

153. "Sir W. Mallet to Chr. Warner," December 22, 1944, AOA, FO 371/48319/R98547.

154. Banac, *Diary of Georgi Dimitrov*, 345; Baev, *O Emfylios polemos*, 71–89; Farakos, *B' Pagosmios Polemos*, 145.

155. Churchill, *Triumph and Tragedy*, 369; Iatrides, *Revolt in Athens*, 221; Roberts, "Moscow's Cold War," 63.

156. "Houston-Boswall (Sofia) to FO," December 13, 1944, AOA, FO 371/43772/R19944.

157. Dedijer, *Tito Speaks*, 238; Ristović, "L'Insurrection de Décembre," 272–74.

158. "Houston-Boswall (Sofia) to FO."

159. Farakos, *B' Pagosmios Polemos*, 147.

160. "Kostov to Dimitrov," December 13, 1944, and "Kostov to the KKE," December 19, 1944, in Kondis and Sfetas, *Emfylios polemos*, 159–60.

161. "Kostov to Dimitrov," January 9, 1945, in Kondis and Sfetas, *Emfylios polemos*, 167.

162. Banac, *Diary of Georgi Dimitrov*, 352–53.

163. "Siantos to Dimitrov and Tito," January 15, 1945, ASKI, box 145, F. 7/32/292.

164. "The Conferences at Malta and Yalta, 1945," FRUS, 1945, 781–82.

165. "Aris Velouchiotis to the PB of the CC of the KKE," February 14, 1945, in Farakos, *Aris Velouchiotis*, 333–35; Ioannidis, *Anamniseis*, 373; Kainourgios, *Sta adita tou Emfyliou*, 61–62, 77; Baev, *Mia matia ap'exo*, 93.

166. *Rizospastis*, May 29, 1945.

167. Gerolymatos, *International Civil War*, 23–24.

168. Roberts, "Moscow's Cold War," 64.

5. Balkan Decisions

1. "MacVeagh to State Department," June 22, 1945, NARA, RG 59, 868.00/6–2245.

2. Iatrides, "Birth of Containment," 6.

3. *Rizospastis*, May 31, 1945.

4. Nikolakopoulos, *I kachektiki dimokratia*, 86–94.

5. Kalyvas and Marantzidis, *Emfylia pathi*, 336.

6. "MacVeagh to State Department," July 4, 1945, NARA, RG 59, 868.00/7–445.

7. "Baranov to Panyuskin," December 20, 1945, RGASPI, fond 17, opis 128, delo 762, ll. 228–29.

8. "Baranov to Molotov," January 19, 1946, RGASPI, fond 82, opis 2, delo 1186, ll. 56–60. Also see Ulunian, "Soviet Union," 146.

9. Partsalidis, *Dipli apokatastasi*, 195, 199.

10. Banac, *Diary of Georgi Dimitrov*, 396.

11. Iatrides, "Revolution or Self-Defense?," 18.

12. KKE, "The 2nd Plenum of the CC of the KKE," February 12–15, 1946, in KKE, *Episima keimena*, 6:178.

13. Sfikas, "'Almost Unique Isle,'" 6.

14. "Note on Conversation between Ambassador Rodionov-Zachariadis," May 4, 1946, in Kondis and Sfetas, *Emfylios polemos*, 237–38.

15. Kondis, *Sosialistika krati*, 293–94; Ulunian, "Soviet Union," 146.

16. Eleftheriou, *Sinomilies*, 35; Iliou, *O Ellinikos Emfylios Polemos*, 23; Iatrides, "Revolution or Self-Defense?," 22–25; Kondis, *Sosialistika krati*, 295.

17. "Baranov and Mosetov on Zachariadis Notes," April 26, 1946, RGASPI, fond 17, opis 128, delo 889, l. 66; "Suslov to Malenkov, Zhdanov, Beria," April 27, 1946, RGASPI, fond 17, opis 28, delo 889, l. 60.

18. "Suslov [and Baranov] to Zhdanov," October 7, 1946, RGASPI, fond 17, opis 128, delo 889, ll. 125–27, 145–46.

19. "Suslov [and Baranov] to Zhdanov," l. 127.

20. Ulunian, "Soviet Union," 147; Papadatos, *Akros aporrito*, 226.

21. "Ioannidis to Zachariadis," November 10, 1946, ASKI, box 146, F. 7/33/115.

22. "Ioannidis to the KKE," February 1, 1947, ASKI, box 146, F. 7/33/125; "Ioannidis to the KKE," n.d., ASKI, box 146, F. 7/33/132.

23. Rossos, "Incompatible Allies," 55.

24. Sfetas, "Anepithimitoi summachoi," 220–21; Mihailidis, *Ta prosopa tou Ianou*, 164; Rossos, "Incompatible Allies," 60–62; Lagani, "Les Communistes des Balkans," 64.

25. Gibianskii, "Soviet-Yugoslav Conflict," 224; Gibianskii and Naimark, *Soviet Union*, 21; Perović, "Tito-Stalin Split," 40.

26. Majstorović, "Rise and Fall," 145; Papathanasiou, "Itimenos protagonistis," 260; Banac, *With Stalin against Tito*, 35.

27. Ristović, *To peirama Bulkes*, 16; Lagani, "Les Communistes des Balkans," 67; Nachmani, *International Intervention*, 33.

28. Ristović, "Yugoslavikis stratiotikis voitheias," 99.

29. Baev, *Mia matia ap'exo*, 97; Baev, *O emfylios polemos*, 107–8.

30. "Kostas [Siaperas] Report on Our Work," January 26, 1948, ASKI, Digital Archive, DSE/001.08.019.00086.

31. "Vasile Posteucă, Memories, October 10, 1978," in Şiperco, *Confesiunile elitei Comuniste*, v. 5.

32. Ioannidis, *Anamniseis*, 373; Kainourgios, *Sta adyta tou Emfyliou*, 61–62, 77; Lalaj, "I embloki tis Alvanias," 86–87; Nilaj, "Civil War in Greece," 100. On the participation of Chams in the DSE ranks and Albania's position, see also "Proceedings of the Meeting of the Politburo of the Party of Labor of Albania," March 25, 1949, AQSH, Politburo, v. 1949, fondi 14, dosja 16.

33. Lagani, "Les Communistes des Balkans," 68–69; Burks, *Dynamics of Communism*, 99–101.

34. Banac, *Diary of Georgi Dimitrov*, 421; Banac, *With Stalin against Tito*, 37–41; Gibianskii, "Kak voznik Kominform," 141; Anikeev, "Idea for a Balkan Federation," 170.

35. "Zachariadis to Stalin," May 14, 1947, ASKI, box 383, F. 20/33/10 (also in Iliou, *O Ellinikos Emfylios Polemos*, 91); "Suslov to Zhdanov," May 15, 1947, RGASPI, fond 77, opis 4, delo 58, ll. 5–13.

36. "Minutes of the Meeting of Comrade Zhdanov with the Comrade Nikolayev," May 22, 1947, RGASPI, fond 77, opis 3, delo 143, ll. 1–13; "Ioannidis to Anastasiadis," June 4, 1947, ASKI, box 146, F. 7/33/164. On the Moscow meetings, also see Zubok and Pleshakov, *Kremlin's Cold War*, 127–28; Iatrides, "Revolution or Self-Defense?," 24.

37. "Molotov to Stalin," September 23, 1947, RGANI, fond 89, opis 48, delo 2, l. 1.

38. *Rizospastis*, June 28, 1947.

39. "Zachariadis to the CC of the All-Union Communist Party (Bolshevik)," April 24, 1950, RGASPI, fond 82, opis 8, delo 1189, ll. 9–10.

40. "Suslov to Stalin, Molotov, Beria, Mikoyan, Malenkov, Voznesensky," September 15, 1947, RGASPI, fond 17, opis 128, delo 1079, ll. 136–45. Also see Mastny, *Soviet Insecurity*, 35; Iliou, *O Ellinikos Emfylios Polemos*, 204–11.

41. "Democratic Army of Greece, GHQ," July 20, 1949, LC, Dossier Grèce–Papier Vlandas Guerre Civile, Fo.D. Rès. 405/6. Also see Iatrides, "Civil War," 213.

42. Gibianskii, "Kak voznik Kominform," 134–43; Di Biagio, "Establishment of the Cominform," 14; Di Biagio, "Marshall Plan," 208–9; Kramer, "Consolidation of a Communist Bloc," 80–81; Zubok and Pleshakov, *Kremlin's Cold War*, 125.

43. Marcou, *Le Kominform*, 1–2, 73–75.

44. Reale, "Founding of the Cominform," 257; Sadekova, "Andrei Jdanov."

45. Andrei Jdanov, "Sur la situation internationale," *Pour une paix durable pour une démocratie populaire*, November 10, 1947.

46. Gibianskii, "Soviet-Yugoslav Relations," 270; Swain, "Cominform"; Majstorović, "Rise and Fall," 148–50.

47. Iazhborovskaia, "Gomulka Alternative," 135–37; Marcou, *Le Kominform*, 53.

48. Marcou, *Le Kominform*, 55–58; Di Biagio, "Establishment of the Cominform," 20–22. Also see the testimony of the Italian representative: Reale, *Duclos au banc des accusés*.

49. Marcou, *Le Kominform*, 43; Gibiansiki, "Kak voznik Kominform," 141–43; Di Biagio, "Establishment of the Cominform," 25.

50. Marcou, *Le Kominform*, 80. During 1948–49, however, the attitude of the Cominform changed and there were more than fifty mentions of Greece in the Cominform's journal. See Papathanasiou, "Cominform," 62.

51. Gibiansiki, "Kak voznik Kominform," 141–42.

52. Anson, "Limits of Destalinization," 48–49.

53. "Kardelj's Speech," September 26, 1947, in Procacci, *Cominform*, 301.

54. "Tchervenkov's Speech," September 23, 1947, in Procacci, *Cominform*, 103.

55. "Gheorghiu-Dej's Intervention in the Discussion of the Draft Resolution," September 28, 1947, in Procacci, *Cominform*, 403.

56. "Gomułka's Speech," September 22, 1947, in Procacci, *Cominform*, 425.

57. Banac, *Diary of Georgi Dimitrov*, 442–43.

58. Banac, *Diary of Georgi Dimitrov*, 443.

59. "Apostolou to the Secretariat of the Politburo of the Romanian Workers' Party," Bucharest, January 14, 1948, ANR-SANIC, fond of the Central Committee of the PCR, Foreign Relations, Dosar 1948, ll. 7-37; "Resolution of the Politburo of the BKP, no 112," June 3, 1948, CDA, fond 1b, opis 6, arhivna edinica 501; "Kolarov to the UN Representative Evet," September 7, 1948, CDA, fond 147b, opis 2, arhivna edinica 1025.

60. Hradečný, "Zdrženlivý internacionalismus."

61. Paczkowski, "'Greek Operation,'" 77.

62. Paczkowski, "'Greek Operation,'" 77; Sanford, *Military Rule in Poland*, 58-59; de Sola Pool, *Satellite Generals*, 76-77.

63. Banac, *Diary of Georgi Dimitrov*, 435; Baev, *Mia matia ap'exo*, 154-55, 228; Kramer, "Split with Yugoslavia," 30.

64. "Report of Major-General Jovan Kapicić to Al. Ranković on Yugoslavia's Aid to the Democratic Army of Greece during 1948," n.d., in Kondis and Sfetas, *Emfylios polemos*, 125-27.

65. "Report of Roussos to the KKE Leadership," ASKI, box 156, F. 7/43/21; "The KPY to the KKE," March 3, 1949, in Kondis and Sfetas, *Emfylios polemos*, 131; "The KKE to the KPY," March 6, 1949, in Kondis and Sfetas, *Emfylios polemos*, 132; "Roussos to the CC of the KPY," April 1, 1949, in Kondis and Sfetas, *Emfylios polemos*, 135-39; Also see Vukmanović, *People's Liberation Struggle*, 111-23; Iliou, *O Ellinikos Emfylios Polemos*, 304-12.

66. Papadopoulou and Ouroumidou, "O Ellinikos Emfylios Polemos," 49.

67. "5th Plenum of the CC of the KKE," January 30-31, 1949, in KKE, *Episima keimena*, 6:337.

68. Kofos, *Nationalism and Communism*, 180-81; Vukmanović, *People's Liberation Struggle*, 77-78.

69. Kondis, *Sosialistika krati*, 282-83.

70. Ulunian, "Soviet Union," 152.

71. "Geminder to Pavlov," Prague, n.d., CDA, fond 1, opis 7, arhivna edinica 7515; "Ponomaryov to Molotov," April 7, 1949, RGASPI, fond 82, opis 2, delo 1186, ll. 95-102; "Minutes of the Meeting," Bucharest, March 10, 1949, ANR-SANIC, fond Central Committee of the PCR, Foreign Relations, dosar 36/1949, ll. 32-41. Also see Ulunian, "Soviet Union," 152; Papadatos, *Akros aporrito*, 111-12.

72. Hradečný, "Czechoslovak Material Aid," 366-68.

73. "Ponomaryov to Molotov," April 7, 1949, RGASPI, fond 82, opis 2, delo 1186, ll. 95, 101; "Minutes of the Meeting," Bucharest, March 10, 1949, ANR-SANIC, Fond Central Committee of the PCR, Foreign Relations, dosar 36/1949, ll. 32-41.

74. "Ponomaryov Notes on Meeting with Ioannidis," RGASPI, fond 82, opis 2, delo 1186, ll. 103-5.

75. "Report of General Komar Bryg," April 23, 1949, IPN, 001103/3; "Report of the Head of the Second Office of the General Command to the President of the Polish Republic Bolesław Bierut," January 19, 1950, IPN, 0298/848. Also see Paczkowski, "'Greek Operation,'" 91.

76. Wudalas, "Greek Political Refugees."

77. "Report on the Czechoslovak Aid to the Greek Communists," September 18, 1951, NAP, KSČ, ÚV, 100/24, Klement Gottwald, k. 99, n. 1142, ll. 1–14. Also see Hradečný, "Czechoslovak Material Aid," 366.

78. "Zachariadis and Vafeiadis to the CC of the Communist Party of Albania," July 7, 1948, AQSH, CC Correspondence with the KKE, v. 1948, fondi 14, dosja 2; "Ioannidis to Comrade Koci," August 5, 1948, AQSH, CC Correspondence with the KKE, v. 1948, fondi 14, dosja 1; "Ioannidis to the CC of the Communist Party of Albania," October 12, 1948, AQSH, CC Correspondence with the KKE, v. 1948, fondi 14, dosja 2.

79. Lalaj, "I embloki tis Alvanias," 89.

80. "Proceedings of the Politburo Meeting of the Communist Party of Albania," March 3, 1948, AQSH, Politburo, v. 1948, fondi 14, dosja 64; "For the Defense of Albania from Greek Monarcho-Fascist," March 13, 1948, RGASPI, fond 17, opis 128, delo 472, ll. 84–89; "Record of I. V. Stalin's Conversation with E. Hoxha concerning Albanian-Yugoslavian Relations and the Foreign and Domestic Policy of Albania," March 23, 1949 (Archive of the President of the Russian Federation, fond 45, opis 1, delo 249, ll. 55–74), in Murashko et al., History and Public Policy Program Digital Archive, 2:44–57, http://digital archive.wilsoncenter.org/document/134384.

81. "To the Secretariat of the Polish Workers' Party," November 19, 1947, Archiwum Akt Nowych, KC PPR, 285/XX, v. 52; Matthaiou and Polemi, "I diethneis scheseis," 13.

82. "Soviet Red Cross to the International Red Cross," May 19, 1948, RGASPI, fond 17, opis 428, delo 181, l. 44.

83. Shrader, Withered Vine, 254–55.

84. Banac, Diary of Georgi Dimitrov, 447.

85. Jones, "New Kind of War," 205, 208.

86. Vontitsios-Gousias, I Aities gia tis ittes, 501; Partsalidis, Dipli apokatastasi, 199; Stavrakis, Moscow and Greek Communism, 181–85; Kondis, Sosialistika krati, 281–82.

87. "Appeal of the Provisional Democratic Government," April 20, 1949, RGASPI, fond 82, opis 2, delo 1186, ll. 92–94.

88. Sfikas, "I 'Eirinopolemi' Diastasi," 75.

89. "Instructions to Comrade Gromyko for the Meeting with MacNeil and Rusk," RGASPI, fond 82, opis 2, delo 1186, l. 122.

90. For a good account of the April–May discussion, see Jones, "New Kind of War," 205–8, 211–12. On this issue also see Mëhilli, From Stalin to Mao, 94; Kondis, I Aggloamerikaniki politiki, 384–89; Kondis, Sosialistika krati, 281.

91. Ulunian, "Soviet Union," 155.

92. Margaritis, Istoria, 2:235–38; Kousoulas, Revolution and Defeat, 270; Kalyvas and Marantzidis, Emfylia pathi, 498.

93. "Zachariadis to Stalin," September 8, 1949, RGASPI, fond 82, opis 2, delo 1187, ll. 103–5; also in ASKI, box 383, F. 20/33/74.

94. Dimokratikos Stratos, September 1949, 597–601; "The Greek Democratic Army has Not Surrendered; [We] Have Our 'Guns at the Ready,'" "DSE Daily Order," October, 28, 1949, ASKI, box 109, F. 4/1/94.

95. On Zachariadis's position on the "northern Epirus issue," see "Zacha-riadis's Speech on the 12th Plenum of the CC," *Rizospastis*, July 3, 1945. Also see Dayos, *I diethnis diastasi*, 87–88.

96. "Resolution of the Politburo on the Battle of Vitsi," August 20, 1949, AQSH, CC Correspondence with the KKE, v. 1949, fondi 14, dosja 3; "The Po-litburo of the KKE to Enver Hoxha," October 31, 1949, AQSH, CC Correspon-dence with the KKE, v. 1949, fondi 14, dosja 1.

97. Iatrides, "Revolution or Self-Defense?," 31; Dayos, *I diethnis diastasi*, 219–20.

98. "Zachariadis to the Party of Labor of Albania," October 27, 1949, ASKI, box 353, F. 20/3/54.

99. "Information on the Disagreement between the Leaders of the KKE and the Party of Labor of Albania," RGASPI, fond 82, opis 8, delo 1188, ll. 17–19. See also Meta, *Albania and Greece*, 48; Karpozilos, "Defeated," 64–74.

100. "Enver Hoxha's Memorandum on the Meeting with the Greek Repre-sentatives in Moscow," January 10, 1950, AQSH, CC Correspondence with the KKE, v. 1950, fondi 14, dosja 1; "Minutes of the Meeting between Comrades Enver Hoxha and Nikos Zachariadis," January 14, 1950, RGASPI, fond 82, opis 8, delo 1188, ll. 37–52; "Enver Hoxha's Notes on the January 14 and January 16 Meetings with Zachariadis," AQSH, CC Correspondence with the KKE, v. 1950, fondi 14, dosja 1.

101. "Record of Enver Hoxha's Conversation with Nikos Zachariadis," Jan-uary 16, 1950, RGASPI, fond 82, opis 8, delo 1188, l. 50.

102. "Record of I. V. Stalin's Conversation with V. Chervenkov, P. Damya-nov, and A. Yugov on the Issues of Bulgaria's Internal Political Life," July 29, 1949, in Murashko et al., History and Public Policy Program Digital Archive, 2:192–202, https://digitalarchive.wilsoncenter.org/document/134386.

103. Iatrides, "Revolution or Self-Defense?," 25.

104. Sfikas, "Almost Unique Isle," 21.

6. The Displaced People's Republic

1. Young, "To Russia with 'Spain,'" 400.

2. "Grigorian to Stalin," April 17, 1950, RGASPI, fond 82, opis 8, delo 1189, l. 6. In 1953, the Albanian government declared that it detained in its territories 385 Greek prisoners of the civil war. See Skoulidas, "I politiki pros-fyges," 121.

3. Tsekou, *Ellines politiki prosfyges*, 52–77; Daskalov, *I Elliniki politiki pros-fygia*, 46; Wojecki, "Clusters of Greek Immigrants," 156; Patelakis, *O emfylios polemos*, 113; Tsivos, *O megalos kaimos*, 30–31; Dordanas and Kalogrias, *I zoes ton allon*, 65–88.

4. "On the Communist Party of Greece," September 23, 1949, RGASPI, fond 17, opis 162, delo 41, ll. 10–12. According to the Soviet authorities, there were 8,441 men, 3,245 women, 38 children, and 296 adolescents. "Kruglov to Molotov," February 28, 1950, RGASPI, fond 82, opis 2, delo 1186, ll. 156–59.

5. "Kruglov to Molotov," February 28, 1950, RGASPI, fond 82, opis 2, delo 1186, l. 156.

6. "Komar to Polish President Bolesław Bierut," January 19, 1950, IPN, 0298/848.

7. Wojecki, "Clusters of Greek Immigrants," 156–60.

8. "Report on the Conditions of the Greek Children and Refugees," June 8, 1948, CDA, Archive Vasil Kolarov, fond 147b, opis 3, arhivna edinica 1399.

9. Tsivos, *O megalos kaimos*, 37–38.

10. "Geminder to Slánský," August 29, 1949, NAP, KSČ, ÚV, 100/1, 1945–1989/59/468, l. 1.

11. "Report of Maria Telanova, Head of the International Department of the CC, Related to the Establishment of the Greek Refugees," September 29, 1949, NAP, KSČ, ÚV, 100/1, 1945–1989/63/509, ll. 1–9.

12. "Karas to Farkas on the Arrival and Establishment of the Greek Children," April 10, 1948, MLO, fond 276, 14/58.

13. "Daniilidis to the Politburo of the CC of the KKE," March 16, 1952, ASKI, box 127, F. 7/14/5.

14. Dordanas and Kalogrias, *I zoes ton allon*, 67, 71.

15. "Zachariadis to Stalin," October 10, 1949, RGASPI, fond 82, opis 2, delo 1187, l. 107.

16. "Ministry of Finance to Molotov," March 19, 1950, RGASPI, fond 82, opis 2, delo 1186, l. 161.

17. "Molotov to Stalin," March 22, 1950, RGASPI, fond 82, opis 2, delo 1186, l. 164.

18. "Council of Ministers of USSR," April 1950, RGASPI, fond 82, opis 2, delo 1186, ll. 183–84.

19. Daskalov, *I Elliniki politiki prosfygia*, 46; Dragostinova, *Between Two Motherlands*, 255–56.

20. "Ministry of Health to Comrade Rákosi," April 4, 1950, MLO, 276/54/93.

21. Hradečný, *I Elliniki diaspora*, 261.

22. Young, "To Russia with 'Spain,'" 401. On the *niños* issue, also see Kowalsky, *Spanish Civil War*, chap. 5; Kirschenbaum, *International Communism*, 198–99.

23. Baerentzen, "Paidomazoma"; Danforth and Van Boeschoten, *Children of the Greek Civil War*.

24. "Proceedings of the Secretariat of the Hungarian Working People's Party," July 1, 1948, MLO, 276/54/3; "Resolution of the Central Committee of the Romanian Workers' Party," June 28, 1950, ANR-SANIC, fond Central Committee of the PCR, Foreign Relations, dosar 6/1950.

25. Kubasiewicz, "Children and Youth," 188; Daskalov, *I Elliniki politiki prosfygia*, 52–91; Tsivos, *O megalos kaimos*, 40–43; Patelakis, *O emfylios polemos*, 76–107.

26. "On Families' Reunification Currently Staying in the People's Republics of Poland, Hungary, Bulgaria, Czechoslovakia and Romania," September 17, 1953, ANR-SANIC, fond Central Committee of the PCR, Foreign Relations, dosar 18/1953.

27. "Loules to the Politburo of the CC of the KKE," October 24, 1952, ASKI, box 127, F. 7/14/7. Also see Tsekou, *Ellines politiki prosfyges*, 157–58.

28. "Zachariadis to the Central Committee of the All-Union Communist Party (Bolshevik)," April 14, 1950, RGASPI, fond 82, opis 8, delo 1189, ll. 9–10;

"Grigorian to Stalin," May 6, 1950, RGASPI, fond 82, opis 8, delo 1189, ll. 15–16; "Molotov to Stalin," May 8, 1950, RGASPI, fond 82, opis 8, delo 1189, l. 19. Also see Labatos, *Ellines politiki prosfyges*, 41–42; Karpozilos, "Defeated," 76.

29. Karpozilos, "Defeated," 76.

30. Kirschenbaum, "Communist Self-Fashioning," 579.

31. "International Department of the Hungarian Working People's Party to the Secretariat," August 16, 1948, MLO, fond 276, 54/58; Mitsopoulos, *Meiname Ellines*; Tsekou, *Ellines politiki prosfyges*, 191–92; Bontila, *"Megale Stalin."*

32. Van Boeschoten, "'Enotita' kai 'aderfotita,'" 50–51; Sloboda, "Language Maintenance," 11; Athanasiadis and Grouios, *Zachariadis*, 65–78.

33. "Report of Maria Telenova to the All-Czechoslovak KKE Conference," December 5, 1950, NAP, KSČ, ÚV, 100/3/132/520. Also see Boeschoten, "'Enotita' kai 'adelfotita,'" 61; Tsivos, *O megalos kaimos*, 90–91.

34. "Greek Immigrants in the People's Republics and the USSR, Ministry of Domestic Affairs, Poland," 1950, IPN, BU 1572/783; KKE, "Report of Bartziotas in the Third Conference," October 10–14, 1950, in KKE, *Episima keimena*, 7:483; "Conclusions from the KKE Meetings in Wroclaw, Ministry of Domestic Affairs, Poland," 1961, IPN, BU 1585/22378. Also see Semczyszyn, "Communist Security Apparatus," 216–21.

35. Kirschenbaum, "Communist Self-Fashioning," 577.

36. "Resolution of the Politburo of the Romanian Workers' Party," January 11, 1951, ANR-SANIC, fond Central Committee of the PCR, Foreign Relations, dosar 3/1951, l. 2; "CC of the Party of Labor of Albania to the CC of the KKE," September 9, 1954, AQSH, CC Correspondence with the KKE, v. 1954, fondi 14, dosja 1. Also see Psimouli, *"Eleftheri Ellada,"* 28; Patelakis, *O emfylios polemos*, 138; Matthaiou and Polemi, *I ekdotiki peripetia*, 41–44, 62–63.

37. "Resolution of the Politburo of the Romanian Workers' Party," January 11, 1951, ANR-SANIC, fond Central Committee of the PCR, Foreign Relations, dosar 3/1951, l. 2; "Resolution of the Politburo of the Romanian Workers' Party concerning the KKE's Budget for 1952," November 15, 1951, ANR-SANIC, fond Central Committee of the PCR, Foreign Relations, dosar 3, dosar 87/1951, ll. 32–35. Also see Tismăneanu, "Intrigi, crime, răni deschise"; Patelakis, *O emfylios polemos*, 111.

38. "Resolution of the CC of the KKE," October 9, 1949, in KKE, *Episima keimena*, 7:13–19.

39. Voglis, *Becoming a Subject*, 63.

40. "Ioannidis and Roussos to Gottwald and Slansky," November 19, 1949, NAP, KSČ, ÚV, 100/24/99/1142; "Grigorian to Stalin," January 4, 1950, RGASPI, fond 82, opis 2, delo 1188, ll. 1–3; "Report on Preparations of the Sabotage School," February 11, 1950, NAP, KSČ, ÚV, 100/3/146/572.

41. Paczkowski, "'Greek Operation,'" 92; Patelakis, *O emfylios polemos*, 125.

42. "The Politburo on the Comrades' Attendance in the Frunze Academy," October 24, 1951, ASKI, box 120, F. 7/7/521; "The Politburo on the Comrades' Attendance in the Frunze Academy," March 19, 1952, ASKI, box 120, F. 7/7/523. Also see Karpozilos, "Defeated," 81.

43. Papathanassiou, *Eniaia dimokratiki aristera*, 26–29; Lambrinou, *EDA 1956–1967*, 16.

44. "Grigorian to Molotov," January 6, 1950, RGASPI, fond 82, opis 8, delo 1188, ll. 7–8; "Grigorian to Stalin," January 10, 1950, RGASPI, fond 82, opis 8, delo 1188, ll. 9–11.

45. "Grigorian to Stalin," April 17, 1950, RGASPI, fond 82, opis 8, delo 1189, ll. 6–7.

46. Preston, *Comrades!*, 307; Anson, "Limits of Destalinization," 29–31.

47. "Zachariadis to the CC of the All-Union Communist Party (Bolshevik)," April 4, 1950, RGASPI, fond 82, opis 8, delo 1189, l. 2; "Grigorian to Molotov," April 9, 1950, RGASPI, fond 82, opis 8, delo 1189, ll. 3–4.

48. "The Third Conference of the KKE," October 10–14, 1950, in KKE, *Episima keimena*, 7:57–98, 465–546.

49. "Third Conference," 7:59–62, 87.

50. "Zachariadis to Gheorghiu-Dej," December 13, 1950, ASKI, KKE box 120, F. 20/28/40.

51. "Partsalidis to the Politburo of the CC of the KKE," October 7, 1951, RGASPI, fond 575, opis 1, delo 199, ll. 214–16.

52. "The 2nd Plenum of the CC of the KKE," October 10–12, 1951, in KKE, *Episima keimena*, 7:189; "Zachariadis to the Central Committee of the All-Union Communist Party (Bolshevik)," October 17, 1951, RGASPI, fond 575, opis 1, delo 199, ll. 210–11.

53. "Partsalidis to Zachariadis," October 16, 1951, RGASPI, fond 575, opis 1, delo 199, l. 220.

54. "Grigorian to Stalin," July 24, 1950, RGASPI, fond 82, opis 2, delo 1189, ll. 146–69.

55. Kramer, "CPSU International Department," 430.

56. "The 4th Plenum of the Central Committee of the KKE," December 12–13, 1953, in KKE, *Episima keimena*, 7:368–69; "Comments of the Central Committee of the CPSU on the KKE's Draft Plan," n.d., ANR-SANIC, fond Central Committee of the PCR, Foreign Relations, dosar 92/1956, ll. 89–94; KKE, "Resolution of the CC of the KKE," November 22, 1954, in KKE, *Episima keimena*, 7:412. Also see Tsekeris, *Mia istoria allios*, 258–59.

57. Vassilis Bartziotas, "The Condition and the Problems of the Political Refugees in the People's Republics," August 1951, in KKE, *Episima keimena*, 7:483.

58. Labatos, *Ellines politiki prosfyges*, 149–50; Tsekou, *Ellines politiki prosfyges*, 102–3; Karpozilos, "Defeated," 83; Tsekeris, *Mia istoria allios*, 260–65.

59. "Ponomarev and Vinogradov to the Central Committee of the CPSU," September 12, 1955, in Afinian et al., *I scheseis*, 37–39; I. Vinogradov, D. Seveliagin, and P. Mandscha, "Report on the Situation of the Party Organization of the Greek Political Refugees Who Live in the Soviet Socialist Republic of Uzbekistan," September 12, 1955, in Afinian et al., *I scheseis*, 40–50.

60. Dimitriou, *Ek vatheon*, 195–98.

61. Antaios, *N. Zachariadis*, 287.

62. "Niyazov to the CC of the CPSU," September 13, 1955, in Afinian et al., *I scheseis*, 57–58; See also Dimitriou, *Ek vatheon*, 199–200; Tsekeris, *Mia istoria allios*, 266–74.

63. "Resolution of the CC of the CP of Uzbekistan," September 9, 1955, in Afinian et al., *I scheseis*, 50-57; Vinogradov, Seveliagin, and Mandscha, "Report on the Situation," 50.

64. A. Nigiasov, "Report of the CC of the CP of Uzbekistan," September 9, 1955, in Afinian et al., *I scheseis*, 57.

65. "Resolution of the CC of the CPSU," September 20, 1955, in Afinian et al, *I scheseis*, 61-62.

66. "Report of the CC of the CPSU," November 3, 1955, in Afinian et al., *I scheseis*, 70-88; "Resolution of the CC of the CPSU," December 15, 1955, in Afinian et al., *I scheseis*, 89-90.

67. "The Fifth Plenum of the CC of the KKE," December 26-28, 1955, in KKE, *Episima keimena*, 7:447-58.

68. Daniilidis, *O Polydoros thimatai*, 242.

69. The six parties were the Bulgarian, the Czechoslovak, the Hungarian, the Polish, the Romanian, and the CPSU. "Zachariadis's Notes on the First Meeting with the Committee," February 21, 1956, in Petropoulos, *I kathairesi*, 59-62. See also Antaios, *N. Zachariadis*, 196; Dimitriou, *Ek vatheon*, 205-6; Daniilidis, *O Polydoros thimatai*, 242; Kasimatis, *I paranomi*, 32; Labatos, *Ellines politiki prosfyges*, 193-94; Sfikas, "'O provoleas fotizei,'" 367.

70. Zachariadis had three meetings with the international committee representatives in Moscow, on February 21, 25, and 26. "Minutes of the Discussion with Comrade Nikos Zachariadis," n.d., ANR-SANIC, fond Central Committee of the PCR, Foreign Relations, dosar 2/1956, ll. 112-34; "Zachariadis to the Committee of the Sister Parties on the Greek Problem," Moscow, February 26, 1956, ANR-SANIC, fond Central Committee of the PCR, Foreign Relations, dosar 92/1956, ll. 135-39.

71. "Zachariadis to the Comrades Bartziotas, Akritidis, Grozos," February 24, 1956, ANR-SANIC, fond Central Committee of the PCR, Foreign Relations, dosar 92/1956, l. 105; "Zachariadis, Bartziotas, Akritidis, Grozos to the Committee of the Sister Parties," Moscow, February 24, 1956, ANR-SANIC, Fond Central Committee of the PCR, Foreign Relations, dosar 92/1956, l. 104; "Proceedings of the CC Meeting of the Party of Labor of Albania," February 29, 1956, AQSH, Politburo, v. 1956, fondi 14, dosja 34.

72. "Letter to the CC of the CPSU from KKE's Members of Tashkent," January 16, 1956, in Afinian et al., *I scheseis*, 119-24; "Letter to the Cominform from KKE's Members of Tashkent," January 17, 1956, in Afinian et al., *I scheseis*, 100-118; "Letter to the International Department of the CC of the CPSU from KKE's Members of Tashkent," February 2, 1956, in Afinian et al., *I scheseis*, 125-28.

73. Fitzpatrick, "Signals from Below," 833.

74. Patelakis, *O emfylios polemos*, 196.

75. Rintala and Hodgson, "Gustaf Mannerheim," 372.

76. "Gheorge Gheorghiu-Dej's Report," March 11, 1956, in Petropoulos, *I kathairesi*, 137; Kasimatis, *I paranomoi*, 292.

77. Marc Marceau, "Le secrétaire général du Parti Communiste Grec a été sacrifié à la 'coexistence active,'" *Le monde*, April 4, 1956.

78. Connelly, *From Peoples into Nations*, 623.

79. "Vinogradov to the CC of the CPSU," May 5, 1956, in Afinian et al, *I scheseis*, 265–66; "On the Letter of Zachariadis to the CPSU," n.d., in KKE, *Episima keimena*, 8:185–87.

80. Vontitsos-Gousias, *I aities*, 2:224–25.

81. Marantzidis, "La deuxième mort," 186.

82. "The Seventh Plenum of the Central Committee of the KKE: On Nikos Zachariadis," February 18–24, 1957, in KKE, *Episima keimena*, 8:173–76; Farakos, *Martyries kai stochasmi*, 127–29.

83. "Report on the Meeting between the CC of the Communist Party of Czechoslovakia and the CC of the KKE," April 19, 1957, NAP, KSČ, ÚV, 100/3/132, l. 526.

84. Tsivos, *O megalos kaimos*, 130–32.

85. Kasimatis, *I paranomi*, 389; Labatos, *Ellines politiki prosfyges*, 201–7; Tsekeris, *Mia istoria allios*, 340–41; Semczyszyn, "Communist Security Apparatus," 218.

86. Antaios, *N. Zachariadis*, 489–536; Marantzidis, "La deuxième mort," 183–89; Karpozilos, "Defeated," 83.

Epilogue

1. Tismăneanu, *Stalinism for All Seasons*, 197–200; Deletant, *Romania under Communist Rule*, 153–72; Connelly, *From Peoples into Nations*, 619.

2. Balampanidis, *Eurocommunism*, 36.

3. Balampanidis, *Eurocommunism*, 6–8, 32–35; Kriegel, *Un autre Communisme?*, 23–25, 68–75; Connelly, *From Peoples into Nations*, 591.

4. Farakos, *Martyries kai stochasmi*, 181.

5. Kalyvas and Marantzidis, "Greek Communism," 667.

6. Balampanidis, *Eurocommunism*, 39–40.

7. Kalyvas and Marantzidis, "Greek Communism," 667.

8. Kalyvas and Marantzidis, "Greek Communism," 669; Stergiou, "Perestroika," 259.

9. Kalyvas and Marantzidis, "Greek Communism," 669.

10. Smith, "Greek Communist Party."

11. Marantzidis, "Communist Party of Greece," 245; Stergiou, "Perestroika," 259.

12. Quoted in Balampanidis, *Eurocommunism*, 8.

13. Marantzidis, "Communist Party of Greece," 250.

Note on Sources

This book is based on a wide variety of hitherto unpublished materials and published document collections, anthologies, memoirs, diaries, and biographies of prominent Greek and Balkan Communists. In particular, my research could not have been undertaken and concluded without access to the archives of a number of Communist parties. This documentary material is indispensable for understanding the inner logic and the process of decision-making within these parties. Among them, the story of the KKE's archives is particularly interesting because it relates to the party's national and international adventures, which are chronicled in the pages of this volume. Originally housed in Athens, after the Second World War the archives were transferred to Moscow, and from there to Bucharest. After the party's split of 1968, the two Communist parties fought over their possession under circumstances of secrecy and deception. After the fall of Communism, a great portion of the KKE archives for the period 1943–68 went to the Archives of Contemporary Social History (ASKI) in Athens. In the KKE files, I found a rich collection of party documents, including records of Central Committee and Politburo meetings, correspondence between the KKE leadership and foreign leaders, memoranda, reports, statistics, and other important materials.

My journey through the world of international archives began in Paris in 2005, when I worked for almost a semester in what was then the Bibliothèque de Documentation Internationale, which in 2018 became La Contemporaine, Bibliothèque, Archives, Musée des Mondes Contemporains. There I made extensive use of the veteran Communist leader Dimitris Vlandas's personal archives (F delta res 405).

Among the most important findings, a Polish document located in the Institute of National Remembrance (IPN) in Warsaw, detailing the material and financial help sent to the Democratic Army of Greece by Poland, Czechoslovakia, Hungary, and Romania, proved to be of critical importance for my research on the Greek Civil War. Written in Polish and signed by President Bolesław Bierut and General Wacław Komar, the report, which was delivered to Stalin, reveals in detail the nature and total cost of the aid procured by the Cominform for the Democratic Army. The report led me to begin a new phase in my research: collecting Polish documents from the IPN in Warsaw and Wroclaw concerning the KKE during the 1940s and '50s. The Polish archives helped me to comprehend the people's republics' critical role in the KKE's concerns and activities during the Cold War. They also led me to consult documentary materials in the National Archives of Prague (NAP), particularly the files of the Central Committee.

Unquestionably, for the study of the Greek Communist movement, state and party archives in the Balkans contain an immeasurable wealth of materials. Already in 1999, the Greek historians Vasilis Kondis and Spyros Sfetas had published important documentary materials from Bulgarian and Yugoslav archives concerning the KKE's politics during the civil war years (1944–49). In 2010, Giorgos Leontiadis and Boriana Bujaska published 107 documents from the Bulgarian Communist Party archives concerning the KKE during 1920–35. Both of these collections of documents were of particular importance for this book. In addition, the Central State Archives of Bulgaria (CDA), particularly the files of the Balkan Communist Federation (f. 10B), the file of G. Dimitrov (f. 146B), and the files of V. Kolarov (107B), include large numbers of documents relevant to this book. Moreover, in the State Central Archive of Albania (AQSH, the Politburo files and Central Committee's files of the Communist Party of Albania) are located materials concerning the relations between the KKE and the Albanian party from 1946 to 1958. Valuable materials were also found in Romania's National Archives (ANR-SANIC, the files of the Politburo and the Central Committee of the Communist Party of Romania). The Romanian archives are especially important for the study of the post-civil-war KKE's history, due to the fact that the party's headquarters were in Bucharest for almost twenty years.

Undoubtedly, and for obvious reasons, the Russian archives were of particular value for this book. For decades, the Greek party kept the Soviets meticulously informed on every aspect of its operations and politics. Since 1993, four collections of documents from Russian archives have been published in Greece. All of these volumes contributed significantly to my research and its conclusions, but I want to make particular reference to Nikos Papadatos, *Akros aporrito: I scheseis ESSD-KKE 1944–1952* (Athens: ΚΨΜ, 2019), which includes 193 Russian documents. Valuable documents were also found in the Russian State Archive of Social and Political History (RGASPI) and the Russian State Archive of Contemporary History (RGANI). In RGASPI, of particular interest were the Comintern's files (fond 495); also consulted were those in fonds 17, 82, and 575. Finally, in the RGANI files, documents in fonds 81 and 89 were also examined.

Among the virtually endless sources in the Western world, particularly valuable for the study of Greece in the 1940s are the British and US archives. Although scholars have been studying them for decades as they have been declassified, their value remains undiminished because of the wealth of information they contain about the KKE and Soviet politics toward Greece during the early years of the Cold War. For my research in British government sources, I worked in the collections of British diplomatic documents housed in the Academy of Athens (FO 371). For US archives, I relied on the General Records of the Department of State at the National Archives and Records Administration (NARA) (CDF 1945-1949, RG 59) and the annual volumes of the series *Foreign Relations of the United States* (FRUS).

Finally, particular attention was paid to the communist press, both Greek and international, for the years covered in this study. Particularly useful were the Comintern's magazines, *Inprecor* (International Press Correspondence, English edition), and *L'Internationale Communiste* (French edition) for the period 1921–38, the Cominform's *Pour une paix durable, pour une démocratie populaire (1947–1956)* (French edition), and the KKE newspapers and magazines *Rizospastis, Neos rizospastis, Kommounistiki epitheorisi*, and *Neos kosmos* for the entire period of my research.

BIBLIOGRAPHY

Archives

AAKT   Archive of New Files (Warsaw)
ANR-SANIC   National Archive of Romania—The Central Historical National
              Archives Department (Bucharest)
AOA   Academy of Athens
AQSH   State Central Archive of Albania (Tirana)
ASKI   Archives of Contemporary Social History (Athens)
CDA   Central State Archives of Bulgaria (Sofia)
FDRPL   Franklin D. Roosevelt Presidential Library and Museum (Hyde
              Park, NY)
IPN   Institute of National Remembrance (Warsaw)
LC   La Contemporaine, Bibliothèque, Archives, Musée des Mondes
              Contemporains (Paris)
MLO   Hungarian National Archives (Budapest)
NAP   National Archives of Prague
NARA   National Archives and Records Administration (Washington, DC)
PRO-FO   Public Record Office—Foreign Office (London)
RGANI   Russian State Archive of Contemporary History (Moscow)
RGASPI   Russian State Archive of Social and Political History (Moscow)

Newspapers and Periodicals

Dimokratikos stratos (KKE)
Inprecor (*International Press Correspondence*), English ed. (Comintern)
L'Humanité (PCF)
L'Internationale Communiste, French ed. (Comintern)
Kommounistiki epitheorisi (KKE)
Neos kosmos (KKE)
Pour une paix durable, pour une démocratie populaire (Cominform)
Rizospastis (KKE)

Collections of Documents

Afinian, V. G, V. Kondis, K. Papoulidis, D. Smirnova, and N. Tomilina, eds. *I
    scheseis KKE kai KK Sovietikis Enosis sto diastima 1953–1977, symfona me ta
    eggrafa tou Archeiou tis KE tou KKE.* Thessaloniki: Paratiritis, 1999.

Banac, Ivo, ed. *The Diary of Georgi Dimitrov, 1933–1949*. New Haven, CT: Yale University Press, 2003.

Bayerlein, Bernhard H., Mikhail Narinski, Brigitte Studer, and Serge Wolikow, eds. *Moscou-Paris-Berlin: Télégrammes chiffrés du Komintern (1939–1941)*. Paris: Tallandier, 2003.

Chourchoulis, Dionyssios, Christos Christidis, Vaios Kalogrias, Periklis-Stelios Karavis, Manolis Koumas, and Sofia Papastamkou, eds. *Greece during the Early Cold War: The View from the Western Archives; Documents*. Thessaloniki: University of Macedonia, 2015.

Clissold, Stephen, ed. *Yugoslavia and the Soviet Union, 1939–1973: A Documentary Survey*. London: Oxford University Press, 1975.

Dallin, Alexander, and F. I. Firsov. *Dimitrov and Stalin, 1934–1943: Letters from the Soviet Archives*. New Haven, CT: Yale University Press, 2000.

Degras, Jane, ed. *The Communist International, 1919–1943 Documents*. 3 vols. London: Royal Institute on International Affairs, 1956–64.

——. *Soviet Documents on Foreign Policy, 1917–1941*. New York: Oxford University Press, 1953.

Dimitrov, Georgi. *Selected Works*. 3 vols. Sofia, Bulgaria: Sofia Press, 1972.

Farakos, Grigoris. *B' Pagosmios Polemos: I scheseis KKE kai diethnous Kommounistikou kentrou*. Athens: Ellinika Grammata, 2004.

Fifth Congress of the Communist International. *Abridged Report*. June 17–July 8, 1924.

FRUS (Foreign Relations of the United States). 1944, vol. 5. *The Near East and Africa*. Washington, DC: US Government Printing Office, 1965.

——. 1945, vol. 8. *The Near East and Africa*. Washington, DC: US Government Printing Office, 1969.

——. 1946, vol. 7. *The Near East and Africa*. Washington, DC: US Government Printing Office, 1969.

——. 1947, vol. 5. *The Near East and Africa*. Washington, DC: US Government Printing Office, 1971.

——. 1948, vol. 4. *Eastern Europe: The Soviet Union*. Washington, DC: US Government Printing Office, 1974.

——. 1949, vol. 6. *The Near East, South Asia and Africa*. Washington, DC: US Government Printing Office, 1977.

Gibianskii, Leonid, and Norman M. Naimark. *The Soviet Union and the Establishment of Communist Regimes in Eastern Europe, 1944–1954: A Documentary Collection*. Washington, DC: National Council for Eurasian and East European Research, 2006.

Iatrides, John O., ed. *Ambassador MacVeagh Reports: Greece, 1933–1947*. Princeton, NJ: Princeton University Press, 1980.

Iliou, Philippos. *O Ellinikos Emfylios Polemos: I embloki tou KKE*. Athens: Themelio, 2005.

KKE. *Dokimio istorias tou KKE 1918–1949*. Athens: Sygchroni Epochi, 2008.

——. *Episima keimena, 1918–1961*. 8 vols. Athens: Sygchroni Epochi, 1974–97.

——. *To proto synedrio tou SEKE, November 4–10, 1918, Praktika*. Athens: Editions of the CC of the KKE, 1982.

———. *To trito ektakto synedrio tou KKE (ETKD), November 26–December 3, 1924.* Athens: Editions of the CC of the KKE, 1991.

Kondis, Basil, and Spyridon Sfetas, eds. *Emfylios polemos: Eggrafa apo ta Yugoslavika kai Voulgarika archeia.* Thessaloniki: Paratiritis, 1999.

Konstantakopoulos, Dimitris, Dimitris Patelis, and Panagiota Materi, eds. *1931–1944 fakelos ELLAS: Ta archeia ton mystikon Sovietikon ypiresion.* Athens: Livanis, 1993.

Kordatos, Giannis. *Arthrografies stin Kommounistiki epitheorisi 1921–24.* Athens: Syllogi, 2009.

Kouzinopoulos, Spyros, ed. *Georgi Dimitrov: Selides apo to aporrito imerologio.* Athens: Kastaniotis, 1999.

Leontiadis, Georgios, and Boriana Bujaska, eds. *To KKE mesa apo ta archeia tou Kommounistikou Kommatos tis Voulgarias: Syllogi eggrafon 1920–1935.* Athens: Novoli, 2010.

Marantzidis, Nikos, and Kostas Tsivos, eds. *O Ellinikos Emfylios kai to diethnes Kommounistiko systima: To KKE mesa apo ta Czechika archeia 1946–1968.* Athens: Alexandreia, 2011.

Murashko, G. P., T. V. Volotikina, T. M. Islamov, A. F. Noskova, and L. A. Rogovaia, eds. History and Public Policy Program Digital Archive. Vostochnaia Evropa. http://digitalarchive.wilsoncenter.org.

Papadatos, Nikos, ed. *Akros aporrito: I scheseis ESSD-KKE 1944–1952.* Athens: ΚΨΜ, 2019.

Papanagiotou, Alekos, ed. *To Kommounistiko Komma Elladas ston polemo kai tin antistasi: Episima keimena.* Vol. 5. Athens: Ekdoseis KKE Esoterikou, 1973.

Petropoulos, Giorgos, ed. *I kathairesi tou Nikou Zachariadi.* Athens: Proskinio, 2003.

———. *Nikos Zachariadis: Istorika dilimmata, istorikes apantiseis.* Athens: Kastaniotis, 2011.

Pearce, Brian, ed. *Congress of the Peoples of the East, Baku, September 1920, Stenographic Report.* London: New Park, 1977.

Pouliopoulos, Pantelis. *Dialechta erga.* Athens: Ergatiki Pali, 2013.

Procacci, Guiliano, ed. *The Cominform: Minutes of the Three Conferences, 1947/1948/1949.* Milan: Feltrinelli, 1994.

Reynolds, David, and Vladimir Pechatnov. *The Kremlin Letters: Stalin Wartime Correspondence with Churchill and Roosevelt.* New Haven, CT: Yale University Press, 2018.

Riddell, John, ed. *To the Masses: Proceedings of the Third Congress of the Communist International, 1921.* Leiden: Brill, 2015.

———. *Toward the United Front: Proceedings of the Fourth Congress of the Communist International, 1922.* Leiden: Brill, 2012.

———. *Workers of the World and Oppressed Peoples, Unite: Proceedings and Documents of the Second Congress, 1920.* 2 vols. New York: Pathfinder, 1991.

Stalin, J. V. *Works.* 13 vols. Moscow: Foreign Languages Publishing House, 1954.

Tiber, Mike, ed. *The Communist Movement at a Crossroads: Plenums of the Communist International's Executive Committee, 1922–1923.* Leiden: Brill, 2018.

Tsouderos, Emmanouil I. *Istoriko archeio 1941–1944*. 6 vols. Athens: Fytrakis, 1990.

United States Senate Committee on the Judiciary. *Yugoslav Communism, A Critical Study*. Washington, DC: US Government Printing Office, 1961.

VII Congress of the Communist International: Abridged Stenographic Report of Proceedings. Moscow: Foreign Languages Publishing House, 1939.

Memoirs and Biographies

Antaios, Petros. *N. Zachariadis: Thytis kai thima*. Athens: Fytrakis, 1991.

Apostolou, Lefteris. *Nikos Zachariadis: I poreia enos igeti 1923–1949*. Athens: Filistor, 2000.

Benaroya, Avraam. *I proti stadiodromia tou Ellinikou proletariatou*. Athens: Kommouna, 1986.

Chatzis, Thanassis. *I nikifora epanastasi pou chathike*. 2 vols. Athens: Papazissis, 1977.

Churchill, Winston. *Triumph and Tragedy*. Vol. 6 of *The Second World War*. New York: Mifflin, 1953.

Cohen, Stephen F. *Bukharin and the Bolshevik Revolution: A Political Biography, 1888–1938*. New York: Vintage House, 1975.

Daniilidis, Polydoros. *O Polydoros thimatai*. Athens: Istorikes Ekdoseis, 1990.

Dimitriou, Panos. *Ek vatheon: Chroniko mia zois kai mias epochis*. Athens: Themelio, 1997.

Dedijer, Vladimir. *Tito Speaks: His Self-Portrait and Struggle with Stalin*. London: Weidenfeld and Nicolson, 1953.

Deutscher, Isaac. *The Prophet Unarmed: Trotsky, 1921–1929*. London: Verso, 2003.

Djilas, Milovan. *Conversations with Stalin*. Mitcham, Victoria: Penguin, 1967.

Eleftheriou, Lefteris. *Sinomilies me ton Niko Zachariadi: Moscha Martios-Ioulios 1956*. Athens: Kentavros, 1986.

Hull, Cordell. *The Memoirs of Cordell Hull*. 2 vols. New York: Macmillan, 1948.

Ioannidis, Giannis. *Anamniseis: Provlimata tis politikis tou KKE stin ethniki antistasi 1940–1945*. Athens: Themelio, 1979.

Kasimatis, Stavros. *I paranomi: Anthropi kai dokoumenta*. Athens: Filistor, 1997.

Khlevniuk, Oleg V. *Stalin: New Biography of a Dictator*. New Haven, CT: Yale University Press, 2015.

Kotkin, Stephen. *Stalin: Paradoxes of Power, 1878–1928*. New York: Penguin, 2014.

Kuromiya, Hiroaki. *Stalin: Profiles in Power*. London: Routledge, 2005.

Lane, A. Thomas, ed. *Biographical Dictionary of European Labor Leaders*. 2 vols. Westport, CT: Greenwood, 1995.

Levy, Robert. *Ana Pauker: The Rise and Fall of a Jewish Communist*. Berkeley: University of California Press, 2001.

Lazitch, Branko, and Milorad M. Drachkovitch. *Biographical Dictionary of the Comintern*. Stanford, CA: Hoover Institution Press, 1986.

Livieratos, Dimitris. *Pantelis Pouliopoulos: Enas epanastatis dianooumenos*. Athens: Glaros, 1992.

Markovitis, Marios. *Ochi, den eimai exthros tou laou*. Thessaloniki: Epikentro, 2017.

Mitsopoulos, Thanassis. *Meiname Ellines: Ta scholeia ton Ellinon politikon prosfygon stis sosialistikes chores*. Athens: Odysseas, 1979.

Nefeloudis, Pavlos. *Stis piges tis kakodaimonias: Ta vathitera aitia tis diaspasis tou KKE 1918–1968*. Athens: Gutenberg, 1974.

Nefeloudis, Vassilis A. *Documento: To Staliniko fenomeno stin Ellada, Zachariadis kai Zachariadismos, o mithos kai i alitheia*. Athens: Delfini, 1993.

——. *Martyries 1906–1938*. Athens: Okeanida, 1984.

Partsalidis, Mitsos. *Dipli apokatastasi tis ethnikis antistasis*. Athens: Themelio, 1978.

Petroulias, Charalambos. *I aichmalosia mou kai i zoi ton politikon prosfygon stin Taskendi 1949–1956*. Athens: Lyhnia, 2012.

Petsopoulos, Yannis. *Ta pragmatika aitia tis diagrafis mou apo to KKE*. Athens: Self-published, 1946.

Piyade, Mosha. *About the Legend That the Yugoslav Uprising Owed Its Existence to Soviet Assistance*. London: Yugoslav Embassy, 1950.

Reale, Eugenio. *Avec Duclos au banc des accusés: La réunion constitutive du Kominform, Szklarska Poreba, 22–27 Septembre 1947*. Paris: Plon, 1958.

Roussos, Petros. *I megali pentaetia*. 2 vols. Athens: Sygchroni Epochi, 1976.

Serge, Victor. *Memoirs of a Revolutionary*. New York: NYRB, 2012.

Stankova, Marietta. *Georgi Dimitrov: A Biography*. New York: Tauris, 2010.

Stavridis, Eleftherios. *Ta paraskinia tou KKE*. Athens: Self-published, 1953.

Stinas, Agis. *Anamniseis: Evdominda chronia kato apo ti simea tis sosialistikis epanastasis*. 2 vols. Athens: Vergos, 1977.

Swain, Geoffrey. *Tito: A Biography*. London: Tauris, 2011.

Vontitsos-Gousias Giorgis. *I aities gia tis ittes, ti diaspasi tou KKE kai tis Ellinikis Aristeras*. 2 vols. Athens: Kakoulidis, 1977.

Vukmanović, Svetozar. *How and Why the People's Liberation Struggle of Greece Met with Defeat*. London: Merlin, 1985. First published in 1950.

Other Sources

Adanïr, Fikret. "The National Question and the Genesis and Development of Socialism in the Ottoman Empire: The Case of Macedonia." In *Socialism and Nationalism in the Ottoman Empire, 1876–1923*, edited by Mete Tuncay and Erick J. Zürcher, 27–48. New York: British Academic Press, 1994.

Aganson, Olga. "The Versailles Order and Perplexities of the Comintern's Policy in the Balkans in the 1930s: Departure from the World Revolution." *Journal of Balkan and Near Eastern Studies* 22, no. 2 (2020): 194–209.

Agtzidis, Vlasis. *Paraefxeinios diaspora: I Ellinikes egatastaseis stis voreioanatolikes perioches tou Efxeinou Pontou*. Thessaloniki: Afoi Kyriakidi, 2001.

——. "The Persecution of the Pontic Greeks in the Soviet Union." *Journal of Refugee Studies* 4, no. 4 (1991): 372–81.

Alivizatos, Nikos. *I politiki thesmi se krisi, 1922–1974: Opseis tis Ellinikis embeirias*. Athens: Themelio, 1995.

Amendola, Giorgio. *Storia del Partito Comunista Italiano 1921–1943*. Rome: Riuniti, 1978.

Anastasiadis, Georgios, Nikos Marantzidis, Chaidi Keramopoulous, and Tatalas Vangelis. *To ergatiko syndikalistiko kinima tis Thessalonikis*. Salonica: EKT, 1997.

Anikeev, Anatoly. "The Idea for a Balkan Federation: The Civil War in Greece and Soviet-Yugoslav Conflict." In *The Balkans in the Cold War*, edited by Vojislav G. Pavlović, 169–83. Belgrade: Institute for Balkan Studies, 2011.

Anson, Beatriz. "The Limits of Destalinization: The Spanish Communist Party, 1956–1965." PhD diss., London School of Economics, 2002.

Applebaum, Anne. *Iron Curtain: The Crushing of Eastern Europe*. London: Penguin, 2013.

Athanasiadis, Andreas, and Elias Grouios. *Zachariadis kai "Makedoniko ethniko zitima" 1949–1956: I periptosi tis organosis Iliden*. Florina: Floriniotikes Ekdoseis, 2020.

Avakumović, Ivan. *History of the Communist Party of Yugoslavia*. Aberdeen: Aberdeen University Press, 1964.

Baerentzen, Lars. "I afixi tis Sovietikis stratiotikis apostolis ton Ioulio 1944." In *I Ellada 1936–44: Diktatoria, katohi, antistasi*, edited by Hagen Fleischer and Nikos Svoronos, 563–95. Athens: Morfotiko Instituto ATE, 1989.

———. "The Paidomazoma and the Queen's Camps." In *Studies in History of the Greek Civil War, 1945–1949*, edited by Lars Baerentzen, John O. Iatrides, and Ole L. Smith, 127–59. Copenhagen: Museum Tusculanum Press, 1987.

Baev, Iordan. *Mia matia ap'exo: O Emfylios polemos stin Ellada; Diethneis diastaseis*. Athens: Filistor, 1996.

———. *O emfylios polemos stin Ellada: Diethneis diastaseis*. Athens: Filistor, 1997.

———. "Ta Valkania: I proti estia Psichrou Polemou stin Evropi." In *Dekemvris tou '44, neoteri erevna, neoteres prosegiseis*, edited by Grigoris Farakos, 165–89. Athens: Filistor, 1996.

Balampanidis, Ioannis. *Eurocommunism: From the Communist to the Radical European Left*. London: Routledge, 2019.

Banac, Ivo. "The Communist Party of Yugoslavia during the Period of Legality (1919–1921)." In *The Effects of World War I: The Class War after the Great War; The Rise of Communist Parties in East Central Europe, 1919–1921*, edited by Ivo Banac, 188–230. New York: Columbia University Press: 1983.

———. *With Stalin against Tito: Cominformist Splits in Yugoslav Communism*. Ithaca, NY: Cornell University Press, 1988.

Barker, Elisabeth. *British Policy in South-east Europe in the Second World War*. London: Macmillan, 1976.

———. *Macedonia: Its Place in Balkan Power Politics*. London: Royal Institute of International Affairs, 1950.

———. "Some Factors in British Decision-Making over Yugoslavia, 1941–4." In *British Policy towards Wartime Resistance in Yugoslavia and Greece*, edited by Phyllis Auty and Richard Clogg, 22–58. London: Macmillan, 1975.

Basciani, Alberto. "Screditare un sistema, delegittimare uno stato: La Fédéra-tion Balkanique e la Grande Romania, 1924-1932." *Krypton: Identità, Potere, Rappresentazioni* 2 (2013): 76-85.

Bataković, Dušan T. "The Communist Party of Yugoslavia, the Comintern and the National Question: The Case of Kosovo and Metohija." In *The Balkans in the Cold War*, edited by Vojislav G. Pavlović, 61-85. Belgrade: Institute for Balkan Studies, 2011.

Beckett, Francis. *Enemy Within: The Rise and Fall of the British Communist Party.* Suffolk: Merlin, 1995.

Bell, John D. *The Bulgarian Communist Party from Blagoev to Zhivkov.* Stanford, CA: Hoover Institution Press, 1986.

Boeschoten, Riki Van. "'Enotita' kai 'aderfotita': Slavomakedones kai Ellines politiki prosfyges stin Anatoliki Evropi." In *To oplo para poda: I politiki pros-fyges tou Ellinikou Emfyliou Polemou stin Anatoliki Evropi*, edited by Eftichia Voutira, Vasilis Dalkavoukis, Nikos Marantzidis, and Maria Bontila, 45-69. Thessaloniki: University of Macedonia Press, 2005.

Bontila, Maria. *"Polichronos na zeis Megale Stalin": I ekpaidefsi ton paidion ton poli-tikon prosfygon sta anatolika krati.* Athens: Metaihmio, 2004.

Broué, Pierre. *Histoire de l'internationale Communiste 1919–1943.* Paris: Fayard, 1997.

Burks, R. V. *The Dynamics of Communism in Eastern Europe.* Princeton, NJ: Princeton University Press, 1962.

Carr, E. H. *A History of Soviet Russia: Socialism in One Country, 1924–1926.* 3 vols. London: Macmillan, 1964.

——. *Twilight of the Comintern.* New York: Pantheon Books, 1982.

Chatzianastasiou, Tasos. *Antartes kai kapetanii: I ethniki antistasi kata tis Voulgari-kis katochis tis anatolikis Makedonias kai Thrakis, 1942–1944.* Thessaloniki: Kyriakidis, 2003.

Cicak, Fedor Ivan. "The Communist Party of Yugoslavia between 1919-1934: An Analysis of Its Formative Process." PhD diss., Indiana University, 1965.

Close, David H., ed. *The Greek Civil War, 1943–1950: Studies of Polarization.* London: Routledge, 1993.

Connelly, John. *From Peoples into Nations: A History of Eastern Europe.* Princeton, NJ: Princeton University Press, 2020.

Connor, Walker. *The National Question in Marxist-Leninist Theory and Strategy.* Princeton, NJ: Princeton University Press, 1984.

Conrad, Sebastian. *What Is Global History?* Princeton, NJ: Princeton University Press, 2016.

Courtois, Stéphane. *Le PCF dans la guerre: De Gaule, La Résistance, Staline.* Paris: Ramsay, 1980.

Courtois, Stéphane, and Marc Lazar. *Histoire du Parti Communiste Français.* Paris: Presses Universitaires de France, 2000.

Crampton, R. G. *Bulgaria.* Oxford: Oxford University Press, 2007.

Dagas, Alekos. "Kommounistiko Komma Ellados, Elliniko tmima tis Kom-mounistikis Diethnous." In *Istoria tis Elladas tou 20ou Aiona: 1922–1940* o Mesopolemos, edited by Christos Chatziiosif, B2, 155–201. Athens: Vivliorama, 2003.

Dagas, Alekos, and Giorgos Leontiadis. Komintern kai Makedoniko zitima, to Elliniko paraskinio 1924. Thessaloniki: Epikentro, 2008.

Danforth, Loring M., and Riki Van Boeschoten. Children of the Greek Civil War: Refugees and the Politics of Memory. Chicago: University of Chicago Press, 2012.

Daskalov, Georgi. I Elliniki politiki prosfygia sti Voulgaria 1946–1989. Thessaloniki: Epikentro, 2015.

Dayos, Stavros G. I diethnis diastasi tis rixis E. Hoxha—J.B. Tito kai i lixi tou Ellinikou Emfyliou Polemou. Thessaloniki: Paratiritis, 2004.

de Sola Pool, Ithiel. Satellite Generals: A Study of Military Elites in the Soviet Sphere. Stanford, CA: Stanford University Press, 1955.

Degerli, Esra S. "Balkan Pact and Turkey." Journal of International Social Research 2, no. 6 (2009): 136–47.

Deletant, Dennis. Romania under Communist Rule. Bucharest: Civic Academy Foundation, 2006.

Di Biagio, Anna. "The Establishment of the Cominform." In The Cominform: Minutes of the Three Conferences, 1947/1948/1949, edited by Guiliano Procacci, 11–34. Milan: Feltrinelli, 1994.

——. "The Marshall Plan and the Founding of the Cominform, June–September 1947." In The Soviet Union and Europe in the Cold War, 1943–1953, edited by Francesca Gori and Silvio Pons, 208–22. London: Macmillan, 1996.

Diac, Cristina. "Între intransigență și complicități asumate: Finanțarea mișcării Comuniste din România de Comintern în prima jumătate a anilor 20." In Relațiile Româno-ruse/Sovietice din secolul al XIX-lea până în prezent, edited by Antoaneta Olteanu and Ana-Maria Cătănuș, 105–23. Bucharest: Editura Universității din București, 2020.

Dimitrov, Vesselin. Stalin's Cold War: Soviet Foreign Policy, Democracy and Communism in Bulgaria, 1941–48. New York: Palgrave, 2008.

Dimou, Augusta. Entangled Paths towards Modernity: Contextualizing Socialism and Nationalism in the Balkans. Budapest: CEU Press, 2009.

Djilas, Aleksa. The Contested Country: Yugoslav Unity and Communist Revolution, 1919–1953. Cambridge, MA: Harvard University Press, 1991.

Dordanas, Stratos N., and Vaios Kalogrias. I zoes ton allon: I Stazi kai i Ellines politikoi prosfyges stin Anatoliki Germania (1949–1989). Thessaloniki: Epikentro, 2020.

Dragostinova, Theodora. Between Two Motherlands: Nationality and Emigration among the Greeks of Bulgaria, 1900–1949. Ithaca, NY: Cornell University Press, 2011.

Dumont, Paul. "A Jewish, Socialist and Ottoman Organization: The Workers' Federation of Salonica." In Socialism and Nationalism in the Ottoman Empire, 1876–1923, edited by Mete Tuncay and Erick J. Zürcher, 49–75. New York: British Academic Press, 1994.

Dunn, David. "Maksim Litvinov: Commissar of Contradiction." Journal of Contemporary History 23, no. 2 (1988): 221–43.

Dymarski, Mirosław. "The Macedonian Question in the Light of the Documents of the Serbian Diplomacy, 1903-1914." *Politeja* 30, no. 4 (2014): 7-18.

Elbaz, Sharon, and Liora Israël. "L'invention du droit comme arme politique dans le Communisme Français: L'Association Juridique Internationale (1929-1939)." *Vingtième siècle* 85 (2005): 31-43.

Elefantis, Angelos G. *I epagelia tis adinatis epanastasis: KKE kai astismos sto mesopolemo.* Athens: Themelio, 1976.

Ellman, Michael. "Soviet Repression Statistics: Some Comments." *Europe-Asia Studies* 54, no. 7 (2002): 1151-72.

Esche, Mattias. "I politiki tis ESSD gia tin Ellada kata ton B' Pagkosmio Polemo." In *I Ellada 1936-44: Diktatoria, katochi, antistasi,* edited by Hagen Fleischer and Nikos Svoronos, 553-62. Athens: Morfotiko Instituto ATE, 1989.

Eudin, Xenia Joukoff, and Harold H. Fisher. *Soviet Russia and the West, 1920-1927: A Documentary Survey.* Stanford, CA: Stanford University Press, 1957.

Farakos, Grigoris. *Aris Velouchiotis, to chameno arheio—agnosta keimena.* Athens: Ellinika Grammata, 1997.

——, ed. *Dekemvris tou '44: Neoteri erevna, neoteres prosegiseis.* Athens: Filistor, 1996.

——. *Martyries kai stochasmi, 1941-1991.* Athens: Proskinio, 1993.

——. *O ELAS kai I exousia.* 2 vols. Athens: Ellinika Grammata, 2000.

Fayet, Jean-François. "Paul Levi and the Turning Point of 1921: Bolshevik Emissaries and International Discipline in the Time of Lenin." In *Bolshevism, Stalinism and the Comintern: Perspectives on Stalinization, 1917-1953,* edited by Norman Laporte, Kevin Morgan, and Matthew Worley, 105-23. New York: Palgrave, 2008.

Firsov, Fridrikh I., Harvey Klehr, and John Earl Haynes. *Secret Cables of the Comintern, 1933-1943.* New Haven, CT: Yale University Press, 2014.

Fišera, Vladimir Claude. "Communisme et intégration supranationale: La revue 'La Fédération Balkanique' (1924-1932)." *Revue d'Histoire Moderne et Contemporaine* 34, no. 3 (1987): 497-508.

——. "La dimension régionale: Slavisme, Fédéralisme et Communisme de la Fédération Communiste Balkanique au Comité Interslave (1920-1946)." *Revue des Etudes Slaves* 51, no. 1-2 (1978): 85-96.

——. *Les peuples Slaves et le Communisme: De Marx à Gorbatchev.* Paris: Berg, 1992.

Fitzpatrick, Sheila. *Everyday Stalinism: Ordinary Life in Extraordinary Times; Soviet Russia in the 1930s.* Oxford: Oxford University Press, 2000.

——. "Signals from Below: Soviet Letters of Denunciation of the 1930s." *Journal of Modern History* 68, no. 4 (1996): 831-66.

Fleischer, Hagen. *Stemma kai svastika: I Ellada tis katochis kai tis antistasis.* 2 vols. Athens: Papazissis, 1989.

Fowkes, Ben. "To Make the Nation or to Break It: Communist Dilemmas in Two Interwar Multinational States." In *Bolshevism, Stalinism and the Comintern: Perspectives on Stalinization, 1917-1953,* edited by Norman Laporte, Kevin Morgan, and Matthew Worley, 206-25. New York: Palgrave, 2008.

Georgantidis, Christos N., and Elias Nikolakopoulos. "I exelixi tis eklogikis dinamis tou KKE metaxi ton dio polemon." *Greek Review of Social Research*, no. 36–37 (1979): 448–68.

Georgiadou-Katsoulaki, A. *I proti syndiaskepsi tou SEKE(K) Februarios 1922*. Athens: Self-published, 1984.

Gerolymatos, André. *The International Civil War: Greece, 1943–1949*. New Haven, CT: Yale University Press, 2016.

Getty, John Arch, and Oleg V. Naumov, eds. *The Road to Terror: Stalin and the Self-Destruction of the Bolsheviks, 1932–1939*. New Haven, CT: Yale University Press, 1999.

Gibianskii, Leonid. "Federative Projects of the Balkan Communists and the USSR Policy during the Second World War and at the Beginning of the Cold War." In *The Balkans in the Cold War*, edited by Vojislav G. Pavlović, 43–60. Belgrade: Institute for Balkan Studies, 2011.

——. "Kak voznik Kominform: Po novym arkhivnym materialam." *Novaia i Noveiishaia Istoriaa*, no. 4 (1993): 131–52.

——. "The Soviet-Yugoslav Conflict and the Soviet Bloc." In *The Soviet Union and Europe in the Cold War, 1943–1953*, edited by Francesca Gori and Silvio Pons, 222–45. London: Macmillan, 1996.

——. "Soviet-Yugoslav Relations, the Cominform and Balkan Communist Parties: Documentary Sources and Some Aspects of Its Research." In *The Balkans in the Cold War*, edited by Vojislav G. Pavlović, 265–301. Belgrade: Institute for Balkan Studies, 2011.

Gotovitch, José. "Histoire du Parti Communiste de Belgique." *Courier Hebdomadaire du CRISP* 37, no. 1582 (1997): 1–36.

Goulter-Zervoudakis, Christina. "The Politization of Intelligence: The British Experience in Greece, 1941–1944." *Intelligence and National Security* 13, no. 1 (1998): 165–94.

Grišina, R. P. "I proti fasi tis drastiriotitas tis Valkanikis Kommounistikis Omospondias (1920–1923) kai i Ellada." *Valkanika Symmeikta* 7 (1995): 171–83.

Gritzonas, Kostas. *Kokkinoi drapetes 1920–1944*. Athens: Glaros, 1985.

Gužvica, Stefan. "Learning Leninism: Factional Struggles in the Communist Party of Yugoslavia during the Great Purge, 1936–1940." MA thesis, Central European University, 2018.

——. "Retrospective Lessons and Generational Gaps: The Impact of Yugoslav Communist Émigrés in Interwar Czechoslovakia on the Postwar Yugoslav State." *Acta Histriae* 27, no. 1 (2019): 35–54.

Harris, George S. *The Origins of Communism in Turkey*. Stanford, CA: Hoover Institution, 1967.

Haslam, Jonathan. *The Soviet Union and the Struggle for Collective Security in Europe, 1933–1939*. London: Macmillan, 1984.

Haug, Hilde Katrine. *Creating a Socialist Yugoslavia: Tito, Communist Leadership and the National Question*. London: I. B. Tauris, 2012.

Hradečný, Pavel. "Czechoslovak Material Aid to the Communist 'Democratic Army of Greece' in the Years 1948–1949." *Balkan Studies* 40, no. 2 (1999): 361–82.

——. *I Elliniki diaspora stin Czechoslovakia: Idrisi kai archika stadia anaptyxis 1948–1954*. Thessaloniki: Institute for Balkan Studies, 2007.

——. "Zdrženlivý internacionalismus: Občanská válka v Řecku a Československá materiální pomoc Demokratické Armádě Řecka." *Soudobé dějiny* 1-2 (2003): 58-92.

Iatrides, John O. "Civil War, 1945-1949: National and International Aspects." In *Greece in the 1940s: A Nation in Crisis*, edited by John O. Iatrides, 195-219. Hanover, NH: University Press of New England, 1981.

——. "Greece and the Birth of Containment: An American Perspective." In *The Balkans in the Cold War*, edited by Svetozar Rajak, Konstantina E. Botsiou, Eirini Karamouzi, and Evanthis Hatzivassiliou, 3-28. London: Palgrave, 2017.

——. "I politikopiisi tis Ellinikis antistasis 1941-1943." In *Anorthodoxi polemi: Makedonia, Emfylios, Kypros*, edited by Vasilis K. Gounaris, Stathis N. Kalyvas, and Giannis D. Stefanidis, 254-76. Athens: Patakis, 2010.

——. *Revolt in Athens: The Greek Communist 'Second Round,' 1944–1945*. Princeton, NJ: Princeton University Press, 1972.

——. "Revolution or Self-Defense? Communist Goals, Strategy, and Tactics in the Greek Civil War." *Journal of Cold War Studies* 7, no. 3 (2005): 3-33.

Iazhborovskaia, Inessa. "The Gomulka Alternative: The Untravelled Road." In *The Establishment of Communist Regimes in Eastern Europe, 1944–1949*, edited by Norman Naimark and Leonid Gibianskii, 123-37. Boulder, CO: Westview, 1997.

Ilicak, Sükrü H. "Jewish Socialism in Ottoman Salonica." *Southeast European and Black Sea Studies* 2, no. 3 (2002): 115-46.

Ionescu, Ghiță. *Communismul în România*. Bucharest: Litera, 1994.

Israël, Liora. "From Cause Lawyering to Resistance: French Communist Lawyers in the Shadow of History (1929-1945)." In *The Worlds Cause Lawyers Make: Structure and Agency in Legal Practice*, edited by Austin Sarat and Stuart Scheingold, 147-67. Stanford, CA: Stanford University Press, 2005.

Jacobson, Jon. "The Soviet Union and Versailles." In *The Treaty of Versailles: A Reassessment after 75 Years*, edited by Manfred F. Boemeke, Gerald Feldman, and Elisabeth Glaser, 451-68. Cambridge: Cambridge University Press, 2006.

——. *When the Soviet Union Entered World Politics*. Berkeley: University of California Press, 1994.

Jones, Howard. *"A New Kind of War": America's Global Strategy and the Truman Doctrine in Greece*. New York: Oxford University Press, 1989.

Kahan, Vilém. "The Communist International, 1919-43: The Personnel of Its Highest Bodies." *International Review of Social History* 21, no. 2 (1976): 151-85.

——. "A Contribution to the Identification of the Pseudonyms Used in the Minutes and Reports of the Communist International." *International Review of Social History* 23, no. 2 (1978): 177-92.

Kainourgios, Christos D. *Sta adyta tou Emfyliou: Stratopeda Rubik kai Bulkes*. Athens: Iolkos, 2003.

Kalyvas, Stathis, and Nikos Marantzidis. *Emfylia pathi*. Athens: Metaixmio, 2015.

——. "Greek Communism, 1968-2001." *East European Politics and Societies* 16, no. 3 (2002): 665-90.

Karpozilos, Apostolos. "The Greeks in Russia: Pages from the Political and Cultural History of Pontian and Mariupol Greeks in Southern Russia." *Archeion Pontou* 47 (1996/97): 16-19.

Karpozilos, Kostis. "Apopeires sigrotisis tou Ellinikou Laikou Metopou: I Dimokratiki Enosi Ellinon Gallias 1937-1939." *Archeiotaxio* 10 (2008): 37-53.

——. "The Defeated of the Greek Civil War: From Fighters to Political Refugees in the Cold War." *Journal of Cold War Studies* 16, no. 3 (2014): 62-87.

——. "Ektos orion: Mia diethniki istoria tou Ellinikou Kommounismou." Work in progress, 2022.

Katsoulis, Giorgis D. *Istoria tou Kommounistikou Kommatos Elladas*. 5 vols. Athens: Nea Synora, 1976.

Kirschenbaum, Lisa A. "Exile, Gender, and Communist Self-Fashioning: Dolores Ibárruri (La Pasionaria) in the Soviet Union." *Slavic Review* 71, no. 3 (2012): 566-89.

——. *International Communism and the Spanish Civil War: Solidarity and Suspicion*. Cambridge: Cambridge University Press, 2015.

Kitchen, Martin. "British Policy towards the Soviet Union, 1945-1948." In *Soviet Foreign Policy, 1917–1991: A Retrospective*, edited by Gabriel Gorodetsky, 111-34. London: Routledge, 1994.

Kocho-Williams, Alastair. *Russian and Soviet Diplomacy, 1900–1939*. New York: Palgrave, 2012.

Kofos, Evangellos. "I Valkaniki diastassi tou Makedonikou zitimatos sta chronia tis katochis kai tis antistasis." In *I Ellada 1936–44: Diktatoria, katochi, antistasi*, edited by Hagen Fleischer and Nikos Svoronos, 418-71. Athens: Morfotiko Instituto ATE, 1989.

——. *Nationalism and Communism in Macedonia*. Thessaloniki: Institute for Balkan Studies, 1964.

Koliopoulos, John S., and Thanos M. Veremis. *Greece: The Modern Sequel*. London: Hurst, 2002.

Kondis, Vasilis. *I Aggloamerikaniki politiki kai to Elliniko provlima, 1945–1949*. Thessaloniki: Paratiritis, 1984.

——. "The Re-establishment of the Greek-Soviet Relations in 1924." *Balkan Studies* 26, no. 1 (1985): 151-57.

——. *Sosialistika krati kai KKE ston Emfylio*. Thessaloniki: Epikentro, 2012.

Kordatos, Yannis. *Istoria tou Ellinikou ergatikou kinimatos*. Athens: Boukoumanis, 1972.

Kousoulas, George. *Revolution and Defeat: The Story of the Greek Communist Party*. New York: Oxford University Press, 1965.

Koutsoukalis, Alekos. *I defteri dekaetia tou KKE 1929–1939*. Athens: Gnosi, 1984.

Kowalsky, Daniel. *Stalin and the Spanish Civil War*. New York: Columbia University Press, 2004. Gutenberg ebook.

Králová, Kateřina, and Kostas Tsivos. *Stegnosan ta dakrua mas: Ellines prosfyges stin Czechoslovakia*. Athens: Alexandreia, 2015.

Kramer, Mark. "The Role of the CPSU International Department in Soviet Foreign Relations and National Security Policy." *Soviet Studies* 42, no. 3 (1990): 429–46.

——. "Stalin, Soviet Policy, and the Consolidation of a Communist Bloc in Eastern Europe." In *Stalinism Revisited: The Establishment of Communist Regimes in East-Central Europe*, edited by Vladimir Tismăneanu, 52–101. Budapest: Central European University Press, 2009.

——. "Stalin, the Split with Yugoslavia, and Soviet-East European Efforts to Reassert Control, 1948–53." In *The Balkans in the Cold War*, edited by Svetozar Rajak, Konstantina E. Botsiou, Eirini Karamouzi, and Evanthis Hatzivassiliou, 29–63. London: Palgrave, 2017.

Kriegel, Annie. *Les Communistes Français: Essai d'ethnographie politique*. Paris: Seuil, 1968.

——. *Un autre Communisme?* Paris: Hachette, 1977.

Kubasiewicz, Izabela. "Children and Youth from Greece in the Realities of the Polish People's Republic: Children's Homes, Education, Upbringing." In *PRL a Wojna Domowa w Grecji/The Polish People's Republic and the Greek Civil War*, edited by Magdalena Semczyszyn, 186–95. Szczecin: IPN, 2016.

Kudrna, Ladislav. "Podivní vlastenectv: Českoslovenští Komunisté a jejich postoj k válce do 22. Června 1941." *Fakta a svědectví* 3 (2011). https://www.valka.cz/14855-Podivni-vlastenci.

Kuniholm, Bruce R. "The Origins of the Cold War in the Near East." In *Soviet Foreign Policy, 1917–1991: A Retrospective*, edited by Gabriel Gorodetsky, 135–45. London: Routledge, 1994.

——. *The Origins of the Cold War in the Near East: Great Power Conflict and Diplomacy in Iran, Turkey, and Greece*. Princeton, NJ: Princeton University Press, 1980.

Labatos, Gavrilis. *Ellines politiki prosfyges stin Taskendi 1949–1957*. Athens: Kourier, 2001.

Lagani, Irène. "Les Communistes des Balkans et la Guerre Civile Grecque Mars 1946–Août 1949." *Communisme* 9 (1986): 60–78.

Lalaj, Ana. "I embloki tis Alvanias ston Elliniko Emfylio Polemo." In *Ellada kai Alvania ston Psichro Polemo: Politikes, ideologies, nootropies*, edited by Nikos Marantzidis and Elias G. Skoulidas, 79–99. Athens: Alexandreia, 2020.

Lambrinou, Katerina. *EDA 1956–1967: Politiki kai ideologia*. Athens: Polis, 2017.

Laporte, Norman, and Kevin Morgan. "Kings among Their Subjects? Ernst Thälmann, Harry Pollitt and the Leadership Cult as Stalinization." In *Bolshevism, Stalinism and the Comintern: Perspectives on Stalinization, 1917–1953*, edited by Norman Laporte, Kevin Morgan, and Matthew Worley, 124–45. New York: Palgrave, 2008.

Lazar, Marc. "Fin de Siècle Communism in Western Europe." *Dissent*, Winter 2000.

Lazitch, Branko. *Tito et la Révolution Yougoslave, 1937–1956*. Paris: Fasquelle, 1957.

Lebedeva, Natalia, and Mihail Narinski. *I Kommounistiki Diethnis ston B' Pagosmio Polemo*. Athens: Ellinika Grammata, 2004.

Lešnik, August. "The Development of the Communist Movement in Yugoslavia during the Comintern Period." *International Newsletter of Communist Studies Online* 11, no. 18 (2005): 25–60.

Liakos, Antonis. *Ergasia kai politiki stin ellada tou Mesopolemou.* Athens: Emporiki Trapeza, 1993.

Linardatos, Spyros. "Antistasi sti diktatoria tou Metaxa." In *I Ellada 1936–44: Diktatoria, katohi, antistasi,* edited by Nikos Svoronos and Hagen Fleischer, 92–97. Athens: Morfotiko Instituto ATE, 1989.

Lukač, Dušan. "I sinergasia metaxi ton ethnikon apeleftherotikon kinimaton tis Elladas kai tis Yugoslavias." In *I Ellada 1936–44: Diktatoria, katohi, antistasi,* edited by Hagen Fleischer and Nikos Svoronos, 480–88. Athens: Morfotiko Instituto ATE, 1989.

Luza, Radomir. "The Communist Party of Czechoslovakia and the Czech Resistance, 1939–1945." *Slavic Review* 28, no. 4 (1969): 561–76.

Macrakis, Michael S. "Russian Mission on the Mountains of Greece, Summer 1944 (A View from the Ranks)." *Journal of Contemporary History* 23, no. 3 (1988): 387–408.

Majstorović, Vojin. "The Rise and Fall of the Yugoslav-Soviet Alliance, 1945–1948." *Past Imperfect* 16 (2010): 132–64.

Marantzidis, Nikos. "The Communist Party of Greece after the Collapse of Communism (1989–2006): From Proletarian Internationalism to Ethnopopulism." In *Communist and Post-Communist Parties in Europe,* edited by Uwe Backes and Patrick Moreau, 245–58. Dresden: Vandenhoeck and Ruprecht, 2008.

——. *Dimokratikos Stratos Elladas 1946–1949.* Athens: Alexandreia, 2010.

——. "Exit, Voice and Loyalty: Les stratégies des Parties Communistes Ouest-Européens Après 1989." *Communisme* 76–77 (2004): 169–84.

——. "The Greek Civil War (1944–1949) and the International Communist System." *Journal of Cold War Studies* 15, no. 4 (2013): 25–54.

——. "Greek Intellectuals and the Fascination with Communism: The Graft That Did Not Blossom (1924–1949)." In *Ideological Storms: Intellectuals, Dictators, and the Totalitarian Temptation,* edited by Vladimir Tismăneanu and Bogdan C. Iacob, 81–97. Budapest: CEU Press, 2019.

——. "La deuxième mort de Nicos Zachariadis: L'Itinéraire d'un chef Communiste." *Communisme* 29/30 (1992): 183–89.

Marantzidis, Nikos, and Giorgos Antoniou. "The Axis Occupation and Civil War: Changing Trends in Greek Historiography, 1941–2002." *Journal of Peace Research* 41, no. 2 (2004): 223–31.

Marcou, Lilly. *Le Kominform.* Paris: Presses de la Fondation Nationale des Sciences Politiques, 1977.

Margaritis, Giorgos. *Istoria tou Ellinikou Emfyliou Polemou.* 2 vols. Athens: Vivliorama, 2000.

Mastny, Voijtech. *The Cold War and Soviet Insecurity: The Stalin Years.* New York: Oxford University Press, 1996.

——. *Russia's Road to the Cold War: Diplomacy, Warfare and the Politics of Communism, 1941–1945.* New York: Columbia University Press, 1979.

Matthaiou, Anna, and Popi Polemi. "I diethneis scheseis tis dimokratikis Elladas mesa sto 1948: Mia ekthessi tou Petrou Rousou." *Archeiotaxio* 2 (2000): 4–40.

——. *I ekdotiki peripetia ton Ellinon Kommouniston: Apo to vouno stin iperoria 1947–1968*. Athens: Vivliorama-ASKI, 2003.

Mavrogordatos, George Th. *Stillborn Republic: Social Coalitions and Party Strategies in Greece, 1922–1936*. Berkeley: University of California Press, 1983.

Mazower, Mark. *Governing the World: The History of an Idea*. New York: Penguin, 2012.

——. *Inside Hitler's Greece: The Experience of Occupation, 1941–44*. New Haven: Yale University Press, 1993.

——. *Salonica, City of Ghosts: Christians, Muslims and Jews, 1430–1950*. New York: Alfred A. Knopf, 2005.

McDermott, Kevin. "The History of the Comintern in Light of New Documents." In *International Communism and the Communist International, 1919–43*, edited by Tim Rees and Andrew Thorpe, 31–40. Manchester: Manchester University Press, 1998.

McDermott, Kevin, and Jeremy Agnew. *The Comintern: A History of International Communism from Lenin to Stalin*. London: Macmillan, 1996.

Mëhilli, Elidor. *From Stalin to Mao: Albania and the Socialist World*. Ithaca, NY: Cornell University Press, 2017.

Meta, Beqir. *Albania and Greece, 1949–1990: The Elusive Peace*. Tirana: Academy of Sciences—Institute of History, 2007.

Mihailidis, Iakovos. *Ta prosopa tou Ianou: I Ellinoyugoslavikes scheseis tis paramones tou Ellinikou Emfyliou Polemou 1944–1946*. Athens: Patakis, 2004.

Morton, Frederic. *Thunder at Twilight: Vienna, 1913–1914*. New York: Scribner-Macmillan, 1989,

Nachmani, Amikam. *International Intervention in the Greek Civil War: The United Nations Special Committee on the Balkans, 1947–1952*. New York: Praeger, 1990.

Narinski, Mikhail. "La politique Soviétique à l'egard des pays de l'Europe Occidentale de 1941 à 1945." *Matériaux pour l'histoire de notre temps* 37, no. 1 (1995): 2–7.

Nation, R. Craig. "A Balkan Union? Southeastern Europe in Soviet Security Policy, 1944–1948." In *The Soviet Union and Europe in the Cold War, 1943–53*, edited by Francesca Gori and Silvio Pons, 125–43. London: Macmillan, 1996.

Naxidou, Eleonora. "Bulgarian Historiography and World War I." *Bulgarian Studies* 2 (2018): 94–112.

Neshovich, Slobodan. "The Correspondence between Tito and Dimitrov on the B.W.P. (c) and Macedonia." *Macedonian Review* 5, no. 3 (1975): 270–80.

Nikolakopoulos, Elias. *I kachektiki dimokratia: Kommata kai ekloges 1946–1967*. Athens: Patakis, 2001.

Nilaj, Marsel. "The Civil War in Greece and Relations with Albania According to the Communist Press during 1948-1949." *European Journal of Multidisciplinary Studies* 3, no. 1 (2016): 95–104.

264   **BIBLIOGRAPHY**

Njagulov, Blagovest. "Early Socialism in the Balkans: Ideas and Practices in Serbia, Romania and Bulgaria." In *Entangled Histories of the Balkans*, edited by Roumen Daskalov and Diana Mishkova, 2:199–280. Leiden: Brill, 2014.

Noutsos, Panagiotis. *I sosialistiki skepsi stin Ellada apo to 1875 os to 1974.* 3 vols. Athens: Gnossi, 1994.

——. "The Role of the Greek Community in the Genesis and Development of the Socialist Movement in the Ottoman Empire: 1876–1925." In *Socialism and Nationalism in the Ottoman Empire, 1876–1923*, edited by Mete Tuncay and Erick J. Zürcher, 77–88. New York: British Academic Press, 1994.

Oren, Nissan. *Bulgarian Communism: The Road to Power, 1934–1944.* New York: Columbia University Press, 1971.

Paczkowski, Andrzej. "'The Greek Operation' by the Second Division of General Staff of the Polish People's Army." In *PRL a Wojna Domowa w Grecji/ The Polish People's Republic and the Greek Civil War*, edited by Magdalena Semczyszyn, 56–93. Szczecin: IPN, 2016.

Palaiologopoulos, Dimitris. *Ellines antifasistes ethelontes ston Ispaniko Emfylio Polemo.* Athens: Filippotis, 1986.

Pantelakis, Giannis. *Los buenos antifascistas.* Athens: Themelio, 2021.

Papadopoulou, Irma, and Victoria Ouroumidou. "O Ellinikos Emfylios Polemos ston Rosiko typo: I optiki tis efimeridas Pravda." In *I eikona tou Ellinikou Emfyliou sto diethni typo*, edited by Nikos Marantzidis and Eleni Paschaloudi, 24–53. Thessaloniki: University of Macedonia, 2015.

Papapanagiotou, Alekos. *To Kommounistiko Komma Elladas ston polemo kai tin antistasi.* Athens: Kazantza, 1974.

——. *To Makedoniko Zitima kai to Valkaniko Kommounistiko kinima 1918–1939.* Athens: Themelio, 1992.

Papastratis, Procopis. *British Policy towards Greece during the Second World War, 1941–1944.* Cambridge: Cambridge University Press, 1984.

Papathanassiou, Ioanna. "The Cominform and the Greek Civil War, 1947–1949." In *The Greek Civil War: Essays on a Conflict of Exceptionalism and Silences*, edited by Philip Carabott and Thanasis D. Sfikas, 57–71. London: Routledge, 2004.

——. *Eniaia dimokratiki Aristera: Archeio 1951–1967.* Athens: Themelio, 2001.

——. "Itimenos protagonistis: To Kommounistiko Komma Elladas sta chronia 1945–1950." In *Istoria tis Elladas tou 20ou aiona*, edited by Christos Chatziiosif, D1:229–75. Athens: Viliorama, 2009.

——. "To Kommounistiko Komma stin proklisi tis istorias 1940–1945." In *Istoria tis Elladas tou 20ou aiona*, edited by Christos Chatziiosif and Prokopis Papastratis, C2:79–151. Athens: Vivlioorama, 2007.

Patelakis, Apostolos. *O emfylios polemos kai i politiki prosfyges sti Roumania.* Thessaloniki: Epikentro, 2019.

Pentzopoulos, Dimitri. *The Balkan Exchange of Minorities and Its Impact upon Greece.* Paris: Mouton, 1962.

Perivolaropoulou, Nia. "La Fédération Balkanique comme solution des problèmes nationaux: Le projet social-démocrate (1909–1915)." *Matériaux pour l'histoire de notre temps* 35 (1994): 29–35.

Perović, Jeronim. "The Tito-Stalin Split: A Reassessment in Light of New Evidence." *Journal of Cold War Studies* 9, no. 2 (2007): 32–63.

Piffer, Tommaso. "Stalin, the Western Allies and Soviet Policy towards the Yugoslav Partisan Movement, 1941–4." *Journal of Contemporary History* 54, no. 2 (2019): 420–41.

Pitsos, Nicolas. "'Peuples des Balkans, fédérez-vous!': Projets pour une résolution pacifique de la question d'orient au tournant du XXe siècle." *Cahiers Balkaniques* 44 (2016): 1–20.

Potamianos, Nikos. "Internationalism and the Emergence of Communist Politics in Greece, 1912–1924." *Journal of Balkan and Near Eastern Studies* 21, no. 5 (2019): 515–31.

Preston, Paul. *Comrades! Portraits of the Spanish Civil War.* London: HarperCollins, 1999.

Psimouli, Vasso. *"Eleftheri Ellada," "I Foni tis Alitheias": O paranomos radiostathmos tou KKE, archeio 1947–1968.* Athens: Themelio-ASKI, 2006.

Reale, Eugenio. "The Founding of the Cominform." In *The Comintern: Historical Highlights; Essays, Recollections, Documents*, edited by Milorad M. Drachkovitch and Branko Lazitch, 253–68. New York: Praeger, 1966.

Rees, E. A. "Leader Cults: Varieties, Preconditions and Functions." In *The Leader Cult in Communist Dictatorships: Stalin and the Eastern Bloc*, edited by Balázs Apor, Jon C. Behrends, Polly Jones, and E. A. Rees, 3–26. New York: Macmillan, 2004.

Rintala, Marvin, and John H. Hodgson. "Gustaf Mannerheim and Otto W. Kuusinen in Russia." *Slavonic and East European Review* 56, no. 3 (1978): 371–86.

Ristović, Milan. "L'Insurrection de Décembre à Athènes: Intervention Britannique et réaction Yougoslave (décembre 1944–janvier 1945)." *Balkanica* 37 (2006): 271–81.

——. *To peirama Bulkes: I Elliniki Dimokratia sti Yugoslavia 1945–1949.* Thessaloniki: Kyriakidi, 2006.

——. "To zitima tis Yougoslavikis stratiotikis voitheias pros to Dimokratiko Strato Elladas 1946–1949." In *O Ellinikos Emfylios Polemos, mia apotimissi: Politikes, ideologikes, istoriografikes proektaseis*, edited by Ioannis Mourelos and Iakovos Mihailidis, 97–121. Athens: Ellinika Grammata, 2007.

——. "The Troublesome Yugoslav-Greek-British Triangle, 1945–1949." In *British-Serbian Relations: From the 18th to the 21st Centuries*, edited by Slobodan G. Markovich, 319–36. Belgrade: Zepter World Books, 2018.

Roberts, Geoffrey. "Moscow's Cold War on the Periphery: Soviet Policy in Greece, Iran, and Turkey, 1943–8." *Journal of Contemporary History* 46, no. 1 (2011): 58–81.

——. *Stalin's Wars: From World War to Cold War, 1939–1953.* New Haven, CT: Yale University Press, 2006.

Rossos, Andrew. "Incompatible Allies: Greek Communism and Macedonian Nationalism in the Civil War in Greece, 1943–1949." *Journal of Modern History* 69, no. 1 (1997): 42–76.

——. "Macedonianism and Macedonian Nationalism on the Left." In *National Character and National Ideology in Interwar Eastern Europe*, edited by Ivo Banac and Katherine Verdery, 219–54. New Haven, CT: Yale Center for International Studies, 1995.

Rothschild, Joseph. *The Communist Party of Bulgaria*. New York: Columbia University Press, 1959.

Roux, Alain. "Annie Kriegel, les Communistes Français: Essai d'ethnographie politique (Paris: Seuil, 1968), compte rendu." *Revue française de sociologie* 10, no. 4 (1969): 541–43.

Sadekova, Souria. "Andrei Jdanov et le mouvement Communiste international." *Communisme* 53–54 (1998): 63–72.

Sanford, George. *Military Rule in Poland: The Rebuilding of Communist Power, 1981–1983*. London: Croom Heim, 1986.

Sassoon, Donald. *One Hundred Years of Socialism: The West European Left in the Twentieth Century*. London: Tauris, 2002.

——. "The Rise and Fall of West European Communism, 1939–1948." *Contemporary European History* 1, no. 2 (1992): 139–69.

Semczyszyn, Magdalena. "The Communist Security Apparatus and Greek Refugees in the Polish People's Republic." In *PRL a Wojna Domowa w Grecji/ The Polish People's Republic and the Greek Civil War*, edited by Magdalena Semczyszyn, 210–23. Szczecin: IPN, 2016.

Sfetas, Spyridon. "Anepithimiti summachi kai anexelegkti antipali: I scheseis KKE kai NOF sti diarkeia tou Emfyliou 1946–1949." *Valkanika symmeikta* 8 (1996): 211–46.

——. "Autonomist Movements of the Slavophones in 1944: The Attitude of the Communist Party of Greece and the Protection of the Greek-Yugoslav Border." *Balkan Studies* 35, no. 2 (1995): 297–317.

Sfikas, Thanassis D. "'An Almost Unique Isle in the Sea of Democratic Europe': Greek Communists' Perceptions of International Reality, 1944–1949." *Cold War History* 14, no. 1 (2014): 1–21.

——. "I 'eirinopolemi' diastassi tou Ellinikou Emfyliou Polemou: Eirineftikes protovoulies kai dinatotites symvivasmou 1945–1949." In *O Emfylios Polemos: Apo ti Varkiza sto Grammo Fevrouarios 1945-Avgoustos 1949*, edited by Elias Nikolakopoulos, Alkis Rigos, and Grigoris Psalidas, 75–101. Athens: Themelio, 2003, 75–101.

——. "'O provoleas fotizei pali tis amarties mou?' O emfylios polemos stin Kathairessi tou Nikou Zachariadi." *Ionios logos* 2 (2010): 367–92.

Shrader, Charles R. *The Withered Vine: Logistics and the Communist Insurgency in Greece, 1945–1949*. London: Praeger, 1999.

Şiperco, Andrei. *Confesiunile elitei Comuniste: România 1944–1965; Rivalități, represiuni, crime . . . Arhiva Alexandru Şiperco*. 5 vols. Bucharest: Institutul Național pentru Studiul Totalitarismului, 2015–16.

Skoulidas, Elias. "I politiki prosfyges tou Ellinikou Emfyliou stin Alvania." In *I politiki prosfyges tou Emfyliou Polemou: Kinonikes kai politikes prosegiseis*, edited by Giorgos Antoniou and Stathis Kalyvas, 118–35. Thessaloniki: University of Macedonia, 2015.

Slijepčević, Djoko. *The Macedonian Question: The Struggle for Southern Serbia*. Chicago: American Institute for Balkan Affairs, 1958.

Sloboda, Marián. "Language Maintenance and Shifts in a Greek Community in a Heterolinguistic Environment: The Greeks in the Czech Republic." *Journal of the Hellenic Diaspora* 29 (2003): 5–33.

Smith, Ole. "The Greek Communist Party in the Post-Gorbachev Era." In *Western European Communism and the Collapse of Communism*, edited by David S. Bell, 87–100. Oxford: Berg, 1993.

——. "The Problem of Zachariadis's First Open Letter: A Reappraisal of the Evidence." *Journal of the Hellenic Diaspora* 9, no. 4 (1982): 7–20.

Stănescu, Marin C. *Moscova, Cominternul, Filiera Comunistă Balcanică și România, 1919–1944*. Bucharest: Silex, 1994.

Stavrakis, Peter J. *Moscow and Greek Communism, 1944–1949*. Ithaca, NY: Cornell University Press, 1989.

Stergiou, Andreas. "Perestroika and the Greek Left." In *Perestroika and the Party: National and Transnational Perspectives on European Communist Parties in the Era of Soviet Reform*, edited by Francesco di Palma, 256–77. New York: Berghahn, 2019.

Studer, Brigitte. "Stalinization: Balance Sheet of a Complex Notion." In *Bolshevism, Stalinism and the Comintern: Perspectives on Stalinization, 1917–1953*, edited by Norman Laporte, Kevin Morgan, and Matthew Worley, 45–65. New York: Palgrave, 2008.

——. "Totalitarisme et Stalinisme." In *Le siècle des Communismes*, edited by Michel Dreyfus, Bruno Groppo, Claudio Ingerflom, Roland Lew, Claude Pennetier, Bernard Pudal, and Serge Wolikow, 33–68. Paris: Editions de L'Atelier/Editions Ouvrières, 2004.

——. *The Transnational World of the Cominternians*. New York: Palgrave, 2015.

Svolopoulos, Constantin. "Le problème de la sécurité dans le Sud-Est Européen de l'entre-deux-guerres: A la recherche des origines du Pacte Balkanique de 1934." *Balkan Studies* 14, no. 2 (1973): 247–92.

Swain, Geoffrey. "The Cominform: Tito's International?" *Historical Journal* 35, no. 3 (1992): 641–63.

——. "Tito and the Twilight of the Comintern." In *International Communism and the Communist International, 1919–1943*, edited by Tim Rees and Andrew Thorpe, 205–21. Manchester: Manchester University Press, 1998.

Ter Minassian, Taline. *Colporteurs du Komintern: L'Union Soviétique et les minorités au Moyen-Orient*. Paris: Presses de Sciences Po, 1997.

——. "Le Komintern et les Balkans." *Matériaux pour l'histoire de notre temps* 71 (2003): 62–70.

Thorpe, Andrew. "Comintern 'Control' of the Communist Party of Great Britain, 1920–43." *English Historical Review* 113, no. 452 (June 1998): 637–62.

——. "Stalinism and British Politics." *History* 83, no. 272 (October 1998): 608–27.

Tismăneanu, Vladimir. "Intrigi, crime, răni deschise: Comunismul Grec si tenebrele Staliniste." *Contributors*, text cu valoara adaugată, August 16, 2011. https://www.contributors.ro/crime-vendete-tradari-comunismul-grec-si-tenebrele-staliniste/.

———. *Stalinism for All Seasons: A Political History of Romanian Communism.* Berkeley: University of California Press, 2003.

Tosstorff, Reiner. *The Red International of Labour Unions (RILU), 1920–1937.* Leiden: Brill, 2016.

Tsekeris, Angelos. *Mia istoria allios: O N. Zachariadis, I Sovietiki Enosi kai i Kommounistes tis Taskendis.* Athens: Taxideftis, 2014.

Tsekou, Katerina. *Ellines politiki prosfyges stin Anatoliki Evropi 1945–1989.* Athens: Alexandreia, 2013.

Tsintzilonis, Christos N. *OKNE 1922–1943: Leninistiko machitiko scholeio ton neon.* Athens: Sygchroni Epochi, 1989.

Tsivos, Kostas. *O megalos kaimos tis xenitias: Ellines politiki prosfyges stin Czechoslovakia 1948–1989.* Athens: Alexandreia, 2019.

Ulunian, Artiom. "The Communist Party of Greece and the Comintern: Evaluations, Instructions, and Subordination." In *International Communism and the Communist International, 1919–1943*, edited by Tim Rees and Andrew Thorpe, 185-204. Manchester: Manchester University Press, 1998.

———. "The Soviet Union and the Greek Question, 1946-53." In *The Soviet Union and Europe in the Cold War, 1943–1953*, edited by Francesca Gori and Silvio Pons, 144-60. London: Macmillan, 1996.

Urban, Joan Barth. *Moscow and the Italian Communist Party: From Togliatti to Berlinguer.* London: Tauris, 1986.

US Senate Committee on the Judiciary. *Yugoslav Communism: A Critical Study.* Washington, DC: US Government Printing Office, 1961.

Vatrin, Alexander. "The Evolution of the Comintern, 1919-1943." In *The Oxford Handbook of Communism*, edited by Stephen A. Smith, 187-94. Oxford: Oxford University Press, 2014.

Vlasidis, Vlasis. "The 'Macedonian Question' on the Bulgarian Political Scene." *Balkan Studies* 32, no. 1 (1991): 71-88.

Voglis, Polymeris. *Becoming a Subject: Political Prisoners during the Greek Civil War.* New York: Berghahn Books, 2002.

Volkov, Vladimir. "The Soviet Leadership and Southeastern Europe." In *The Establishment of Communist Regimes in Eastern Europe, 1944–1949*, edited by Norman Naimark and Leonid Gibianskii, 55-72. Boulder, CO: Westview, 1997.

Weber, Hermann. "The Stalinization of the KPD: Old and New Views." In *Bolshevism, Stalinism and the Comintern: Perspectives on Stalinization, 1917–1953*, edited by Norman Laporte, Kevin Morgan, and Matthew Worley, 22-44. New York: Palgrave, 2008.

Werth, Alexander. *Russia: The Post-war Years.* London: Hale, 1971.

White, Stephen. "Communism and the East: The Baku Congress 1920." *Slavic Review* 33, no. 3 (1974): 492-514.

Wojecki, Mieczysław. "Clusters of Greek Immigrants in Poland (Lower Silesia, Pomerania, Bieszcady Mountains)." In *PRL a Wojna Domowa w Grecji/The Polish People's Republic and the Greek Civil War*, edited by Magdalena Semczyszyn, 148-63. Szczecin: IPN, 2016.

Wolikow, Serge. "Aux origines de la galaxie Communiste: L'internationale." In *Le siècle des Communismes*, edited by Michel Dreyfus, Bruno Groppo,

Claudio Ingerflom, Roland Lew, Claude Pennetier, Bernard Pudal, and Serge Wolikow, 293–319. Paris: Editions de L'Atelier/Editions Ouvrières, 2004.

Woodhouse, Chris M. *Something Ventured*. London: Granada, 1982.

——. *The Struggle for Greece, 1941–1949*. London: Hurst, 2002.

Woodward, Ernest Llewellyn. *British Foreign Policy in the Second World War*. 5 vols. London: HMSO, 1962.

Wudalas, Angelica. "Greek Political Refugees—Medical Care in the Hospital No. 250 in Dziwnów." In *PRL a Wojna Domowa w Grecji/The Polish People's Republic and the Greek Civil War*, edited by Magdalena Semczyszyn, 164–75. Szczecin: IPN, 2016.

Xydis, Stephen. *Greece and the Great Powers, 1944–1947: Prelude to the Truman Doctrine*. Thessaloniki: Institute for Balkan Studies, 1963.

Yalimov, Ibrahim. "The Bulgarian Community and the Development of the Socialist Movement in the Ottoman Empire during the Period 1876-1923." In *Socialism and Nationalism in the Ottoman Empire, 1876–1923*, edited by Mete Tuncay and Erick J. Zürcher, 89–108. New York: British Academic Press, 1994.

Yannakakis, Elios. "To oplo para poda: I egatastasi ton prosfygon stis sosialistikes chores." In *To oplo para poda: I politiki prosfyges tou Ellinikou Emfyliou Polemou stin Anatoliki Evropi*, edited by Eftihia Voutira, Vasilis Dalkavoukis, Nikos Marantzidis, and Maria Bontila, 3–17. Thessaloniki: University of Macedonia Press, 2005.

Young, Glennys. "To Russia with 'Spain': Spanish Exiles in the USSR and the Longue Durée of Soviet History." *Kritika* 15, no. 2 (2014): 395–419.

Zapantis, Andrew L. *Greek-Soviet Relations, 1917–1941*. Boulder, CO: East European Monographs, 1982.

Zečević, Nikola. "The Russian Revolution and Its Impact on the Idea of Balkan Union (1918–1933): National vs. International." *Trames* 23, no. 3 (2019): 323–34.

Zubok, Vladislav, and Constantine Pleshakov. *Inside the Kremlin's Cold War: From Stalin to Khrushchev*. Cambridge, MA: Harvard University Press, 1996.

INDEX

Agrarian Party (Greece), 96–97, 120
Albania: Communist-led guerrilla resistance in, 14, 126, 127, 134; as Communist state, 7; DSE retreat to, 181–82; Greek Civil War refugee crisis and, 187–88, 239n2; Greek Civil War support from, 163–66, 177, 178, 180–82; Soviet Union recognized by, 100; Tito and annexation of, 174; training of KKE military officials in, 151, 159
Albanian Communist Party, 95
Alexakis, Orion, 25–26, 32, 56
Allen, George, 129
Amendola, Giorgio, 112
Angelopoulos, Angelos, 142
Anti-fascist Council for the National Liberation of Yugoslavia (AVNOJ), 134–36
antifascist front, 14; Comintern policy and, 99–100, 117; KKE commitment to, 74, 96–97, 100–101, 105; Ribbentrop-Molotov Pact and, 111, 112
Apostolidis, Thomas, 51–52
Apostolou, Ilektra, 88
Asia Minor campaign, 28, 32, 34–35, 45, 48, 58, 68
Askoutsis, Nikolaos, 142
Association Juridique Internationale, 102, 227n164
Atanasov, Shtreryu, 125

Bakarić, Vladimir, 172
Baku Congress of the People of the East (1920), 26
Balampanidis, Ioannis, 210
Balkan Committee of France, 105
Balkan Communist Federation (BCF), 7–8; Second Congress (1921), 26; Fourth Congress (1922), 42; Sixth Congress (1923), 44–46; Seventh

Congress (1924), 50, 52; Eighth Congress (1928), 81–82; creation of, 12, 19, 23; Dimitrov's leadership of, 13, 54, 55; dissolution of, 107; Fifth Conference (1922), 42; Greek status in, 28–29, 33, 38, 62, 91; KKE's criticisms of, 80–83; Kutvie faction of KKE and, 69–70; Macedonian question and, 41–48, 51, 53, 81; Pouliopoulos and, 48, 69; trends against centralism in, 35–38
Balkan Revolutionary Center, 54
Balkan Secretariat (of ECCI), 22, 80–82, 89–90, 97, 107. See also Dimitrov, Georgi
Balkan Wars (1912–13), 19, 32, 39–40, 70
Balkan Workers' Social-Democratic Federation, 41
Banac, Ivo, 89
Baranov, Leonid, 141, 144–45, 156, 160–61, 163
Battle of Athens (Dekemvriana), 147–51, 153, 154, 209
BCF. See Balkan Communist Federation
Benaroya, Avraam, 32, 70–71
Beneš, Edvard, 112–13
Beria, Lavrentii, 161, 199
Bierut, Bolesław, 173
BKP. See Bulgarian Communist Party
Bled agreement (1947), 165, 171
Bolshevik Revolution, 20, 49
Bolshevization, 9, 12; absolute compliance vs. à la carte, 27, 34, 58; Balkan Communism's shift toward, 52–54, 80–83, 106; Dimitrov's role in, 54–55, 62, 107; elements of, 105–6; of KPJ, 163; Macedonian question and resistance to, 46, 47, 51–53, 58–59; old vs. new guard of SEKE and, 57–59; Pouliopoulos and, 48, 70; removal of KKE's leadership by ECCI (1931),

CPSIA information can be obtained
at www.ICGtesting.com
Printed in the USA
LVHW111740050123
736514LV00002BA/18